Transforming the Delivery of Health Care:

The integration process

Author
Keith M. Korenchuk
Parker Poe Adams & Bernstein
2600 Charlotte Plaza
Charlotte, NC 28244
(704) 372-9000

Published by:
Medical Group Management Association
104 Inverness Terrace East
Englewood, CO 80112
(303) 799-1111

Medical Group Management Association (MGMA) publications are intended to provide current and accurate information and are designed to assist readers in becoming more familiar with the subject matter covered. MGMA published *Transforming the Delivery of Health Care: The integration process* for a general audience as well as its members. Such publications are distributed with the understanding that MGMA does not render any legal, accounting or other professional advice that may be construed as specifically applicable to individual situations. No representation or warranties are made concerning the application of legal or other principles discussed by the author to any specific fact situation, nor is any prediction made concerning how any particular judge, government official or other person who will interpret or apply such principles. Specific factual situations should be discussed with professional advisors.

MEDICAL GROUP
MANAGEMENT
ASSOCIATION

Dedicated to my wife, Darlene,
and my children, Michael, John,
Thomas and Sarah Catherine.

— Keith Korenchuk

Acknowledgments

I would like to thank my secretary Sharilyn Craddock for her invaluable assistance in the preparation of this book, for her patience with the process and for her unfailing good humor in dealing with the author.

This book would not have been possible without the support of the Medical Group Management Association staff members: **Fred E. Graham II, Ph.D., FACMPE**, senior associate executive director, **Dennis L. Barnhardt, APR**, director of communications, **Barbara U. Hamilton, M.A.**, Library Resource Center director, **Brenda E. Hull**, communications project manager, **Stephanie S. Wyllyamz**, communications specialist, and **Ellie J. Cox**, communications administrative secretary.

About the author

Keith M. Korenchuk received his undergraduate degree from Duke University, his law degree from the University of Virginia and his masters in health administration (M.P.H.) from Harvard University.

He is chairman of the Health Care Group in the Charlotte, North Carolina law firm of Parker, Poe, Adams and Bernstein. The firm's clients include medical group practices and hospitals involved in the transformation of the health care delivery system.

Table of contents

Table of contents

Table of contents

Table of contents

Chapter 1

The challenge

Major change is sweeping the medical care delivery system. The essence of how health care is provided is under attack. Medical groups, hospitals, managed care companies and the individuals charged with the responsibility of managing these institutions are challenged by and caught in this monumental transformation. Rising expenditures of state and federal dollars for health care, the problems of the uninsured and underinsured, the ever increasing cost of health care for employers, the graying of the population and the increasing amounts of technology devoted to health care has challenged the system. Health care reform at the federal and state levels has also changed the landscape in which the medical groups and hospitals must operate. This changing environment confronts providers of health care, both medical groups and hospitals, with major challenges to the way they provide health care: challenges to thier very existence. New approaches for the delivery of health care must be developed and implemented. In response to these factors, the practice of medicine and the role of the hospital are being redefined.

The health care marketplace

Responding and adapting to this changing environment is a major challenge for hospitals and medical groups. Physicians, accustomed to practicing individually or in small groups, will find that continuing the status quo of delivering medical care is untenable. Reimbursement changes, the pace of regulatory change, inefficiencies of small operations, growing overhead, increasing debt and the loss of patients caused by managed care or direct contracting, threaten the very existence of these physicians.

Hospitals that continue to treat their medical staff at arms length without forming strategic alliances with key groups will lose the opportunity for transitioning their inpatient facility to an integrated delivery system where the hospital is a cost center and no longer the focus of the delivery of health care. Hospitals that fail to recognize the need for a strong, integrated approach to the delivery of inpatient and ambulatory care will lose managed care arrangements, direct contracts with employers, ancillary revenues and ambulatory care opportunities, and will suffer increasing isolation in an increasingly ambulatory care driven delivery system.

The integration of the delivery of medical care by merging group practices and the delivery of ambulatory care in hospital/medical group affiliations is in an early stage of development. In many ways, the manner in which health care is delivered in this country currently resembles the way machinery was manufactured before the advent of the assembly line. The manufacture of machinery in small shops where different stages of the process were performed in different locations meant that inefficiencies and costs of production were high and output was limited. While the technological advances in the practice of medicine are unparalleled, the method in which this "high tech" care is provided to patients often resembles this "cottage industry" approach.

While health care has always been, and will likely remain, a local, community-focused endeavor, the environment will no longer permit inefficient providers of services to exist. The pace of this change throughout society, and the implementation of health care reform, will only hasten the need for transition to more integrated systems. For individual medical groups and hospitals to survive, more management techniques and business practices must be utilized to allow physicians to practice medicine efficiently and to enhance quality of care. It is this need for both efficiency and quality, as well as the ability to deliver a comprehensive package of health care services for an established budget, that will greatly accelerate the creation of more integrated systems of delivery of health care.

For the individual physician, radical change is assured; the paradigm of the autonomous individual physician/owner who provides medical services individually or within a small group to a loyal group of patients is outdated. Unquestionably, this loss of a frame of reference creates uncertainty for physicians. Coupled with declining revenues and increasing overheads, this changing reality of medical practice may alter physician lifestyles and career satisfaction, and threaten their ability to provide quality care.

For hospitals, the situation is equally challenging. Failing to recognize and respond to the declining importance of providing inpatient care will threaten the future of the hospital. Hospitals are confronted with their own unique set of problems including cost pressures, increasing competition and revenue challenges. They must devise strategies to form effective alliances with physicians for the mutual best interests of all concerned, and to refocus the strategic vision of their institutions.

The situation demands action, but the response to this demand may take many forms. Complaining about change or leaving the field are generally unproductive or unsatisfying. Remaining paralyzed in existing relationships is equally unsatisfactory. Ignoring the challenge in the hopes it will go away by yearning for the "good ol' days" will not improve the situation. All of these approaches fail to recognize that while change brings uncertainty, it also brings opportunity.

The challenge

Responding to the challenge of this changing environment makes it imperative for group practices and hospitals to devise effective strategies. These strategies must allow medical groups to evolve into better organizations by considering the dynamics of group behavior and physician satisfaction. They also must consider the ability of the medical group to relate, compete and organize with hospitals, insurance companies, employers and other third party payers. These strategies must allow hospitals to assist physicians in creating more conducive environments for practice and by strengthening the relationship between hospitals and physicians. The winners in health care delivery in the coming years, therefore, will be those organizations which understand the dynamics of the transformation currently underway and those which can identify and adopt effective strategies to respond to those changes.

Mergers, acquisitions and hospital/medical group affiliations are effective tools in responding to this changing situation. These transactions, often undertaken at much effort and expense, are not answers in and of themselves. These combinations are merely vehicles that will allow medical groups and hospitals to implement the specific strategies for their organizations to respond to the changing environment. Therefore, the very need for these combinations depends on the development of a strategic plan. The strategic plan must look with vision to the future, must respond to system-wide competitive factors and must allow for the continued growth and satisfaction of the participants.

To respond to the changing environment and to utilize merger or hospital affiliation options, medical groups and hospitals will engage in a process in which they have limited experience and perspective to evaluate and implement the strategy successfully. Hence, this book was created to fill this void of understanding. By breaking down the strategies to their constituent parts, and by dealing with the players in the process, the following chapters will provide the guidance and perspective necessary to negotiate these complex, difficult and multi-faceted transactions more successfully. This book, therefore, focuses on the integration process and the people involved. It avoids theoretical explanations or abstract theories about delivery systems, while providing organizations that have decided to integrate a way to identify and resolve the myriad of issues necessary to complete the transaction.

Transforming the Delivery of Health Care:
The integration process

The challenges associated with these transactions should not be underestimated. On an individual level, the importance of the personal relationships between physicians and the hospital management cannot be underestimated. Personal feelings and relationships, as well as individual personalities, make each step in the process an uncertain one, but one that can be completed successfully if due consideration is given to the people involved. All participants must keep two things in mind. First, no matter how difficult and complex the process may be, the parties must remain focused on the reasons that brought them together and the larger strategic aims that will be accomplished by completing the transaction.

Second, the parties must understand that the negotiating process and the implementation of these transactions is merely a prelude to establishing a long-term relationship. Unlike the sale of a business where the seller disappears with the cash proceeds and has minimal contact with the business after the sale, the integration process, regardless of its specific form, is distinguished by the reality that the parties must work cooperatively in a "partnership" after the closing. It is this spirit of cooperation that must form the cornerstone for approaching these transactions. The long-term success of any of these ventures stretches far beyond the three to six month period when these arrangements are typically documented and consummated.

While each party will protect its own interests by seeking the best financial and business arrangements associated with a transaction, neither side can afford, over the long term, to strike too hard a bargain. Nor can either side risk creating an atmosphere of crisis negotiation or ill-will where scars take years to heal. For the strategic advantages of integration to be achieved successfully, it is important to remain focused on the larger issues in the transaction and to allow both sides the ability to gain advantage from the combination. Moreover, it is important to lay a solid framework for future decision-making and conflict resolution that inevitably must be part of the newly created relationship.

Each transaction will have a unique set of business considerations with different ownership arrangements, finances associated with each organization and competitive situations which may dictate both the form and the substance of these transactions. These unique internal and external factors mean that any integration effort cannot proceed in cookbook fashion, but must consider special facts and circumstances, and allow modification of the process along the way. Participants should never lose sight of the reality that the solution proposed for one situation will leave others in similar situations with unresolved issues or unsuccessful conclusions. This fact-specific decision-making means there is often no absolute right or wrong answer. The relative positions of the parties must be carefully weighed in structuring any successful long-lasting venture.

The Integrated Delivery System

As the response to change has developed over the health care delivery system, physicians, hospitals and insurance companies are increasingly viewing their strategic options as being more intertwined and as requiring an integration of previously separate functions. In the old system, physicians provided physician care, hospitals provided hospital inpatient care and insurance companies provided the administrative and risk function that would allow health care to be packaged, delivered, sold and administered to the purchasers of health care and ultimately to patients. With the changing environment, however, these historical roles have begun to break down.

Integrated delivery systems are being fashioned to combine in one organization a seamless continuum of inpatient and outpatient care with the ability to demonstrate quality and to deliver that care by assuming risk for delivering that care within financial budgets. This comprehensive, integrated delivery and finance system is the goal of many health care organizations, and the process of integration is proceeding in various places around the country in order to allow systems to transition to this approach. The goal in creating the integrated delivery system is to assure its participants with control, involvement and accountability for the delivery of health care in their particular community.

Physicians organized their practices in the '70s and '80s to cater to individual choice for selection of providers by patients and to create an environment which catered to physician autonomy, the ability to defer taxes and the creation of a work environment which appealed to the desire of physicians to be their own bosses. This delivery mechanism is no longer adequate in an environment which requires comprehensive delivery of efficient care where quality must be demonstrated, where patient choice is being limited and where the financial risks of that care must be borne by the provider.

Hospitals face an equally challenging transformation with the increasing use of risk-based reimbursement systems found in integrated and managed care environments. The hospital operations, which were historically focused on inpatient care, must transform. Old hospital strategies of catering to surgical subspecialists who would keep the hospital full and revenues growing will no longer work. Integrated systems that are required to take on risk will view both hospitals and the surgical subspecialists who have had historically strong relationships with those hospitals as cost centers. This cost center approach means that when the integrated system is at risk for providing a range of care to enrollees, placing an individual patient in a hospital will cost the integrated system money and will be viewed as a cost item for delivering care rather than as a revenue-generating operation. The old paradigm of hospital as the center of health care delivery is breaking down and hospital executives must meet the challenge of transforming their systems to account for the new reality.

Insurance companies face similar challenges as they historically had relationships with the purchasers of health care through major employers and groups of employers, while administering the health care benefit side of the health care system, but had little involvement in the actual delivery of care. In order for insurance companies to survive the coming transformation in their businesses, they also must begin to seek to integrate the financing and administration of health care benefits with the actual delivery component.

All of these players face the prospect of transforming their historical relationships and roles that they have played in the health care delivery system to the new environment which demands collaboration among the various participants, and demands accountability for the quality of care that will be provided and for the financial consequences of decisions that are made in delivering that care.

The physician integration process

In many medical communities, physicians will not immediately accept a view of the future health care delivery system as being completely integrated with hospital, physician and insurance company components. The process of change is an incremental one. Recommending that independent physicians who have operated as autonomous businesses merge and have that merger then simultaneously create an integrated system with the local hospital has little chance of immediate acceptance. Because the pace of change is incremental and the ability to move individuals to accept change must be based upon immediate, real and, most importantly, perceived need for change, most physicians will look for physician only alternatives in changing practice delivery styles as a viable first alternative.

Physician alternatives, however, fall short of the total package that must be created in an integrated environment. Even though these efforts fall short of total integration, however, taking independent physician practices and put them together in a closer relationship is a fundamental first step in creating effective physician relationships. The process of physician integration is, in most instances, a necessary first step along the integrated delivery system continuum. Particularly in communities where there is no strong group practice, incremental steps in reorganizing these physician relationships are critical. In addition, organizing these physician relationships is often a pre-requisite to begin the larger integration process with hospitals and insurance companies, for without these physician efforts, independent practices will have limited bargaining power in the creation of these systems.

6

The challenge

Physician integration options include a range of strategies. Each of these strategies must be viewed as ways in which the strategic plans of the participants can be established. They are, in many ways, first steps in the gradual evolutionary process in changing how physician care is delivered. From an organizational perspective, the most radical change in the physician integration continuum is embodied in the medical group merger. In mergers, separate physician groups become one, their operations are combined, their benefit plans are standardized and physicians become part of one governing entity. The merger represents the end-stage for physician integration as it is the most difficult, complex and potentially far-reaching change that physicians, by themselves, can accomplish.

Of course, mergers take many forms, some single specialties, some primary care groups and other multi-specialty arrangements. Each type can represent an effective way of combining organizations, yet a combination of a variety of groups will often be required to position the medical care delivery system to be a strong partner with hospitals and insurance companies in the integrated environment. The end-stage is likely, in many communities, to consist of a multi-specialty arrangement, primary care based and subspecialty physician supported. This likely scenario, however, will often be subject to modification and alternative approaches, depending upon the facts of each local medical community and the history of physician relationships in that community.

This combination of medical groups may be technically called a merger, in which the corporate existence of one organization is absorbed into the other, or it may be an acquisition where one group acquires the assets of another group and hires, as employees, the most valuable asset of the other group, its physicians. In either event, the combined medical group represents a larger, more complex, more competitive entity, regardless of whether the new group is created by merger or acquisition. Throughout this book, this medical group combination by merger or acquisition will be collectively referred to as a merger.

The reasons to consider mergers to fulfill strategic goals are numerous. First, groups may desire to strengthen their position in the medical care delivery market. By combining with another group, additional services, specialties or subspecialties may strengthen the competitive advantage of a group by allowing a more comprehensive range of services to be provided by the group.

Second, a larger group also may be an important goal in and of itself, since the ability to negotiate with managed care organizations or directly with employers will depend upon the negotiating position and attractiveness of the group from both a coverage and quality of care perspective. Larger groups allow third party payers to secure access to a wider range of physicians, and allow employers forming direct relationships to provide the fullest range of services to their employees. Small groups have neither the attractiveness from a service perspective nor the clout from the negotiating perspective to implement these types of relationships effectively.

Third, the management of a combined group may allow substantial economies of scale and the development of advanced administrative systems. Positions can be consolidated in a merger, supplies can be purchased in greater volumes, and a wider range of benefit plans will be available. These economies of scale can only be achieved over a significant period of time, and no immediate cost savings should be anticipated, however. Experienced management will be able to implement many administrative techniques that previously might have been beyond the scope of operations of the smaller premerger groups. To the extent a coordinated administrative structure can be established, the combined groups will be able to create a more efficient organization and management system.

Fourth, the quality of medical practice can be enhanced. The larger group will have the resources and expertise to implement and sustain an expanded peer review and quality assurance program. As the number of physicians in a group increases, the ability to devote resources to this process will increase and implementation of these programs can be refined more highly. These quality programs will be demanded increasingly of medical groups from third party payers and employers. The combined group, because of its size, will be better positioned to demonstrate quality outcomes and cost-effective treatment. These programs, therefore, will allow another competitive advantage for the combined group by coupling this external demonstration of effectiveness with the internal sense of pride of performance.

Finally, the local environment will have a significant impact on the need for a merger. Relationships with other groups, the mix of specialties in a community and the growth and combinations of other groups and their access to patients will impact the group as to the necessity of a merger. The strengths or weaknesses of various hospitals, and potential strategic alliances with those hospitals, may also make a combined group a much more attractive partner for these institutions. These local environmental factors will be critical in fashioning the most appropriate strategy for the combined medical groups and for compelling groups to consider the merger option.

Other physician integration strategies exist that are short of the merger option. Often, the word "merger" in and of itsel, creates great fear in individual physicians about loss of autonomy, loss of benefits and loss of the historical practice environment which those physicians have become accustomed. Accordingly, a merger may not always be the first option that physicians may consider.

The challenge

The least integrated approach for physician integration is that of the creation of a contracting network. A contracting network can be called by many names, including physicians' organization, independent practice organization, physicians' alliance, or practice network. Regardless of the name employed to describe the effort, the concept of a contracting network is that independent physicians join together for managed care contracting purposes by creating a central organization that can respond to managed care initiatives by directing an increasing volume of business to physician practices through this network. Only the contracting network patients go through this network. Physicians remain employees of their own medical group, they maintain their own employees and conduct their own billing and collection efforts. Employee benefits, work hours, office locations and all the other indicators of private practice remain the same and unaltered by the creation of this network. As such, the network appeals to physicians who have a concern of doing "too much" and appeals to the sense that "doing something" is better than nothing. As an integration strategy, however, the network has limited utility, particularly if what is designed is not desired by the purchasers of health care. Specialty networks, networks that do not take on risk, or networks that do not provide a desirable package may accomplish little other than make the participants feel proactive in the development process. Efforts that are not designed for the purchasers of health care will often find that they have no customers when the development process is concluded.

The contracting network, however, is in some communities an effective way to begin to allow physicians to work together, and accordingly, it should not be dismissed without consideration. Its usefulness will depend upon the nature of the network, the nature of the competitive environment in a community, and the new products and services which this network can offer. As long as it is constructed in a proper manner in light of local circumstances, and as long as it is viewed as a transition vehicle to a more integrated approach to physician delivery of medical services, it will remain a viable, if limited, option.

An intermediate approach along the physician integration continuum is that of the creation of a "group practice without walls." These group practices without walls are known by a variety of names. Whether they be independent practice organizations, loosely structured organizations, clinics without walls or other names, the essential function is to straddle the fence between autonomous independent practice and the creation of a group practice operation. The function of the group practice without walls is to create an environment whereby management structures and centralized decisionmaking are created, but are balanced against the ability of physicians at each practice site to make fundamental decisions concerning how their practice site is administered.

Transforming the Delivery of Health Care:
The integration process

Because of increasing concerns about self-referral legislation and the restrictions caused thereby, and because of the increasing need in the managed care area to facilitate the collective negotiation of managed care contracts, these group practice structures have evolved into tighter organizational relationships. Accordingly, most group practice without walls development activities have focused on creating an employment relationship for all physician participants by one organization. This employment relationship means common benefits, common employment status and the creation of an entity with a common governance structure and board of directors. Group practice employees who were previously employed by the independent practices become employees of the new organization.

This central authority is balanced against the need to cater to individual autonomy. Within this overall framework, therefore, divisional or office decisionmaking is created. Physicians at each practice site are given authority over a variety of issues. These issues may include physician compensation, as generated by a cost accounting method of allocating revenues and expenses to the practice site, hiring and firing decisions with respect to physicians at each practice site, administrative aspects of the operation of each practice site in the actual delivery of patient care and such other items as may be negotiated in the development process.

This group practice without walls concept seeks to balance the need for central control with the need for individual autonomy. For example, rather than merging all the assets and liabilities of the constituent groups into one seamless organization as in a merger, the group practice without walls approach often allows the existing medical groups to retain their assets and hold them in a separate entity, making them available by lease to the new organization.

This type of approach will make the other central element of a group practice without walls easier to achieve. That element is the creation of an exit strategy for practice members. To the extent that a merger combines the assets of the constituent organizations into a new entity and makes dismantling that organization very difficult, the group practice without walls approach is, in general, to allow the relatively easier process of exiting the practice to occur. Leasing facilities and equipment and not combining assets in the central organization are examples of this approach of creating an exit strategy.

In general, the group practice without walls concept will likely not withstand the need for further integration of the various constituent practices over time. The lack of central control, the need for the organization to be more capitalized and the need for more efficient operations will mean that successful group practices without walls will ultimately transition into tighter controlled organizations such as a fully integrated group practice. The primary purpose of the group practice without walls is probably to serve in most communities as a transition vehicle to a more integrated environment. As such, it is an effective strategy in some circumstances to facilitate incremental change, where that change is the only viable method of proceeding with the integration process.

The physician-hospital integration process

The physician integration process represents but one step in the continuing development of integrated delivery systems. The natural evolution of this physician initiative is to expand it to include relationships with hospitals. Integrating physician and hospital care gives the critical delivery components necessary for the creation of an integrated delivery system. The process of being able to combine the full scope of care will allow the ultimate development of mechanisms by which this continuum of care can be combined with the insurance and financing aspect of health care delivery.

Just as the physician integration options span a wide continuum of integration levels and complexity, the physician-hospital integration process spans an equally wide continuum. Which integration options are selected is a function of the historical relationships in a community between physicians and hospitals, the dynamics of the health care delivery marketplace in that community and the willingness of the parties to create a new vision for health care delivery in their community. Incremental change in the physician-hospital relationship is also a likely result when both physicians and hospitals begin to think for the first time that their existing practice styles must transition to a more integrated environment.

The range of integration activities begins in its simplest form with the creation of the physician-hospital organization. The PHO, as they are called, often has as its principle focus the organization of physicians into a physician-contracting relationship, the creation of a joint governing mechanism whereby physicians and hospital representatives can come together for joint decision making, and the creation of a managed care contracting network consisting of both physicians and hospitals which can provide a coordinated approach for managed care contracting and the delivery of care in a managed care environment. As such, the PHO represents the most conservative and least controversial approach to organizing physician-hospital relationships.

The PHO model requires that physicians and hospitals agree to cooperate for managed care contracting purposes. It keeps physicians in their private practices, allows physicians to continue to remain employed by those private practices and to keep intact their own salary, benefit and employee relationships. The PHO structure only changes the mechanism by which a portion of managed care patients are received into the practice. As such, it changes little about the internal mechanics and operational issues confronted by medical groups. It also changes little the way in which physicians and hospitals will look at each other in terms of developing a much more coordinated approach to the delivery of health care in a managed care environment.

Because the PHO model asks the parties to give up so little, it is naturally attractive and PHO development around the country is proceeding at rapid pace. Because it does not fundamentally change the way in which health care is being delivered, however, it creates significant risk that the completed effort will not be attractive to the purchasers of health care. Accordingly, the limited scope of a PHO may have little long-term significance in the way in which health care is delivered over the next decade. It does provide an incremental approach to begin to allow physicians and hospitals to work together. It is this effort of physician-hospital cooperation that may have the most lasting impact on how the parties relate to each other. To be effective over the coming years, the PHO must be able to transition into a more integrated relationship.

In many instances, however, the level of integration between physicians and hospitals must go beyond merely the contracting network represented by most PHOs. A new partnership with the hospital, with respect to the actual way in which care is organized, administered and delivered, is the goal of many organizations. For many medical groups, joining with a hospital or management company can provide administrative expertise and capital that may enable the group to vertically integrate its existing services with new ancillary services, create strategic alliances with inpatient providers and at the same time, employ efficiencies and management expertise.

Both hospitals and management companies are important players in this integration concept. Hospitals are a natural partner with which to consider an affiliation. Hospitals seek stronger alliances with medical groups to integrate the health care services they offer the hospital. Hospitals must recognize that health care delivered in the ambulatory setting represents an area of potential which extends far beyond the future growth of inpatient care. Medical groups, on the other hand, will be attracted to the capital and resources of a hospital along with the new range of services this combination can offer.

Management companies are the other players in this affiliation scenario. A management company, owned by outside investors in a for-profit setting, may allow medical groups advantages not present in the hospital affiliation option. These management companies may offer significant experience in ambulatory care, which hospitals, as inpatient providers, often lack. Management companies may also offer access to capital through the public stock markets. In addition, these companies, through multiple locations, can bring an added level of experience and expertise to solve common problems that local efforts rarely see. Finally, a larger organization may be able to obtain volume discounts and other efficiencies unavailable to local efforts. Insurance companies are also becoming increasingly active in the integration scenario. Insurance companies already have expertise with respect to the financing and actual administration of health care benefits, and they are involved actively in seeking relationships with physicians, particularly primary care physicians. These insurance companies recognize that providing a full range of integrated services to their customers will be a way to position themselves for maintaining their integral role in health care delivery of the future.

In general, the discussion of a need for a non-physician partner by a medical group often causes emotional discussions among physicians in any group. Fears of loss of independence and loss of control over the practice of medicine are threatening, yet very real concerns for individual practitioners. This perceived loss of independence must be balanced against the many advantages that an integrated alliance with a hospital will create for medical group participants. Regardless of which form an affiliation may take, both physicians and hospitals must understand that maintaining the status quo in health care delivery is not a viable option, and that loss of independence through affiliation must be put in the context of the threat to the very existence of these organizations.

A variety of factors will lead the leadership of a medical group and a hospital to consider integration beyond PHO development as a viable option. The first factor is that overhead associated with the practice of medicine is subject to constant upward pressure. This increase in overhead is associated directly with erosion of physician earnings. This situation generally encourages shortsighted cost cutting or delay of improvements which increase the inefficiencies and lack of sound management systems that can hold these skyrocketing costs to a minimum.

Second, the number of physicians in many markets, particularly in urban areas, continues to rise. Many medical groups face loss of market share due to new competitors, lost managed care contracts, patient shifting by direct contracting and marketing programs that result in the shifting of patient loyalties.

Third, medical practices have traditionally paid out all of their earnings to their physicians as compensation. As a consequence, most groups have little capital to expand or modernize their businesses. Without capital for investment, no business can survive, expand and prosper. The need for expanded ancillaries, for refurbishment of existing space, for additional satellites and for acquisition of equipment puts severe strains on the ability of the group to access capital. Withholding additional funds from physician income is an undesirable, unpalatable and risky way to raise capital, since the ability of physicians to invest in these items through actual dollar investment or through reduced take home pay is unpopular. Equally unpopular is the growing trend of financial institutions to request individual guarantees to be executed by those physicians as security for the repayment of any bank loans.

Fourth, the increasing complexity of medical practice often has left groups with management structures that need revision. Experienced managers are needed to run these larger and increasingly complex businesses, but physicians view increasing administrative salaries as an inappropriate increase of overhead. Hospital integration can provide more access to administrative experience necessary to run medical groups by the recruitment of additional ambulatory care management personnel to assist the existing group practice administrators. The affiliation also may ease the imposition of change in medical group operations by avoiding internal medical group politics and decision-making limitations.

Fifth, reimbursement from third parties including Medicare, managed care organizations and from direct contracting is under severe downward pressure. The decreasing revenue from the practice of medicine may increase the pressure for management assistance to search for new sources of income.

Sixth, in addition to revenue reductions generated by third party payer relationships, the growth of alternative delivery systems will present additional challenges for medical groups. To manage the risks associated with capitation reimbursement, and to develop management reporting, utilization review and quality assurance activities, groups will need to affiliate with parties that offer the experience and depth to provide these services competently or that have the ability to hire such expertise.

Finally, physicians are dissatisfied increasingly with the practice of medicine in general. Frequently internalizing that dissatisfaction and frustration by directing it towards the group, more physicians are leaving their practices. These physician departures negatively impact group revenue, result in increased recruitment costs and create replacement physician start-up expenses which all lower the profitability of the medical group and, most importantly, the compensation of the remaining physicians. A hospital affiliation can provide stability to the group, education regarding the external environmental changes which occur rapidly, and a renewed sense of confidence that may be necessary to boost physician morale as difficult practice environmental conditions are confronted.

Hospital integration options can provide alternatives to address many of these issues. A new discipline and business approach can be brought to group practice. Access to an administrative structure and team can supplement the single group manager who, in the past, has been forced to confront a multitude of tasks without sufficient backup. Affiliations also can provide access to the depth of experience necessary to negotiate alliances successfully with other providers and contracts with third party payers and managed care entities. Access to capital is also a major benefit. The affiliation should provide capital for future group expansion, for new ventures and for improved operations. Funds can also be supplied as part of the initial formation of a venture which can be used to buy out senior physicians and to lower the amount of buy-in needed by new physicians to become group members.

The structure of a relationship with this hospital/management/ insurance company essentially can take several forms. The concepts are essentially the same, and accordingly, except where necessary, this option will be referred to as a hospital affiliation or integration, regardless if the relationship is with a hospital, a management company, or an insurance company. All references to a hospital also include reference to a management company or an insurance company.

The hospital integration process can take one of three basic forms. Each represents a different level of integration with the hospital and each has its own set of nuances and difficulties to overcome in the formation, implementation and operation phase. While there are countless variations of these models, all can be broken down essentially into three types. These options are as follows:

1. The Management Services Organization Model — The Management Services Organization Model (MSO) is the least integrated of the physician-hospital integration options. It requires the establishment of a separate management organization whose function is to provide comprehensive management services to the independent medical group. The MSO, as it is called, provides comprehensive management services and hires most of the former employees of the medical group. The medical group continues its separate existence and is the "provider" of physician care to its patients. The medical group continues to own the medical records, it continues to own fees that it generates and are collected, and it continues to be responsible, in a legal sense, for the quality of care that it delivers. The MSO operates in a support role to the physician practitioners in the medical group. As such, its comprehensive management services provide a service to the medical group.

   The MSO option is appealing to physicians because it allows them to continue in their own organization, which is physician-owned and governed. It provides the most autonomy, but it also has the most risk. Physician groups that enter into the MSO relationship will ultimately remain responsible for the fiscal results of its operations. It is difficult, if not impossible, for MSO organizations to subsidize medical group income and this model does not provide any security to physician income.

In addition, this model, because it relies upon two separate entities coordinating the practice and administration of medicine, will come under scrutiny both from a fraud and abuse, and a self-referral perspective. To the extent that the medical group continues to provide ancillary services, self-referral laws will require those ancillaries to be provided in the group practice setting rather than in a separate management company. This legal restriction will hamper the ability to provide integrated management services, as those ancillary services must continue to be owned and operated by the medical group. In addition, the MSO must provide its services at fair market value in light of fraud and abuse concerns of paying physicians in effect for referrals to a hospital that owns the MSO.

2. The Foundation Model — The foundation model is an intermediate integration model. It provides care through a separately established medical foundation which is the "provider" of medical care. This provider arranges for the care, has the patient relationship, and employs many of the personnel necessary to render that care. The foundation, however, relies upon physicians who are organized in a separate medical group to provide physician services. This separate medical group does not have patient relationships in and of itself, but acts as an independent contractor to service the patients of the foundation. This model is an outgrowth of regulatory requirements in states such as California with strict corporate practice of medicine restrictions. The foundation model keeps intact the internal work-ings of a medical group, allows physicians to have autonomy with respect to group governance, compensation systems and with hiring and firing individual practitioners who are members of the group. The model has significant integration aspects, however, as the actual care is rendered not to the patients of the medical group, but to the patients of the foundation. As such, it is an intermediate model, allowing the foundation to be the provider, but also allowing the medical group to continue to exist as well. Fraud and Abuse and Anti-referral legislation will impact this model as well.

3. The Medical Division Employment Model — Under this model physicians actually become employed by the hospital or a hospital subsidiary. The critical aspect of this relationship is that physicians become employees of the hospital. As such, they are completely integrated within the overall delivery system. The challenge in this organizational model is to create a "medical division" where group practice skills and the administration of ambulatory care are con-ducted in a way that recognizes that ambulatory care is an entirely separate business from inpatient business.

From an operational perspective, an effective medical division relationship will consist of three components: First, physicians elect representatives to a governing body. Second, this governing body, sometimes called a policy council or governing board, sets the overall policy for the ambulatory care operations of the medical division. The policy council should consist of a physician majority or at least an equal number of physician and hospital representatives. Third, a separate committee, entitled a medical practice committee or executive committee, is organized to deal with exclusively medical practice issues. The medical executive committee should consist entirely of physicians, reflecting the medical practice issues that this committee will confront. With an effective governance mechanism, group practice principles can be encouraged and fostered and the development of an integrated system can proceed with the recognition of the important attributes of each component of the system. This model also has the added advantage of facilitating compliance with the fraud and abuse and self-referral laws.

The process

Medical groups and hospitals that embark upon the integration process will engage in a challenging and rewarding journey that will enhance the opportunities to accomplish their strategic goals. Combinations of medical groups or affiliations with hospitals will offer significant advantages to the participants over practicing in a smaller uncoordinated environment. The ability to create a more efficient operating environment, preserve individual physician relationships in a larger organization and improve business operations and financial strength will lead many medical groups to consider these options to achieve their strategic aims. Hospitals also must recognize these challenges and devise strategies to assist medical groups confronting the challenges of group practice, while at the same time formulating an effective strategy to allow their own institutions to grow, prosper and evolve into integrated delivery systems.

Without significant planning and a strategy to implement these integration efforts, however, many ventures will go astray. This loss of momentum can lead to confusion, delay, unnecessary expenses and perhaps loss of an opportunity for a relationship that improves not only medical care delivery, but patient care itself. Strong leadership by medical groups and by hospitals that explore these options will enable them to confront, with confidence and some sense of perspective, the merger/affiliation integration process, and to accomplish the myriad of details that must be identified and resolved to formalize the relationship. To implement the transaction, a broader perspective and problem-solving environment are necessary to create a long-term strategic alliance that will redefine the way health care will be delivered in the 21st century.

Chapter 2

The players in the process

Despite the attention paid to organizational behavior in health care organizations, the health care delivery integration process is, in essence, a challenge for the individual, and the success or failure of these combinations often rests upon the ability of individuals to master the process and to confront successfully the personal challenges they face. The appropriate roles of the individuals involved in the process must be examined, as how these roles are understood and performed are critical to the success or failure of a particular transaction.

The individuals involved in an integration project will have various objectives. It is the complex interplay between these personal agendas and the ability of the leadership of the parties to marshall and harmonize these different viewpoints that will determine whether the transaction is implemented successfully. As part of the planning process, the various roles that the players will have in the process must be analyzed, along with the decision-making structure and history of each party. The leadership of each party must understand the roles that must be performed to complete the transaction and must fill these roles in light of their own circumstances.

Once this planning process is complete, the leadership of a party must communicate the roles it envisions particular individuals playing to all those who will be involved in the process. Without understanding their various roles in the process, participants inevitably will have inaccurate expectations which will impair the establishment of good working relationships. The decision-making process also will be threatened and the ability to effect organizational change accordingly will be impaired.

There are many benefits of good planning to specify the assignments of the participants. Individuals will understand their roles, both in making decisions and in shaping the decision-making process. The leadership will be able to decide policy issues and to influence the decisions of the individual participants. The process itself will be assisted because clear lines of negotiating authority will be established. Dispute resolution and opinion formation can be assisted greatly as individual physicians and their own hidden agendas can be discovered, analyzed and harmonized. Communication efforts can be assisted, keeping those who are outside of the day-to-day decision-making process informed of the progress of the project, thereby encouraging their support by making them feel a part of the overall endeavor.

The board of directors

The role of the board of directors of a medical group in decision making for a group is a function of history, size and the evolution of that group. This development inevitably requires, as a group grows in size, the delegation of individual autonomy to a smaller decision-making body. For many medical groups, the board of directors may consist of all the physicians in the group. Other medical groups may have begun the transition from a "pure democracy" to a representative form of government. In any event, the board of directors, as the legal governing body of a group, will have a central role in any integration project. The major issues that affect physicians of a group will be discussed and decided at meetings of the board. It is likely that the board, as the decision-making body, will decide the basic issues concerning the transaction. The leadership provided by the board will be essential in deciding such fundamental issues as compensation, future governance and strategic plan.

With such a central role, board members can expect weekly meetings throughout the implementation phase. Extra hours will be required to understand the issues to allow for proper decisions to be made. Careful instructions must be given to those who will implement decisions, such as the negotiating committee and the administrative team of the group. The role of an individual board member will extend far beyond preparing for and attending the formal meetings of the board, however. Board members should be prepared to discuss in the hallways, in the doctors' lounge and in various other locations, questions from concerned staff members, and must be prepared to be strong advocates for the position of the group concerning the project.

The board must assume a leadership role, delegating, as appropriate, the details of the transaction to the administrative team, while at the same time being familiar enough with the concepts to give adequate direction to allow negotiating timetables to be met and other issues to be decided. The direction given to the merger/negotiating committee, which will usually be a separate group from the board, will be critical, and a two-way exchange of information and guidance must be established with that committee which will make the decisions concerning the integration project. Without direction from the board of directors on fundamental issues, the merger/negotiating committee will be left powerless to decide many implementation details.

The board also will play an essential role in communicating with the physicians and employees of the group. In this role the board will act as an advocate for its individual physician colleagues, while at the same time acting as a lobbyist to influence individual physician opinions on issues. This dual role will require board members to balance their loyalties between the organization to which they now belong, and the new organization that may be created in the integration process. Board members must agree, early in the project, that while differences in opinion undoubtedly will arise concerning specific details of the implementation process, once the board collectively has decided an issue, all board members must support, wholeheartedly, the decisions that have been made. Without this cohesive action, mixed messages will be conveyed to individual physician group members who will rely on the board to show leadership. Boards that are divided, and fail to support the consensus decisions arrived at the board level, will destroy the successful implementation of any project.

Board members will be challenged to represent their group in their relationships with the employees of the group and with third parties. The consensus building approach to decisions at the board level must be carried through to interactions with group employees who will, given the major changes happening in the group, experience significant anxiety concerning their future at the group. The role of the board regarding its employees will be to communicate appropriately, on a formal and informal level, the positions of the group. While this communication process at the formal level may be delegated to the administrator of the group and the physician executive, it is clear that numerous informal communication opportunities will occur. Board members must recognize the importance of their role in this communication plan. The board should discuss and develop consistent policies with respect to communication of information and should end every meeting at which decisions are made by determining the way in which those decisions will be communicated to both the physicians and non-physician employees of the group.

The negotiating/merger committee

To implement any transaction, it will be necessary for the board of directors to delegate their work to a smaller working group of three to five individuals which will have a more active role in the day-to-day negotiations. This negotiating/merger committee must, therefore, be composed of the key decision and opinion makers. Included within the committee should be the medical director/physician executive of the group, influential members of the board of directors who have the respect of, and ability to influence behavior of, the group and the administrator of the group. In order to represent the group successfully, the committee must have the ability to implement decisions concerning the policy established at the board level, and should encourage all involved in the process to proceed in a timely fashion to identify and resolve the multitude of issues that will arise.

The importance of this role of the committee as an intermediary cannot be overemphasized. On one hand, it will serve as the conduit by which positions of the group are communicated to the other parties. This process will require an exchange of views with the board and with individual physician members. The overlap of individuals on the board and on the committee should improve this communication process. On the other hand, this committee will have the primary interchange with the other medical groups or hospitals. This exchange of views with the other parties to the transaction will set the tone for the future relationship of the new operation. The role of this committee in negotiating successfully for its group will be to identify objectives that are critical for its group to achieve, to identify alternative ways in which those goals may be met in order to effect any necessary compromise, and to accommodate the needs of the other parties on goals which are critical for those parties to achieve as part of the negotiating process.

Each negotiating committee member must be comfortable working with the other members of the committee. The committee selection process, therefore, should include not only considerations about the formal position that each potential member may have in the governance of the group, but also the ability of a potential member to articulate and harmonize his positions with other members of the committee. It is this interplay of group members that can lead to a successful team approach to negotiating. Negotiating committee members must give serious consideration to the way in which they conduct themselves during this process. Negotiations must be held from a constructive rather than destructive point of view. The positions of others must be thoroughly heard and considered, and the ability to compromise must be practiced. Harsh, unyielding and aggressive positions taken in the process will leave scars for the future, and while negotiating positions occasionally may need to be taken that will cause tension, the way of communicating a negotiating position, and the respect for the individuals involved on the other side, must be demonstrated clearly. With several committee members expressing the position of the group, it will be possible to establish negotiating positions by allowing one member to take an aggressive, but not impolite, stance, that is moderated by other members of the group. If effectively orchestrated, this negotiating strategy can present the position of the group, while at the same time, avoid an overly adversarial approach that will alienate the other parties.

The players in the process

A negotiating/merger committee is needed in most transactions. Without a committee, there will be no formal mechanism which can bring the parties together in a common forum to facilitate decision making. While the size and complexity of a transaction may dictate a different approach, all parties should consider creating this smaller group to facilitate the transaction. Members of the committee should push their constituencies to delegate enough decision-making authority to this committee to allow decisions to be made and positions taken. Without this empowerment, it will be difficult to complete the transaction in a timely manner. Without this delegation of power, the negotiating committee will be unable to decide issues and will be reduced to a messenger service delivering positions formulated elsewhere. If this situation is allowed to develop, the ability to identify, resolve and proceed in a timely fashion with a project will be impaired. While the negotiating committee will receive guidance from its constituency, the way it implements that guidance should be left largely to its discretion.

Positive working relationships developed among negotiating committee members for all of the parties involved also will help the new organization at large. The decision-making process that will be created in any integration effort will depend upon the personal relationships built among individuals in the organizations. The merger/negotiating committee interchange probably will be the first significant and sustained contact between the parties. To the extent that positive decision making and negotiating methods can be fostered in the negotiating process, the framework for future success of the venture will have been laid. The familiarity which grows from constant interpersonal contact in this setting will help create a new combined organization mentality necessary for the new entity to survive and prosper.

The negotiating committee must be prepared to meet frequently to maintain momentum for the project. Weekly meetings will be likely. Committee members for each party also will need to meet internally to fashion their positions before meeting with the other parties to conduct actual discussions. Committee members should be prepared to commit a significant amount of time to the transaction, both with respect to meetings of the committee, internal and external, and with respect to the time necessary to communicate committee actions to the board of directors and physicians in their respective organizations.

The physician executive/medical director

Most medical groups of significant size will have selected a physician executive/medical director who performs a variety of functions. In smaller groups, the physician executive/medical director often will have an overlap of clinical and administrative duties to perform in fashioning the approach of the group to the practice of medicine. In larger groups a dichotomy will exist in the business role of the physician executive and the clinical role of the medical director, and in fact two individuals may fill this role. While the integration process will impact the roles of the medical director/physician executive on both the clinical and business side, it is the business skills this person has that will provide great assistance in the business transaction itself. Accordingly, all future references will be to the physician executive rather than the medical director. Without strong physician leadership in the implementation process, a project will never be consummated. The role of the physician executive in this process is multidimensional and is one of the most critical aspects of determining the success or failure of a project. The physician executive will be required to perform a variety of functions. Often this individual will act as lead negotiator, representing the position of the medical group. While the negotiating committee will meet in formal sessions with the other parties, the day-to-day interaction and give-and-take on various issues often will occur outside a formal meeting, and it is the physician executive who will usually be charged with performing this critical role. The approach taken to this process should set the tone for the development of a constructive working atmosphere. The physician executive will play a key role in formulating the position of the group based upon his vision and experience, but also will be called upon to listen to the group, to harmonize the discordant voices from the group, and to communicate with and listen to the other parties. The physician executive will act as communicator to the board of directors, reporting on progress, making recommendations as to positions to be taken, and identifying, clarifying and summarizing positions upon which the board must act.

As the chief representative of a group, the physician executive will play an important role communicating with physician members of the group who will look to the physician executive for an explanation of why individual physicians should support the transaction, and with the employees of the group who will seek any available information they can about the integration plans and their future in it. This role, as communicator and listener, will place inordinate demands on the time and leadership skills of the physician executive.

The physician executive will be called upon frequently to be the primary spokesman of the group with third parties and with the media. This role will require the physician executive to balance information that is available to the group at large, with the need to control carefully, if possible, the way in which the integration effort is portrayed to third parties and in the media.

Another important role that the physician executive will play is that of directing and supervising the efforts of the internal administrative staff of the group, in conjunction with the administrator of the group. This partnership with the administrator of the group will be critical for the preparation of the various analyses and preparatory work that must be undertaken to implement successfully a venture. Both the physician executive and administrator must develop a process by which decisions can be delegated to various members of the administrative staff. The work of outside consultants also must be coordinated. These consultants must be informed of the scope of their work, the strategic objectives of the group that must be obtained in the process and the need for timely and accurate responses to requests for information that are made by the physician executive and the administrator of the group. Coordinating work with respect to such issues as pension plan/benefits, employee relationships, discussions with lending institutions, and with important vendors who may be impacted by the transaction, can come within the scope of the executive or the clinic administrator depending upon the division of authority between these two positions. The other role of the physician executive is the traditional clinical role which a medical director fills. In any integration project, the medical practice style of the other medical groups or the philosophy of the hospital must be evaluated, for even where physicians may be comfortable from a business perspective with the combination, the relationship will be successful only if the clinical practice of medicine of the new relationship is consistent with the quality and style that a group is committed to practice. No amount of business organization will be able to smooth over differences in practice style philosophies. A primary role of the medical director will be to evaluate the practice philosophy of the other parties and to identify issues that need to be resolved. This evaluation must be accomplished early in the process as part of determining whether the parties do, in fact, fit together. In a hospital affiliation, the medical director also must determine the "corporate" philosophy of that non-physician partner to determine whether the philosophy of delivery of health care that is held by that partner is consistent with that of the medical group. This evaluation of physician credentials and of corporate philosophies must be communicated to the board of directors of the group, as well as to physicians in the group at large. All of these individuals will be interested in the clinical aspects of the new relationship and the potential impact on their practice of medicine as much as in the impact on business operations.

The administrator

The role of the administrator of a group in any integration effort is as important as the role of the physician executive. In groups where no physician executive position exists, nearly all of those tasks that would have been performed by the physician executive will be the responsibility of the administrator. The manner in which the administrator performs that role will largely determine whether the project can be implemented effectively and whether the new entity will begin operations successfully. The integration process, therefore, will present a significant challenge to the personal and leadership skills of the administrator.

Balancing conflicting loyalties will be a major challenge for the administrator, who must be responsive to the interests of his current employer, while at the same time be aware that for the success of the integration effort, confidence in the administrator must be engendered from all physicians in a physician integration project, or from the hospital that will be involved in an affiliation. These conflicting loyalties of new and old will place significant stress upon the administrator who must be an advocate of the interests of the physicians in his/her existing group, but who also must have the best interests of the new organization in mind when making decisions that will have a long lasting structural impact on the future viability of the new organization.

Successfully implementing a medical group merger or hospital integration project will be a major career achievement for the administrator. The challenges presented in the process should be viewed in a positive light by the administrator and as an opportunity to demonstrate excellence in the field. By viewing the combination as a career challenge, by exhibiting leadership and by demonstrating a positive attitude that anything is possible, the administrator will be able to achieve success and advancement for the group as well as personally. As a new, more complex position usually will be created after the completion of the integration effort, an administrator who has won the respect of all those involved in the process will be able to accept that job or will be an attractive candidate in a growing field where experience and demonstrated competence are highly sought after attributes. During the process, therefore, the administrator should be aware that his/her performance will be scrutinized by all involved, including physicians and hospital personnel. All of these individuals will be evaluating continuously the skills of the administrator in leading the operational aspects of the transaction. The way an administrator responds to this challenge will dictate, in large measure, the ability of the administrator to remain employed by the new organization one year after the creation of the new relationship.

The role of the administrator must be multifaceted. The administrator will be challenged to present the business perspective of the project to the board and to the medical staff of the group. The administrator will need to be responsive to the needs of the board and the negotiating committee by adequately preparing issues for their decision which will include analysis and collection of the necessary data, and a summary of the issues and recommendations with respect to actions. This type of analysis will greatly facilitate decision making by the board.

The administrator will be confronted with the challenge of directing the analysis of the financial implications of the proposed relationship for the group. If assets or stock are to be sold or exchanged, the administrator must be prepared to direct the analysis of that transaction. This financial analysis should include identifying the assets and appropriately placing values upon them or the stock of the group, preparing the assets so they may be transferred without liens or encumbrances, and coordinating the communications with banks, lenders and other third parties. The administrator will be required to provide input, direction and information on a timely basis, to accountants, lawyers and other consultants who will require guidance and information concerning their assigned tasks in the transaction. As the administrator will be present day after day during the transaction, he/she will be able to provide guidance on the myriad of small issues which arise and usually will be the only person who can locate the business records and other information concerning the group.

The administrator also will be confronted with coordinating the reorganization of the employees of the group. This effort will require that the administrator prepare a plan for the new operations which may result in downsizing or may result in the modification of employee job descriptions for some employees in a new organization. The administrator must be prepared to redefine the organizational structure of the staff, to assess the financial impact of this restructuring and to communicate the decisions made regarding restructuring to all employees. A smooth transition to the new entity will be enhanced greatly through an effective plan that will organize the human resource component to accomplish the integration project in an efficient and effective manner.

Individual physicians

Medical groups, of course, are made up of individual physicians and it is the reaction to the proposed integration effort on the individual level that will dictate whether the combination can be achieved, and once achieved, whether it ultimately will be successful in creating a better practice environment. The reaction of the individual physician who has not been involved intimately in the process by way of a position on the board of directors or negotiating committee must be addressed by the leadership of the medical group in the planning process. The moment of truth in the implementation of the project may occur when individual physicians are asked to sign new employment agreements and, therefore, be required to commit personally to the merger or affiliation. Without adequate preparation by the decision makers in a group, individual physicians may not feel part of the process and may not accept the proposed combination. Loss of significant numbers of physicians in the process may doom the project to failure. To minimize this risk, a new identity must be forged at the individual physician level by convincing physicians of the strategic importance of the combination and by convincing those physicians that the physician culture of the combined group, or the culture of the group as impacted by the hospital, will be consistent with the environment in which the physician will be comfortable practicing.

Individual physicians, however, must be led to recognize the benefits associated with the combination, and also must be apprised of the sacrifices that must be made along the way. This communication process means that meetings must be held frequently to apprise the individual physicians as a group of the rationale for the integration effort, the impact upon the clinical practice of medicine that the combination may bring about, and the financial implications of the relationship. In addition, groups of individuals, by department or working group, must be gathered together to allow specific concerns to be addressed and diffused outside of a more formal and potentially intimidating group meeting. This informal process will help ensure that all concerns of the constituent members of the group are addressed.

Physicians should be given the opportunity to express their concerns on the individual level as well. Board members, the physician executive and administrator must make themselves available for this type of interchange. Inevitably, the leadership will need to adjust positions or make accommodations for those physicians who express significant concerns about certain aspects of the venture. These concerns must be dealt with effectively, either by incorporating the concerns and a proposed solution in the overall project, by explaining to the physician how the perceived concern is not a problem, by explaining that the process is in the overall best interests of the group even in light of these concerns, or by dealing with the problem more effectively after the consummation of the proposed combination.

Hospital personnel

The individuals employed by the hospital often will be part of an organization with clearer and shorter lines of decision making than in a medical group, making the process of arriving at positions to be taken in the integration process less complex to determine and implement. Even though a reporting mechanism to a board of directors will exist, this reporting process usually is better established than the same process in a medical group.

While the internal dynamics of the operation of a hospital are not without their challenges, the two main challenges in the integration context for hospital personnel are understanding the complexities of medical group dynamics and the business issues associated with ambulatory care. With respect to medical group dynamics, hospital personnel must understand that, unlike business organizations with clearer lines of decision making and authority, medical groups and individual physicians are much more difficult to organize or control. Attention to this process must be given throughout by recognizing physician concerns, and by understanding and utilizing the formal and informal channels of decision making and opinion formation in medical groups.

With respect to ambulatory care operations, many hospitals will lack the experience to understand and manage ambulatory, as opposed to inpatient, care. Hospital personnel should be prepared to spend time learning the ambulatory care business, to work cooperatively with medical group administrators to develop combined systems, and to expend sufficient resources to fill gaps in ambulatory care managerial talent.

Legal counsel

The role of legal counsel must be performed well to implement any project successfully. Initially, the medical group must satisfy itself that its legal counsel is suited to the task. The choice of counsel may have already been made because of long-standing historical relationships. As the project begins, however, medical leadership should consider the appropriateness of that counsel to the task. First, familiarity with medical groups and their operations is absolutely critical. Without an understanding of how the health care system works, and how the medical groups function within that industry, a lawyer often will miss critical points in representing a medical group. Failing to understand governance of medical groups, the importance of physician contracts or the impact of managed care upon operations will leave a medical group under-represented in areas in which legal counsel can provide significant guidance.

Coupled with the knowledge of the health care industry, however, legal counsel for the group also must have significant experience with mergers/acquisitions and other combinations. Relationships which involve mergers, the sale of assets or stock and/or long-term affiliation agreements have their own unique set of legal issues, and legal counsel should have experience in similar transactions in health care to enable the best interests of the medical group to be served and to negotiate effectively with the other parties. Attorneys who are unfamiliar with the nuances of structuring these transactions will put their groups at a significant disadvantage by being unaware of the various alternative ways the strategic goals of the group can be obtained.

Legal counsel must be instructed to approach the transaction without the adversarial approach employed by many lawyers. The fundamental basis on which the new combination will operate is one of mutual trust and respect. The approach taken in negotiations and implementation of the project by legal counsel, therefore, should be one of cooperation and consideration, as opposed to confrontation. While tough positions may need to be taken during this negotiating process, legal counsel must recognize that the parties will live with each other after the transaction is consummated, and that wounds caused during the negotiating process often take years to heal.

Effective legal counsel can provide much more than a review of the documents necessary to consummate the transaction. The role of counsel should be defined to include not only protecting the interest of the group in the documents, but also identifying the most appropriate structure for the organization of the group, suggesting how the relationship should work, and acting as a coordinator for the various mechanics of implementing the transaction. Legal counsel should, therefore, be in a position to anticipate pitfalls that may be unrecognized by a group because the group likely will not have engaged in this type of transaction. The counseling aspect of the role of the lawyer also should not be underestimated. Legal counsel can play an effective role in the process by planning, encouraging and reassuring the medical group along the way. Legal counsel should be expected to have a close working relationship with the accountants and financial advisors of the medical group.

The role of the legal counsel in the transaction will include being able to work cooperatively with the other legal counsel involved. While each group must be ably represented and its position advanced, neither group will benefit from legal counsel that attempts to extract too many concessions from the other side. Perceived imbalances in the integration process will lead only to long-standing suspicion and resentment.

Accountants and financial advisors

The financial analysis that must be undertaken in any integration project will place heavy demands on the financial advisors of a medical group. To the extent that the group has in-house financial expertise, a significant amount of the basic work concerning the analysis of the proposed financial combination can be performed by that personnel. Independent financial advisors will be necessary, however, to perform a variety of functions. These financial advisors will be asked to undertake the preparation of forecasts regarding the financial implications of the integration. Accountants with which the group has an ongoing relationship should be in the best position to facilitate the analysis that must be made.

Each party will have its own set of financial statements which must be reviewed and analyzed. In addition to the existing financial situations of the participants that must be examined, financial statements and projections must be prepared that will allow a party to analyze correctly the financial position of the other parties, and to forecast the impact of the new structure upon expenses, operations, physician incomes and other matters. Finally, accountants can perform a useful role in analyzing the existing financial condition of the other parties.

Financial advisors should be closely consulted with respect to the tax planning associated with the sale of any assets or stock, and distribution of any proceeds to individual physicians. Accountants should provide, prior to closing, a preliminary analysis which incorporates the impact of the transaction on the tax situation of that party. Equally as important, accountants should be asked to provide a post transaction analysis coupled with a pro forma tax return that can forecast accurately the potential tax liability for the transaction. These two activities should not be disregarded, as the potential gains of any transaction can be eliminated if poor planning and inaccurate tax analysis are allowed to occur. The group and its leadership must place significant importance on, and be willing to expend resources for, the performance of this important advisory role, as no tax planning is possible after a tax year has concluded.

The facilitator

In implementing an integration project, the parties may wish to consider utilizing a facilitator who will act as an advocate for the new organization or relationship. This facilitator can serve an effective role in scheduling the transaction, providing leadership on difficult issues, and ensuring that all the other actors in the process are adequately performing their tasks. The facilitator brings the added advantage of being viewed as impartial. By acting as an advocate for the "new relationship," the facilitator can speak without past relationships impairing perceived fairness and will lessen the adversarial nature of the parties. This facilitator may be a health care consultant, financial expert or attorney. Whatever the occupation of the facilitator, it is clear that he or she must possess strong organizational and leadership skills.

The parties must be willing to empower the facilitator to make decisions regarding how issues are analyzed and decided, and must be willing to provide the facilitator latitude about how the transaction should proceed, as the parties will confront for the first time many difficult issues in creating the new relationship. A facilitator may be effective in any integration effort regardless of the form and regardless of the parties involved.

Chapter 3

Medical group acquisitions and mergers

Medical groups that integrate completely with other groups either engage in a merger or an acquisition. From a strictly legal perspective, a merger is generally referred to as a combination of two or more organizations which results in a single surviving entity. An acquisition, on the other hand, describes when a larger medical group purchases a smaller group which joins the larger group. In most medical group combinations, however, the process is best described as a merger, since the common connotation of that term implies a combination among relatively equal parties.

This tone of equality is important for physicians who, in most instances, do not wish to be "acquired" by another medical group. While some combinations are no doubt an acquisition by the larger group (e.g., a 70 person medical group combining with a four person medical group), there is a wide range of medical group sizes where the combination of the two groups will be appropriately called a merger.

While the issues in either a merger or acquisition are largely the same, the process is most complicated when a true legal merger exists. Therefore, this chapter will discuss the full ramifications of a merger, terming any combination of medical groups a merger, and specifically raising issues unique to acquisitions where appropriate.

The merger process creates many challenges. Groups that engage in the process must be prepared to undertake an intensive and comprehensive effort to achieve the combination. Groups will confront a multitude of factors, but these factors must not be viewed in isolation. The participants must remember that the merger process itself is only a legal mechanism to achieve the strategic goals of the participants. The art of implementing any merger is to combine these various considerations into a cohesive whole, identifying and resolving issues that arise along the way, while maintaining the momentum created by the initial enthusiasm for the merger concept and the development of the strategic vision which originated the merger strategy.

Identification of candidates

The initial merger idea may come from a variety of sources. The medical marketplace in a particular locality may force a group to consider a combination. Other integration activities, competition, hospital relationships, the demands of third party payers, or individual personal relationships may cause the development of a strategic plan which includes a merger with another group.

The initial starting place for any merger is the identification of a viable merger candidate. Cultural similarities are important, as groups having a common culture will find combination easier. A common strategic vision is also critical. While a common culture and strategic vision may not be present at the beginning, the realistic opportunity to create that common vision must exist. Combinations that will allow the creation of a strategic mass of physicians for hospital or third party payer negotiations often make good sense. Combinations that add strategic services that a single group has lacked, or that provide access to existing relationships with hospitals, third party payers, or with industry, are other factors that should be examined. The type of the practice is also an important factor, as primary care combinations will generally have more strategic value than single subspecialty mergers. Finally, not to be underestimated, are the practice styles of the individual physicians. Commitment to excellence and patient service are all factors which can lead groups to identify common ground upon which groups can come together.

Groups must survey their community for candidates. The method of identifying candidates should be done in a confidential manner. Informal approaches through casual conversations are the best method to proceed after a group has identified a candidate. A nonthreatening approach, suggesting an exploration of common interests and values, is one way to begin the dialogue. This low-key approach will be effective in creating a way in which the groups can feel a part of the process. Informal approaches also will not prematurely harden positions of the physicians of one group or another, or appear so aggressive that the group approached will be intimidated or discouraged from proceeding. In addition, if the target group is uninterested, the informal approach will not put the prestige of the approaching group on the line if the overture is rebuffed.

Finally, groups should approach the candidate identification process as a long-term endeavor, working to make contacts, building relationships and planting the seeds for future development. Once begun, conversations may stretch over a long period of time — perhaps even years. Detailed discussions or formal negotiations may finally be precipitated by external events that raise the consciousness of the groups that a combination is now compelling in light of changed circumstances.

How it works

To accomplish a merger, a merger agreement must set forth the legal basis on which the groups will be combined. Typically, the merger agreement will provide that the corporate existence of one or more groups will be merged into the surviving group, and that the surviving group will be the entity that goes forward after the merger. From the legal perspective, all of the rights, responsibilities, assets and liabilities of each group are combined and transferred automatically to the surviving group. Each group must examine carefully the assets and liabilities of the other groups prior to the merger, because merging the groups together means that these liabilities transfer automatically without further action by any of the parties. In addition, the physician shareholders of the medical groups will have their shareholdings combined so all physicians have an ownership interest in the new group after the merger.

The acquisition process differs in a conceptual way from that of a merger. In an acquisition, a smaller group in effect joins the larger group. The physicians of the smaller group execute employment agreements with the larger group, thereby becoming employees of the larger group under the same terms and conditions as the physician-employees of the larger group. These acquisitions often focus on an asset acquisition which requires the evaluation of the assets, the establishment of the purchase price and the transfer of those assets to the larger medical group.

Group culture

A critical issue in identifying potential combination candidates, in structuring the merger and in prospering as a newly combined medical group, is the evaluation and melding together of the culture of each group. Initially, both groups must determine whether their values, work styles and vision for the future are compatible. Without a common culture, or at least a commitment to blend the respective cultures of the groups together, the merger may be mechanically implemented, but the formation of a single group which prospers in the long run will never be achieved. Groups, therefore, must identify the major components of their culture and whether the other group and its value systems are compatible with their own.

The evaluation of group culture can proceed in a variety of ways. Under ideal circumstances, the groups will have worked together and will know each other well, given their presence in the local medical community. In other situations, the groups may not have a longstanding relationship and the comfort level with which they proceed can be expected to develop slowly over time. A consultant can assist in the culture identification process by interviewing the physicians of both groups to determine work styles, values and personalities. Using a "neutral" third party to gather this data can be an effective non-threatening way to assess the groups and ask the "hard" questions that even groups well known to each other will be reluctant to explore. Interviews and questionnaires can be used by this third party to develop a composite view of the culture of the respective groups. The groups should expect a report which identifies, without specific names, the personalities of the groups, their work habits, their vision for the practice of medicine and their individual plans for the future. Determining if there is a proper fit will be well worth the cost of this project.

Having obtained this data, the leadership of the respective groups must undertake an honest, straightforward appraisal of the strengths and weaknesses of group members. To determine a strategy to combine these groups on the personal level, the leadership of each group must have candid discussions about their compatibility. This personal equation may well spell the success or failure for any merger.

Once the compatibility of the groups is determined, strategies should be devised to blend the cultures of the groups. To foster personal relationships, it is important for the groups to get to know each other better. Dinners or other social gatherings should be scheduled to assist in this process.

Strategic plan

As important as group culture and personal equation issues are for the viability of any merger, the strategic vision of the respective groups and the manner in which they desire to practice medicine will have an equally significant role in determining the feasibility of a merger. As part of the initial identification of candidates and discussions, many planning issues will have been identified that will need to be addressed. The strategic vision that a combined group may have for its future and how it will achieve those goals must be a part of any merger process. Once the initial conversations have taken place and the parties conclude there is serious interest in proceeding, a process must be instituted to complete the strategic plan.

To fashion this strategic vision, a combined planning retreat of the groups may be warranted early in the merger process. This planning retreat can allow group members to begin working together effectively and help them develop combined strategies for their future. A facilitator may be necessary to keep the groups focused on the larger strategic issues. This facilitator could be the individual who performed the initial cultural review to determine the compatibility of the groups. This session should be held early in the process because of the importance of an effective strategic plan. Planning allows the groups to work closely together and communicate with each other. Groups that ignore this team-building process do so at their peril, as this process will help to mold a single-group mentality.

In forming any strategic plan, groups must begin by considering four separate concepts: strengths, weaknesses, opportunities and threats.

Strengths

Each group must identify its current strengths. These strengths may include personnel, practice locations, hospital affiliations or specialties offered. Identifying these strengths will enable the groups to evaluate critically how they achieved the market position they now have, and will help the groups focus on what they do well. Expanding upon these strengths is an effective way for the new group to achieve its goals.

Weaknesses

The weaknesses of each group must be examined. The merger, in fact, may assist in eliminating some weaknesses by creating certain benefits. Weaknesses must be honestly and openly assessed. For example, specialty coverage in a given practice or subspecialty area may be lacking. The need to recruit additional physicians for coverage or service considerations may be apparent. The payer mix of a particular group may be overly dependent upon Medicare or a single third-party relationship. Multispecialty groups may not have the appropriate primary care focus. All of these issues must be addressed in a strategic plan to allow coordinated action to be taken to improve these weaknesses.

Opportunities

Opportunities may exist for both groups separately. In addition, many new opportunities may present themselves to the new combined group. A combined group may make a much more attractive candidate for hospital affiliation. The combined group may offer a significantly wider range of services that can attract the attention of managed care entities, insurance companies or direct contracting initiatives. Combined groups may provide a greater range of care that improves overall quality of patient care offered by the group. Opportunities also may exist to institute comprehensive utilization review or quality assurance programs to encourage a group practice concept.

Threats

To respond with an effective strategy, groups must also perceive the realistic threats to their practices. Some of these threats may be national in scope and are ones which cannot be changed or diverted, but only planned for. Other threats may come in the form of competitive medical groups, loss of physicians, growing hospital, ancillary or ambulatory care business, and employer or managed care initiatives. The ability of a group to respond to these competitive threats must receive significant attention in this planning process.

Groups that can identify their strengths, weaknesses, opportunities and threats will be in a good position to fashion an effective strategic plan. This conceptual process will help identify common goals, opportunities and strategies which can be used to forge group consensus and identity. A strategic vision which prioritizes steps to be taken should be enunciated. Groups should expect a strategic plan to cover such issues as:

- scope of specialties to be provided by the combined group;
- practice locations at which the group should deliver its services;
- potential hospital affiliation and the identification of a strong partner;
- a compensation system that can enable the group to function as an effective whole;
- direct contracting strategies with employers;
- managed care strategies;
- practice style considerations;
- utilization review, quality assurance and research activities; and
- other merger candidates or needs.

Identifying this strategic vision will form the blueprint for new group operations, and will guide the thinking of individual physicians who participate in the merger process. This long-range vision can provide the physicians with the perspective to look beyond single, troublesome issues and focus on larger, strategic goals which the merger will achieve. Allowing physicians to meet and jointly develop a strategic plan will provide the "consensus building" that is often necessary for the participating physicians to embrace the goals achieved by the merger.

The merger framework

In the merger, the simplest structure is for one medical group to combine or merge with the second medical group, with the rights and responsibilities of the first medical group becoming automatically vested in the second medical group. The corporate existence of the first group automatically ceases upon combination with the second group. This form of merger is illustrated as Exhibit 1. This simple form of transaction will be applicable in most situations of medical group mergers.

In specific health care situations that may be dictated by peculiarities of state law, or in shareholder dispute situations, a third corporation could be used as part of this overall merger process. Generally, the use of the third corporation to create a "triangular" merger structure will allow the removal of certain shareholders with whom the medical groups no longer wish to have a relationship. Most medical groups should have appropriate shareholders' agreements or employment agreements governing the resale of stock, and state law concerning medical practice may often require resale of that stock upon termination of employment. These factors mean that the use of a triangular merger structure is, for the most part, unnecessary in medical group mergers. A description of this triangular merger process is set forth on Exhibit 2.

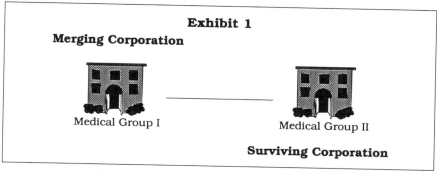

Exhibit 1

Merging Corporation

Medical Group I   Medical Group II

Surviving Corporation

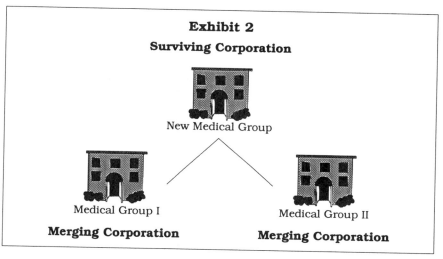

Exhibit 2

Surviving Corporation

New Medical Group

Medical Group I   Medical Group II

Merging Corporation   **Merging Corporation**

The acquisition framework

When a medical group acquires the assets of another group, the usual structure is for the purchaser of the assets, by way of an asset purchase agreement, to buy the assets of the medical group for a stated price, and to assume specific liabilities that are listed in the agreement. The general advantage of this structure is that, in most instances, the sale of assets permits the purchaser to assume only those liabilities specifically set forth in the asset purchase agreement. This ability to limit liability is an attractive provision of an asset purchase transaction, as the purchaser does not assume all liabilities, disclosed and undisclosed, as in a merger transaction. Asset acquisitions cut off, in most instances, this undesirable liability assumption. This limitation of "transferee" liability for undisclosed liabilities has been eroded in several areas such as environmental and employee relations, which means that even in some asset acquisitions these type of liabilities of a seller may be imposed by law upon a purchaser. While the range of these liabilities that are assumed automatically by a purchaser, however, remains small, these risks should be examined carefully during the due diligence process. This process is illustrated on Exhibit 3.

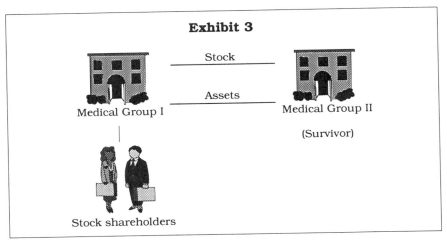

Exhibit 3

Stock

Assets

Medical Group I

Medical Group II

(Survivor)

Stock shareholders

Another mechanism to accomplish an acquisition may be the outright sale of the corporate stock of a medical group to another medical group or hospital. This process is illustrated on Exhibit 4.

Under this structure, a medical group or hospital acquires all of the assets and liabilities of another medical group by purchasing its corporate stock. In general, this structure will be used only in limited circumstances, as medical group transactions structured as a tax-free merger will be preferable to this structure which may involve a taxable event. Because a sale of stock involves the automatic assumption of all liabilities, disclosed or undisclosed, this mechanism has no tax advantage and contains all of the risks found in a merger with respect to an assumption of unknown liabilities. In most medical group combinations, a merger, as opposed to a sale of stock, will be the appropriate structure.

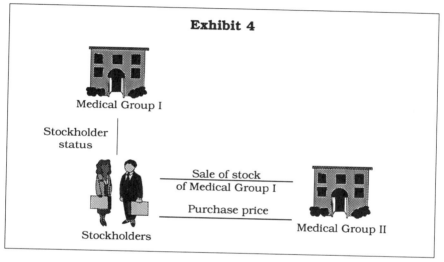

Exhibit 4

Medical Group I

Stockholder status

Sale of stock of Medical Group I

Purchase price

Stockholders

Medical Group II

Combining ownership

For most mergers, two separate combination issues must be resolved. First, a plan must be devised to combine the professional corporations or other entities in which the physicians practice medicine. To devise this plan, a review of the respective ownership interests and their value for each group must be made. It will be necessary to value, on a consistent basis, the assets and liabilities of the respective groups. Financial statements of the participants must be prepared and evaluated on a consistent and comparative basis. These statements determine the respective value of the interest of each physician in a group.

Once this valuation process is complete and the value of each physician has been determined, the groups can develop an appropriate combination strategy. As a general proposition, mergers will be structured most effectively if the physicians in each group can participate in the new group on the same relative basis that they participated in the old group. In the best case, all physicians should have equal ownership in the new group or a specific plan that moves all physicians to equal ownership should be adopted. The plan must create an ownership structure to allow physicians to feel that they have a significant voice in the affairs of the combined group. The ease in which this combination may be accomplished depends upon the relative differences in individual physician ownership of each group, expressed as a dollar value.

Small discrepancies in ownership will make a combination quite easy, as equal ownership by all physicians can be achieved by distributing small payments to those physicians with a more valuable ownership interest. In the situation, for example, where the value per physician of one group exceeds the value per physician of the other group, the valuation of the first group could be reduced to equal the lower valued group. In this way, the lower valued group will not be required to pay anything to go forward with the merger. This absence of any up front payment will smooth the way to a combination by eliminating the need for physicians to contribute funds to participate in the new group.

If, on the other hand, a wide disparity exists in valuation between the respective groups, more creative ways will be needed to move physicians toward equal ownership. For example, physicians in the lower valued group may be asked to pay a fixed amount over a period of years to achieve equal stock ownership. This mechanism would allow, as in the case of new physicians joining the group, a gradual buy-in process. Another alternative is to obtain financing to allow these contributions to be made. The general aversion to adding debt under these circumstances would, however, reduce the attractiveness of this option. Finally, it may be possible to achieve the merger by accepting that a different stockholder interest will be held by physicians. This is generally not recommended as it may create the perception of two classes of physicians in a practice; those with a higher number of shares and those with a lower number of shares. A combination of these approaches ultimately may be necessary to achieve an acceptable combination plan.

The second aspect of merger structure that must be addressed is real estate ownership. For many groups, real estate will be held in a partnership or corporation separate from the medical practice. This separate ownership of property and a more likely disparity of ownership interests, even among the partners of an existing group, will often require different approaches than those used to combine the medical group practice organizations. Because of the complexity of this real estate factor, it is separately discussed in Chapter 7.

Regardless of the combination plan contemplated, to encourage physician support for a merger, physicians should not be asked to make significant monetary investments, either in the corporation or in real estate. Requiring a substantial initial buy-in will dampen the enthusiasm of physicians who personally must contribute funds, thus jeopardizing the success of the merger. Members of the constituent medical groups must not be faced with a large buy-in, or the long-range benefits of the merger will be overshadowed by concerns over initial short-term cash requirements.

Merger design issues

Building upon the strategic plan and merger structure, a merger design process must be developed. To accomplish this goal, key financial issues must be assessed by reviewing budgets, financial reports and other materials to develop a consistent data base of information about each organization. This financial information and the merger design issues raised below will be used to develop projections and options concerning the proposed merger. The financial assumptions made in the merger design process will impact significantly how the merger is achieved and accepted by physicians.

First, the parties must consider whether the proposed merger, as designed, will realize the strategic advantages identified in the strategic plan. A strategy must be developed to maximize the chance of success and to make basic decisions regarding the location of the group, existing and additional specialties and ancillary services to be provided by the group.

Second, basic assumptions should be made regarding combined group expenses and physician compensation models. These assumptions will allow the evaluation of various scenarios concerning economies of scale and compensation. Compensation issues are more fully discussed later in this chapter.

Third, the parties must make certain basic assumptions about the revenue projections for the combined group and about charges for its medical services. Accurate financial forecasts must be made for the combined group. To begin that process, assumptions must be made concerning pricing to be employed by the new group. Adjustments to prices and a combined pricing policy must be adopted to achieve accurate operational forecasts.

Fourth, certain other basic assumptions must be made. The impact of combining real property and assets of the medical practice must be included in financial modeling to test basic assumptions and the feasibility of the combinations. Cash flow projections must be made to prepare for combined operations and to forecast the need for additional equity to sustain the operations of the new group. Basic decisions also should be made concerning the long process of recruiting and hiring of physicians. A more in-depth discussion of the financial projections that are necessary in the design process is contained in Chapter 19.

Selecting a name

A critical issue in any merger is the name under which the new group will practice. This issue, as much as any other, may create significant discord. Each group likely will have a vested interest and emotional attachment to its own name. Each group will have the tendency to view the selection and perpetuation of its own name as a victory in the "merger battle." While the competitiveness of physicians will have both sides looking for ways to claim "victory" over the other, the leadership of the medical groups must try to minimize any dispute concerning a name. A strong effort must be made to depersonalize the name selection process, and to employ sound marketing principles to pick a new name.

The parties must understand that the most significant purpose for any name of a group is to convey a message about the group. The name should be selected with a marketing focus that will allow the name to inform the public, in an effective and distinct way, about the group with respect to the delivery of medical care. The new name must project the image of the practice to the public at large and particularly to self-referring patients. These patients will often select their physician based upon the name of a group, and this name should facilitate that selection by patients who refer themselves to the group.

Most referral relationships with other physicians are not based upon the name of a group. Physician colleagues tend to refer based upon personal relationships and past interaction. These referral relationships, in many instances, will continue after the merger and while it will be necessary to inform the physician referral source of the new name, it will be an easier task in comparison to informing the public at large.

Some groups may resolve the name selection issue on their own. In those fortunate circumstances, both groups may realize that the name of one group may be clearly superior in the marketplace, or that a totally new name is appropriate in light of the circumstances. In some instances, physicians will be diverted from considering marketing principles in the name selection process, and the expertise of a marketing/public relations firm will need to be employed to select or guide the name selection process. The role of a marketing firm will be to study the appropriate market and to assist the groups in evaluation of names that convey the desired message. Using this "independent third party" has advantages where there is a dispute over the name. First, it avoids political squabbles. Second, it legitimizes the decision-making process through the use of an outside expert. Third, it allows the name selection process to employ sound marketing principles to ensure that the appropriate message is broadcast to the marketplace. Finally, the marketing firm can devise an effective communication strategy that will smooth the transition to a new name and will highlight the selected name as being appropriate for this newly combined medical group.

Selection of a well-experienced and qualified marketing group will do much to convince physicians that a true "expert" has been retained. This expert status will allow medical groups to have confidence in the decision that is made and will defuse the "we" vs. "they" mentality that may develop over this issue. Putting the name process on a professional level will set the proper tone for the selection of the best name.

The name selection process should be broken down into several steps. Initially, the strategic plan of the group should be examined to determine its future direction. The name selected should be part of the integrated plan to communicate the future growth and direction of the group. It is necessary to select several options for a group name. Any name considered will need to be acceptable for use in the state. State licensing authorities, both medical and corporate, must approve the use of a corporate name. A check of name availability is the first step before any list of potential names is compiled. The reservation of a corporate name with state authorities is an important adjunct to this process, as any potential name should be protected from future use by third parties. By taking this fundamental preliminary step, the group can be assured that the resources expended in examining and testing a name will not be done in vain, and that the name will, in fact, be available after the selection process is made.

The second part in the name selection process involves selection of alternative names. Various principles may be utilized in this process. The ultimate goal, however, is to have the name serve a marketing purpose. Geographic names may be effectively used. Wider geographic areas that go beyond a section of a city or the city itself may convey the message that the group desires to be the recognized provider of medical care in a given region. The name also should convey the appropriate practice specialty of the group. Again, patients who will self-select the group are those most sensitive to a name, and, therefore, the name selected should reflect the type of service provided by the medical group. Given that the goal of the name is communication to nonphysicians, technical names of medical specialties should be avoided as lay persons are often unfamiliar with medical terminology.

Finally, groups should be reluctant to use the name of an individual to describe the new practice. While there are classic examples of well-known national medical groups that have utilized the names of their founders in a most effective manner, most medical groups will not be in this enviable position. The name of an individual usually will not convey the desired message and will not be known readily to patients who will self refer to the group.

Having selected a variety of alternatives by employing these principles, the next task is to analyze the message conveyed by those names to both the physician members of the group and to the general public. Public perceptions of the existing names and the other names on the list should be assessed. This data can then be presented to physicians in the respective groups and recommendations made about the appropriate name to be utilized.

After this preliminary presentation, the medical groups should authorize further market testing of two or three names. This testing can take the form of a focus group in which narrowly defined questions and reactions can be elicited from members of the general public. The reaction of individuals who likely will refer themselves for medical care should be analyzed. Focus group results can then be conveyed in a final meeting of the physicians to present the data and final recommendations.

Having laid the groundwork for a professional approach to the selection of a market-sensitive name, the decision should be positioned effectively to minimize potential disputes concerning this name. Not all name selection processes may go smoothly, however. Loss of confidence in the marketing approach or emotional attachment to particular names may hamper the process. The eventual outcome, however, may spell success or failure for the merger efforts. It is important, therefore, to recognize the sensitivities of those involved, to utilize effectively dispute-resolving techniques to minimize concerns about this process, and to employ peer pressure to build support for the name ultimately selected. While this strategy can be used in resolving other disputes in the merger, the volatility of name selection demands the attention of all involved to defuse the emotional aspect of this issue.

Examining the parties

To begin the merger process, it is important for groups to gather information about the other merger participants. While this information may be gathered on the personal level through contacts and other interchanges, the examination of the medical practices themselves goes far beyond this personal interaction. Both groups must understand the parties with whom they are about to enter a long-term relationship. Financial, legal and business organization details of both groups must be understood to allow an informed decision to be made about completing the process.

To make this informed decision, and to prepare for effective operations of the newly combined group, medical groups should gather, organize and transmit data to the other side. This exchange of "due diligence" information should be scheduled early in the process. The information revealed will help direct the analysis of the merger by the parties and will identify potential problem areas that must be confronted. Information requests should be divided roughly along the following lines:

Medical group acquisitions and mergers

Corporate records

Each group should be prepared to deliver corporate information including its certificate of incorporation, bylaws, stock records and shareholders' agreements. The group also should be expected to provide a list of all subsidiary, partnership or joint venture relationships. Also to be included is the meeting minutes of the board of directors and executive committees, reports or communications to stockholders and written reports to the board of directors concerning material corporate matters. The time period covered by this document request may vary, but at least minutes covering the immediately preceding two-year period should be examined.

Authorization

The group should provide a detailed list of all lessors, lenders or creditors from whom consent may be required for the medical group to enter into the proposed transaction.

Financial statements

Audited financial statements, if available, should be provided for at least the last four years. Monthly unaudited financials should be provided for interim periods after the date of the last audited financials. If audited financials are not available, comparable unaudited financials should be provided. Auditor's letters to management, auditor's inquiry letters and responses, and other correspondence with lenders should be supplied for at least the last four years. Long- and short-term debt should be identified with respect to amount, major financial covenants and date of maturity. A review of accounts receivable with respect to quality, aging and other provisions, as well as accounts payable and annual depreciation costs should be identified. Finally, contingent liabilities should be specified.

Tax matters

Each group should be willing to provide copies of federal, state, and local tax returns, again for the last four years, and any correspondence or other unusual information with respect to these tax filings.

Employees and benefit plans

Groups should provide copies of employment, confidentiality, or restrictive covenant agreements that may have been entered into with their nonphysician employees. Agreements also should be provided concerning pension, profit sharing or other employee benefit plans. Nonphysician employees earning salaries in excess of an established amount should be described with respect to hire date, age, current salary and job description. Finally, a listing of all fringe benefits, insurance coverage, holidays and vacation accrued or owed to employees should be provided.

Material contracts and commitments

Each group should provide copies of documents and agreements that evidence loans or credit agreements, leases of real property or personal property, sales or purchases of businesses, management agreements, managed care contracts and other material documents.

Licenses, permits and other filings

Copies of material permits, licenses and governmental consents necessary for the operation of the medical group or the practice of its physicians should be provided to the other group. Any reports filed or correspondence with these regulatory agencies also should be supplied.

Insurance

A detailed list of all material insurance policies utilized to protect the group against various risks, including malpractice policies, should be provided.

Litigation

A complete list and summary of all litigation involving the medical group and any of its physicians should be provided. Copies of pleadings and court documents should be provided if requested. Notices, citations or other communications received from governmental agencies also should be disclosed.

Properties

The groups should provide a list of all assets and material mortgages, liens and security interests affecting their property. Copies of options to purchase or leases of property should be included, as well as copies of all claims relating to any change in zoning or other adverse circumstances affecting any real property utilized by the group. While this document collection process places a burden upon the administrator of each group, there can be no substitute for an organized approach undertaken early in the process. Many of the facts and potential problems that may be uncovered in any transaction will be discovered through the collection of this information and the analysis undertaken by the other parties. The goal of the due diligence process, therefore, is to spot problem areas and resolve them before they become major merger-threatening issues.

The merger documents

To accomplish the merger, it will be necessary to document the agreement of the parties. In the technical "merger" context, a merger agreement will set forth the details of combining the groups. In the asset acquisition context where one group purchases the assets of another group and employs its physicians, an asset purchase agreement will effect this combination. The details of a merger agreement and the related documentation are discussed below. The details of an asset acquisition are the same as an acquisition of the assets of a medical group by a hospital and therefore are discussed in Chapter 11.

In a merger agreement, seven separate sections will contain the necessary details to accomplish the merger. The first section of a merger agreement describes the mechanics of the merger. This section will set forth the date on which the merger agreement is to be signed, the day the merger is effective, and the requirement of a meeting of the shareholders to ratify the merger. To accomplish the merger, the procedure dictated by applicable state law must be followed. This procedure generally requires the board of directors of each group to authorize the execution of the merger document. This signing, or closing as it is referred to, is held so the documents may be executed simultaneously by all the parties. Immediately following the execution of this document, a meeting of the shareholders is held to approve the merger. Following shareholder approval, the merger will become legally effective after filing the articles of merger with the state corporation agency.

On the effective date of the merger, the first medical group is merged into the second group, and the separate corporate existence of the first group ceases, with the second group continuing as the surviving corporation. By operation of law, all the rights, responsibilities, obligations and assets of the first group are automatically transferred to the second surviving group. This surviving medical group then operates under the name selected by both parties. Where multiple groups are involved, the process is the same, resulting in the survival of one medical group.

The second issue to be addressed in a merger agreement is the establishment of the corporate governance of the surviving corporation. The Articles of Incorporation of this ongoing corporation should be restated and attached as an exhibit to the merger agreement. Any special provisions regarding corporate governance, voting requirements or other matters should be placed in these revised articles. Also specified in this section of the merger agreement should be the bylaws of the new organization. These bylaws should contain provisions in accordance with the review of the bylaws undertaken as part of the overall review of the organization of the medical group. Finally in this section, the new directors and officers of the surviving corporation should be specified. It is important for the merging groups to have agreed in advance regarding the identity of their new representatives and these representatives should be specified in this section of the merger agreement.

The third section of a merger agreement will cover the method for the conversion of the securities of the respective groups into a stock ownership interest in the surviving medical group. As part of the merger, the stockholders of each organization will have their shares in the existing corporation converted into shares in the new organization. The method of the combination and the conversion ratio will depend upon the method chosen to equate the ownership of stockholder interests for all the physicians. It is desirable to have a conversion factor that will equalize ownership so all the physicians will own the same number of shares in the surviving medical group.

This section of a merger agreement also should discuss the method by which a shareholder may object to the transaction. Under the corporation laws of many states, shareholders who vote against a merger may be entitled to "dissenter's rights." These rights give a physician who votes against the merger the option to dissent and have his shares appraised and repurchased by the corporation at the appraised value. It is important to examine, as part of the merger process, the potential liability a medical group may have to repurchase shares from dissenting physicians, and to review thoroughly the provisions of the applicable state corporation act concerning rights of dissenters. In any event, the language of the merger agreement must account for this dissent process and the agreement must allow the parties to call off the merger if too high a percentage of shareholders dissent from the transaction.

The fourth section of a merger agreement should contain the representations and warranties that both groups will make concerning their respective operations. In this section, medical groups will disclose a wide variety of information about their operations. These disclosures cover diverse matters such as the number of shares outstanding, the accuracy of financial statements, the disclosure of certain liabilities, the pendency of litigation, and various employee and employee benefit matters. The purpose of these disclosures is two-fold. First, the process of making the disclosure will inform the other groups of any significant liabilities or problems that exist. Disclosure will allow the other groups to obtain an informed evaluation of the financial strengths and weaknesses of the group making the disclosure, as well as other key operational details. The second purpose of these representations and warranties is to protect the other party in the event the warranties are not true. Liability will occur if the representations and warranties made by the disclosing group later turn out to be false.

The fifth section of a merger agreement will contain other agreements of the parties. The organizations should agree to conduct their business during the merger process in accordance with past practice and to avoid making material changes in operations that might affect the value or operations of their practices. This section of the merger agreement also should require the parties to allow access to the properties, records and business operations of the other party.

Medical group acquisitions and mergers

The sixth section of a merger agreement should set forth the various conditions that must be met before each of the groups is required to complete the merger. These requirements, listed below, are called "conditions precedent" because they are the circumstances which must occur before a party is obligated to go forward with the merger.

Shareholder approval

In order to go forward with the merger, the shareholders of each medical group must approve the merger.

Representations and warranties

The representations and warranties made in the merger agreement must be true in all respects at the effective date of the merger. The usual time lag between the signing of the document and the effective date of the merger should not permit anything to have occurred which would make those representations set forth in the merger agreement false as of the effective date of the merger.

Physician employment agreements

It is likely that new physician employment agreements will be entered into as part of the merger. The number of physician employment agreements required to be signed by the other medical group should be set forth in the agreement, as should any related restrictive covenant agreements.

Real estate

Any provisions regarding the agreed treatment of real estate in a separate entity should be referenced here as having occurred prior to the merger.

Litigation

As a condition precedent to the merger, there should be no action or lawsuit pending that seeks to challenge the transaction contemplated by the merger.

Dissenting shares

As stated previously, a limitation on the number of dissenting shares should be specified so if the number is too high, the other medical group may be relieved of going forward with the merger.

The seventh and final portion of a merger agreement should contain a provision regarding the survival of representations and warranties, and the indemnification process. This section of an agreement will provide that the representations and warranties made by a party in the agreement are not extinguished at the closing and that they survive after the effective time of the merger. The concept is that anything a party specifies in the merger documents also should be true after the merger, and the parties should remain responsible if any representation is untrue.

This final section also will contain a provision stating that the shareholders of a medical group will indemnify the surviving medical group if any of the representations and warranties are later found to be false, and the surviving medical group suffers loss because of that misrepresentation. This indemnification requirement means that if a warranty is false and the surviving medical group is required to make a payment or suffers loss because of this untruth, then the shareholders of the original medical group will reimburse the surviving medical group for this loss. The loss should include not only the actual loss incurred by the surviving medical group and its officers, directors or agents, but also related expenses, such as attorney fees.

The parties should consider whether the amount of liability that a shareholder may incur because of the indemnification provision should be limited. The theory is that a shareholder by owning his or her shares of stock is only at risk for the amount of funds that are invested in the medical group. The limited liability of a stockholder as a shareholder is inconsistent with this unlimited indemnification liability that may be present in a merger agreement. The parties likely will agree to an appropriate limit on the liabilities their individual shareholders may incur because of a breach of warranty.

Chapter 4

The group practice legal structure

Medical groups that engage in mergers are in transition. This transition to a larger, more complex organization requires the group to undergo certain structural changes. To prosper in this changing environment, organizations will need to evolve from democracies whereby every physician may have an equal voice in decisions regarding the business of the group to organizations where power is centralized and decision making is delegated. Centralization of authority and the transformation to a more complex structure puts stress upon the legal basis on which the group is organized.

Many organizations that undertake a merger will have basic legal organizational documents that were prepared by individuals to protect physician autonomy and as a consequence will have neglected guarding the interests of the group as a whole. For example, employment agreements will often have been drafted to protect individual physician rights by specifying generous benefits and salaries that cannot be changed without the consent of the individual, and by making termination of the relationship difficult for the group to invoke. In these employment agreements, restrictive covenants will be non-existent, will be very narrow in scope, or will contain a small amount of liquidated damages. Concern for the right of the individual to practice medicine and the mobility of that practice will prevail against the interests the group has in protecting its goodwill, guarding its patient base, and protecting it from the loss of revenue that inevitably will occur if a physician leaves the group and takes patients away from the group as a result of that departure.

The governing structure of many of these "individually focused" groups often will be non-existent, as all physicians may make decisions in a general staff meeting that allows participation by all in attendance. In other groups, a large board of directors may have been created which includes a high percentage of physician group members, and the size of this board may preclude the fast, efficient action necessary in a changing health care environment. Groups in this phase of development with a large board of directors likely will have failed to delegate sufficient authority to the administrator, physician executive, or a small executive committee that may meet between board of directors meetings.

Shareholders' agreements which govern the purchase and sale of the stock of the group also demonstrate how individual interests predominate in many of these "democratic" groups. In these groups the rights of the individual are again protected, allowing the individual to have his stock repurchased upon departure at a favorable rate, and requiring the group to pay out this repurchase price in a short period of time. This slant of shareholders' agreement toward an individual perspective must also be examined in light of the organizational change that will occur in the merger.

Finally, many groups will have neglected over the years to formalize their relationship with their administrator, or will have done so without adequate provisions for protection of the group and for the administrator. In many situations, these key players in the operation of a group will be operating without a contract.

Groups undergoing a merger will be presented with the opportunity to re-examine the legal basis of their organization. In implementing the transaction, the group must proceed with a heightened awareness of the importance of protecting the group. This re-evaluation will make the group concept stronger by protecting group rights and at the same time lessening the ability of the individual to cause damage to the group. To implement a merger successfully, and to lay a solid foundation upon which the new organization will operate, many familiar documents will need to be revised and take on a new perspective. This new group perspective must be incorporated as a common theme throughout all of these documents. As revised, these documents will serve as the legal basis for implementing change in groups from the democracies they may have been to a group with centralized authority where the group is strengthened in its ability to confront the challenge of individual threats to its health and well being.

Physician employment agreements

The merger process will bring into focus the relationship of the individual physicians to the medical groups to which they belong. To create a strong new medical group, an effective employment agreement that gives the group the power to govern its individual members must be signed by all physicians.

The need to reexamine physician employment agreements is based on a variety of factors, all of which are brought into sharper focus by the great change that a merger may bring to the group and its physicians. First, physicians no longer spend their entire career in one group or in one city.

The group practice legal structure

If a physician severs his relationship with a group, disputes are likely to arise, and the employment contract in effect will be examined closely in an effort to resolve these disputes.

Another factor that increases the need to re-examine physician employment contracts is the increasing size of the group occasioned by a merger. This risk of physician departure exists in general, but is increased where a fundamental change will cause physicians to reevaluate their role in the organization. As groups grow past the number of six to 10 physicians in size, individual physicians feel less a part of management and more like employees. This feeling of being an employee continues to grow as group size increases. To the extent that this difference in perspective develops or continues to grow, disputes will arise in the employment relationship and reference to the written contract to resolve the dispute will occur more often. After the employment contract has been prepared, it is important to circulate a draft to physicians for discussion and revision. A process must be established to respond to concerns raised and to harmonize the responses to achieve an effective document. While some compromise can be expected with respect to the contract, the group must be cautioned about weakening the contract so much that the group cannot deal effectively with its individual physicians.

Individual physicians may resist the infringement upon their personal rights by this new group contract, but all group members must be convinced that by protecting the group, individual members are also protected. It is often the actions of only one individual that will create significant harm to the entire group due to the inability of the group to deal effectively with that individual.

While an employment agreement should reflect the history, personality and work philosophy of the new group, certain basic elements should be included in every document and should be designed to move the organizational structure to a different level of group development. The following paragraphs present some suggested guidelines that may be utilized in the process of revisiting the basis on which the physician-medical group relationship is maintained.

Introduction

The employment agreement should begin with introductory wording which describes the parties involved, their addresses, a legal description of the organization and the overall intent of the employment contract. The agreement should set forth that as a condition of the merger that the physicians and the group are being required to enter into a new agreement. In addition, if the physician is a shareholder in the group, that status should also be specified. These recitations are necessary because contracts can only be changed in a binding manner by the parties if they exchange something of value. The requirement of "consideration" means that merely signing a new agreement will not be binding on the physician for such an important item as a restrictive covenant. This "value" requirement means that a merger will present groups with the opportunity to effect new and binding agreements by allowing physicians to benefit from the merger as a shareholder or as employee with a new work environment or new compensation system.

General statement of employment

Each contract needs to contain a general statement that the physician and the medical group are creating an employment relationship that is based upon the terms and conditions set forth in the employment agreement. This general paragraph is the basis for defining the rights and obligations of the parties and specifically references the other provisions of the agreement.

Duties

The employment agreement also should contain a section which describes the duties which the physician is expected to perform. These provisions may have in the past been limited to describing generally the duties of the physician and requiring that these duties be performed within the policies, rules and procedures of the group that are established from time to time. While this general language should be retained, it needs to be supplemented by adding a requirement that the physician should agree to serve the group faithfully and to devote such time as may be necessary for the adequate performance of his duties.

In addition, in light of the need for more centralized management in the new group, stronger language should be placed in this section which would require the physician to perform his or her duties in such areas and at such times and locations as may be required by the medical group, and which would make the practice of the physician subject to such review processes and procedures as may be established by the group from time to time. These type of provisions will allow the group to adopt and modify utilization review quality assurance programs and to review individual physician participation and compliance. This contractual basis to review physician performance will establish the legal authority for the review programs of the group and preclude later questioning of that authority by an individual physician.

Other activities

Physician employment contracts also benefit from having provisions which prohibit the physician from engaging in any activity which is determined to be detrimental to the group or which results in the physician not devoting his full time to the practice of medicine for the medical group. From the perspective of the medical group, it is important to establish that the physician is devoting his or her full time to the business of the group. It is also important for the group to obtain the agreement of the physician that he or she will not engage in other work for anyone else without the prior written consent of the medical group.

Larger groups created by mergers will contain more individuals, and the risk of activity occurring which takes away productive, revenue-producing activity must be closely monitored. Budgetary considerations, revenue projections and space allocations may all be impacted by the other activities of a physician. The group must have oversight duties on the amount of effort devoted by its physician employees. From the viewpoint of the individual physician, to the extent that the physician desires to engage in other practice related activities or independent teaching or research, specific reference to these activities should be made so no questions will arise in the future regarding the propriety of the physician engaging in these activities.

Compensation

Another major goal of the revised employment contract, both from the group and physician perspective, is to set forth the method of compensation of the physician. The compensation system for the new group will be established or modified as part of the merger process. With regard to contract content, however, it is in the interest of the medical group to leave discretion to its board of directors to make modifications in the compensation system. Without this flexibility to make modifications, a new contract or amendment must be executed each time a change in the compensation system is implemented.

While a flexible compensation provision gives the individual physician less certainty in his relationship with the medical group, the medical group should consider this approach to enable it to respond rapidly to changes in the finances of the medical group. Historical reasons regarding group governance and lack of trust in the new organization may result in significant individual physician resistance to giving up this certainty. Medical group leadership, however, should be aware of the significant advantages from a governance and financial operations perspective of a more flexible expression of the compensation obligation. Even in circumstances where a full delegation to the board cannot be achieved, the strategy should be used to centralize decision making about as many aspects of the compensation system as possible.

Professional meeting time, vacation, sick leave

The specifics of professional meeting time, vacation and sick leave benefits should be contained in the personnel policies of the group. From the position of the medical group, therefore, no further obligations with respect to professional meeting time and related expenses, or with respect to additional vacation or sick leave or their accrual should to be made in an employment contract. While individual physicians may desire to see these matters set forth in writing, the group will have more flexibility to modify the policies if the board of directors is free to modify these provisions without seeking the approval of each physician.

Disability

Although many existing physician contracts spell out, in detail, the effects of the partial or total disability of a physician, it will be more beneficial, from the perspective of the medical group to specify disability provisions in a policy manual which can be updated and changed rather than in the contract. The merger process may also highlight weaknesses in the existing disability provisions of a group.

As a general matter, groups should no longer act as an "insurance" company by providing benefits out of group revenues to individual physicians. By allowing payments to disabled physicians that are in addition to the disability insurance policy of the group, income of the remaining physicians is put at risk. Physicians should be encouraged to obtain individual policies consistent with their own level of risk concerning their health that they are able to assume. Group assumed contractual obligations with respect to disability not covered by separate insurance should be limited.

Fringe benefits

The revised physician contract should contain a section covering fringe benefits. From the perspective of the medical group, the provision should state that the physician can participate in employee benefits generally provided by the group, but that no special fringe benefits are provided for the physician. To the extent that the group has decided to provide other fringe benefits such as a car allowance or additional life insurance, those provisions may be generally referenced in this fringe benefit provision, but the details should be established by the board of directors from time to time.

Administrative and practice considerations

The relationship of a physician with the business operations of the medical group is also an important topic to be included in a "group centered" physician employment contract. A variety of concepts should be considered for this section to strengthen the ability of the medical group to manage its affairs. First, the paragraph should establish that all fees, billings and collections are to be established by and remain the property of the medical group. Departing physicians should not be able to make the claim that they are entitled to some general interest in receivables, unless this interest is specifically granted in the termination section of the agreement.

Second, the agreement should specify that the group, and not the physician, has the full authority to administer the business of the group and to hire and fire all personnel. Individual physicians should not be given the authority outside of the board and the administrative team to make these decisions.

Third, the agreement should provide that all accounts and medical records are the property of the medical group and that the physician is required to keep accurate records of all professional work performed or supervised by him.

Finally, the contract should state that the group will provide all office space, equipment and other items necessary for the practice of the physician, but that the group alone has the authority to determine what is necessary and what is to be purchased. All of these provisions will enable the new group to operate the practice from the business perspective without granting the individual practitioner a veto power over the decisions of the collective leadership of the group.

Automobiles and insurance

Physician contracts may contain paragraphs pertaining to automobiles and automobile insurance. While many of the details of automobile insurance should be determined at the board level without reference in the contracts, many groups require that their physicians maintain an automobile and maintain appropriate insurance regarding liability and property damage and therefore believe that such a provision is necessary in the contract. If such a paragraph is utilized, flexibility on limits of coverage should be maintained, allowing the board of directors of the group to specify from time to time the coverage levels.

Regardless of whether the insurance issue is covered in the agreement or in a separate policy statement, attention to insurance is necessary, as physicians who are traveling on medical group business, even in their own automobiles, will be deemed to be doing so in the course of their employment for the group. This means that the medical group is responsible for the actions of the physician if an accident occurs while the physician is driving the automobile. To coordinate the coverage that a medical group may have in its umbrella policy which will cover excess liability for the group and its employees, individual physicians will be required, pursuant to the terms of those umbrella policies, to maintain a baseline of coverage before the umbrella policy takes effect. Because uninsured liability actions may pose a major threat to their financial integrity, groups undergoing mergers should reexamine their policies on this issue as they may have been neglected over the years.

Term

The term of the contract is one of the most important provisions to be considered in the preparation of the employment agreements to be utilized in the merger. A review of the principles to be employed in determining the appropriate term of a contract should be made. For example, if a contract with a long term (more than one year) is utilized, the medical group and the physician are obligated to satisfy their respective obligations for that entire stated period of time. Generally, the longer the term of the contract, the more favorable it is for the physician. Physicians who desire to leave a situation are in most instances of less value to the medical group, and the medical group has little to be gained in seeking redress for the breach of the obligation of that physician to perform services for the entire term of the obligation of the physician. Physicians who decide to leave for other positions may not provide adequate notice and usually feel free to do so without any great risk of liability.

If a medical group decides to terminate the services of a physician in the first year of a three year agreement, on the other hand, the medical group will be obligated (unless it has cause to terminate the agreement, and is prepared to establish that cause) to continue to pay the physician for the full term of the agreement. While the physician has an obligation to seek new work to lessen the damages the medical group would be required to pay for the remainder of the contract term, this type of provision is in fact quite favorable to the individual physician.

It is usually in the best interest of the medical group, therefore, to provide for a much shorter contract term. Accordingly, a short contract term (certainly not more than one year) with liberal termination provisions as discussed below would protect the interest of the medical group by permitting the release of a physician in an undesirable situation, without having to establish that the physician, in fact, breached the agreement.

Another issue to be decided in determining the appropriate term of an agreement is whether the contract should contain language that automatically renews the contract at the end of the term, unless one party notifies the other that the contract will terminate at the end of that current term. These automatic renewal or "evergreen" clauses are usually desirable.

Most medical group contracts should contain this automatic renewal provision after the parties have worked with each other for some time and an ongoing relationship is anticipated. In that context, the automatic renewal clause has the advantage of not requiring a new contract to be executed at the end of each term. On the other hand, it is recommended that a contract not contain this automatic renewal clause where the contract is with a new physician and the medical group· utilizes a "probationary" period to evaluate the practice of the new physician. Inadvertent renewal of contracts for these new physicians should be avoided, as the end of the contract will provide a convenient time at which to evaluate the performance of the physician. In the merger, it is likely that most, if not all of the physicians to be retained under the new arrangement, will be existing employees of the medical groups. In those circumstances, it is recommended that the clauses prepared for those physicians contain the automatic renewal provision.

Termination

An equally important provision in the employment agreement is how the contract may be terminated prior to the expiration of its term. If, for example, a physician is employed for a one year term, but the contract may be terminated on 30 days notice without any reason, the contract really has a term of 30 days, as opposed to one year. The employment contract provision which allows a contract to be terminated by either party without any reason is called a termination "without cause" provision. It is generally in the best interest of the medical group for its employment agreements to contain a termination without cause provision that has a short (30 to 60 day) notice period. The rationale for this type of provision is that it allows the medical group to sever relationships without specifying the reason for termination. In many circumstances, medical groups will prefer to avoid disclosing in a public forum the reasons for termination.

Many individual physicians and, in particular, participants in the merger process may view such short notice termination provisions with some skepticism. Attempts may be made to limit the discretion of the board of directors to act on this termination. In fact, some groups may feel that a higher vote requirement or a vote of all the shareholders should be obtained before severing a relationship without any reason. Such provisions are thought to protect the individual from the arbitrary behavior of the group at large.

In general, the leadership of the merger process should resist these limitations on the authority of the new board of directors. It is likely that the collective wisdom of the board would not allow it to act arbitrarily in the termination of a physician, and most termination situations arise under a set of circumstances where the behavior or practice style of the physician has created serious problems for the group. Because the "problem" behavior is the most common reason for the termination of a relationship by a group, physicians should be reminded that it is this type of problem, rather than an arbitrary decision, which causes the termination to occur.

From a legal perspective, the ability of the group to terminate the agreement in those "problem" situations is greatly enhanced if the agreement contains provisions that allow termination of the relationship without the need for giving any reason for termination. The adverse publicity or difficulty in proving behavior and practice concerns in a public forum can be minimized greatly by use of these provisions. While compromise may be necessary to have an agreement to be acceptable to the group at large, the merger committee process should guard against the tyranny of the individual rather than the tyranny of the group.

Another difficult question raised in termination sections of employment agreements is under what circumstances the agreement may be terminated "with cause." The phrase "with cause" means that the contract can be terminated at any time if a reason exists which would allow the non-breaching party to terminate the agreement prior to the conclusion of the term of the agreement. Cause provisions that specify how the medical group has failed to live up to its obligation in the contract are relatively straight forward. The interest of the physician in this situation is for the group to continue to pay the salary, provide the fringe benefits and abide by the policies and procedures established in the medical group. "Cause" in this context is often defined as the failure of the group to satisfy its obligations under the agreement.

On the other hand, the reasons the medical group may rely on to establish "cause" may be more difficult for the merger committee to detail. The group is vitally interested in having the duties performed by its physicians in a competent manner. To the extent the physician is not performing his duties, the medical group has an interest in and, in fact, should be required to terminate the relationship. How the reasons giving rise to the right of the medical group to terminate the agreement are expressed will depend in large part upon the perspective of the merger committee and its balancing of individual vs. group rights. In most instances, a group-centered agreement should define "cause" as:

- willful or repeated failure of the physician to comply with the reasonable directives of the board of directors;
- impairment due to drugs or alcohol;
- disability;
- loss or suspension of license; or
- loss or suspension of hospital privileges or other practice privileges.

While some medical groups may wish to consider adding a statement that allows termination of the agreement for lack of quality of care, the difficulty in proving lack of quality in most instances means that medical groups will be reluctant to try to establish this lack of quality in a public forum such as in court. Because quality is difficult to attack, even most medical groups that decide to put this type of provision in the agreement rarely will utilize it as the basis to terminate the relationship. Terminating physicians with quality of care problems will more often be achieved by using the termination without cause provision, which allows a medical group to sever the relationship without establishing any reason or revealing physician behavior to the public.

Effect of termination

Once the agreement is terminated, the parties must specify their respective rights and obligations which arise as of the effective day of termination. It is important for the medical group to focus on the adverse impact that a termination has upon its fiscal health. While it is impossible to prevent a departure of a physician, the merged medical group should consider including some version of the following concepts in its agreements to cushion the group from the adverse effects of departure:

1. A provision should be included that all uncollected charges and accounts receivable will remain the sole property of the medical group and that the physician has no rights in any of these amounts. In many instances, the departing physician will claim that revenues created from the work performed during the last several months of his or her employment should be rightfully his/her, and that he/she should be paid for that effort when the amounts are ultimately collected. The medical group leadership should consider, however, that there are significant costs associated with a physician departure, including loss of revenue, replacement costs and start up time for replacement physicians. The accounts receivable of the departing physician can be used to help defray the costs associated with finding a replacement for this departing physician. While this amount of money will rarely, if ever, fully compensate the medical group for the loss, it is better than the alternative of having an

additional obligation to make payments to the departing physician on top of recruitment and start up costs for the replacement for that physician.

2. A provision should also be added that the physician is responsible for the payment of any malpractice premium that may be necessary to provide extended coverage to the medical group for the actions of the physician. This endorsement on a malpractice policy converting the policy from a "claims made" to an "occurrence" basis is often an expensive item for a group and this expense should be borne by the departing physician who caused this expense to occur. The rationale for imposing this expense upon the physician is that without making this transfer to an occurrence basis, the physician will be uncovered (although the medical group will retain its coverage) and, therefore, the medical group will be more likely to be the target of any potential litigation than the physician. Separate limits and different levels of coverage from the group to the physician also may impact the amount of dollars available to protect the group if no physician coverage is available. The occurrence basis conversion therefore adds another layer of coverage and the cost to convert a policy to an occurrence basis is usually a warranted expense.

3. The agreement should also specify the amount of compensation owed to the physician. The exact nature of the compensation due the physician upon departure should be specified, otherwise the risk exists that a physician may claim amounts due beyond what is intended by the medical group.

4. Finally, the agreement should contain references to both the obligation of the physician to resell his stock in the medical group upon departure pursuant to a shareholders' agreement and a reference to the obligation of the physician to be bound by the terms of any restrictive covenant provision that may be applicable to a physician.

Restrictive covenants

Restrictive covenants (or covenants not to compete) usually prohibit a physician from practicing medicine within a certain area (for example, a county or within a 50 mile radius of an office) for a specified period of time (one to two years after employment ends). Restrictive covenants have often been used by medical groups to protect the good will and patient loyalty that the group has established over the years in the community. Often medical groups and their physicians think of restrictive covenants only where an established group hires a new physician and establishes that physician in the practice, thereby conferring a great benefit upon that new physician. Equally, if not more important, are the situations like mergers where the medical group engages in a new endeavor and where the success of the new effort depends upon, to a great extent, the combined efforts of all the constituent physicians. Mergers will create a larger group with increased risk of damage caused by a physician departure.

In these situations, a properly drafted restrictive covenant can allow the group to prevent individuals from establishing a competing practice. In many states the legal requirements that a restrictive covenant must meet to be enforceable are generally similar, and in these states in order for a covenant to be enforceable, it must have been entered into in exchange for something of value and must be reasonable. In other states, specific statutes may prohibit the enforcement of a restrictive covenant, except in narrowly defined circumstances or only where liquidated damages are to be paid. In designing an appropriate covenant, therefore, reference must be made to both the specific statutes in the state in which the transaction will occur and the applicable cases that have been decided in that state in order to determine specific guidelines concerning the enforceability of a particular covenant.

The process of determining what covenants are enforceable in the employment context has been impacted by the competing policies surrounding restrictive covenants. On the one hand, courts must consider the public policy in favor of allowing people to work and contribute their skills and abilities to the community. This policy would, therefore, limit the enforceability of covenants and this policy is particularly applicable in the employment context. On the other hand, courts must consider the general principle of freedom of contract and the public policy in favor of encouraging employers to hire employees in a particular community.

A great number of cases have been decided across the country concerning restrictive covenants. This considerable body of case law has developed governing the interpretation and enforcement of restrictive covenants. In determining whether a particular covenant is reasonable and therefore enforceable, courts have applied a number of rules. The following guidelines give a brief overview of the type of considerations that will lead to more enforceability in a particular contract:

Writing required

The covenant should be in writing and signed by the physician. Oral restrictive covenants are not enforceable in many states, and in any event it is critical that the covenant be in writing and signed in order to establish in a reliable fashion the terms of the covenant.

Business interest protected

The covenant must be related to the protection of the legitimate business interests of the medical group. Examples of this legitimate business interest include the patient relationships and name recognition developed through the investment of the time, effort and resources of the group. Covenants must be narrowly drawn to protect only this interest.

Consideration

The covenant must be supported by valuable consideration. Physicians cannot merely agree to refrain from practicing in a particular area. This promise will not be enforceable because it lacks legal consideration, which means that in exchange for agreeing to refrain from practice, the physician must receive something with an economic benefit, such as salary or payment, a portion of which can be thought of as being given in exchange for the covenant. In the merger context, the new employment agreement derives consideration from the benefits received by a physician in entering into a merger with a combined group. For new physicians hired by the new group after the arrangement has been consummated, the situation is simplified as the requirement of legally sufficient consideration will be satisfied when the physician enters into an employment contract in connection with accepting the offer of employment and before the physician begins work.

In general, if improvements or strengthening of restrictive covenants are to be made in the merger, it is important that they be done in conjunction with the consummation of the transaction. Any deviation from this procedure, such as waiting until "the dust has settled" to address the physician contract issue, may result in a court finding that the covenant was given without valuable consideration and, therefore, unenforceable. Many courts have invalidated covenants when they were entered into after the employment relationship had commenced. To strengthen the enforceability argument for restrictive covenants, therefore, the employment agreement should be entered into during the course of the implementation of the merger.

Activity

The covenant must be reasonable with regard to the scope of activity prohibited. In order to be reasonable and, therefore, enforceable, a covenant must be drafted so it only restricts the physician from a reasonable scope of activity. Standards of what is reasonable concerning the scope of permissible activity vary from state to state. Regardless of the specific standard that may apply, however, the following guidelines should be considered.

Multispeciality groups should consider whether the group needs protection over the full range of practice encompassed in the phrase "practice of medicine," or whether a restriction limiting the physician from practicing only his specialty is sufficient. The medical leadership should determine what interests of the group need to be protected. Often this interest is one which requires the protection of the group's goodwill, patient relationships and financial well being. Because the reality of most large groups is that the physician staff member is quite specialized and only sees patients in a limited area of practice, it is prudent for the group to consider restricting the physician from working only in the practice area in which the physician worked while employed with the medical group. While a broad prohibition against the departing physician from "practicing medicine" may be enforceable in a particular state, the added protection of this broad prohibition may not be worth the uncertainty it raises in the specialized practice of medicine of today. It is strongly recommended that single specialty groups limit the practice of the departing physician to the specialty being practiced for the same reasons.

Time

The covenant must be reasonable as to the length of time of the restriction. Recent cases across the country have indicated that courts have narrowed the time period which is considered to be a reasonable restriction on the practice of the physician. Time periods that extend beyond a two or three year period following the termination of an employment agreement may be challenged as being too long to protect the legitimate interest of the medical group. While the exact period of enforceability may vary from state to state, a conservative approach should be used in selecting the appropriate time period. The main purpose of a time period is to disrupt the practice of a physician who leaves a group, thereby making it impossible for that physician to transfer his patient population to a new competing practice.

Territory

The covenant must also be reasonable as to the territory in which the activity is prohibited. Covenants are often phrased in terms of prohibiting practice within a county or city, or within a radius of miles from an office or city. The exact extent of the territory to be restricted, however, should be based upon the business activity of the medical group. If the group draws patients from a county or series of counties or a wide geographic area, the restriction should be based upon the attraction of patients from that wide referral area. On the other hand, if the covenant extends beyond the reasonable drawing area of a medical group, it will likely be deemed to be unenforceable as not being related to the interests of the medical group that needs to be protected. In most instances, a 25 to 50 mile radius from an existing office site will be sufficient to cover the bulk of most patients that are seen by the physician, and requiring that the physician practice outside of that area will disrupt sufficiently the practice of that physician to protect the interest of the group.

Public policy

The covenant must not be against public policy. The parties will be allowed to make agreements between themselves, except when the public interest in not enforcing the agreement outweighs this freedom to contract.

This public concern arises when enforcement of the restrictive covenant may harm the general public. An example of this type of issue and one that may jeopardize enforcement of restrictive covenants with highly trained specialists are situations where a medical group employs a specialist which is the only physician of that kind in a community. In some cases courts have ruled that the covenant was invalid on public policy grounds. These cases have concluded that if ordering the physician to honor the contractual obligation would create a substantial question of potential harm to the public, then the public interest outweighed the contract interest of the parties and the court would refuse to enforce the covenant. If, on the other hand, ordering the physician to honor the agreement would merely inconvenience the public without causing substantial harm, courts have concluded that the medical group should be entitled to have the contract enforced. The small number of decided cases have provided limited guidance in this area, and, accordingly, great uncertainty remains in this area. This developing area of the law will impact some groups who hire specialists that are unique in a community. While this development should not discourage medical groups from continuing relationships with these rare specialties, it does add another element of uncertainty in the already uncertain area of restrictive covenant enforcement.

As an alternative or supplement to a restrictive covenant, many medical groups will consider the use of a liquidated damage provision. Liquidated damage clauses provide that a physician must pay the medical group a specified amount if the physician practices within a prohibited area or if the physician leaves the group. The rationale for a liquidated damage provision is that the exact damages caused by the departure of a physician will be difficult to establish and, therefore, a fixed amount set in advance is the only way to determine these damages.

The group practice legal structure

While physicians have different perspectives on establishing a liqui-dated damage amount, many will find these clauses preferable to an all out prohibition against practice. It is this softened effect of liquidated damage clauses that may give physicians in leadership positions cause to consider them more seriously than is warranted. These provisions may also receive additional interest because of the mistaken belief that while restrictive covenants may be difficult to enforce, payment of liquidated damages is an uncomplicated process resulting in easy payment for the group.

Liquidated damage provisions, however, are not easy to enforce. In addition, the ability of the group to collect payment is not as clear cut as many physicians would believe. Liquidated damages may be attacked as vigorously as restrictive covenants and a physician who desires to practice in breach of a liquidated damage provision will have only the payment of monetary damages as the downside risk, as opposed to being put out of business by the enforcement of a restrictive covenant.

In comparing restrictive covenants to liquidated damage provisions, medical groups should consider the following. As an alternative to a restrictive covenant, the liquidated damage clause reimburses the medical group for expenses associated with recruitment and establishing a re-placement in practice. Liquidated damage clauses, however, may be subject to attack, as in most states a clause is not enforceable if it is a penalty. The determination of whether the clause is a penalty or truly a liquidated damage amount is a hazy distinction and subject to varying interpretations. Because liquidated damages are only enforceable where the actual amount of damages are difficult to determine, the medical group that seeks to collect a liquidated damage provision must also meet this burden. These abstract concepts are difficult to establish in any enforce-ment action and disputes about the use of liquidated damage clause are likely to occur just as often as disputes concerning the enforcement of a restrictive covenant. Other difficulties with liquidated damages exist. Often they are set at a fixed amount and do not increase over time. What may seem to be an appropriate liquidated damage amount when it is established, will lessen over the years and in many instances may seem to be insignificant by the time a physician is prepared for departure. Second, it is very likely that with higher paid specialties, a liquidated damage amount that approximates some significant percentage of annual income will be deemed so high that the ability to convince physicians to sign it will be jeopardized. This high liquidated damage amount provision may in fact create serious opposition to the merger and physicians will seek to have the number negotiated downward as part of the negotiations. In an effort to accommodate the short-term interest of the wide number of physicians who may oppose a higher liquidated damage amount, the group may impair its ability to protect itself in the future. A lower liquidated damage amount will encourage physicians to view departure as a less painful process and if departure is made too easy, this ultimately may jeopardize the long term survivability of the group.

Selection of a restrictive covenant as opposed to a liquidated damage clause will depend upon the goal of the group in using these options. If the goal is to prevent a physician from entering into competitive practice, a restrictive covenant clause in some fashion should be utilized. If the goal is merely to seek reimbursement for costs expended when a physician leaves, a liquidated damage provision should be considered. Most medical groups will conclude that the real goal is to prohibit competition from being created and therefore will opt for a restrictive covenant.

Medical group governing structure

After a merger, there will be a critical need for the medical group to maintain and further develop a governing structure for the group practice. As the medical group organization evolves in terms of size and organizational orientation, the structures which the group uses to govern its affairs must evolve to accommodate this development. In the evolution of any medical group, it is clear that the governing structure must move from a pure democracy to the delegation of authority to individuals who will be guided by what is in the best interest of the group. When a group undertakes a merger the usual result is a significant increase in size, and the structures which may have been utilized before the transaction no longer will be adequate to the task. In the planning for the merger, it is important to consider the effect of the new combination upon the governing structure, and to make plans to institute effective lines of authority to allow the new organization to function in an efficient manner.

Many groups that have made decisions on a collaborative basis will find that system no longer workable in a larger organization created by a merger. A governing body must be created to respond to this situation and all physician-owners should be encouraged to accept that a board of directors will make basic decisions about how the practice is operated. This delegation of authority from shareholders to a board of directors is a well-known and well-accepted concept in the business world. Physicians who practice in groups, however, have more difficulty delegating authority to their colleagues to make decisions on their behalf. Groups must be encouraged to accept this delegation because of the many advantages it brings for quicker decision making and efficient governance. This centralization of power should occur in any growing group, but in the merger, the sudden infusion of large numbers of physicians makes this delegation even more important to achieve.

Just as it is important to establish the concept of delegation of authority, it is equally as important that the size of board of directors be reduced to a workable number of individuals. Groups should resist the argument that all physicians in the new group should remain on one large board. This large board needlessly complicates the decision-making process at a time when many groups must react quickly and efficiently to the changing health care marketplace. Ideally, the new board of directors should consist of no more than five to seven individuals, regardless of the group size, or the size of any previous board of directors. A board larger than seven creates a decision-making process that impairs the efficiency at the board level.

To achieve optimum size for the board of directors, most groups who combine will need to reduce significantly the number of individuals who will remain on the board of directors. Although a five to seven member board is ideal, some groups may find it impossible to achieve at the outset. In these situations, many groups will be faced with a transitional arrangement which will accommodate the many political concerns that arise with the merger. Obtaining an agreement at the outset to reduce gradually the size of the board may be one way to effect a compromise in the event of resistance to a significant reduction in the size of the board.

As medical groups grow and develop, another concept that should be introduced is that of an executive committee. The executive committee, consisting of perhaps the administrator, the physician executive and one or two officers can function very well as the decision-making body empowered to make decisions between board meetings. By using an executive committee, the larger board can avoid having to meet on a weekly basis. The implementation and use of an executive committee is another step in the centralization of decision making that is necessary as a group transforms to a larger organization. For many small- to medium-size groups, however, the transition from a pure democracy to a fully implemented executive committee concept will be too much of a change to achieve all at one time. Groups should understand, however, that the importance of the transition to this smaller ruling body is a necessary development for decisions to be made in an effective manner.

In the merger, selection of members of the boards and committees should reflect the political realities of the combination of the medical groups and seek to strike a balance between members in both groups. The combining groups also should consider in advance the issue of selection of officers for the newly combined group. The process of selection of these directors and officers often will require that a compromise slate be selected. The directors and officers selected should reflect a balance between the two groups, and the individuals asked to serve should have significant leadership and administrative skills. By agreeing to a slate, the merger committee can minimize the chance of a dispute concerning individual candidates, thereby reducing the divisive effects an open election might have on the merger process.

Transforming the Delivery of Health Care:
The integration process

In addition to the traditional offices of president, vice president, secretary and treasurer, a medical director position should be considered if that position is not already in existence. The job description of the medical director must be developed by the merger committee. In the ideal situation, the medical director should report and be accountable to the board of directors, but not be on the board itself, thereby increasing accountability of the medical director to the board and making replacement easier if that were to become necessary. If both groups already have medical directors, a combination of the functions of the medical directors into one individual may be desirable, or the size of the group or the volume of work may be such that two medical directors may be challenged to confront the many medical practice issues that are faced by the large medical group.

Finally, medical groups should examine the committee structure that has evolved through its history, with the goal of streamlining the types and numbers of committees that may be used to address issues. Excessive reliance upon committee structures will necessitate delays in the decision-making process. Committees will need to be organized and then meet, followed by preparation of reports and actual reporting to the board of directors. The committee decision-making process is overly cumbersome for large medical groups and the scope of activities of committees should be limited to those in which a wide sampling of opinion is necessary or where a short response time is not necessary.

Bylaws

As part of the reorganization of the group in the merger process, the bylaws should be reviewed and revised. Corporate bylaws, in general, reflect the provisions of the corporation law in the state in which the group is organized. Medical groups must examine their bylaws to make sure that they are consistent with current corporate practice in their state. It is likely that many groups have ignored their bylaws over the years and that an update of these materials is warranted during the implementation process. Many of the changes that would be incorporated in a revised set of bylaws are likely to be standard provisions that have no particular specific relevance to the merger process.

Groups should engage in the effort, however, to include special provisions necessitated by decision making made in conjunction with the merger. Often the bylaws of the group will be the preferred place to specify a variety of decisions regarding the governing structure of the organization. Special provisions on the election of the board of directors, whether the terms are staggered and the number of individuals on the board will be items to be specified in these revised bylaws. In addition, the special provisions for the board to elect officers should be specified, with any special qualifications being set forth in the bylaws. Any higher vote requirements needed by a board, such as may be necessary for changing compensation systems or terminating physician employment agreements, should also be specified so physicians will know in advance that a greater-than-majority vote may be required for certain decisions.

Stock ownership and shareholders' agreements

The way physicians buy and sell stock in the new organization is also a significant matter to be addressed in advance of the consummation of any merger. While the medical groups will have existed before the consummation of the merger, and will have established a mechanism by which physicians purchase and sell their stock upon their departure, the merger process will require that a consolidated approach be taken. The merger implementation period is a perfect time to reevaluate the role of stock ownership in a medical group. While all physicians who were shareholders in a group prior to a merger will continue to be shareholders, the new group must decide the basis on which physicians new to the group should become shareholders. In many groups, a long apprenticeship and significant buy-in, in which physicians buy-in over time and ultimately accumulate the same number of shares as a senior physician, is a concept under attack. While this phase-in makes sense in terms of continuity of leadership, and in giving the new physicians the opportunity to become accustomed to the history and tradition of the group, many young physicians believe that they are entitled to equality more immediately in the medical group hierarchy. A short period of time to equal stock ownership after the physician becomes eligible for stockholder status is therefore becoming accepted practice.

While many factors may go into how the merger committee ultimately decides the stock ownership issue for the new group, it should keep in mind the competitive realities of attracting new physicians to its practice. The goal, given these recruiting pressures, should be to minimize the amount of a physician buy-in, to allow equality in terms of number of shares owned so all physicians feel equal, and to achieve that equality over a short period of time.

Having decided these buy-in issues by establishing a buy-in amount and payment timetable, those decisions can be formalized in a separate shareholders' purchase agreement whereby a physician agrees to purchase shares. As an alternative to a separate document, a provision or paragraph could be placed in the employment agreement for the physician which specifies the obligation of the physician to make purchases of shares over a certain period of time. This obligation should be placed on the physician after the decision has been made to admit the physician as a shareholder, rather than at the new employment relationship stage where a final decision has not been made on the future of the physician with the group.

An equally important issue pertaining to ownership of stock is preparing for a physician departure through a shareholders' agreement. Shareholders' agreements set forth the conditions upon which the interest of a physician in the professional corporation may be sold by that physician or repurchased by the corporation. Without this agreement, there will be no binding agreement that details under what circumstances and terms a medical group will be entitled to repurchase the shares of the stock of the group from a physician.

A shareholders' agreement should cover a number of issues concerning the relationship between the individual physician and the group. The agreement should restrict the transfer of stock in the medical group by prohibiting a physician shareholder from selling, or in any other manner disposing of the stock, without complying with the terms of the agreement. This restriction is important, as it protects the group from having its stock pass to third parties without the consent of the medical group. This restriction is also important because state law often restricts ownership in a professional corporation to physicians who are authorized to practice medicine in that state.

An equally important issue to be addressed in the shareholders' agreement is the circumstances under which stock owned by a physician must be repurchased by the medical group. Shareholders who sever their relationship will desire to have their investment returned. The medical group also will want to reclaim the shares from its former employee because it does not want a physician who is not associated with the group to have the right to be active in its affairs. The shareholders' agreement should detail the events which cause the corporation to become obligated to repurchase these shares. Events which should give rise to the obligation of the medical group to repurchase the shares usually include the following:

- death of the physician;
- termination of the employment of the physician by the group;
- inability of the physician to perform his duties as an employee, officer or director of the group for a certain period of time, perhaps six months or more;
- retirement of the physician;
- conviction of the physician of a criminal offense;
- an event of bankruptcy with respect to the physician;
- the entry of an order by a court that the spouse of the physician has acquired an interest in the stock under the applicable divorce or separation laws of the state; or

- the physician being found to be disqualified under the applicable state law to practice medicine.

Other events may be added depending upon the individual preferences of the group. When any one of these events occurs, therefore, the medical group is required to repurchase the stock upon the terms and at the value specified in the shareholders' agreement.

The value placed upon each share of stock in the medical group is, perhaps, the most critical provision to be found in the shareholders' agreement. Without an agreement in advance concerning the repurchase price of the stock owned by a physician, the risk of disagreement concerning value and perhaps even litigation is greatly increased. Various methods may be used to value the interests of the physician in the corporation and, for sake of consistency, the valuation method for repurchase should be the same as the original purchase obligation.

Many issues should be considered in determining how the valuation of stock is established. One issue to be determined is whether physicians are entitled to receive value for the accounts receivable of the group. In general, physicians should not be entitled to accounts receivable as part of their stock interest in the corporation. Whether accounts receivable are paid to a departing physician should depend upon the provisions specified in the employment agreement, not the shareholders' agreement.

Groups also should realize that in most circumstances and in most communities, physicians will be unwilling to pay large amounts associated with the good will or "franchise" value of a particular practice. While some competitive situations may allow existing physicians to charge a premium for entry into the group, the ability of most groups to receive that premium valuation is limited. The reality of changing medical practice is that even those groups in the country which in the past have charged a premium will find that physicians will go elsewhere if those premium demands continue to be made. The group also should examine whether real estate is included in the valuation process. In general, as discussed in Chapter 7, real estate should be held in the partnership or limited liability company form, which will avoid double taxation upon sale or other disposition of property. In any event, if the property is in the corporation, it should be valued and the valuation method should be specified as either cost or market value.

Apart from the valuation of real estate, which should be considered separately, several different methods of valuing stock may be used. First is the book value method of valuation as determined by the corporation's accountants, in accordance with either generally accepted accounting principles in the case of accrual basis medical groups, or in accordance with cash receipts and disbursements methods of accounting for those medical groups on a cash basis system. This valuation method can give a conservative value to the assets of the corporation which are listed at the acquisition price of the assets minus depreciation. Good will is not given a value under this method.

Other options include establishing a fair market value each year or having the board of directors designate a value. Determining fair market value requires a determination of what a willing buyer would pay a willing seller for the stock, with the determination being made by an independent third party. Alternatively, the board of directors can establish a value each year. This method places a burden each year on the board, which should be coupled with an appeal process if a shareholder disagrees with this determination.

Finally, in light of the changing reality of medical practice, many medical groups may reconsider the practice of valuing the assets of the organization by determining the book value or some other valuation formula and switch to a fixed buy-in price that is not directly tied to fluctuations in value. This method of stock valuation has the advantage of eliminating financial concerns at the end of every year that might impact the stock value determination formula and frees physicians to make business decisions without undue concern about the decisions they make having an adverse, or overly positive, impact on the yearly valuation of stock.

Just as in the front end purchase price valuation, a conservative valuation for physician departure will help attract physicians, for in the departure context, the remaining physicians must be in a position to continue practice in the medical group, while at the same time undertaking to repurchase the interest of a departing physician.

After establishing the value of the shares, the terms of payment for those shares purchased from a departing physician should be established. The medical group should be given great flexibility to determine how payment is made. The shareholders' agreement should give the group the option either to pay the full price for the shares at closing or to pay the purchase price over a number of years on an installment basis. The number of years during which payment should be made, as well as the interest charged on the unpaid balance, also should be determined in the agreement. A long period of time to repay this obligation to departing shareholders is the preferred method for protecting the interests of the group. A 10-year or longer promissory note should spread out the payment obligation of a group sufficiently, thereby protecting the cash flow of the group and physician incomes which may be affected adversely if a shorter time period such as three years is used.

Another issue that should be addressed in the shareholders' agreement is an authorization to allow insurance to be placed upon the life of physician shareholders. Life insurance can be a useful funding vehicle to allow the repayment of the capital investment of the physician at the time of the death of a physician. The shareholders' agreement, therefore, should provide that a shareholder will agree to allow the corporation to obtain insurance upon the life of the shareholder. In the event of the death of a shareholder, the insurance proceeds would then be applied to the purchase price for the shares. Medical groups, however, should avoid being lulled into a false sense of security that, by providing insurance coverage for its physicians, it will have funded its buy-out obligation. Many more physicians retire or depart from a group than have their employment relationship terminated by death. Upon termination of the agreement or transfer of the stock, physicians should be given the option to purchase the insurance if the physician so decides, or the group should be allowed to maintain the insurance if the physician decides that he or she does not wish to purchase the insurance.

Finally, the provisions of the shareholders' agreement should allow for termination of the agreement if the business of the medical group ends, if the medical group becomes bankrupt, or if a number of the shareholders of the corporation die within a relatively short period of time, thereby making it very difficult to fund a repurchase of the stock.

Administrator employment agreements

During any merger, the relationship of the current administrators of the groups will be brought into focus. In general, the same considerations that apply to physician employment agreements apply equally to the administrator contracts. New employment agreements may be negotiated, however, during this time period to reflect accurately the position of the parties in going forward with the new transaction.

Although it may be difficult for many administrators to make the case that they should be treated differently from their physicians who are in the group, administrators should not hesitate to make the argument that in light of their unique position in the group that a different contractual relationship should be fashioned. For most administrators, therefore, it is reasonable to request a contract with a longer term that will allow many of the problems of a transition to be resolved without creating undue job insecurity. While the group may desire to keep the term short, and to retain flexibility to make any desired changes without a long notice period, the relationship of the administrator to the group that existed before a merger often will dictate in all fairness that a contract should provide protection for the administrator during this turbulent period.

The interest of the medical group must be balanced with that of the administrator in evaluating the appropriateness of other provisions of the contract for the administrator. Administrators increasingly have requested, and received from their groups, such provisions as long term notice of termination, severance pay depending upon years of service, and severance benefits that can extend the benefit of the contract to provide a "golden parachute" to those administrators who are asked to be relieved of their obligations during this transition period. Because of the need to attract and retain good managerial talent, groups may find it in their best interest to agree to some of these requests made by the administrator. A reasonable balance should be struck between job security for the administrator and the need for the new group to protect itself from an undesirable situation.

Evaluating potential physician departures

In fashioning any evaluation of the merger process, the negotiating team and the medical leadership of the group must be prepared for the eventuality that some physicians may find the proposed venture unacceptable and, therefore, leave the group. To be prepared for these potential departures, a medical group must examine its existing employment agreements to understand the negotiating position that it may take with these physicians. While every effort must be made to retain the core of physicians to participate in the new group, it is likely that some physicians will use the new proposal as a catalyst to begin a new practice.

Many of these physicians may have been reluctant group practice members already, and the prospect of major change in the organization or operations of the new group will be too much for these individuals to accept. Groups that have strong group-centered contracts in place already will be the beneficiaries of a stronger negotiating position with these departing physicians. For those groups that have weak individual-centered agreements, the only solace can be that it has learned first-hand the importance of having a group-centered contract, and that by this experience it will maintain the resolve to have the remaining physicians enter into a stronger contract that comprehensively protects the interests of the group created by the merger.

Chapter 5

The merger implementation process

T he process of implementing a merger often is overlooked by the individuals involved, as medical groups usually have little, if any, experience with the process. Uncertainty can seriously undermine the efforts of those involved to anticipate and resolve effectively issues that might prevent a successful conclusion. In all of these transactions, however, the issues that will arise can be predicted with some certainty. Attention to the implementation process will greatly facilitate the successful consummation of the merger. Without this attention, the transaction may drift aimlessly without direction, causing delay and additional expense. This delay creates the opportunity for loss of momentum, loss of group consensus, and for a breakdown in negotiations that may be permanent. Developing a comprehensive implementation strategy is an important task to be undertaken by the merger participants.

Letter of intent

To implement any merger, the parties first must understand the scope and nature of the business relationship. In many instances a letter of intent will set forth the basic principles of the proposed merger. Using a letter of intent serves several purposes.

First, the letter of intent will require the parties to focus on the main points on which they agree, and will require them to decide whether a basic agreement has been reached before considerable effort and expenditure of funds are made. The anticipated structure of the combination, how the parties will relate to each other for governance, physician compensation and stock ownership combination principles are all subjects which should be included in a letter of intent.

A second important reason for a letter of intent is that it serves as a psychological tool to enlist the support of physicians for the change. Medical group leadership that announces that a letter of intent has been signed will create the impression that an important first step has been made, and this sense of progress will enable the leadership to marshal support for the merger.

The third reason to employ a letter of intent is to allow the parties to identify those issues on which they currently agree and, to hold for further discussion, those issues which cannot yet be resolved. This process of issue-narrowing and definition will allow parties to begin to work out their difficulties on issues on which they have not yet agreed. Purposefully keeping vague some of the difficult issues faced in the transaction will allow the parties to go forward in a common problem-solving mode to resolve those issues.

There may be valid reasons not to use a letter of intent, however. First, letters of intent are noncontractual, and they may be viewed as a meaningless exercise on which the parties focus undue attention. This focusing of effort can derail the process by allowing lawyers and other advisors to negotiate the language in the letter of intent too heavily. This misplaced energy may result in the entire merger project becoming bogged down. The time spent negotiating may be another significant drawback, because if the parties spend weeks negotiating a letter of intent, issues must be negotiated twice, as opposed to once in the final documents. Finally, a letter of intent may push issues to decision when they are not yet ready for resolution. The parties may be far apart on several substantive issues and their ability to build a consensus will take time, experience and growth in the relationships between the individual members of the merger committee. Prematurely rushing issues to a conclusion may result in polarization, rather than cooperation, and proceeding to negotiate a letter of intent which attempts to cover these issues may be destructive of the entire process.

Whether a letter of intent is used depends upon the facts and circumstances of each transaction. If a letter of intent is used, however, attention should be paid to the format of the letter. It is important to recognize, and the letter should state, that the letter of intent does not bind the parties to the transaction. Language which states the agreement to proceed is noncontractual, but represents the good faith intent of the parties to finalize the transaction, is appropriate. Otherwise, the risk arises that a binding agreement to proceed may be created in the letter which can be used as a basis for a claim of damages should the merger later fail. It is in the interests of all parties to avoid having a contract for the merger arise based upon the execution of the letter.

Another important provision to be included in the letter of intent is a confidentiality provision. Both parties should agree to keep confidential all financial information and other confidential materials that are exchanged. This part of the letter should be made contractually binding on the parties and language to that effect should be added to the letter. Making this obligation binding addresses the risk that information which is exchanged in the negotiating process could be leaked to third parties or used to the detriment of the party that provided the information. This paragraph also should contain a provision that requires all this information to be returned immediately if the negotiations terminate.

A final provision to include in the letter of intent is an exclusivity provision. Exclusivity provisions bind both parties to proceed in negotiating their transaction, usually for a specific period of time, without negotiating with a third party. Exclusivity provisions allow the parties to proceed with some confidence that third parties will not interfere with an orderly process of negotiating. This provision also should contain a reference to a continuation of the exclusivity period if the parties are proceeding in good faith toward final negotiations at the expiration of exclusivity. The time period for exclusivity should be relatively short in most instances, and should coincide with a reasonable estimate of how long the transaction will take to conclude. Including an exclusivity provision in a letter of intent is usually reasonable as the effort and expense of engaging in a merger means that the parties should use their best efforts to complete their transaction without outside distraction. The exclusivity provision also should be made contractually binding on the parties.

The schedule

For groups to understand fully the process before them, a schedule should be prepared for every transaction which identifies the issues to be confronted, categorizes the tasks to be performed and sets an appropriate timetable in which to accomplish these tasks. Schedules serve several purposes. First, they allow all of the issues to be identified by the participants by providing an overview of the merger process. The schedule illustrates that there is a beginning, middle and end to any merger implementation. Second, the schedule helps the individuals charged with implementing the transaction to plan to confront the issues and the process in a coordinated manner. This planning process will improve greatly the chance of success for implementing the transaction. Finally, the schedule helps to create a sense of accomplishment and momentum as the parties proceed through the process and accomplish the tasks contained on the list. It is important to update the schedule every several weeks to reflect this progress. During the process, the schedule will need to be revised to reflect unanticipated problems, inevitable delays and other issues that will arise. Using the schedule as the operative document, however, can help minimize these disruptions and put them in perspective while achieving the larger goal.

Transforming the Delivery of Health Care:
The integration process

While each transaction will have issues that are unique to the parties involved, a typical merger can be achieved in a 90- to 120-day period, beginning from when the parties conclude conceptually that they should proceed. Prior to beginning the intensive implementation process, a significant period of time may have elapsed whereby the parties have identified each other, discussed in general the terms that will bind them together, and then focused more specifically on the details of their merger. This exploratory period may have lasted another 90 days, but may extend over a longer period, given that knowledge of particular opportunities and relationships often evolve slowly and in response to a variety of factors.

Once the decision is made to proceed, however, the 90- to 120-day implementation period probably is ideal. A shorter period of time makes building group consensus difficult to achieve and makes covering the myriad of details necessary for successful implementation nearly impossible to accomplish. A longer period of time has its own set of risks and problems. Momentum may be lost as the parties become bogged down in detail, losing a sense of urgency to accomplish their goal and becoming sidetracked on ancillary issues that may result in loss of perspective on the strategic importance of the overall merger. The uncertainty caused by the transaction will be increased significantly by a longer time period, as employee anxiety and turnover increases, rumors are generated, and the stress and tension about job security are not resolved. This uncertainty is inevitable in any major change, but a longer time period magnifies these negative aspects. Finally, a longer time frame will allow those who are opposed to the transaction to find ways of raising ancillary issues that may threaten progress on the transaction.

While most parties will find ample excuse to delay the process beyond this 90- to 120-day period, given the "unique" set of factors present in their situation, this argument should be resisted. Most issues faced by the parties are not unique and can be reduced to the fundamental issues which must be decided before the transaction is finalized. Those charged with implementing the transaction must be prepared to convince those who seek delay that the schedule should be adopted. Often, the desire for more information and more data can mask the real motive of delaying the process which is to avoid making critical decisions. Usually, the additional information obtained by this data will not give the "ultimate" answer that those who request the data are seeking. The decision-making process should provide enough data to make decisions, but the judgment and analysis that must be employed usually will not be improved by this additional data.

The merger timetable

While the exact sequence in which a merger will be implemented often depends on the specific circumstances of each transaction, the process will fall roughly within three distinct phases. A detailed list of issues to be covered and a suggested timetable is set forth on Table 1 on page 91. This process can be summarized as follows:

First period

During the first period of the merger process, the parties must be prepared to identify and begin work quickly on a number of significant issues. These issues include physician compensation, the merger structure, and the name of the organization. Data will need to be collected during this time period to identify all of these issues and that process should begin as soon as the parties decide to proceed. During this initial time period it is important to identify banking and lending relationships which may require modification to complete the merger. These lending institutions will not operate with the same sense of urgency that the parties to the merger will, and, therefore, a significant amount of advance notice will be necessary to allow these institutions to respond. Identifying these relationships at the outset will allow the group sufficient time to make these contacts. Another important issue that must be addressed during this initial period is whether appraisals of real estate will be required to combine the real estate holdings of the respective groups. Appraisals typically take 30 days to 60 days to complete, and in order not to delay the entire merger process, it will be important to order them early to facilitate receiving the results in a timely fashion.

Second period

During the second period, work that already has begun on critical issues of physician compensation, merger structure and name should be finalized, allowing the parties to find out relatively early in the process whether agreement can be achieved on these significant issues. Communication with all physicians must continue. Also during this second period, work should begin on identifying the new governing structure for the combined group, for reviewing pension plan and employee benefit issues and for preparing cash flow projections for the new group. These issues will require a significant amount of administrative work to complete. During the second period, it also is important to begin preparation and circulation of the legal documentation that will be necessary to consummate the merger. During this time period, the physician employment agreements that will be used by the combined group must be prepared and circulated for comment, first to the merger committee, then to the respective groups, and finally to all physicians for comment.

Allowing sufficient time for these employment contracts to be reviewed, modified and circulated will minimize complaints that physicians are not given sufficient time to review these important documents. Merger documentation such as the merger agreement which combines the professional corporations and partnership agreements which combine the real estate also must be prepared during this time period. Because of the expense involved in the preparation of these documents, the parties should begin this process during the middle portion of this time period. The final items to be identified during this time period are licenses of the group that must be assigned or modified, and relationships with vendors that may change with the combination. Again, sufficient advance notice must be allowed to account for lack of a timely response by these parties and vendors.

Final period

During the final period, the legal nature of the transaction will predominate with the finalization of all necessary documents. During this process, continued communication with all physicians will be necessary. Drafts of the documents will continue to be circulated and the work on benefits, banking and lending relationships and cash flow projections will need to be concluded. Physicians will be expected to execute their new employment agreements near the end of this period. All licenses and vendors' relationships must be identified and transferred as of the effective date of the merger if they do not transfer automatically. Finally, during this time period, the appropriate meetings of shareholders and directors must be held to approve the process pursuant to applicable state law.

The negotiating process

Inevitably mergers will entail negotiations with the other parties to the transaction. The ability to create a situation in which all the parties feel they have won, and to create a spirit of compromise, are essential elements for creating a successful combination. Unlike the sale of a house or even the sale of a business, the parties to a merger do not disappear after the closing. If an adversarial approach that often is taken in conjunction with a sale of a business is employed in implementing these transactions, the merger may fail, or this confrontational approach may become the method of operation for the new group in the future. All parties must recognize that the manner of negotiating will establish the foundation of future cooperation in resolving difficult issues. A spirit of cooperation to solve a problem in the implementation phase should be encouraged by all concerned. The leadership of the parties must be cognizant of the need to utilize this approach and must monitor the approach utilized by their respective legal counsel who may use the adversarial approach. The parties must convince their respective legal counsel that an overly adversarial approach will be counterproductive in mergers.

Equally important in the negotiating process is the way a party decides to assemble its negotiating team. Physician-to-physician relationships will be critical in implementing a merger successfully. The concept of one negotiating team versus another may create undesirable polarization in the formation of the new medical group. In the merger context, a single body known as a merger committee can be selected which will consist of representatives appointed by each group who will represent that group on the merger committee. While inevitably negotiating will occur at this committee level, this combination in a single body will help create the mentality of a combined group that is important to foster in the merger process.

Members of the merger committee will be charged with providing the leadership necessary to complete the merger. It is important, therefore, to include physicians in leadership positions in each group on this decision-making body so support for decisions made in the merger committee can be passed through to the individual medical groups. In addition, in some instances it may be beneficial to include those individuals who are initially hostile to change in order to have them become part of the process of devising solutions and approaches, thereby becoming supporters, as opposed to opponents, of the merger.

To be effective, a merger committee must be granted some decision-making power from the original appointing groups. The ideal process is for the merger committee to set the agenda of significant issues that should be decided, and to suggest possible solutions. The respective constituents of the merger committee will then return to their groups with the proposed solution and seek their support. While the individual groups will give guidance throughout the process to their merger committee members, it is the ability of this committee to propose solutions by compromise that will greatly enhance the process.

If the merger committee is not delegated sufficient authority to enable it to fashion solutions, every decision that will need to be made by the combining medical groups will need to be referred back to each group. This method of decision making will create a powerless merger committee that will serve merely as a messenger. Significant delay will occur in the process if this messenger syndrome is allowed to develop, as allowing the constituent groups to make all decisions will mean inevitably that a merger committee meeting will need to be followed by group meetings, followed again by a merger committee meeting where group decisions are reported, in an endless cycle that will prolong unnecessarily the process.

Decision making

Inevitably in the merger process, conflict will arise over various issues. How this conflict is resolved will set the framework for future conflict resolution in the new group. A process by which conflict can be resolved effectively must be established for the creation of a healthy working relationship. Each party will have developed over the years its own conflict resolution process. Medical group decision making may take many forms. For example, some groups may use the well-respected senior leadership to fashion and direct physician support. Others may use the team approach whereby physicians with special relationships with the constituent physician departments will be used as a liaison between those departments and the larger group. Others may use a group meeting concept where decisions are discussed in true democratic fashion, with consensus forming from those interactions.

Whatever the mechanisms that have been utilized by the respective parties, the new merged group must develop its own strategy. This strategy can be developed only by examining, in a historical fashion, how the constituent parties have made these decisions. A combination of efforts, and a balance of old and new approaches, is likely to be successful for the new effort. In the resolution of conflict, it is important that decisions be achieved by allowing all in the decision-making process to feel a part of the decision in order to secure support for decisions ultimately made. It is important, therefore, that majority votes not be used to decide critical issues. Discussion, identification of common ground and consensus building are essential for achieving these decisions. This process of consensus building at the decision-making level, however, should not be used for all group decisions involving all group members, where attempting to build a consensus with too many individuals will be prone to delay and failure.

The merger committee must consider the changing dynamic between decision making by consensus versus for the merged group. A smaller group may find that the consensus building process of individual communication and molding of views based on that communication is an effective way to enlist physician support. Groups that grow beyond seven to nine physicians will find themselves in a transition where the ability to achieve consensus of all physicians in the process, and the time entailed in achieving that result, will seriously impede decision making. As groups begin to grow beyond a certain size (perhaps 10 to 20) the ability to achieve consensus of all physicians will be significantly impaired and may disrupt the decision making necessary for larger groups. Larger groups must, therefore, develop a centralized decision-making process. The size of such groups makes the ability to solicit individual decisions and opinions from physicians virtually impossible to achieve, and a centralized management

86

with power delegated by individual physicians often will be in a better position to make decisions and report those decisions to its constituents. As long as the decision makers keep that trust, physician support is usually sustainable. The transition between these two poles of organizational behavior is an uneven one and medical groups in the merger context will need to examine seriously where they are in the organizational development process, and where the new organization to which they will belong will be in this transition. Yet this delegation of authority to that leadership group means that the leadership group itself must struggle to build consensus for decisions that this leadership is charged with making.

Within each medical group, decision making also should receive attention so support for the transaction can be built. Regardless of the size of a group, the medical group leadership must identify issues, propose solutions, and guide physician thinking on these issues in order to implement these decisions. While input from physicians is a necessary component to this decision-making process, the physician leadership must develop its agenda for implementing the change and as part of that implementation process incorporate physician feedback on various issues.

As part of the decision-making process for merger implementation within a medical group, discussion of issues must continue outside of formal meetings. Private discussions must be held with those who may be reluctant to support the group position, as this type of individual lobbying will be necessary to build support. This approach also allows physicians to feel a part of the process, enabling them to support with some enthusiasm decisions that are ultimately made. Without appropriate involvement of these physicians and attention to their opinions, the risk exists that groups or individual physicians will not support the merger and will either leave or become agents of discontent in the newly formed organization.

Communication

To implement a merger successfully, significant attention must be given to communication. This communication dilemma is multi-faceted, as it covers not only the process of informing physicians about a transaction, having the merger committee report to the board of directors, or having the board of directors report to its physician-staff, but also includes contact with a variety of other interested parties including medical group employees, the parties with whom a medical group has ongoing relationships, and the public at large. The rumor mills that exist in many medical groups and in the physician community at large are often well established and must be managed rather than ignored.

Transforming the Delivery of Health Care:
The integration process

A strategy must be developed to confront this information dilemma. A central element to that strategy is the need to control information and confidentiality. In one respect, confidentiality means the ability to keep details of the transaction from those who are outside of the medical group. To accomplish this goal, physician leaders must impress upon the group members the need for secrecy. Details of the transaction may be discovered by the media, competitors, or other medical groups or hospitals, with the risk that the transaction may be inappropriately characterized or prematurely disclosed. All players in the process must guard against inappropriate disclosure of the details of the transaction.

An equally important concept that leadership of the parties must confront, however, is the amount of communication given to various participants in the process. This control of information is critical to the success of implementation. The leadership must strike a balance between withholding information from others in the group to allow a clear consistent message of information when it is finally communicated, and providing sufficient amounts of information to enlist support, understanding and feedback concerning the proposed transaction.

When communication is made, the leaders must be prepared to summarize the information that is conveyed to their constituent members. Information should not be conveyed in such detail that individuals who are not intimately familiar with the process become bogged down in details. Clear and concise summaries that leave out the various negotiating positions and nuances are helpful.

Equally important as the nature of the disclosure is the timing of that disclosure. Information must be disclosed at the right time. Premature disclosure of information may cause undue alarm by focusing on issues yet to be resolved, or by focusing on a variety of options that the merger committee currently confronts. Raising issues that have yet to be decided, and that may prove to be difficult to resolve, also may heighten insecurity or tension if the recipients of this information are not part of the conflict resolution process. Medical group leadership should plan how information will be conveyed among various players. At the beginning of the process, the merger will be extremely confidential. Throughout the process, various decisions and negotiating positions that are taken also will be confidential, and the leak of that information or the mechanism by which a decision will be made may hamper the ability to form a consensus around the compromises that inevitably will be made.

While the individual context of each decision will dictate the strategy employed, leadership of the group must understand that in many situations, the complexity and volatility of many positions dictate that the information be kept confidential and that when in doubt, preference should be given to maintain confidentiality rather than premature disclosure. Seasoned leadership experienced in making changes and implementing decisions will understand the need for a cautioned approach.

As part of the communication plan for a medical group, briefing sessions should be scheduled with physicians. Discussions must be held with physicians concerning proposed new employment arrangements, physician compensation and the details of the merger. This communication, on a routine and regular basis, is important to build support for the process, and to identify danger signs which may evidence an erosion of physician support. Another critical aspect of this communication program will be to clarify to individual physicians the risks associated with not completing the transaction. To accomplish a merger successfully, it will be necessary to focus physicians on the larger issues confronted in the transformation of medical care delivery. Information concerning changing medical practice patterns, and the changing economies of that practice, must be conveyed to physicians. The message must be communicated that the status quo and a return to the days past are not viable alternatives, and that change and evolution inevitably will occur. This message will, if properly conveyed, convince physicians that planning for change is as important a process as any in a medical practice, and that the ability to adapt to that change, as represented by the proposed transaction, will allow their practice to operate more successfully in the changing health care marketplace.

With respect to its employees, a medical group must be aware that the benefits in the proposed merger which the physicians have so readily identified as being available to them will not be as readily apparent to the nonphysician employees. Employees will be concerned about a variety of matters. They may view the merger as a threat to job security, recognizing that combining groups may result in loss of, or modification to, job duties. These employees also will be concerned about modifications to benefits that may arise given the combination of work forces, with minor changes in minor benefits being viewed with exaggerated apprehension by those employees. This employee uncertainty must be dealt with effectively by the groups.

A strong communication program must convey information to employees in a form that allows employees to have their questions answered in as timely a fashion as possible. Both group meetings and written communication programs should be utilized to accomplish this effort. Without a program sufficiently attuned to employee concerns, rumors and gossip will replace facts, increasing the risk of confusion and the likelihood of harm to employee morale and employee retention. The medical leaders should develop a communication program that only deals with the basic issues of the proposed merger and that will treat, in summary fashion, many of the nuances that will have been covered in greater detail with the physician staff members. Broad statements about the type of relationship that will be created, coupled with more specifics about benefit changes and redirection in staffing will be the right mix of detail to satisfy these concerns. Negotiating positions or difficulties and any recitation of problems associated with the merger should not be part of this communication process, the focus being on positive information provided in a general format.

With respect to the general public, another level of the communication plan must be devised. First, a plan must be developed to deal with inquiries from the media and other parties about the inevitable rumors that will arise about a pending transaction. Each of the parties to the transaction should appoint a central spokesperson who will provide information or answer questions concerning any potential combination. The response to these general inquiries should be discussed in advance by all the parties to the transaction, with the understanding that parties will communicate with each other about the nature of the inquiry and the response given. The nature of this response must be agreed to in advance so consistent positions can be taken with the media.

In addition to this preventive strategy with respect to immediate inquiries, it is critical for the parties to spend sufficient time in the preparation and development of a plan to announce the merger. Appropriate attention should be given to the drafting of press releases, to the site of the news conference, and to the timing of that conference. In many instances, public interest will be high in the venture, and the message to be conveyed should be planned in light of the strategic plan of the new group. This announcement will be one of the initial steps in a coordinated marketing plan that will be necessary to communicate the new message of the merged group to the general public and the medical community.

Groups must focus not only on the general public, but also on the medical community given the referral relationships that are essential to the fiscal success of many groups. Public confusion about the proposed combination must be minimized and a consistent message must be developed for communication. As part of this effort, the groups should consider any change in letterhead, logo and name, and must undertake sufficient planning in order to implement those changes in a timely and orderly fashion. The ability to plan effectively for the communication of the message of the new organization to the community at large is a critical component to the successful launching of the new venture. Special attention must be made if the name of the group will change as part of the process. Public confusion about this name change will inevitably occur and a general awareness campaign about the new name must be planned. Without this campaign, patients may become confused in the process and this confusion may result in loss of market share by the new group until confusion is eliminated.

The merger implementation process

Table 1
The merger schedule

Key: **Tasks Completed (boldface text)**
Tasks Remaining (normal text)
Changes From Previous Report Are Underlined

	Sept.	Oct.	Nov.	Dec.	Jan.
1. Physician compensation:					
— Commence work	1st				
— Preliminary report distributed		1st			
— Comments received re: report		15th			
— Final report		30th			
— Compensation system finalized			15th		
Status report:					
2. Merger structure:					
— Commence structure work		1st			
— Preliminary report distributed		10th			
— Development of legal analysis of structure and meetings with groups' counsel & accountants		14-21st			
— Structure presentation		30th			
— Medical group structure finalized			8th		
— Real estate partnership structure finalized			24th		
Status report:					
3. Name:					
— Merger committee authorizes process	15th				
— Report to merger committee		1st			
— Report to all physicians		15th			
— Name finalized		30th			
Status report:					
4. Governance:					
— Merger committee selects candidates for president-medical director-board of directors		1st			
— Candidates for position finalized		15th			
— Subcommittee to nominate slate for vice president, secretary and treasurer		30th			
— Vice president, secretary and treasurer approved by merger committee				5th	
— New candidates installed					1st
Status report:					

91

	Sept.	Oct.	Nov.	Dec.	Jan.
5. Pension plan-employee benefits-personnel:					
— Select subcommittee	23rd				
— Preliminary report circulated to sub-committee on pension plan-benefits		10th			
— Preliminary report circulated to sub-committee on personnel consolidation	20th				
— Discussions on progress		30th			
— Present final report to merger committee		5th			
Status report:					
6. Banking and lending relationships:					
— Submit search request for liens and identify loans	1st				
— Identify areas to discuss with lenders	15th				
— Meet with lenders as necessary			15th		
— Finalize all lender issues				15th	
Status report:					
7. Appraisal of real estate:					
— Appraiser selected	15th				
— Appraisal results received by merger committee		15th			
Status report:					
8. Cash flow projections for new group:					
— Commence cash flow projection on combined group		10th			
— Circulate preliminary draft of projections		5th			
— Incorporate results of financial statements			7th		
— Finalize cash flow needs			12th		
Status report:					
9. Physician employment and administrator agreements:					
— Circulate 1st draft of employment agreements to merger committee		1st			
— Comments regarding drafts received		10th			
— Circulate revised employment agreement to merger committee and counsel			20th		
— Discussion of revised drafts at groups respective board meetings			25th		
— Circulate execution copies to physicians			1st		
— All agreements returned				15th	
Status report:					

The merger implementation process

	Sept.	Oct.	Nov.	Dec.	Jan.
10. Merger documents and ancillary documents:					
— Circulate 1st draft of merger agreement to merger committee and counsel		20th			
— Receive comments re: 1st draft		30th			
— Circulate 2nd draft of merger agreement and 1st draft of partnership agreement			10th		
— Receive comments on 2nd draft of merger agreement and on 1st draft of partnership agreement			20th		
— Circulate ancillary documents			25th		
— Circulate all drafts			31st		
— Receive final comments on all documents				10th	
— Circulate execution copies on all documents				15th	
— Board meetings to approve plan of merger				15th	
— Notify board of medical examiners of merger				15th	
— Execution of merger documents				16th	
— Formal notice to shareholders				16th	
— Shareholders- meetings				26th	
— Merger effective					1st
Status report:					
11. Financial statements of existing PAs:					
— Commence preparation of financial statements for PAs		1st			
— Each group receives internal drafts of its own statement		25th			
— Groups receive drafts of both statements		31st			
Status report:					
12. License-vendors:					
— Begin inventory of vendors and licenses		1st			
— Finalize list of licenses and vendors	15th				
— Begin notification as needed			1st		
— All licenses and vendor contracts assigned effective this date					1st
Status report:					

Chapter 6

Nuts and bolts of
merger implementation

Surrounding any merger of medical groups there are a variety of issues that must be confronted, analyzed and resolved in order to implement the project. Many of these business issues form the foundation on which the future operation can be built, and accordingly represent great planning opportunities to improve the previously standard way of dealing with these issues. A proactive approach to confront these issues early in the merger process will avoid unpleasant surprises near the closing date which can seriously delay completion of the transaction. Identifying these issues, assigning appropriate administrative team members to these tasks, and creating effective reporting mechanisms that allow communication to be made to group leadership, will form the basis for the successful resolution of these issues.

Physician compensation

It is no surprise that the most difficult, and potentially most divisive, issue in any medical group relationship is that of physician compensation. Mergers put the compensation system in a spotlight, as change in the compensation system often may need to be made in the process. In a merger, the combination of the two compensation systems of the medical groups will be required unless, by good fortune, the constituent groups have already, on their own, adopted the same compensation system.

The compensation systems of the medical groups will probably have already created a significant amount of tension because of the impact of that compensation system upon the various physicians and because certain physicians, regardless of their income, will perceive the system currently utilized as unfair. The proposed combination of two systems will increase significantly this tension in each group and, coupled with the tension between the two groups themselves, the chance for disagreement and controversy will be great.

Transforming the Delivery of Health Care: The integration process

In beginning the process of compensation system analysis for a merger, the groups should set forth in writing an explanation of their current systems. This written document will allow both groups to understand thoroughly the system as implemented by both groups. The merger committee and the medical group leadership must then identify a system which will achieve the goals of the new group. The policy reasons behind the adoption of a particular compensation system must be examined to determine whether the incentives created by that system in fact do foster the overall philosophy of the group with respect to group practice, quality of care and hours worked. Groups should examine the way in which the following possible compensation system components should be used to reflect their philosophy. These factors can be expressed in the following six components:

Productivity

Productivity systems reward physicians on the basis of the amount of work they perform. The harder a physician works, the more that physician will earn as income. These productivity systems may be based on collections, that is being based on actual dollars received by a medical group, on charges, with the recognition that the charge made will need to be adjusted to a net amount to reflect the funds actually available for distribution as compensation, or on relative value units, that being a system which, regardless of payer source credits physicians for the same work they do on the same basis. Collection based systems may put a premium on a patient-mix of a particular physician, whereas charge-based systems with a general adjustment for uncollectable amounts will spread the risk of uncollectibility evenly over all physicians regardless of their particular payer mix. Relative value unit systems eliminate payer source as a factor in compensation, but are complex to implement and administer. Productivity systems in general, however, will discourage physician involvement in group activities that are nonrevenue-generating and may encourage work to be performed in an increasingly capitated environment.

Equality

Equal compensation systems divide the amount of money available for distribution to physicians equally regardless of the work formed by the various physicians of the group. These systems recognize the nature of group practice and, therefore, will encourage physicians to engage in other activities that may be in the best interests of the group, such as administrative or community activities, without fear of reduction of compensation. Equal systems also may undermine the incentive to work harder because of the lack of reward for that extra work.

Nuts and bolts of merger implementation

Capitation

Some managed care systems may be implemented in group practice through the use of a capitation model. Physicians who have the obligation to treat patients in a managed care environment may be compensated based upon a set fee per member per month that will not vary depending on the type or intensity of services rendered by a particular physician to any particular patient. Under these systems, a physician will face the volume and intensity risk associated with being responsible for the patient panel. To the extent that some physicians in a group are disproportionately at risk for a large patient panel, it may be necessary to adjust the system to take into account that the volume and intensity is not borne equally by all group members. In general, this system is not used frequently.

Administrative compensation

Some systems may also recognize, with a separate compensation component, that physicians who perform administrative tasks should be paid extra for that work. In effect, these systems require the revenue producing physicians to give up a portion of their revenue to subsidize the nonrevenue producing work of other physicians serving in an administrative capacity. The rationale for including this component is that it serves to encourage those with administrative skills to give up revenue producing time for the greater welfare of the group. By allowing these payments to be made, the group also will signal that it values the services rendered and that those who do not devote this time should be asked to contribute to the payment for those services.

Seniority

Other compensation systems may recognize that senior physicians have contributed disproportionately to the development of the group and the goodwill associated with its practice, and, therefore, add an element of compensation to allow physicians who are in a senior status to receive an extra allocation of revenue for these past efforts.

Salary

Medical groups also may compensate their physicians on the basis of a salary. The salary system allows each physician to be paid a fixed amount, plus perhaps a bonus based on individual productivity or group profitability. The ability of many groups to pay a salary, however, will be limited as a salary means paying that amount regardless of how well the group does financially. This system has the advantage of giving predictability to physician income and encouragement to participate in group activities, but may not provide sufficient productivity incentives to individual physicians unless appropriate bonus criteria can be structured.

Any combination of these compensation systems can be made. In the merger context it is important to examine from an historical basis the various compensation systems and their components, identify the incentives created by these systems and decide upon a system that will meet the philosophy of the new group toward the practice of medicine. The precise mix of compensation components selected will be a function of the history of the groups, specialty type, mix of subspecialists, payer mix and group size. Selecting the proper mix will depend upon the cooperation of the merger committee and the leadership of each medical group as they balance the needs of the new group with their old royalties to their existing groups.

The system used for the compensation of individual physicians in the merger will receive the greatest amount of scrutiny of any portion of the transaction by individual group members. The physician leadership must understand that any change in a compensation system will create winners and losers. It is critical, therefore, to collect sufficient data and construct models which will forecast the impact that the new compensation system will have on physician income. Identifying winners and losers, and making modifications to a proposed system to address perceived inequities, will be an important part of the fluid process of designing a system that generally is perceived to be fair by all physicians involved. The analysis necessary for construction of this fair system must be started early in the process of considering a merger as most, if not all, physicians will not agree to support the proposed transaction until they have an opportunity to review and evaluate the potential impact on their take home pay. Subcommittees must be set up quickly to formulate the structure necessary for this work, and to create accurate models evaluating the system.

Banking and lending relationships

A merger will bring about a major change in the business operation of the medical group, which means that a change in banking or lending relationships may occur. In order to assess the impact of this change, banking and lending relationships must be identified and documents that embody those relationships reviewed. This exercise is necessary because these loan documents often will contain provisions that will require the approval of the lender before any changes are made in the business of the medical group. The structure of the merger, the modification of the structure of the medical group, the operation of the real estate partnership, or the transfer of assets may give the lender the ability to approve or veto these fundamental changes. In order to secure the approval of a lender and to formulate an effective strategy for strengthening the banking relationship, groups must develop an effective communication strategy to explain the transaction to bankers and must be prepared to meet personally with banking representatives. This strategy should include an explanation of the proposed merger, the impact that it will have upon the medical care delivery capabilities of the group, the impact upon health care delivery in the community, and any available projections about the financial implications of the transaction, along with plans for future growth and expansion. The strategy to be utilized is to explain to the bankers why the proposed merger represents a positive move for the group and, therefore, why the bank should view it as in its best interest to cooperate with any requested change. This face-to-face meeting should include the leadership of the group along with any appropriate representative from the other medical group.

Utilizing an approach that conveys information and explains the merits of the proposed transaction will assist medical groups in securing the necessary approvals. Groups must allow for this information to be conveyed a significant time in advance to allow the bankers to become familiar with the proposed transaction, and to secure the needed consent. Many lenders, particularly those, such as mortgage lenders, who are not in the community in which the new group will operate, will have little or no incentive to cooperate quickly with these requests. Planning for this communication and consent process must be undertaken early to avoid potential delay in finalizing the merger.

Personnel

Making effective personnel decisions in the planning process will be a challenging task to all who confront it, but making those decisions for the newly merged medical group will do much to ensure its success. Without sufficient attention to personnel issues, the risk will increase that while the merger may be completed successfully, the business operations that are conducted thereafter will be damaged seriously or impaired because the personnel function has not been addressed adequately.

The primary and most substantial personnel task will be to combine two separate office staffs. This combination must receive significant attention from the administrative leadership of the combined groups. Administration must evaluate its personnel critically, coping with the bias that each respective administrative team will have for its own personnel. First, the administrative teams must develop a prototype organizational chart which will allow the combined group to function effectively. To the extent possible, this organizational work must be completed without reference to individual personnel and must be viewed as a flow chart that can accomplish in a functional, as opposed to a theoretical, way the many tasks that will be required of the new organization.

Once this organizational planning has taken place, the administrative team must be prepared to evaluate critically the individuals that will fill the new organizational plan. Inevitably, the loyalties of the administrators to their respective staffs will interfere with the process. The administrators must recognize this element of bias, but nonetheless must attempt to make decisions with respect to experience, competence and ability of the staff to grow in expanded positions. The administrative team must be prepared to make difficult choices about the suitability of their staffs for various roles, as some positions will require consolidation, and some employees will have their positions eliminated through downsizing, even if not at once, then over a gradual transition period. In other areas, the extent and complexity of the work of the new medical group will require that a new level of specialization be engaged in by certain employees. Some employees who may have performed several functions will now, because of increased volume of work, be required to specialize in one area.

The combination of two staffs is a difficult task and one that most administrations would like to avoid. The economies of scale of the merger, however, can only be achieved if the administrative team looks for these types of staff consolidation savings, as personnel costs remain a major overhead factor for any group. Any projected savings of the merger must be accompanied with a detailed plan of how to achieve economies of scale in the personnel area. These savings in personnel costs must be balanced against the need to implement the process so it is perceived in as positive fashion as possible by the employees of the respective groups. As a consequence, economies of scale are not likely to be achieved immediately, but only after several years of consolidation.

Just as administrative staffs must be combined in a merger, medical groups must come to grips with the reality that a combined group can only have one chief administrator. The selection of this administrator will, in many instances, be a difficult process. This issue, however, must be dealt with early in the merger process. The ability to organize effectively a combined staff can only be accomplished if clear lines of authority are established, and a hierarchy of decision making put into place. Without selecting the chief administrator who can direct the many details in the merger, the process of the merger and the ability to combine office staffs may be threatened. Physician leadership of the respective groups must determine which administrator will direct the combined group, and this decision should be based on performance, experience, self-confidence, judgment and ability to grow to a position with significantly more responsibility. While both administrators can be expected to want and lobby for the position, all involved must recognize that an early resolution to the decision is needed and, that once the decision is made, it must be accepted by all involved.

From the perspective of the individual administrator, the ability to accept the decisions made by the combined group often will dictate the way in which the relationship of the administrator with the new group will develop. Demonstrated competence in different situations and solid performance of whatever task is assigned to the administrator are accomplishments which will improve the standing of the administrator with both constituent groups. Administrators who successfully implement a merger and who retain the confidence of both the old and new physician groups throughout the process will find themselves in a position that can significantly enhance career opportunities regardless of whether that opportunity exists within or outside the group. A long term view of career development is necessary for administrators in the merger process, and if viewed in that light, the day-to-day difficulties of the merger can be put better in perspective.

Employee benefits

Linked closely with the personnel issue is that of the benefits that must be provided to employees. Any change in benefits that are provided to the physician staff will be viewed with great concern by the physicians who must understand the need for any proposed change. The modification of benefits will be a significant issue that must be addressed in the pre-merger implementation phase.

Medical groups will have their own separate plans and benefit levels for their employees and physicians. Just as significant job insecurity may be created because of the merger, the merger will also create uncertainty about employee benefits, as any change from the status quo will be perceived as a threat by employees who will assume immediately, without the benefit of receiving any information, that reductions or modifications of benefits will be a result of the merger. The groups must move to identify quickly what changes will be made in this area to combat this uncertainty and the negative impact that uncertainty will have on employee morale and retention.

First, the respective types, levels and related costs of benefits from each group should be identified, compiled and prepared in report form to make accurate analysis possible. After that compilation task has been completed, a benefit subcommittee should discuss and fashion a philosophy to be adopted by the merger committee and the respective boards of directors that will enable many of the implementation details to be decided with reference to that philosophy.

In adopting a benefit combination strategy, the following options should be considered:

First, the employees of both groups could be treated so none will have a reduction in benefits due to the merger. This philosophy will require the adoption of the most comprehensive (and, therefore, in most instances, the most expensive) benefit option for each group. Given the cost pressures and increasing overhead experienced by medical groups in general, this philosophy will be difficult to implement without a severe adverse impact on physician compensation. Because the benefits of each group will likely differ in many ways, adopting the highest common denominator will increase costs at a time when the groups are trying to decrease overhead and demonstrate cost savings from the merger.

A second approach would be the opposite of the first, that being the adoption of the least expensive benefits provided by each group. In this scenario, reductions in employee benefits from each group may create morale problems. The maximum amount of savings may be achieved, but it may be at the expense of making significant benefit cuts. This approach provides little incentive to employees to welcome the merger enthusiastically, and employee retention also may suffer if this strategy is used. To the extent, however, that cost pressures have become severe, some benefit reductions may be in order. If the group will be forced to make benefit reductions regardless of whether the merger is accomplished, planning must center on how to communicate the benefit reduction decision. The task in communicating benefit reductions must focus on a strategy of explaining why these cuts are necessary and avoid blaming the decision on the merger itself.

A third philosophy to be considered is to limit expenditures for benefits to the level of that in the previous year. This "no growth" philosophy can be expressed in a variety of ways. These options could include no growth in per employee costs or no growth in absolute dollars expended by the combined groups. This philosophy will result in some benefit cuts given the gradual increase of benefit costs from year to year. The advantage, however, is that it may provide some flexibility to increase some of the lower-end benefits provided by the groups.

A final philosophy would be to hold benefit package increases to a percentage increase over the previous year. A percentage increase of benefits could be made to allow for some increases, but the rate of increase could be kept well below the average annual increases experienced by the groups over the previous years. There is a cost containment element to this approach that could be utilized to explain to employees that benefits will be increased in some areas, but that cost pressures preclude wholesale adoption of all benefit plans concerned. This percentage increase can be expressed as a per employee cost percentage increase or as a percentage increase in total benefit costs for the combined group.

Whichever philosophy is adopted by the combined group, the administrative team must perform an important function (in conjunction with benefits consultants that can assist with the implementation process) to conduct an orderly review with respect to benefit cost and design. As part of this benefit review process, administrators can expect to receive a variety of overtures from various benefit vendors and consultants who all will be attempting to sell their products to the combined group. The

Nuts and bolts of merger implementation

"political" process of combining benefits will mean that many consultants with long term relationships of providing insurance or other benefits to various physicians will have those relationships challenged. The challenge for the administrator is to channel these inevitable marketing pressures away from individual physicians and staff members to a central decision maker who will receive proposals and field inquiries with respect to potential business. Administrators also should be prepared to rely on legal counsel experienced in benefits design in order to become fully informed about the legal nuances of combining benefits and any collective bargaining restrictions that may impede benefit changes. Because benefits remain a significant portion of medical practice overhead, administrators must be prepared to look critically at all proposals in order to avoid losing any potential cost-saving opportunities that may be present in the merger.

The communication process also must receive attention in the implementation of the merger. Because employees will be concerned about benefit issues, as soon as a substantive progress report can be made, employees should receive an update on the progress of that work to decrease this uncertainty. In addition, as soon as final decisions are made regarding benefits, a final report should be made to employees.

Licenses and reimbursement considerations

Commencing new business operations in the merged group may impact the licenses under which a group has previously operated. As part of the implementation process, it is important to identify and categorize licenses and permits that the group currently may utilize to function. Appropriate steps should be taken to notify these regulatory agencies of the impending change. Many of these licenses will automatically transfer to the organization as a result of the merger. To maintain regulatory compliance for the new operation, an action plan must be developed early in the implementation process so with respect to licenses and permits that must be changed, all necessary steps will be taken by the beginning of the start-up of the new operation.

Particularly important in this area is the relationship the new group will have with third party payers. An analysis will need to be undertaken concerning how the new organization will be able to bill for the medical and ancillary services that are provided. In light of the basic decision about the structure of the relationship, the parties must review the legal requirements that must be fulfilled for the new organization to receive reimbursement. To the extent a change in provider number is deemed necessary, the parties must apply for new provider numbers. Medicare intermediaries, for example, will often require a waiting period before processing the change, and the medical group should be in constant communication with the applicable intermediaries to assure a smooth transition. Interruption of cash flow and other negative implications may occur if these steps are not followed.

Third party contracts

All medical groups receive a variety of services pursuant to vendor contracts. As part of the merger process, it will be necessary to identify these relationships and analyze them. The two groups inevitably will have a duplicate set of arrangements which cover such activities that range from janitorial relationships to leasing of medical equipment. It is important to develop a detailed plan to deal with these relationships.

The challenge will be to make comparisons of service and price, and analyze cost savings opportunities in order to cut duplicate services and achieve economies of scale. Existing vendors should be approached to seek a modification of their prices, given the potentially larger volume of business that may be channeled through a merged group. Duplicate arrangements should be consolidated, with due attention being given to notice of termination provisions contained in these agreements to determine the steps necessary to terminate a relationship legally. The identification of these termination provisions must be done early so any required notice can be given. These notice provisions should be utilized even if a final decision has not been made concerning a particular vendor because the negotiating position of the medical group will be improved greatly if it negotiates a revised relationship without asking at the same time to be relieved of an existing contractual relationship. Even where this notice is not given, medical groups should not be reluctant to renegotiate, as the vendor will usually try to make every effort to accommodate this new larger customer.

The merger planning process also should identify those contracts which formally must be assigned to the new group. In most mergers, the contracts and obligations of both groups will be assumed automatically by the surviving corporation and no formal assignment may be necessary. In the acquisition context where one group acquires the assets of the other group, this formal assumption process must occur. The administrative team must delegate this contract assignment process to appropriate individuals on its staff. Much of this detail work requires aggressive contacting of third parties and those who are asked to accomplish this task must have impressed upon them that this process is an important part of the overall transaction.

Security interests

In the course of operating its medical practice over the years, medical groups will have entered into a variety of relationships whereby a third party will have extended credit or provided equipment on a lease basis. In order to secure its right to have its loan repaid, or to perfect its right to repossess the equipment if the debt is not repaid by the medical group or if lease payments are not made, these third parties will have filed liens on the property of the medical group. These security interest filings made under the Uniform Commercial Code protect the interest of a creditor or lessor to the equipment.

These third party filings may apply to specific medical equipment purchased by the group, to equipment leased by the group (and therefore rightfully owned by the lessor) or to such general categories of assets as equipment or accounts receivable. For example, a security interest will likely have been created when a group purchased its computer with the proceeds from a loan. In this process, the group will have granted a security interest in the computer which would allow the lender, who advances funds for the purchase, to "repossess" the computer if there is a default in the loan. The theory for allowing this repossession is that the lender can then sell the equipment and take the proceeds from that sale to apply to the reduction of the debt. The documents creating the obligations which give rise to the security interest will need to be reviewed to determine whether consents of these third parties who have these security interests are necessary where a merger occurs. In many instances, the consent will not be necessary.

Quality of medical practice and utilization review/ quality assurance programs

In the merger, an additional significant activity that must be considered is the combination of the respective utilization review and quality assurance programs of the merging groups. How these programs are operated or to the extent they exist at all often reflects the larger philosophy of the groups with respect to medical practice issues. As part of the merger process, the groups will have identified their respective philosophies concerning the practice of medicine and, in most instances, will have satisfied themselves that they are compatible in the practice of medicine. The internal utilization review/quality assurance programs that have been used by the groups or the way that medical practice issues are confronted are reflective of this practice philosophy and also will need to be combined in the merger. Differences in program operations and duplicate personnel will create opportunities for combination and improvement in programs, while at the same time will create additional uncertainty regarding philosophy of operations and for personnel.

In order to address these difficulties adequately, the combined leadership must agree conceptually about the medical practice philosophy of the new group, along with general philosophy of the role of utilization review and quality assurance programs in group practice. Once this philosophy has been adopted by the groups and the merger committee, adequate steps can be taken to combine and modify the approaches using a comprehensive plan to combine program functions and staff members with a commitment to achieving cost savings. Combinations of larger groups that have well established programs may create special problems because staff roles will have been developed already. It is likely, however, that the combination of medical groups of sufficient size will create an additional volume of work that will mean that the programs must be enlarged over the scope of the former programs. It is also likely, however, that the medical director position, as well as various other positions, will need to be consolidated.

Patient care issues

While medical groups may be consumed with staff combination and medical practice issues throughout the merger transaction process, the parties must also pay attention to an analysis of patient demographics and payer mix in the new practice. The parties should identify applicable patient population demographics information, identify third party payer mix and specify collection data. This raw data should be compiled by each group to a merger to provide strategic information about the future direction of the medical group. This information, for example, may reveal that the groups have significant disparities with respect to participation in managed care programs, or may have significant differences in Medicare population statistics. All of these factors will have implications upon the combined operation of the group. The development of this database will be a useful planning tool to be used in both the implementation period and in the future operation of the medical group.

Chapter 7

The real estate factor

The question of how real estate, which a medical group uses to perform its medical practice, should be owned has been answered in many different ways. Some groups, feeling that it is important to own the place in which they practice, have utilized an ownership structure. Others have always leased space, preferring to pay rent, rather than become involved in ownership issues. In mergers, the complex issues that come with dealing with the ownership of real estate are further complicated by the modifications in that ownership structure that may be made or required as a result of the transaction. To the extent that the group does not own real estate and merely leases it from a third party landlord, the only issues present in a merger are the assumption of those leases by the new entity. This chapter, therefore, will focus on the issues raised by medical group ownership of real estate and the suggested approaches to dealing with this difficult problem in the merger process.

Medical groups desire to own real estate for a variety of reasons. These reasons include having equity grow in the practice, having control over rent, and providing a nest egg for retirement of physicians who have invested in the real estate. The role of real estate in medical group practice has changed, however, and the current role of real estate has raised significant problems. In the 1990s, many areas of the country no longer have attractive real estate investment climates, and commercial real estate buildings, including single tenant medical offices, are no longer the attractive investment vehicles they once were in light of this changing investment climate and changing tax laws. The rationale for including real estate as part of a group practice accordingly has been decreased.

Ownership of real estate also has created problems for young physicians who may be required to buy into the real estate as a condition to joining a practice. The ability of groups to attract new physicians may be impeded if there are significant buy-ins associated with the medical practice. The inability or unwillingness of young physicians to buy into a practice has exacerbated the problem of providing an effective mechanism for physicians who leave a practice to be paid for their investment. Without new money coming in as new physicians join a group, the medical group will have difficulty funding the repurchase of the interest of physicians who depart. While in the past it has been possible to access the equity of a building by refinancing the property and distributing the proceeds to those physicians who have the highest ownership interest in the building, this practice has become more difficult to accomplish with the slowdown of commercial development, declining or stagnant building values and a tighter lending climate.

A variety of real estate ownership structures will have been created by groups over the years based upon varying philosophies and the attempts to respond to the changing tax laws. Some groups will have owned their office space in the medical group corporation. The advantage of this form of ownership is that it simplifies the number of parties that must be dealt with in the medical practice, since the medical group is, in effect, both the landlord and the tenant at the same time. By establishing a stock ownership policy, the group solves its ownership problems in both the medical practice and the real estate. The disadvantage to the ownership of real estate in the medical group practice is that the sale of real estate will create the risk of double taxation. This problem arises because the corporation will be required to pay tax on the sale of the building, calculated as the difference between the cost basis of the property and the amount of money received for the sale, and the shareholders for the corporation, to the extent they are not able to receive extra bonuses in the form of compensation, will be required to pay tax on any dividends that are made to the individual shareholders from the sale proceeds.

Ownership of the real estate in the partnership or limited liability company form has, under current tax law, significant advantages over ownership in the corporate form. The sale of real estate by a partnership or limited liability company creates only one level of taxation to the partners or members themselves, as the gains and losses of the partnership or limited liability company are passed through directly to the individuals who are partners or members. The partnership form also has the benefit of added flexibility with respect to how the partnership is structured. Rather than having individual shareholders, the partnership can have various classes and returns on investment that can create a much more flexible way of dealing with the real estate. It is for these reasons that the current recommended ownership of real estate is in the partnership form, whether that form is an actual limited or general partnership, or the limited liability company, which is treated for taxation purposes as a partnership.

Separating real estate ownership from the medical group, however, is not without its complications, as separate ownership creates a landlord-tenant relationship. Accordingly, the individuals who own the real estate may not be the same as, or may have varying interests from, those who produce revenues or are shareholders in the medical group. The resulting tension between landlord and tenant is created by several factors. The first factor is rent. The owners of the real estate will desire that the rent, in general, be as high as commercially possible, because the return on their investment will be based upon the rent that is charged for the building owned by them. The medical group, however, will seek to lower its cost and its overhead by paying a below market rate with respect to the leasing of the practice site. Because the ownership of the medical group, the earning power of the physicians who are in the group who may contribute disproportionate amounts to overhead, and the ownership of the real estate, often will not be identical, there is significant room for dispute about the level at which the rent should be established. The initial rent, the rent charged in subsequent terms, and the exact term of the relationship will be subject to discussion and negotiation.

Another drawback to the separation of the real estate from the medical group is that the ability of the medical group to move its location may be seriously jeopardized. The leadership of the medical group may determine that the current site of the practice is no longer suitable to the strategic plan of the medical group. To the extent this occurs, the leadership of the group will desire to move the group to a new location or to several other sites. The owners of the building, however, may be diametrically opposed to that of the medical leadership, because if the group decides to move elsewhere, the owners may be saddled with a vacant building fit for a single purpose that will be difficult to sell or rent. The value of the property, the ability to service the debt on the property and hence the value of the ownership interests held by the individual physicians will suffer dramatically. The lack of liquidity of real estate may seriously impair the ability of the medical group to do what may be in its strategic interests.

Regardless of whether ownership of the real estate is in a separate entity or in the medical group, the leadership must grapple with the issue of funding physician buyouts upon physician departure, retirement or death. Because the mobility of physicians has increased dramatically over the past decade, groups can anticipate a number of physician departures for a variety of reasons, and this mobility will place stresses on the ability to fund real estate buyouts.

In addition to the issues associated with having adequate funds to pay any buyout obligation, groups must re-examine the terms on which they will be required to repurchase the real estate interest. Allowing physicians the ability to demand a buyout upon any separation from the group should be reevaluated. While it is clearly in the best interest of the group to require that physicians no longer practicing in the group be required to sell their interest in the real estate, the decision to require a buyout should only be made by the group. Provisions that mandate a buyout should be modified to give the group the option to determine at the time of separation whether it should exercise its option to fund a buyout for a particular physician.

Groups also should consider the need for an extended period of time in which to repay the repurchase price. Groups that originally may have structured three to five year payment periods for repurchase of real estate interests must reassess this short debt payment schedule. The ability to pay the purchase price out of cash flow will be enhanced greatly if the debt repayment schedule can be extended. Extended payment periods, perhaps 10 years or longer, can permit this debt to be amortized over a longer period of time and not impact severely current physician income.

Another concept that should be considered for use is the creation of "value" for physicians who remain in the group for a longer period of time. Under this "value" creation concept, physicians should be allowed to participate fully (vest) in those benefits of real estate value only over an extended period of time. This concept of "vesting" means that a physician must serve a certain period of time, perhaps five years, before being entitled to the full value of his interest in the real estate upon departure. A vesting schedule could be used that allows a physician to obtain the benefits on an incremental basis. For example, a physician might be allowed to retain 30 percent of any increase in value after three years, 70 percent of any increase in value after five years, and 100 percent of any increase in value after seven years. Any combination of vesting schedules is possible and this schedule should reflect the philosophy of the group about what an appropriate tenure is before benefits are bestowed upon the physician.

Any valuation method should incorporate the reality that at any given time the real estate may be worth less than the original contribution by this physician. Any buyout formula must take into account that the vesting of benefits to a physician must be tempered by a reduction in the interest of the physician due to market considerations or other operations of the ownership entity.

The ability of the group to take on new members for real estate ownership also must be reexamined. Recruiting new physicians to join a group and then advancing them to "senior" status is an important component of the ability of a group to grow, to become more competitive, and to provide a continuing source of new talent to make the group prosper. Physicians who have just completed their training and are devoting significant resources to establish their families and homes will be reluctant to make significant contributions to real estate. It is important to devise a strategy to allow these physicians to become senior members of the group without placing an unrealistic burden on them in the process. Devising an effective strategy to accomplish this goal will enhance greatly the ability of the medical groups to attract new talent.

A variety of options exist for bringing in new participants in the real estate of the group. These options include at least the following:

Equal ownership

The most straightforward, yet most costly, mechanism of adding new owners is to divide the available assets of the real estate among all the owners and allocate an equal portion to a new physician, to arrive at the buy-in for that physician. The advantage of this mechanism is that a physician becomes an equal participant early in the process, thereby eliminating the different economic interests of landlord and tenant that can cause disputes about the appropriate level of rent to be charged to the medical group. The significant disadvantage of this approach is that it requires a significant capital outlay from a young physician. While the dollar amount will depend upon the facts and circumstances of a particular case, it is likely that such an investment will be substantial and that young physicians will be reluctant to commit to such an obligation. While the financing of a buy-in can be made part of the proposal, it is likely that the magnitude of the dollar amount will discourage physicians from participating, even though the monthly payments amortized over a reasonable period of time will not result in substantial monthly payments.

Fixed contribution

The second alternative for bringing new physicians into the real estate is requiring a fixed contribution of dollars. A fixed contribution may be set in advance by the group at a level affordable to a new physician and, therefore, have the advantage of providing certainty to a physician considering the buy-in. Fixed contributions have the disadvantage of being selected in a somewhat arbitrary fashion, of not achieving equality, and of still requiring a substantial contribution if any significant ownership interest is to be achieved. The fluctuating values of the ownership interests over time also may complicate this process by modifying the percentage ownership that a new physician may have in the assets of the ownership entity.

Mark to market

Another mechanism to add a new physician may be described as the "mark to market" method. This mechanism requires a revaluation of the ownership interests of the existing owner just prior to the addition of a new owner. The capital accounts, or ownership interests, of the existing owners are valued at the current fair market value of the property, with all of the value of the property being allocated to the existing owners. This valuation process means that in essence a physician who buys into the real estate can be admitted without any payment because there is no equity of the property for that physician to purchase, it having been just previously allocated to all the existing owners. The goal of making an inexpensive or cost-free buy-in is achieved.

New physician owners who are added in this manner are then given a share of the future appreciation of the real estate at no cost. This future appreciation benefit is given to the physician so the physician shares equally in all future appreciation. This mechanism is, in effect, a gift from the senior physicians who share the appreciation potential of a building with the new physician. The justification for this "gift" is that physicians who become participants in the practice of the medical group pay a portion of the overhead for the rent, and this payment, in effect, acts as a contribution to the ownership entity.

The advantage of this mechanism is that it allows an easy, low cost method of entry for new physicians. The disadvantage is that it allows a disparity in the ownership of the real estate to remain. Even with these drawbacks, however, the mechanism does allow an attractive alternative for bringing in new physicians on a low-cost basis to the ownership entity.

Preferred return

A final mechanism for bringing in new physicians is a modification of the third alternative. This "preferred return" method allows the existing physicians who have their capital accounts "marked to market", as described above, to have a preferred return on those capital accounts before any benefits are given to a new physician. A new physician is added in the same manner as in the "mark to market" method and accordingly is allowed to share in the future appreciation of the group for a minimal buy-in because the existing fair market value of the property has been allocated to existing physician owners immediately prior to the entrance of the new physician to the ownership entity. Rather than sharing future appreciation equally, however, this method restricts the return of the new physician to that which may occur after the existing physicians receive a preferred return on their investment. This mechanism creates an interest-bearing account whereby the ownership interest of the existing physician receives a preferred return, for example, of seven percent, before the future gain of the property is allocated equally among all existing owners, including the new physician.

The "preferred return" method has the advantage of being fairer to existing physicians who have made significant contributions to the real estate by creating a mechanism for them to receive a return on the investment of capital that they have made in the property. The disadvantage to the younger physician is that while buy-in is minimal, the presence of the preferred return may dilute any future appreciation benefit so significantly that little, if any, gain may be achieved by the new physician except in real estate markets with rapidly rising values. While many would argue that if the new physician made no contribution, little benefit should be obtained. The reality is that new physicians who see their interest grow only marginally, if at all, will not feel like they are a part of the ownership entity. Accordingly, medical groups must make a philosophical decision concerning addition of new owners in light of the changing role of real estate in medical practices and perhaps sacrifice some of their personal gain for the interest of the group and its new members to achieve a more significant interest or position in real estate.

Groups that are about to engage in a merger must incorporate these general considerations about real estate ownership into their transaction planning. Even if no change is required to be made to real estate ownership as a condition of closing the transaction itself, these general principles of medical group real estate ownership should be considered, for the merger process may give rise to the opportunity to implement some of these principles.

In the merger process, special considerations arise in addition to the general real estate principles discussed above. The initial issue to be confronted by the combining groups is whether the real estate should be combined or whether it should remain separate. The overriding consideration in a merger is to create a common bond and identity of interest in the physicians who will practice in the new group. To build this group identity, it is important to seize the opportunity to combine real estate so all groups own a portion of the real estate and the new group will rent its property from a combined cross section of the new physicians. The ability to combine the real estate will help create a new identity, will foster new group consciousness and will tend to reduce the animosity that will occur when the landlord and tenant in a medical practice are different entities.

As the groups conceptualize the basis on which they will merge, it is important to consider the direction of the new group. The group leadership must develop a plan which allows the real estate to be viewed as the property of the combined group, develop a mechanism to achieve that joint ownership, and devise a procedure to allow ease of entry for new physicians.

The first step in the process of combining the real estate is to evaluate the properties owned by the existing groups. This evaluation involves a critical examination of the existing facilities, their condition and the location of these facilities. As part of the strategic planning for the future of the group, the combined groups must consider the appropriateness of these various locations for their practice by determining how the existing locations fit in the long range strategic plan of the combined group. The evaluation also must consider the existing rental rates paid by the group for the property, the tax basis of the property, the debt on the property and the condition of the property. A determination should be made whether a combination of the real estate of the two groups may cause a taxable event, causing physicians to be taxed without receiving any cash to pay that tax. All of this information must be gathered and evaluated to determine the feasibility of a combination.

Once the decision has been made that it is feasible to combine the properties and achieve the goal of creating common ownership, it will be necessary to value, on a consistent basis, all of the real estate. This valuation process will allow a dollar figure to be attached to each parcel which can be combined with all other property. The aggregate amount of value calculated in this process will then become the value of the ownership entity, and the interest of an individual in the ownership entity will depend upon his percentage ownership interest in the property as combined. In order to arrive at the total value of the property as combined, it is important to have accurate appraisals of the properties. The opinion of an outside expert on the value of the properties is necessary, and a decision on the selection of an appraiser should be made quickly as appraisers often need a significant time period to complete their work. While the engagement of an appraiser may be an expensive endeavor, obtaining an accurate appraisal is necessary before significant planning and modeling of a combined real estate project can proceed. To accomplish the merger within a 90 to 120 day time period will require the appraiser to complete the process within a 30 to 45 day time frame.

Selection of an appraiser must be made carefully. A truly independent appraiser should be selected and, if necessary, resort to a third party who will make the selection of an appraiser should be contemplated if the parties themselves cannot agree. It is possible that one side or the other will be disappointed with the review of the appraiser concerning the property evaluation. It is important, therefore, to avoid a claim that favoritism has occurred for one party or another. Care in selection of the appraiser will avoid the possibility that another appraisal will need to be obtained with the additional delay and expense a second appraisal will entail.

Several combinations of the property are possible and should be considered in any strategy to combine the respective real estate holdings of the medical groups. The first and perhaps easiest option is to combine the properties and the respective interests of the physicians, thus spreading the ownership interest that an individual physician has in the property over all the parcels. A physician who has a certain percentage of an existing building will take that interest as appropriately valued and combine it with the remainder of the property to be combined. While the ownership of the parcels may be scrambled, this mechanism does not allow for any equalization or narrowing of differing ownership interests.

The second available option is to create equality of ownership interests. This mechanism proceeds with a valuation of the properties to calculate the existing respective interests of the physicians. It then requires physicians to contribute sufficient funds to make their interests equal. The advantage of this mechanism, of course, is that it creates equality of ownership, thereby minimizing disputes about the appropriate level of rent and what should be done with the property. The disadvantage of this approach is that it may create a significant buy-in for some physicians. The disparity in buy-in may exist along group lines, but it also may exist along generational lines within each group. Young physicians may be faced with the same prospect of a significant buy-in that they confronted when they joined the group. Older physicians may face the prospect of a significant buy-in if their interest in the real estate in their group is significantly less than the interest of physicians in the other group. Requiring significant payments from some physicians to others to achieve equality of ownership will create a significant impediment to completion of the merger. An effective strategy to implement a merger successfully must avoid significant payments of funds from one party to another.

The final option in the merger context is to consider a mechanism to narrow the disparity in the ownership interests. Under this option, the parties can determine the appropriate investment level that each physician should make. After determining the goal, those below this level will contribute a certain amount each year until the goal is reached. The amount of the annual contribution can either be a fixed amount or a percentage amount of the difference between the capital account balance of that physician and the established ownership goal. This method can be expressed in a number of different options and financial modeling is necessary for an accurate comparison of options to be made.

Chapter 8

Other physician integration strategies: The physicians' contracting network

Physician integration strategies often begin at the least integrated option. To physicians who are accustomed to being in their own business and to having significant operating autonomy, the integration process serves as a challenging and disconcerting time over their practice future. On the integration spectrum, the least integrated approach and the one that is often most attractive to physicians is a contracting network. This contracting network has, as its principal focus, the organization of physicians in a loosely affiliated alliance whose primary purpose is to cooperate for managed care contracting. As such, it is the least integrated option for physicians to consider in their search for effective strategies to react to the changing health care delivery scene. This chapter outlines the steps necessary for the creation of a physicians' contracting network or physicians' organization.

The physicians' organization structure

Creating a physicians' organization, sometimes known as a PO, independent practice organization or physicians' alliance, requires that several basic steps be taken by the physicians organizing this relationship. To form a PO, articles of incorporation must establish the organization, the organization must adopt bylaws, and to the extent the organization has shareholders, the control of the ownership interests must be detailed in an agreement among the shareholders. The PO ownership and governance structure is illustrated in Exhibit 1 on the next page. These issues and organizational steps will be discussed in this section.

The first issue that is often faced in the development process is selecting the proper form of the organization to be established. In general, there are several basic options. The first decision is whether the organization should be organized as a for-profit entity or a nonprofit entity. A for-profit entity has the advantage of giving the shareholders an opportunity

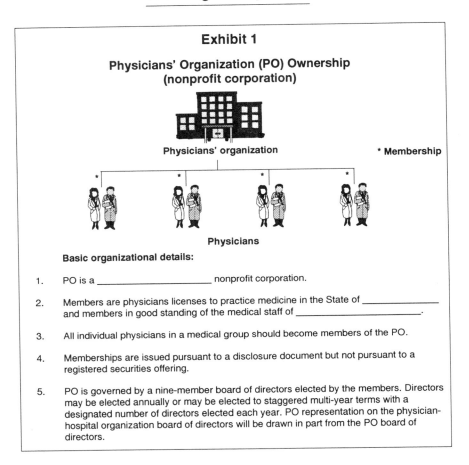

Exhibit 1

Physicians' Organization (PO) Ownership
(nonprofit corporation)

Physicians' organization   * Membership

Physicians

Basic organizational details:

1. PO is a _____ nonprofit corporation.

2. Members are physicians licenses to practice medicine in the State of _____ and members in good standing of the medical staff of _____.

3. All individual physicians in a medical group should become members of the PO.

4. Memberships are issued pursuant to a disclosure document but not pursuant to a registered securities offering.

5. PO is governed by a nine-member board of directors elected by the members. Directors may be elected annually or may be elected to staggered multi-year terms with a designated number of directors elected each year. PO representation on the physician-hospital organization board of directors will be drawn in part from the PO board of directors.

for a return on their investment in the PO. This advantage may exist more in theory than in practice, however, as the primary purpose of the physicians' organization is to create a mechanism that will benefit the independent practices of the participating physicians. This benefit means that the practice itself will benefit from the generation of revenues rather than the physicians' organization being created. It also means that revenues are likely to flow to the individual practices by way of additional fees for services rendered, rather than to the shareholders as a return on their investment. From that perspective, the decision between a for-profit and a nonprofit organization has little consequence, because the main goal of the organization is to benefit the practices rather than the physicians' organization itself.

The physicians' contracting network

If a nonprofit form of organization is selected, it is clear that even if the organization is organized as a nonprofit, it will still be required to pay taxes in most instances. This result is obtained because entities may be organized as a nonprofit entity under state corporate law, but if they desire to qualify as tax exempt, they will be required to undertake the additional step of applying for and meeting strict criteria established by the Internal Revenue Service for a tax exempt organization. These criteria require the entity be formed for broad charitable purposes that go far beyond the relatively narrow scope of the managed care contracting which is the primary purpose of creation of the physicians' organization. Tax exempt status will not be achieved by these organizations, and hence the decision to select nonprofit status will not avoid taxation of any profits that remain in the physicians' organization. Physicians who organize on a nonprofit basis, however, must be prepared to have the funds they pay to the physicians' organization be considered as a contribution to their practice as opposed to an investment in the physicians' organization.

Another consideration in the choice of the organizational form are the securities laws implications of raising money from physicians. To collect money from physicians to form a PO, it is important to comply with the state and federal securities laws that govern the sale of stock. Either an exemption from registration under the securities laws must be found or a registration process must be undertaken. In some states there is an exemption from the securities laws for organizations that are organized as a professional corporation. This professional corporation exemption means that physicians who purchase stock in a physicians' organization will not be required to undertake a securities registration at the state level in order to accomplish the capitalization of the physicians' organization. If available under state law, this securities exemption will assist greatly in facilitating the development process for the physicians' organization. In other states it may possible to avoid the securities registration problem where there is not an exemption for professional corporations by allowing the physician organization to be organized as a nonprofit organization. Nonprofit organizations may be exempt under applicable state law from these types of registration requirements, although under the law of some states the exemption is only granted to tax-exempt organizations as opposed to just nonprofit organizations. State law must be reviewed to determine the most efficient way of raising funds from physicians without resorting, if possible, to the often expensive securities registration process.

Because the primary role of the PO is to assist in the creation of benefits for the independent physician practices, the final form of the physicians' organization should remain a facts and circumstances determination for the organizing physicians. Accordingly, the final recommendation will be a function of the legal requirements in raising funds from individual physicians, the personal preferences of the organizing physicians, and the overall role or functions which the physicians' organization will be performing as envisioned by the physician and medical group leadership.

If the decision is made to create a for-profit entity, the form of that entity must then be considered. The options include creating a partnership for the physicians' organization, establishing a limited liability company, utilizing a business corporation or utilizing a professional corporation. In general, a partnership creates potential unlimited liability for its general partners and is not a form of organization that should be used. Limited partnerships have the advantage of limiting liability and the advantage of avoiding two levels of tax at the corporate and shareholder level, but do little to assist physicians in becoming actively involved in the management of the organization. Recently many states have adopted limited liability company statutes. Limited liability companies may offer an attractive option for the creation of a physicians' organization. To the extent that profits are generated at the PO level, it can be distributed to the members of the limited liability company without first being taxed at the organization level. This is a valuable attribute for those organizations. Because not many profits are expected to be generated, however, this advantage may be outweighed by the relative unfamiliarity with these types of organizations that physicians may have. Accordingly physicians are likely to feel less comfortable with this organizational form.

A corporate form of organization is therefore likely and the choices include a regular business corporation or a professional corporation. From the perspective of taxation, it is likely that either type of organization will be required to pay taxes at the corporate level and an additional level of tax to the shareholders for any distribution of profits. Accordingly, that issue will not impact the organizational form selection process. More appropriate may be the determination on the securities issue which may provide a professional corporation exemption from a securities compliance perspective. From a managed care contracting point of view, it may be preferable to have a professional corporation arrange for the medical services to be performed rather than a regular business corporation. From a policy point of view, it is more appropriate for the organization to be able to provide physician services and it is this ability that perhaps is dispositive in selecting a professional corporation to be the form of the entity that is utilized for the physicians' organization. A review of applicable state law, however, is necessary to evaluate these options.

Once the decision regarding the organizational form is made, it will be necessary to create the organization itself. As the form of the organization is likely to be corporate, the organization will be established through a document called the articles of incorporation. These articles establish certain basic decisions concerning the organization itself. The exact form of the articles of incorporation will be specified by the law of the state in which the organization is formed.

The physicians' contracting network

In general, however, there are several basic decisions that must be made with respect to these articles. The first decision is the selection of an appropriate name. Before any name is selected, the availability of the name should be cleared with the state corporation commission, secretary of state and/or board of medicine to make sure that the name is not too similar to a name already approved for use in the state. The name selected should be descriptive of the physicians' organization itself. It is likely that it will have the word "physicians" in it and that some geographic description of the location of those physicians also will be included. The main purpose for this name, however, will be identification of the physician members with the organization. From a marketing perspective, this name likely will not be used in any marketing of materials to prospective patients. It may, however, be used in discussions with the payers of health care, including major employers and managed care companies.

The articles also should specify the number of shares to be authorized for the stock, if a for-profit entity is used. In some states, a minimum number of shares is required to be set forth in the articles of incorporation and any additional shares authorized must be done so with the payment of an additional fee. Because the number of shares authorized as the minimum amount available under state law will, in almost every instance, be sufficient to provide shares for all interested physicians, this minimum number should be specified rather than incurring the payment of an additional fee.

In selecting the form of the stock to be authorized by the corporation, consideration should be given to whether one or two classes of stock should be issued. A single class of stock requires all physicians to vote equally on matters. This type of voting may be appropriate where the goal is to be inclusive and to require physicians to work together in the process. This is a positive goal and should be considered seriously by those who are engaged in the development process.

On the other hand, two classes of stock may be considered for issuance. These two classes can be used for various purposes. Under one possible scenario, one class of stock could be issued to primary care physicians and the other to specialty care physicians. This dichotomy would allow primary care physicians to elect a certain number of directors and to establish their ability to select their own directors for the physicians' organization. This approach will, however, institutionalize the division between physicians and potentially cause future divisions between primary and nonprimary care physicians.

Another potential use for the two classes of stock is to allow a single class to be purchased by all physicians for a minimum amount of purchase. The second class, which could be nonvoting, would be available to physicians on an investment basis, whereby physicians would be entitled to a greater ownership interest in the organization based upon their willingness to invest in that organization, but would not be given any greater voting rights. Where additional capital is needed for the organization, use of two classes of stock may facilitate the raising of capital from physicians.

In the articles of incorporation, the organizers also must consider whether cumulative voting should be allowed for the election of directors. Under the laws of many states, shareholders may vote for directors by cumulating their votes for a single director. For example, if there are three directors being elected, the shareholder may cumulate three votes for those three positions being elected by casting three votes for one director. Because this voting protects minority shareholders, it is preferable that this cumulative voting should be waived, because individual physician shareholders should not be viewed as minority shareholders. This conclusion is reached because individual physicians likely will be required to purchase the same number of shares of voting stock to require each physician to have the same voice in the governance of the organization. Protection of shareholder interests may be served better by designating certain categories of directors by practice or specialty lines.

The articles of incorporation also require that the physicians' organization specify the purposes for which the corporation is formed. In general, most state corporation laws allow the articles to specify that the entity will engage in such activities as may be permitted under state law. Most laws are permissive and allow a corporation to perform any activities that may be allowed under the general state law, rather than just the specific purposes. Accordingly, specifying the purposes of the organization serves more of an educational and a communication function than an actual legal function. The professional corporation can list as its purposes rendering professional services related to the practice of medicine, owning or leasing real or personal property, investing funds and doing such other acts or engaging in other activities as may be allowed by state law.

A final issue to be considered in the preparation of the articles of incorporation for the physicians' organization is whether to include a provision that absolves a director from liability to the fullest extent of state law for monetary damages for breach of duty as a director. Many states allow this limitation of liability to be included in the articles of incorporation. If this type of provision is available in a state, it should be utilized as it will provide some protection to directors who will usually serve the physicians' organization in an uncompensated capacity.

When the organizational decisions discussed above have been made, appropriate articles of incorporation can be prepared. The corporate existence of the physicians' organization begins when the articles of incorporation are filed with the state secretary of corporations.

The physicians' organization bylaws

Fundamental governance decisions then must be made to determine how the physicians' organization will be operated. It is in these fundamental operational areas which the bylaws will embody the basic operating philosophy of the physicians' organization. Under most state laws, the organizing physicians are given great flexibility in a variety of these areas. A discussion of these areas follows immediately below.

The first significant issue to be considered for inclusion in the bylaws concerns the shareholders or members of the organization. In either the for-profit organization, where shareholders are in existence, or in the nonprofit organization, where members are utilized, basic decisions must be made with respect to the participation of these individuals in the PO and the method for their selection. The initial issue for determination is who may become a shareholder or member. If a professional corporation is used, generally only professionals licensed under the same section of the state licensing law can be a participant in the organization. This means under many states only physicians can become members of the organization, and other professionals such as oral surgeons must have their own organization.

Other limitations on shareholder or member status that may be considered are requiring licensure by the particular state in which the physicians' organization is organized, or requiring or allowing only certain practice categories to be members or shareholders (such as primary care). Generally physicians should be licensed under the law of the state in which the physicians' organization is organized, as this is often required by state law for professional corporations.

Another significant issue in the shareholder or member qualification area is the decision regarding whether all physicians or only primary care physicians should participate in the physicians' organization. The issue here is whether the physicians' organization should be inclusive, allowing all physicians who are otherwise qualified to be members in the organization or whether only primary care physicians should be allowed membership. In part this decision is impacted by the purpose of the PO; broadly based physicians' organizations will have this issue, single specialty physicians' organizations will not. The rationale for the first approach is that all physicians who are members of the organization and likely to be participants in the PO contracting network should be given a voice in its governance. This approach seeks to encourage cooperation, minimize division, and recognize that all physicians must establish collaborative relationships.

Other physicians believe, however, that the organization should have a completely primary care focus. This decision will in part be made by the dynamics and makeup of a particular medical community, but some primary care physicians may feel that as primary care will be the principal focus of the managed care initiatives in a particular community, they should be the only ones with voting participation in the physicians' organization. In addition, given the suspicion that some primary care physicians have regarding their specialist colleagues, some may feel that allowing the specialists a vote will put at risk the primary care focus of a physicians' organization which is necessary for a successful network to be built, marketed and sold in the managed care marketplace. Under this scenario, specialists would be treated as physicians who may participate in managed care contracting aspect of a PO, but have no voice in governance. In general, however, the recommended approach on this issue is to include all physicians as voting members, but to make specific allocations in the governance area to ensure a primary care focus on the PO board of directors. The governance of the physicians' organization and the mechanism for implementing governance will be embodied in the bylaws of the organization. In addition to the fundamental issues discussed above, these bylaws will contain provisions that will mirror the rules for the operation of a corporation under the specific state law under which the physicians' organization is incorporated. Many of the provisions with respect to notice, annual meetings and other basic organizational issues will be specified in the state corporation law, and the role of the bylaws will be to set forth those specific details in a place where the shareholders and directors of the organization can have ready reference to them.

Another important issue to specify in the governing materials is the structure and procedure for holding shareholders' meetings. While many of these particular provisions are specified by applicable state law, some organizational decisions can be made that will reflect the wishes of the participating physicians. For instance, annual meetings are required to be held at which the directors can be elected for the board of directors. The annual meeting date is usually specified in the bylaws. The issue presented here is whether the individuals who act as the organizing committee continue to serve for a period of time after the organization has been formed, or whether the shareholders or members immediately should elect their representatives by vote. Postponing the meeting at which elections are held ensures continuity of the organizing leadership. Having a meeting immediately upon formation of the physicians' organization allows the members to select by vote their representatives that they desire to continue. This conflict between continuity and popular vote is a decision that must be made under the particular facts present in organizing the physicians' organization. In general, however, the recommended approach is to allow a sufficient period of time for continuity of service so those physicians most intimately familiar with the development of the physicians' organization can continue in that role for some period of time, perhaps for six to 12 months.

A technical consideration, yet an important one for the governance of the physicians' organization in the bylaws, is the number of shareholders or members who are necessary to be present at any particular meeting for valid action to be taken. This concept of a quorum has minimum guidelines established by state law. In general, the rule is that a majority of the shareholders or members should be present for a quorum to be achieved. Specific considerations, however, may make this quorum higher or lower. For instance, a lower quorum requirement may be necessitated where the physicians' organization is extremely large and where attendance at meetings is generally poor. Requiring a majority of members or shareholders in a 600 physician organization may result in a quorum not being achieved if 300 physicians must be in attendance for that to occur. In this instance, a 20 percent or 30 percent quorum requirement may deserve consideration. On the other hand, a higher quorum requirement may be warranted where there is some concern that a minority of the shareholders or members can make basic decisions in a smaller PO. By requiring a higher percentage of the shareholders or members to appear and vote, a representative decision can more easily be assured. Another way to address this concern may be to adjust the voting requirements for action by the shareholders or members as explained more fully below.

The voting requirements for shareholder action also should receive considerable attention in the bylaws. The basic right of shareholders or members to vote on an action is what makes the physicians' organization representative of its members within the guidelines that may be established by the corporate law of the state in which the organization is incorporated. The bylaws will specify the vote required for shareholder or member action. For shareholder or member action to be effective, bylaws often provide that such action must be authorized by a majority of the votes cast at the meeting. While this is the general rule, variations can be utilized to make shareholder or member action (other than for election of the board of directors) more difficult to achieve. One option is to require a higher vote requirement of those in attendance. Under this scenario a two-third or three-fourth vote can be required for significant corporate action such as a merger, sale of assets, dissolution or other fundamental change in the organization.

Another option is to require a higher percentage of the shareholders as a whole, rather than just the shareholders or members in attendance at a shareholders' meeting. This option accordingly would require a two-third vote of all issued and outstanding shares or of all members for affirmative action to be taken, rather than just that same proportion of shareholders or members in attendance. The advantage of this type of provision is that it allows all shareholders or members to have a voice in the potential change. The disadvantage of this type of high vote requirement is that it may make it difficult, if not impossible, to achieve any binding action, where merely not attending the meeting is in affect a vote "no." `

The principal governance function for the physicians' organization is undertaken by a board of directors. This board of directors is given the power to exercise all powers vested in the corporation and to undertake the management of the business and other affairs of the corporation through the board of directors. Unless the corporation law of the particular state requires the action of shareholders on a particular issue, all issues may be decided by the board of directors. Directors stand in a fiduciary relationship to the corporation and are required to perform their duties in good faith in a manner that the director believes to be in the best interests of the corporation and with such care, skill and diligence as a person of ordinary prudence would use under similar circumstances.

The significant issues to be decided by the organizing committee with respect to the board of directors are the election, term and qualifications for membership on the board. The first issue to be considered is qualification. Qualifications for directors can be specified in many ways. The most permissive approach is to make no restriction on qualifications for a director. This allows the shareholders to elect physicians, nonphysicians and other persons who may be interested in the physicians' organization.

Other organizing efforts, however, insist upon further qualifications. Some of these qualifications for consideration include requiring the director to be a shareholder of the physicians' organization, requiring the shareholder to be a licensed physician, requiring the director to be a participant in the managed care contracting network, and requiring the director to be obligated under one managed care contract that the physicians' organization may have. Each of these requirements address a particular concern about the focus which a director may have in undertaking his or her duties to the corporation. Requiring shareholder status or physician status focuses the organization toward a physician perspective. Requiring participation status in the contracting network and actual participation in managed care agreements ensures that the director will be exposed to the types of practice concerns that may be confronted by physicians participating in the managed care plans. The rationale for these specific restrictions is that for directors to be effective, they should participate fully in the principal obligations of the physicians' organization. The specific requirements selected by a physicians' organization organizing committee should take into account that the more specific the restrictions regarding who may be a director, the less flexibility the shareholders will have in electing particular representatives.

The most critical aspect of the board of directors is determining the number of directors and the categories into which those directors may be divided. The size of the board first must be determined. It is important for

126

the physicians' organization to have a relatively small board of directors. A large board means that working sessions will be difficult to achieve. Once the board grows beyond about nine individuals, the interactions of the board members become limited and the board becomes less effective. Larger boards usually rely upon an executive committee to perform the work necessary for a board of directors.

In general, because the physicians' organization will be representative of a number of constituent medical groups, achieving a small board may be very difficult. Certainly a three to five member board may be ideal for decision making, but it usually will be viewed as unrepresentative of the constituencies of physicians which comprise the physicians' organization. Having ruled out in all likelihood a three to five person board, the next level is in the seven to nine person range. This size of board is probably the smallest that is practically achievable, yet large enough to have enough representatives to allow for broad representation. This size should be sought after as it has the most chance of becoming an effective working board.

In most instances, the physicians' organizing committee will consist of many more physicians that seven to nine. Accordingly, large numbers of physicians in the 15 to 20 range may have been asked to participate in this organizing committee, depending upon the scope of the effort, the need for broad representation, and the desire to build broad support for the effort. Narrowing this larger organizing committee to a smaller board of directors will be extremely difficult, because the concern of those who are not asked to continue will be of being disenfranchised in the process. This concern over leaving physicians out after they have been served on a physicians' organizing committee means that some care should be taken in selecting the original committee. It is often difficult, however, to have a small number of physicians serve on the organizing committee, because the primary concern in the development effort is to make sure that there is broad cross-representation of a number of physicians on the organizing committee. One compromise strategy may be to allow the larger number of physicians to be selected as the initial board of directors and to have the first election six to 12 months after the commencement of operations, at which time the board can be reduced to a smaller number through the election process. The proper solution for this issue is a function of local medical politics and the composition of physicians involved.

Having determined the size of the board in absolute terms, the next issue faced by the organizing committee is to determine the mix of directors on the board. The question of mix for the board is literally a function of the scope of the physicians' organization. Single specialty organizations will not have this issue, while multispecialty or community wide organizations will by design need to consider this issue. One option is to specify no practice categories for representation on the board. In this approach, physicians who otherwise meet the qualifications of directors can be elected to the board. In general, this approach will be unacceptable to primary care physicians who will look for significant representation on the board before deciding to participate in a multispecialty organization. Accordingly, most multispecialty physicians' organizations are now being developed with a primary care majority specified for the board of directors. The rationale for having primary care physicians in a majority position is that managed care plans will be more likely to deal with the organization when the gatekeepers under managed care programs are in control of the organization. The design of the organization therefore should focus not on embodying the status quo, but in meeting the needs of the payers and other purchasers of health care who are searching for primary care driven type organizations.

While a primary care controlled board may be difficult for specialty care physicians to accept, if the needs and concerns of primary care physicians are ignored in the development process, they will not choose to become involved with or join the organization, with the result that the organization will be less successful. The long-term perspective for specialty care physicians should be that by allowing a primary care physician majority to control voting, the organization and hence the practices of the specialty care physicians will be benefited more than in an unsuccessful organization controlled by specialists. The precise mix between primary care directors and specialty care directors should be determined in the organizational efforts. While some physicians' organizations may choose an even split between these two categories, most will pick a primary care majority.

Once the mix of primary care and specialty care directors is determined, the next issue to be decided is the definition of what is a primary care physician. While for managed care contracting purposes, the purchasers of health care will determine who can serve as a primary care gatekeeper under a managed care plan, the issue here is what type of physician will be elected to serve in a particular category on the board of directors. The organizing committee for the physicians' organization must define a primary care physician. There is little dispute that family practice physicians, pediatricians and general practice physicians are included in the definition of primary care. Less clear are physicians practicing internal medicine. Internists who practice general internal medicine are generally included within the definition of primary care. Determining the practice mix of internists between general internal medicine and subspecialty internal medicine is more difficult. Precise guidelines are very difficult to achieve, but the general goal is to require that those physicians who are practicing general internal medicine do so for at least a majority of their time. Others may take the view that a general internists should practice two-third, three-fourth or even 100 percent of the time in general internal medicine. The precise determination must be decided on a community specific basis as local practice patterns and general practice styles may dictate different approaches.

Perhaps the most difficult issue in defining primary care pertains to obstetrics-gynecology. In many communities Ob/Gyn physicians serve as the primary care giver for a significant portion of the female population. In other communities this role is more limited and Ob/Gyn physicians are viewed as specialists. The decision whether to include Ob/Gyn physicians within the definition of primary care, and hence be entitled to designated positions on the board of directors, is largely a function of the local medical care delivery system, the relationships among physicians in a community and the role assigned to those physicians by managed care plans. The decision whether to classify Ob/Gyn as primary care for governance purposes is a decision independent of whether those physicians serve as primary care gatekeepers under managed care plans. In general Ob/Gyn physicians will lobby to be included, while internal medicine, family practice and specialty physicians will resist including these Ob/Gyn physicians within primary care. The ultimate decision may come down to the beliefs of other primary care physicians given that the primary focus of organizing the physicians' organization should be to make it as attractive as possible for the core primary care physicians, meaning family practitioners, pediatricians and general internists, to join the organization.

The election of directors is also a critical issue to be determined by the organizing committee. The general rule is that the board of directors is elected by a vote of the shareholders or members of the organization, with candidates receiving the highest number of votes in each category of primary care or nonprimary care being elected. Under this voting method, elections occur by a vote of all the shareholders or members of the organization. These individuals can vote for both primary and nonprimary care categories of directors. Accordingly, specialty care physicians can vote for primary care physicians of their choice and vice versa.

The election of directors also could be facilitated by the creation of two classes of stock whereby primary care physicians elect primary care directors and specialty care physicians elect specialty directors. As discussed previously, however, the better view is to have all physicians participate in any election of directors in an effort to have physicians become accustomed to working together as opposed to building permanent barriers between primary care and specialty care physicians.

The term of office of each director also should be determined. The simplest approach is to have each director elected at each annual meeting of the shareholders or members. This process allows the shareholders or members to elect the entire board each year, thereby facilitating immediate responsiveness of the directors to the shareholders or members. Another option is to stagger the board of directors, electing directors by class and having each class serve a term of two or three years. At each annual meeting of the shareholders or members, one-third or one-half of the directors of the entire board of directors is elected. Terms of two or three years provide some continuity for the board. This continuity may encourage stability in the operation of the physicians' organization. The physician organizing committee may determine however that an annual election process may serve the best interests of the organization initially. This decision hinges upon the trust and willingness of the physician members at large to delegate their decision making to a board that is more independent in its operations.

In addition to determining the term and length of term for each director, consideration should be given to whether there should be a limitation on the consecutive number of terms that a director may serve. Some organizations put a two term limit on serving, although the general view should be that if directors can be re-elected by the shareholders or members each year, it may be preferable to allow those directors to continue serving in that capacity if so elected. Directors also should be able to be removed from the board by vote of the shareholders or members. In general this removal should be accomplished by the same body that has the ability to elect a director. Thus if all physicians are entitled to elect a primary care physician director, for example, that same group should be entitled to remove that director. Filling vacancies created by this removal should be handled in the same way as the original election, with the specification that primary care physician slots should be filled by a primary care physician.

The manner of acting of the board of directors should be specified in these bylaws. First, quorum requirements must be specified for holding a valid meeting. In general a majority of the physician directors should be required to be present for a quorum to exist. Higher quorum requirements make action more difficult, and lower quorum requirements make action less difficult to achieve. In addition, consideration should be given to having two separate quorum requirements, that being a majority of primary care physicians and a majority of specialty care physicians. This type of dual quorum requirement will ensure that a sufficient number of primary care physicians are present for valid action to be taken. The extent to which this type of specification occurs, however, is a function of the relationships among physicians and the perceived need to specify those relationships.

Just as the quorum must be established, the organizing committee also must establish the mechanism by which the board of directors will make decisions. Again the simplest approach is to have the vote of the board consist of action of a majority of the directors present and attending a meeting. This approach recognizes that directors once elected should vote their conscience with respect to decisions faced by the physicians' organization.

For board of directors voting, it is also worthy to consider that certain matters must be passed by a higher vote requirement. For example, managed care agreements authorized by the board of directors may require a two-thirds or three-fourths vote of the directors. Managed care contracts have a significant impact on physicians as practitioners and some physicians' organizations feel that a higher vote requirement may be advisable on these matters.

A second area where a higher vote of the board may be required is a termination of an individual physician's participation as a participating physician with the physicians' organization. Some physicians' organizations feel that protection should be given to physicians so they are not terminated arbitrarily from participation in the network. Accordingly, these termination or nonrenewal decisions concerning participating physician agreements are sometimes required to be made upon a recommendation of the credentials committee and/or by having the board vote upon such action by a two-thirds or a higher vote. By putting in these safeguards, the process is designed to ensure individual physicians will not be asked to leave the organization on an arbitrary basis, but will be asked to do so only upon the request of a credentials committee. While both of these issues concerning managed care and renewal of physician relationships are critical, the decision making with respect to these issues and the sensitivity by which they are made often will dictate whether a higher vote requirement is deemed to be necessary. In general the rule of a majority vote should be utilized in all but the most extraordinary circumstances.

Other options exist for board of directors votes, however. First, higher vote requirements for all decision making may be considered. A higher vote requirement means that more of the primary care physician majority of the board will need to favor an action for it to receive approval. While this higher vote requirement does not ensure a primary care majority, it does allow a greater number of those physicians to vote on a matter for it to pass. Another option is to have two voting classes for action by the board of directors. One voting option would require a majority of the entire board, while the other would require having a majority of the primary care physicians who serve on the board. The concern sought to be addressed by this approach is that primary care physicians may not always be present or may be diluted by combining their votes with specialty care physicians to pass certain actions. By requiring a majority of primary care physician directors to vote, primary care interests are required to speak with a collective voice, that being determined by a majority vote of all of the primary care physician directors. This approach will ensure primary care control of board decision making, whereas a vote of the entire board will only ensure that a sufficient majority of the board, which can consist of as few as one primary care director plus all remaining specialty directors, can pass corporate action. Whether this specification is necessary is again a function of the community, its decision making and the message the organization wishes to send to all physicians who are potential participants on the physicians' organization.

The organizing committee also should select its leadership who will serve as officers for the board. In general, officers of the physicians' corporation include the president, the secretary and the treasurer. These individuals need not be directors, shareholders or members of the organization, but should be elected annually by the board of directors and serve in such office for a term of one year or until a successor has been selected. Officers serve at the pleasure of the board of directors and should be able to be removed at any time by the board with or without cause or reason for that removal. The authority of the officers should be specified in the bylaws, and the authority given to those officers should be consistent with the role which they will play in the physicians' organization. Accordingly, if the president of the organization will have administrative and executive authority to hire and fire employees of the physicians' organization, those powers should be specified. If the board is uncomfortable with giving that power to another physician in the event that a full-time staff person is not hired by the physicians' organization, those restrictions should be specified in the governing documents.

Another subject to be specified in the bylaws are the rights of indemnification for individuals who serve as directors and officers of the physicians' organization. State corporate law will specify the permissible requirements for a corporation to reimburse officers and directors for expenses they personally may incur as a result of serving the physicians' organization. In general the basic provisions to be embodied in the bylaws should allow the organization to reimburse all participants to the fullest extent allowed by law for expenses and liabilities that may be incurred by that individual as a result of serving as a director or officer for the corporation. While this reimbursement or indemnification right is only as good as the assets of the organization are available to reimburse these expenses, there is usually very little dispute among organizing committee members that these types of provisions should be included in the bylaws.

Another issue to be confronted in the bylaws pertaining to the governance of the physicians' organization is the process by which the bylaws may be amended. Amendment of the bylaws can allow the rules to be changed and significant attention should be given to this procedure. In general the amendment or repeal of bylaws will be subject to the requirements of state law. The first decision to be made about the amendment process is whether the board of directors should have the authority to amend the bylaws or whether that authority should be reserved to the shareholders or members alone. As a matter of corporate governance, the general rule is to give flexibility with respect to amendment to the board of directors. Because the governance and control provisions are critical to the functioning of the physicians' organization, however, most physicians' organizations make bylaw amendment relatively difficult to achieve by requiring a shareholder or membership approval of any bylaw amendment. This restriction means that a meeting of the shareholders or members must be called to approve any suggested changes. The vote required for the amendment to be approved also must be specified. Because of the impact of the potential change on the governance of the organization, a greater than majority vote requirement is often utilized. A two-thirds vote is the most likely choice, as a three-fourths vote will make amendment of the bylaws very difficult to achieve. However, to ensure the primary care focus of the organization, another option for maintaining control would be to require any change in the bylaws in the number of directors, the definition of primary care, or the mix between primary care and specialty care to be allowed with only a super majority vote.

The stockholders' agreement

In for-profit physicians' organizations, another fundamental issue that must be considered is the control of the transfer of interests in the physicians' organization. Typically these transfer restrictions are embodied in a shareholders' agreement, which prohibits the sale, transfer or disposition of the stock by a physician stockholder in the physicians' organization unless it is done in accordance with the provisions of the agreement. The first significant issue is to determine the events which give rise to the right or obligation of the physicians' organization to repurchase the stock. A decision must be made to identify those instances when the repurchase obligation is mandatory upon the physicians' organization and those which just give the physicians' organization an option to repurchase the shares. The goal for the determination of whether the repurchase is mandatory or optional is in part dictated by state law. If a professional corporation is used, certain resale or repurchase requirements are required by state law. Thus, upon the death of a stockholder, loss of licensure, or the stockholder being found disqualified to practice medicine under state law, the corporation will be obligated to repurchase the shares of the physician. In addition such events as conviction of the stockholder of a criminal offense against the corporation, an event of bankruptcy or adjudication that the spouse of a physician has acquired interests in the stock of the corporation probably also will trigger the obligation to repurchase this stock.

There are other circumstances, however, where the physicians' organization may wish only to have the option to repurchase the stock, it being within the discretion of the organization whether to exercise those repurchase rights. Those events include termination of the physician's participation agreement from managed care contracting by either the physician or the physicians' organization. Physicians who drop out of the network will no longer be wanted as a stockholder by the physicians' organization. The departure, however, may strain the resources of the physicians' organization to make the repurchase, and accordingly this repurchase obligation should be made optional for the physicians' organization. The basic concept in any of these events should be that the physicians' organization should only consist of those members who are actively participating in its affairs. As such, ownership in the physicians' organization differs somewhat from ownership in a regular business corporation.

The organizing committee should determine whether the physicians' organization should allow the sale of the shares of the physicians' organization to a third party. In general physicians should not be allowed to acquire more than a single ownership interest in the organization, as the one person one vote rule is most appropriate for an effective democratic election of representatives. If the physicians' organization does not purchase the shares automatically, however, it may allow a transfer of that stock to occur as long as the physician receiving the transferred interest agrees to abide by rules, regulations and qualifications established by the physicians' organization. These rules can include qualification to be a member of the contracting network established by the physicians' organization, licensure under applicable state law, and not owning more than one ownership interest in the organization.

The valuation methodology for the repurchase of the stock should be specified in the shareholders' agreement. Valuation of the stock is often considered the most critical aspect of a shareholders' agreement. The valuation method and the purchase price determined pursuant to that method sets forth the economic value of the stock to the parties involved. The physicians' organization must specify clearly the valuation of this stock to minimize any potential valuation disputes.

To place a value on the stock requires the selection of a valuation methodology. Valuation of stock can be performed one of several ways. The first is allowing a fair market value appraisal of the stock. This valuation method may seem at first glance the fairest way to value stock, that being on the open market. But this valuation method is probably inappropriate to value the interest in the physicians' organization. The primary benefit to be obtained in joining the network is access to patients for the private practice of the physician. It is not to obtain a return on an investment. Because the physicians' organization has a network focus rather than an operational focus, the inherent value of the network will not be great, as it would if it included a health maintenance organization or other business with revenue and profit generating potential. An expensive evaluation process may have to be conducted under this scenario, as each time a shareholder leaves, the fair market value of the stock must be determined. This is an undesirable and expensive procedure to undertake and should be avoided.

A second method for determination of the stock value is to place a fixed value on that stock. For example, a physician paying $1,000 to join the physicians' organization would have a $1,000 valuation placed upon the stock. This valuation would limit the upside potential of any investment and would eliminate disputes with respect to a valuation methodology. The drawback of this approach is that it may in essence guarantee the principal return for a shareholder. Because the organization likely will not accumulate capital and the initial capital contributions will be used to fund start-up operations, this methodology may create an expensive buy-out obligation. Accordingly it is probably the less preferable of the valuation options.

A final valuation option is valuing the stock at net book value. A book value valuation methodology requires a determination of the assets of the organization as maybe fully depreciated, subtracting liabilities on the balancing sheet of the organization and arriving at a net equity figure. Because this methodology results in a conservative valuation for those organizations which will not have hard assets such as the physicians' organization, it is probably recommended because the valuation will ebb and flow based upon the hard assets of the organization and the age of those assets. Accordingly physicians who invest $1,000 will have less or more of that returned upon resale depending upon the assets contained in the organization. Because this valuation methodology only includes hard assets, excludes accounts receivable and excludes good will valuation, it should be a favorable valuation formula from the perspective of the physicians' organization.

The valuation per share is multiplied by the number of shares to be purchased to determine the aggregate purchase price of the stock. It is important for the parties to agree that the value determined under the shareholders' agreement is conclusive upon all the parties. The agreement may allow for arbitration of the determination of the purchase price in accordance with arbitration provisions contained in the agreement. The agreement also may provide that any closing for the purchase of the stock will be postponed during the pendency of any arbitration proceedings. Including arbitration is a method by which an element of fairness may be put into the agreement, because it allows a third party to confirm that the valuation has been performed in accordance with standards specified in the agreement.

The last significant issue covered in a shareholders' agreement should be the terms of payment. The physicians' organization should be given the option to pay the purchase price at the closing for the stock by cash or certified check. As an alternative, the physicians' organization should be allowed to pay a portion of the purchase price on the installment basis. This method will allow the purchase price to be spread over time and to conserve the cash that may be needed for the operation of the physicians' organization. Accordingly, a nominal amount, perhaps 10 percent, of the purchase price could be paid at the closing, with the balance due pursuant to a promissory note which could provide payment over a period of years, perhaps five to seven, with an interest rate as specified in the agreement. A longer payout period will facilitate the repayment of this debt and will conserve the cash position of the physicians' organization.

Subscription agreement

The final principal document used in the creation of the physicians' organization is the subscription agreement. This subscription agreement is used where the physicians' organization will be a for-profit entity, as it allows the physician to subscribe for the purchase of the stock in the physicians' organization. A similar document may be used to acknowledge receipts of funds where a nonprofit corporation is used. The subscription agreement is the means of obtaining the commitment of physicians to purchase an interest in the physicians' organization. It sets forth the purchase price or formula for establishing the purchase price for the interest in the physicians' organization. The agreement also requires where stock is being sold that the physicians make certain statements and agree to certain conditions in order to comply with federal and state securities laws. The main purpose of the subscription agreement will be to specify the purchase price for the interest in the organization. The parties must determine how much money should be raised from the physicians. This dollar amount is a direct function of the business plan of the physicians' organization. The goal should be to require sufficient funding of the physicians' organization to forestall any need in the immediate future to ask for funds again from participating physicians. Going back to physicians a second time within a relatively short period will make that type of fund raising very difficult to conclude successfully.

The agreement also should require that the full purchase price should be paid before any shares are issued. It is in the best interests of the physicians' organization to require payment in full at the time of the subscription and before issuance of any shares. Some states have escrow provisions requiring proceeds from an offering of stock to be placed in an escrow account until a certain percentage of the aggregate purchase price for all of the shares has been received. In the event the subscription agreement allows for payment over a period of time, the funds from the offering may be inaccessible until the final payment is made under the subscription agreements. Accordingly full payment should be required upon submission of the completed subscription agreement by the participating physician.

The subscription agreement also should contain representations concerning the intent of the subscribing physician regarding the stock or membership interest being purchased. State and federal securities laws may require that certain representations be made. Generally these representations are that the physician is duly licensed in the relevant state, that the physician understands that the shares are not registered, and that the physician is acquiring the shares for the physician's own account, and is not buying with the intent of reselling the shares or membership to another party. The physician should certify that no transfer of the shares will be made in violation of any securities laws and the physician should acknowledge that the securities are issued relying on specific exemptions or other requirements under the federal and state securities laws. Finally, the agreement should provide that the physician will reimburse or indemnify the physicians' organization and other parties to the offering in the event that any representation made by the physician in the subscription agreement is untrue.

A time limit should be placed upon receiving the funds from the physicians. As part of the overall development process, therefore, the subscribing physician will be required to return the shareholders' agreement as executed, the executed subscription agreement and the executed network participation agreement whereby the physician becomes a member of the contracting network and to enclose the required amount of funds.

Managed care contracting network

The final step in the development of the physicians' organization is the creation of the contracting network. Once the physicians' organization has been formed, the final developmental piece should be to create the managed care contracting network. As one of the principal purposes for the creation of the PO will be to organize physicians in a contracting network, a contractual relationship must be created with the physicians as providers. The managed care contracting network for the PO is illustrated in Exhibit 2 on page 138. The development process requires that the physicians' organization enter into network participation agreements for the physicians to provide services under managed care contracts. Accordingly, this network must be built by several documents that include the two items on the next page:

1. **The physician application**. This form requires physician members of the physicians' organization to provide certain practice specific information about themselves.
2. **Physicians' network agreement**. This network agreement requires physicians and medical groups to participate in the contracting network established by the physicians' organization. As such, it contains many managed care contracting type provisions typically found in managed care relationships.

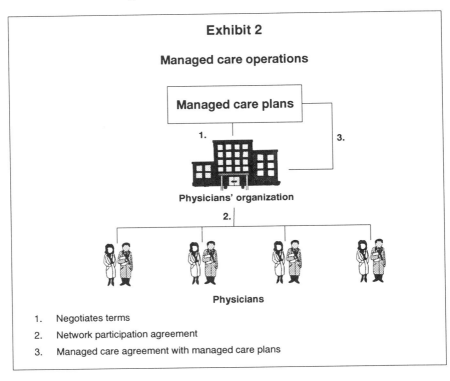

Exhibit 2

Managed care operations

Managed care plans

1.

3.

Physicians' organization

2.

Physicians

1. Negotiates terms
2. Network participation agreement
3. Managed care agreement with managed care plans

The first step in the creation of the physician contracting network is to require participating physicians to complete an application for participation in the physicians' organization. The main purpose of the application is to obtain information about the practice of the physician and to obtain authorization of the physician for the physicians' organization to make such inquiries as it deems appropriate in establishing the qualifications of the physician to participate in that network. The form should contain a release from liability of the physicians' organization to assure that potential liability for the physicians' organization is as limited as possible.

The physicians' contracting network

The application should require general information concerning the physician, such as educational and training information, specialty certification, office practice information and licensure information. The application should contain a series of questions with respect to quality. Questions regarding limitation, suspension or revocation of licenses, permits or other actions should be included. Malpractice history questions should be included. CME activity and hospital and other medical organization committee activities should be listed. A listing of recognition, awards, and membership in professional societies and civic responsibilities should be provided. Practice information should be detailed and participation in managed care plans should be specified. Hospital privileges should be listed. Medicare and Medicaid participation should be designated, and call group members should be specified. Insurance and liability information should be detailed along with policy limits. Medical references should be provided.

The application also should contain a statement of the applicant. It should require the applicant to confirm that acceptance for membership in the physicians' organization is within the sole discretion of the physicians' organization. The application should require the physician to abide by the rules and regulations established from time to time by the physicians' organization. The application should require the physician to certify that the information provided is accurate in the questionnaire. The application also should require that the physicians' organization be notified of any change in the information provided and should contain a release which allows the physicians' organization to consult with hospital administrators, other medical staff members, malpractice carriers and others to verify information concerning practice styles. The statement should release the physicians' organization, its agents and employees from any liability for their acts performed in good faith in obtaining and verifying the information. Finally, the physician should consent to the release by any person to the physicians' organization of any information it may request which it deems relevant in the evaluation of the professional competence, medical practice patterns, ability to work well with others, and moral and ethical qualifications with respect to the participating physician. This consent should be followed by a release of such persons who provide this information from any and all liability.

The network agreement

The contracting network to be established by the PO is based upon the relationship with the individual physician as a provider of physician services. The network participating physician agreement is an agreement between the physicians' organization and the physician in which the physician agrees to provide services to managed care plans through his or her participation in the physicians' organization. As such, it is the primary document which organizes the physicians into a relationship for managed care. By setting forth a comprehensive managed care contracting relationship in this agreement, it will not be necessary to duplicate most of these provisions again in the managed care agreement with a health plan. This approach will give the physicians a negotiating advantage with managed care plans because if the provisions set forth here are not negotiated again with the managed care plan, the manner in which these obligations are expressed will have been established by the physicians rather than the health plan.

The first series of issues that must be addressed in the creation of the participation agreement for physicians is the services to be provided by the physician and the method by which the physician becomes obligated to provide those services. To have an effective contracting network, the physician must agree to provide services under contracts entered into by the PO. When the physicians' organization enters into a contract with a third party to provide physician services to certain groups or individuals as negotiated by the PO, an issue arises whether the physicians' organization can bind the individual physician or whether that physician can opt out and decline to participate in the managed care contract. From a business point of view, creating an effective contract network will mean that the physicians' organization must obligate individual practicing physicians to participate in network arrangements as negotiated by the PO. To the extent that this obligation arises automatically, the PO can market its network as a cohesive whole, without the risk to the managed care plan or employer that a large number of participants may opt out of a particular arrangement that may be negotiated by the PO. By prohibiting this opt out, a physician is obligated by the terms of the contract negotiated by the PO to provide services in accordance with its terms and in accordance with the terms of the participating agreement with the physicians' organization.

While the business perspective of the issue of whether physicians are bound by the decisions of the PO clearly indicates that a physician should be bound automatically, many physicians may resist that wholesale delegation of authority to the PO. Accordingly, negotiating corridors may be developed whereby the physicians agree to provide services for contracts that contain reimbursement rates within specified corridors. This limited granting of authority can help the PO know the extent of its network that it can offer, while at the same time provide protection to the physician that within a given range, reimbursement will be acceptable to that physician.

The ability of the physician to become obligated by the terms of a PO negotiated agreement also depends upon the antitrust laws. In general, independent competitors cannot negotiate collectively with respect to

The physicians' contracting network

price. Accordingly, independent physicians who have not created an integrated operation or who do not assume risk will not be able to have the PO automatically bind them, and will require a messenger-type approach whereby any pricing terms must be negotiated directly between the HMO and each of the physicians. While a messenger can be used to facilitate these negotiations, the messenger must not communicate inter-physician pricing positions to the independent physician practices.

The options to avoid this messenger-type approach all revolve around the ability of the physicians and the PO to be integrated in developing a new business which can then withstand antitrust scrutiny and negotiate prices collectively. Either a new business must be created where physicians put substantial capital at risk and integrate their practices, or a mechanism must be derived by which physicians are collectively at risk through capitation or sufficient withholds. These options all require significant funds being put at risk by participating physicians. In the capitation context, if the physicians are at risk for providing care, this new business imperative of integration will have been achieved. To the extent that fee for service reimbursement is used, a significant withhold in the 20 percent range may allow the requisite integration to be achieved, if the withhold will be paid to physicians only if certain cost containment goals and operational efficiencies are achieved on a collective basis before this money is returned. This "at risk" nature of reimbursement is a difficult and changing concept, and any final decisions with respect to this issue should be made with guidance from antitrust counsel. Accordingly, the opt in or opt out nature of contracts with managed care plans is dependent upon not only the business aspects of having a cohesive network, but also the antitrust limitations placed upon independent competitors to go forward with any particular arrangement.

When agreeing to provide services, a physician probably should be given the ability to opt out of providing additional network services if that physician provides at least 30 to 60 days advance notice to the physicians' organization that the physician has no capacity to accept additional patients under any payer agreement. A sufficient time period should be allowed so notice can be given to managed care plans to allow those plans to remove their physicians from the subscriber list.

Because this network agreement will be signed first and the actual agreement with a managed care plan will be signed sometime in the future, it is important to consider that the participation agreement entered into between the physician and physicians' organization may conflict with a provider agreement which the PO enters into with a managed care plan. In order to protect the integrity of the managed care relationship and because each plan will be slightly different, the actual relationship will be governed in cases of ambiguity by the contract with the managed care plan. This preference recognizes the reality that it is the plan relationship itself that will govern the overall relationship. Creating the managed care network first, however, should give physicians a negotiating advantage with managed care plans who are confronted already with a network agreement drafted in more favorable terms to the particular physician.

While physicians will be credentialled as part of the overall physician organization development process, a network agreement should allow the physician to provide covered services to eligible persons within the scope of the practice of the physician in accordance with the terms of the agreement with the physicians' organization and the plan arrangement with the managed care plan. The agreement should recognize that these physicians are only eligible to provide covered services to members of a plan upon satisfaction of credentialing requirements imposed by the plan.

The agreement should contain provisions with respect to the standard of care utilized by a physician to provide covered services. Accordingly, the physicians' organization participation agreement should include a provision requiring the physician to provide physician services using the standard of care required by the law in the relevant state. In managed care contracts, physicians are often asked to agree to a higher standard of care than may be required under applicable law. Physicians should not agree to a higher standard than required by law since that could increase their exposure to malpractice liability by raising the standard of care required of them under an agreement. In addition, the agreement probably should contain a nondiscrimination clause. This clause would require physicians to treat patients governed by the managed care agreement no less favorably than all other patients of the physician. Illegal discrimination should be prohibited. The participation agreement should require physicians to admit patients to participating hospitals, to provide encounter data in a form acceptable to both the physicians' organization and plan showing services provided to eligible persons, and to obtain prior authorization for covered services where required.

In addition to the section requiring a detailed explanation of how services will be provided for a plan, the agreement should detail provisions concerning compensation and billing. Under a participation agreement, compensation payments to physicians from the managed care plan may be handled in several different ways. The physicians' organization may limit its risk of nonpayment by not being responsible for making any payment to a participating provider. If the physicians' organization receives funds and agrees to pay the participating provider, however, it must avoid assuming the risk of nonpayment by the health plan. In general, it may be favorable for the physicians' organization to have these funds channeled through it rather than directly to the physicians. This approach may assist in the control of the managed care relationship.

Another provision with respect to payment that is often required by state law is that physicians cannot seek reimbursement from eligible persons under a plan if those persons are covered by a health plan. Accordingly, agreements often contain provisions that the physician agrees that in no event, including nonpayment or insolvency or breach of agreement, that physician will bill, charge, collect or have any recourse against any eligible persons other than through the agreement with the physicians' organization or with the managed care plan.

Physicians are allowed, however, to bill individuals directly for any services following the date the individual ceases to be an eligible person. When these eligible persons become ineligible for covered services, a physician may bill that patient directly. The challenge in the managed care contracting realm is to have sufficient notice from the managed care plan to determine when this coverage ceases. Accordingly, the managed care agreement negotiated by the PO will seek to limit the ability of the health plan to delete retroactively-covered individuals. This retroactive deletion would allow health plans to notify physicians of lack of coverage long after the occurrence of a loss of coverage. Because health plans themselves often do not receive notice from employers concerning loss of coverage for individual employees on a timely basis, health plans will seek to put this risk upon participating providers. Often, the best that can be achieved in this area is a limitation on the time period during which health plans may make this retroactive deletion. These limitations should be negotiated in the specific agreement with the health plan.

Payment provisions in the participating provider agreement also should contain very specific requirements with respect to the payment obligation. For instance, capitation payment reimbursement typically requires the payment of a predetermined periodic payment for specific covered services for each eligible person who is a member of a patient panel. This capitation reimbursement means the payment of a fixed sum in advance in return for the agreement by a physician to assume the risk of the volume and frequency of providing a stated range of services to those eligible persons. In order to circumscribe this risk, it is important to have several words clearly defined in this payment obligation. First, covered services must be defined accurately. The actual agreement with a managed care plan should set forth in as much as detail as possible the health care services to be provided by a physician. Any ambiguity in what is covered will likely be resolved by the managed care plan in its favor.

The expression of the capitation amount also is important in that age and sex-based capitation for particular services should be specified, otherwise the physician will take the risk that the patients assigned to the physician will meet the actuarial assumptions constructed by the managed care plan in determining the blended capitation rate paid to the physician. This blended capitation rate that was constructed is based on certain actuarial assumptions concerning the mix of age and sex of a particular patient panel. By breaking down a blended undifferentiated age and sex capitation amount into specific age and sex categories for reimbursement, the physician takes less of the actuarial risk undertaken by the managed care plan when it sets a fixed rate for the premium it charges to all its potential enrollees.

Finally, in the compensation area, it is important to specify that the physicians' organization itself will not be responsible or liable for any decisions to deny payments of any claims submitted by any participating physician for furnishing services to eligible persons. The physicians' organization should not be an insurer or underwriter of the responsibility of any managed care plan to provide benefits or to provide payments to any physicians. The role of the physicians' organization is to provide a physician perspective in the affairs of the physicians' organization and the managed care relationship.

Another critical portion of the individual physician participation agreement with the physicians' organization is a section requiring compliance with laws and program requirements. Under this section, physicians agree to comply with all applicable laws and regulations that may be applicable to the practice of the physician. In addition, the physician may be required to prescribe or authorize substitution of generic pharmaceuticals when appropriate and may be required to cooperate with any program for prescribing the use of pharmaceuticals. While these provisions take away some autonomy from physicians, the purpose of the PO is to negotiate these general program requirements with a health plan so they are fair to all participating physicians.

Another critical component for the participation agreement for individual physicians is physician credentialling. Physicians should be required to adhere to credentialling standards and procedures adopted by the PO or a payer. While this may be an open-ended provision with respect to the individual physician, the input of physicians in a representative capacity in the PO process will make this agreement fairer than if it were negotiated in the abstract without physician input. The agreement also should contain a provision that the physician warrants the accuracy of all credentialling information and imposes an obligation upon the physician to notify the physicians' organization of any change in any of that information. Finally, this section on physician credentialling should contain the acknowledgment of the physician that credentialling information concerning the practice of the physician will be submitted by the physicians' organization to any payer that may require that information.

The agreement of an individual physician to participate in the physicians' organization also should specify several key points concerning records. Clinical records should be regarded as confidential and the agreement should require compliance of all parties with applicable federal and state laws and regulations regarding such records. Physicians should maintain and furnish those records as may be required by applicable federal and state law, regulations and plan requirements. The physician should cooperate with the physicians' organization and the plans to facilitate information and record exchanges that are necessary for the quality assurance and utilization management programs established by the physicians' organization or the managed care plan. Finally, this section should allow the physicians' organization, or their designees with reasonable access during regular business hours to specified clinical and medical records of persons covered by a plan that are maintained by a physician. Prior to the release of such information, however, the party requesting the records must obtain the appropriate consent or approval from the patient before such access is granted. This is an important provision to be specified in the agreement, because often this obligation is imposed upon the physician as opposed to the party who is requesting access. The agreement should place the obligation where it is most properly rests, that being on the party requesting the access itself.

The agreement should require physicians to purchase and maintain policies of comprehensive general liability and professional liability insurance. Physician participants in the physicians' organization are not employees of that organization. They maintain their own practices. Therefore, it is essential that the physician members of the physicians' organization maintain, at their own cost and expense, comprehensive general liability and professional liability insurance. These policies should be in amounts reasonably determined by the physicians' organization. In addition, the policy should provide that the insurer will give the physicians' organization written notice prior to any cancellation, termination or material alteration. Cancellation, termination or material alteration of insurance should be a default under the agreement. The physicians' organization should not be placed in the position of having to accept terms of a modified insurance policy unless it agrees to the terms of such modification. Because the physicians' organization will be composed of physicians and will represent the best interests of the physicians, the requirements imposed on physicians in this area should be reasonable. The same discretion should not be given to every health plan in its agreement with the PO.

Somewhat related to the insurance question is the liability issue. Liability for malpractice is always a concern in the managed care context. Often, managed care plans will require, or at least attempt to require, physicians to enter into indemnification agreements. These indemnification clauses allow a managed care plan to be reimbursed for its out-of-pocket expenses that may be occasioned by it being named as a defendant in lawsuits of professional malpractice against participating physicians. This indemnification obligation is deemed to be a "liability assumed under contract" and insurance coverage for the expenses associated with this assumed liability is often denied by malpractice carriers. Because of the lack of coverage for these indemnification clauses, physicians and the physicians' organization should try to avoid making these types of commitments. Any agreement to make these payments will often require the physician or organization agreeing to these payments to make the payment out of their own funds rather than from insurance proceeds. The best defense to this type of situation is to include a statement that all parties should be responsible for their own liabilities. Under this type of provision, neither party indemnifies the other and neither is responsible for either the liability itself or for defending or paying for the defense of another party.

The participation agreement between the physician and physicians' organization also should anticipate the managed care company requirement that a physician participate in grievance procedures for plan complaints. The participation agreement should require the physician to cooperate with the physicians' organization in the implementation of a grievance procedure that may be established by the PO and to comply with appropriate corrective action taken by the physicians' organization under any of these grievance procedures. By structuring the arrangement in this way, the involvement of the PO in the grievance process is encouraged in what is typically the exclusive domain of the health plan. As such, the PO will have an expanded role in this area and will have a more physician-focused perspective than is typically found in most health plan grievance programs. Because grievance procedures are often required by state law regulating health maintenance organizations, a review of that law will be necessary to determine the specifics regarding the role the physicians' organization can have in this process.

To construct a strong contracting network for managed care purposes, it is also important to address the quality assurance, utilization management and rules and regulations necessary for participation in managed care plans. The goal to achieve in the participation agreement with individual physicians in the physicians' organization is to lay the groundwork for a more expanded role for the physicians' organization in the quality assurance, utilization and management and rules and regulations established by the managed care plan. This expanded role will be a positive development for PO participants in general and physicians in particular, but will be resisted by the managed care plan in the negotiating process.

The ability to amend quality assurance, utilization management and rules and regulations also should be specified in the participation agreement. In general, there are a variety of approaches that can be taken. It is important to allow the physicians' organization the ability to change rules and regulations with written notice to a physician regarding these changes. At least 30 days advance notice should be given by the physicians' organization of any change in these programs, and the amendment should be effective at the end of that 30 day period unless the physician provides written notice of rejection during that period. If the physician does not agree to the amendment, the physicians' organization should probably have the option to terminate the agreement. During the period prior to termination, however, the rules and regulations should be conducted without giving effect to the proposed amendment. This type of provision allows the general programs of the physicians' organization and the managed care network to be modified during the course of a contract year. As such, it is unfavorable to a physician as it gives the physicians' organization the ability to change its rules during the course of the year. Such a provision is probably necessary, however, to allow the physicians' organization and managed care network to proceed with modifications to its programs without seeking amendment to the contract with its entire network. This provision seeks to strike a balance between fairness to the physician by requiring advance notice and by not requiring automatic acceptance, and fairness to the physicians' organization by allowing modification of these programs without seeking the approval of every physician. It also should be noted that this amendment process only should apply to quality assurance, utilization management and other rules and regulations rather than the entire contract. Accordingly, it is more favorable in this respect than many managed care contracts which seek to give the managed care plan the ability unilaterally to modify other substantive provisions in the agreement, including price.

To construct the network, the physicians' organization also should require the participating physician to participate in the network for a period of time. The length of commitment of the physician to the physicians' organization contracting network should be reviewed carefully. From a marketing perspective, the ability to sell the panel to managed care plans will depend in part upon the ability of the panel to be utilized for sale of the network to employers and managed care plans. This need for a long term commitment must be balanced against the desires of the physician to maintain flexibility and the potential desire of the physicians' organization to reduce the size or modify its contracting panel by not renewing agreements, rather than being required to terminate the relationship during a longer term by establishing "cause" for the termination. In general, the initial relationship between the physicians' organization and the physician should probably be in the one to two year range. Any shorter agreement will not give continuity to the network which will be asked to provide care to managed care plans.

Having established a term for the initial relationship, consideration should also be given to whether the agreement and commitment should be renewed automatically at the end of each term. In general, continuity of the network will be improved by requiring that the agreement renew for additional terms automatically unless written notice of the termination is given at least 90 to 120 days prior to the then current expiration date of the agreement. This type of automatic renewal will facilitate continuation of the network and will avoid the rather large task of having physicians sign new participation agreements at the end of each term. Some physicians' organizations may feel that requiring this recredentialling and recontracting process every year or two is an important vehicle to allow modification of the network. On the other hand, nonrenewal from a legal perspective can achieve the same goal and should be considered as the more feasible alternative.

Consideration also should be given to whether the physicians' organization should be permitted to not renew the agreement only if the physician fails to comply with certain standards. Participating physicians may be concerned that the physicians' organizations will be arbitrary in its nonrenewal process. Accordingly, some physicians' organizations may obligate themselves to not renew the agreement only upon recommendation of termination by a credentialling committee and a vote of the board of directors to terminate the relationship. In general, in most physicians' organizations, these additional restrictions on termination and nonrenewal should be avoided because they limit the flexibility of the organization and may create grounds for dispute in the termination context.

The relationship between the physician and the physicians' organization should be terminated if either party fails to perform under the agreement. From the perspective of the physicians' organization, it should be allowed to terminate the agreement if certain events concerning the physician occur, such as loss of licensure or insurance. If these circumstances occur, the physicians' organization should have the ability to terminate the agreement immediately. In other circumstances, however, such as failure to comply with the terms of the agreement, the physicians' organization should have the ability to terminate the agreement only upon giving prior notice of the default and allowing a period of time to cure the default before the agreement is terminated.

The physicians' organization also should consider whether a provision allowing for termination of the agreement without cause should be utilized. These types of provisions permit either party to terminate without specifying any reason. In effect, if a 90 day notice period for termination without cause is utilized, the agreement is in fact a 90 day agreement as opposed to a longer two year term that may be specified in the agreement. Termination of the relationship without cause will often reduce the risk of a legal challenge to termination, but having such a short commitment for participation in the organization may reduce the effectiveness of the network for managed care plan purposes.

Consideration also should be given to the effect of termination upon the obligations of the parties. The question here is whether the obligation of the physician to continue to treat patients under managed care plans continues after the termination of the agreement. In general, provisions should be utilized which require the obligations of the parties to terminate as of the termination date of the agreement. This is a fairly limited provision with respect to obligations that may occur after termination of the agreement. Managed care plans can be expected to require a longer period of time for the transfer of their patients out of the relationship. In fact, many managed care plans require up to one year to have their patients moved out of managed care relationships with a particular provider. Because the individual employer groups and eligible persons are covered by one year agreements, many managed care plans desire to assure the coverage of those individuals under the provider panels that were initially made available to the employers and eligible persons at the beginning of their enrollment period. These provisions will likely be negotiated between the PO and the managed care plan in terms of the extent of the ongoing relationship or obligations that are required of the physicians' organization and the physicians after the termination of the agreement. Accordingly, it is prudent to place in the participation agreement with the individual physician the obligation that they will bound by any continuing care requirements as specified in the particular managed care plan.

A fundamental concept to be embodied in the relationship between the physicians' organization and the physician is that their relationship is one of independent parties. Any other relationship might impose liability on one of the parties for the actions of the other. Employer-employee and agent-principal relationships should be avoided because of the liability which such relationships would create. Independent contractors are not responsible for the actions of the other party to the agreement. Physicians also should be solely responsible for exercising their judgment in medical matters.

In constructing the relationship with the physician, the physicians' organization should consider whether the relationship should be exclusive between the physicians' organization and the physician. Under the exclusivity concept, the physician would be prohibited from joining other networks. In almost every circumstance, this exclusivity will be rejected. In some instances, it will be rejected for antitrust reasons, which would limit severely the size of the panel that could be engaged in an exclusive relationship. In most other circumstances, the exclusivity will be rejected because of the need for physicians to maintain their flexibility in their practices and not limit the organizations which they join. Requiring an exclusive commitment probably would limit the acceptance of the organization and accordingly for marketing purposes, it is likely that this exclusivity will not be utilized.

The parties should consider, however, what should be done with the existing contractual relationships that physicians may have in the event the PO enters into an agreement with a managed care plan. Under these circumstances, it is probably appropriate for the physician to agree not to enter into separate agreements with that payer during the term of the PO agreement. If a physician is a party to an agreement with that managed care plan that is already in existence, the physician should either terminate the agreement with the managed care plan following the execution of the PO agreement with that managed care plan or the agreement should terminate at the conclusion of its term.

Finally, in the participation agreement with individual physicians, the physicians' organization should consider the interrelationship between the network that is it forming pursuant to the participation agreement and the network that will be utilized by the managed care plan. In order to encourage a managed care plan to accept the provisions of the participation agreement between the physician and the physicians' organization, it will be necessary to allow a payer to enforce the terms of that agreement. If the PHO and the physicians' organization have the direct contractual relationships with the managed care plan, that plan will likely only agree to that framework if it can assured that it can enforce compliance with its programs against the physician if the physicians' organization fails to enforce those obligations. Accordingly, the managed care plan should be allowed to enforce the agreement if the physicians' organization fails to enforce it under a third party beneficiary concept.

Chapter 9

Physician integration strategies: The group practice without walls

While the merger represents the most integrated option for independent medical groups to consider in the physician integration process, other options exist that represent less comprehensive changes to the way physicians practice medicine. While the integration process itself is making clear that physicians need to combine into larger organizations to be able to negotiate effectively with insurance companies and with hospitals in the development of integrated systems, most physicians are in small practices which will resist dramatic change to a large integrated system. In many markets, physicians are becoming aware of the need for change, yet are reluctant to make drastic change in advance of the perceived need to make such change. In many markets, managed care, while present, is growing. In many of these markets, integrated delivery system developments by hospitals, insurance companies and other larger medical groups are in the formative stages.

This gradual evolution and the natural resistance to change means that a merger may be beyond the change that many groups are willing to make. The desire for change is tempered by the reluctance of those physicians to give up many of the indicators of autonomy that they found attractive in their single-specialty practice. Even multi-specialty groups of a smaller size will find that this level of comfort and autonomy is difficult to give up to a larger organization. With this assessment of the market place in their own community, many physicians and group administrators have concluded that change must be gradual to retain some of the autonomy that is so cherished.

In this context, the idea of the "group practice without walls" arose. The essence of the group practice without walls concept is that physicians create a central governing authority with limited control and also construct local site governing options that keep significant operating autonomy at each office. In many ways, the group practice without walls or clinic without walls, as it may be called, satisfies the need to allow physicians to have significant involvement in governing their own affairs.

The history of the group practice without walls development began with the concept that has, by necessity, evolved over the years. Originally, the group practice without walls concept was structured as follows: First, a central management organization was separately incorporated and owned by the participating physicians. The participating physicians remained in their separate professional corporations and practiced medicine within that corporate entity. Each of the professional corporations purchased services from the central management entity, and the extent of those services and the types of those services was determined by the parties. Flexibility was given to balance the needs of autonomy for the individual practice versus the needs of the central organization to manage the entire operation. This structure allowed physicians to have their own professional corporations which employed the physicians, but gave them the option of placing the other non-physician employees under the employment of the central management company. This clinic without walls historical structure is illustrated as follows in Exhibit 1.

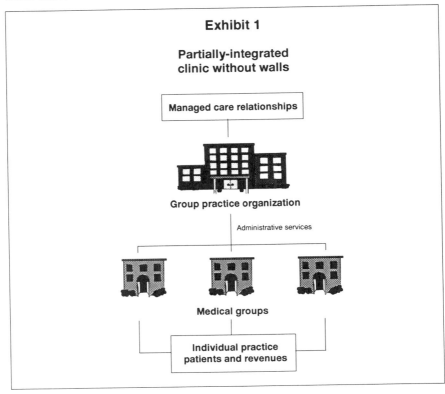

Exhibit 1

**Partially-integrated
clinic without walls**

Managed care relationships

Group practice organization

Administrative services

Medical groups

Individual practice
patients and revenues

The *group practice without walls*

In general, the original clinic without walls governing structure provided limited and loose overall coordination of the respective participants in the group practice, and this central management organization had limited ability to direct the function and operation of each separate professional corporation. Separate professional corporations remained the operating entity through which the revenues of the practices flowed and through which patients were seen. Accordingly, the central management organization provided the management services, subject to the limitations of each independent professional corporation in making decisions. The experience of these early group practice without walls organizations, however, was less than satisfactory. Decision making was slow to evolve and the needs of the overall group practice suffered at the expense of giving individual practice organizations autonomy with respect to their operations. Capitalization was often lacking and the ability of the organization at large to respond to the changing health care marketplace was limited by the attenuated decision-making process.

Over the years, however, the group practice without walls concept persisted, because it met a basic organizational need for autonomous physicians to begin the transition to a more coordinated group practice. The structure of the group practice without walls also needed to be changed. The emphasis for change was in part legislative. In connection with the establishment of the Stark Legislation and state anti-referral laws, it no longer became permissible legally to have ancillaries operate at a central organization level with the physicians practicing in separate corporate entities. Under the Stark Law and many state anti-referral laws, physicians could refer to ancillaries in which they had an interest only if those ancillaries were owned and operated within the same group practice. The historical formulation of the group practice without walls with a separately incorporated management corporation and independent separately incorporated professional corporations failed to meet this group practice test.

Accordingly, in any group practice without walls development which consolidates ancillaries such as clinical laboratories, imaging, pharmacy and ambulatory surgical operations, another mechanism had to be created for physicians to have ownership and compensation arrangements with the organization that, in fact, owned and operated these ancillaries. In addition, as managed care became more prevalent in markets, the limitations from an antitrust perspective on the operations of the separately incorporated professional corporation became apparent. Independent physician practices could not agree to common pricing strategies, both for managed care and for fee-for-service patients. While some limited collective activity could take place in the managed care context where physicians were at risk for the services they provided, this somewhat piece-meal approach to collective action was not sufficient to meet the growing needs of physicians to act collectively in a legally permissible manner and in a growing competitive environment.

The group practice without walls concept, therefore, has slowly evolved into another form. This form can be described as follows: One separate professional corporation or limited liability company is formed. All physicians enter into an employment agreement with this organization. All employees of the previously independent practices also become employees of the new entity. Operations are conducted by the new entity which bills and collects physicians' services in its own name, and, in fact, owns these funds and revenues created by the work of its physicians. Thus, a central organization that employs all the individuals that operates the group practice is created.

The distinguishing factor which allows this structure to be called a group practice without walls is the governance structure created within this single entity. The governance structure within this group practice without walls entity has, as its essence, a site-specific governing mechanism. At each site, physicians who are members of the group at that site construct their own governance organization and committee. Each committee is charged with fulfilling and undertaking a variety of obligations concerning its site. At the central organizational level, the group has a board of directors. This board of directors is authorized to make decisions on a collective basis on a variety of issues which are negotiated between the individual physicians and the group governing organization. Physicians are compensated at each site based upon the revenues generated at that site, minus the expenses incurred at that site, and minus a central allocation of the common overhead generated by the central governing organization.

Rather than merge together the assets and real estate of the constituent and previously independent professional corporations owned by the physician participants in the group practice without walls, these assets are often kept within their previous corporate entities. By keeping these assets at arms length and outside the newly created organization, a leasing arrangement is created whereby the existing group practice continues to own the assets of the practice and leases those assets to the newly created group practice without walls. The expenses associated with the lease of those assets are allocated to the site at which the physicians use those assets. From a structural and organizational perspective, the group practice utilizes one corporate entity with common employees, benefit plans and common billing and collection system. Yet, while the purpose of the merger of medical groups is to create a unified whole with common governance and common ownership of the assets of the group, the purpose of the group practice without walls is to provide limited central control, assets held at arms length, and enhanced ability of the participants to exit the organization. This planned exit strategy is one that is not present in most well-designed mergers which make the exit of individual physicians out of the relationship a very difficult process. The current structure of the group practice without walls is illustrated in Exhibit 2.

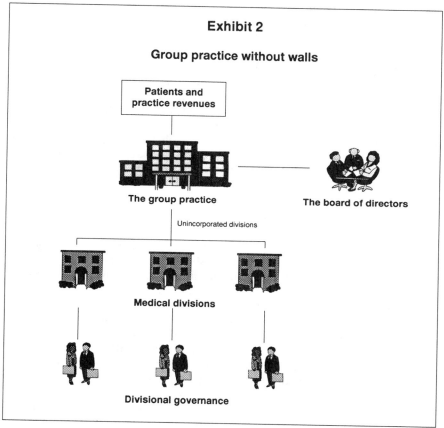

Exhibit 2

Group practice without walls

Patients and practice revenues

The group practice

The board of directors

Unincorporated divisions

Medical divisions

Divisional governance

In many ways, the cumbersome governance structure created by the group practice without walls will only be a transitional vehicle as it is likely to be unworkable in an increasingly competitive marketplace. The attenuated decision making, the pre-eminence of the individual and the ability to exit rapidly from the organization all mean that the central organization is put at a tremendous disadvantage and is designed to appeal to the internal needs of the participating physician rather than to confront the external environment created by the purchasers of health care. This same type of prospective resulted in the creation of small physician organizations where the need for the organization was to meet the individual needs of participating physicians, rather than the overall practice environment.

Transforming the Delivery of Health Care:
The integration process

In many ways, then, group practices without walls are likely to fail and the question arises: why do them in the first place if that failure is likely? The response in many instances, however, is that without this form of development, many changes will not occur because of the reluctance of individual physicians to make radical departures in their practice style. If the group practice without walls model can be successful, it should be viewed as a transitional development which begins the basis for larger physician cooperation beyond the managed care network but yet short of a completely integrated merger. It is the establishment of working relationships and a recognition of the need to work together in ways that have historically not been possible that represent the value of this development. Yet if physicians enter into the relationship without the recognition that this concept is a transitional one, they will likely be disappointed and the organization that is created will likely be pulled apart by the same forces which have caused them to consider doing something beyond the status quo in the first place.

The development process

In developing a group practice without walls, many of the same principles utilized in the merger also should be used. In general, the development process will be more successful if a smaller number of groups and a smaller number of physicians are incorporated initially. The numbers to be incorporated in the development process will dictate the ease of making a change. There are two ways to approach development practice. The first is to look for strategically well-positioned partners and to approach those individual physicians on a confidential basis to secure their support and willingness to undergo the development process. In this way, the group practice can develop by integrating strategic partners on a selective basis. This type of development process has a greater chance of success as the numbers involved and the strategic value of the potential partners being combined will create an organization with more tangible value. Development on a selective basis also will facilitate the development process by not allowing it to become so large that the process fails.

Another common development scenario, however, is that physicians in a medical community at large desire to develop a group practice without walls. Invitations are issued to the community at large to come to organizing sessions and large numbers of physicians, not wanting to be left out of any development, come to the development meetings. The result is a large group, often consisting of numbers of solo practitioners and a wide variety of physicians who may or may not bring real value to the new group being created. This type of development process is more difficult to structure properly and may lead to an unsuccessful conclusion. A wide open development process will be faced immediately with the prospect of having some physicians that the rest of the group does not wish to have participate. In addition, large numbers of the physicians may cause the development process to proceed very slowly and the willingness of physicians to participate in a process where they give up real autonomy may be limited.

Regardless of which development option is selected, that being the small group with gradual growth or the wide community effort, certain organizing principles should be utilized to develop a group without walls. While the development process will be shaped in part by the number of practices and the number of physicians who participate, it should first proceed with the establishment of a committee system that will guide the process. This committee system can consist of one large committee, which can approximate the functions of the merger committee used in the merger process. More often, however, it is likely that the number of practices and the number of individuals in the process will require a somewhat more complex approach to the development process. Accordingly, a committee structure can be established which will direct the process.

The first committee to be appointed should be the steering committee. While this committee can be named a variety of other names, the main function of this committee should be to act as a clearing house for other working committees and to approve, veto or recommend changes to the suggestions of the other working committees. It will be the primary working group charged with moving the project forward and communicating progress to all physicians who are interested in the development process. The committee should meet periodically to give guidance and to hear reports by the various other committees. This committee should be charged with determining the overall structure of the relationship and to assign additional tasks to the working committees as those needs arise from time to time. This steering committee should take a lead role in reviewing and negotiating the physicians' and administrators' employment agreements.

The number of physicians serving on this steering committee is in part dependent upon the number of physicians and independent practices who are participating in the project. In general, a steering committee of seven to nine physicians is probably appropriate, with a smaller number being utilized when a smaller number of physicians and practices participate and potentially a somewhat larger number where a great many physicians and practices participate. The goal, however, should be to create a working environment where efficient decisions and productive discussions can be made. When the steering committee goes beyond approximately nine members, this ability to work in an effective fashion may be lost. Accordingly, the steering committee should be limited to a relatively small number of physicians.

The makeup of the steering committee will be dependent upon the nature of the project to be undertaken. In a multi-specialty development process, a majority of the committee members should probably be primary care physicians. Development of these group practices with a primary care focus should recognize that primary care physicians will add great benefit to the overall development process. To encourage input and participation by primary care physicians, they should be given a lead role in the overall committee structure. Where single specialty developments are undertaken, the committee should reflect the overall direction that the group practice needs to take in order to develop a successful operating entity.

The steering committee also should be charged with establishing the other committees to be used to develop the details of the development process. In general, the steering committee should consider establishing five other committees. While the number of committees is dependent upon the size of the development process and the number of physicians and practices that are going to participate, the functions of these committees must be performed by someone during the development process and if separate committees are not utilized, these functions must be undertaken by the steering committee at large. The five committees to be considered for appointment by the steering committee include the following: governance, compensation, benefits, finance and quality assurance/utilization review.

The governance committee should be charged with the development of the basic structure of the governance system for the new group, including the size and composition of the governing body. The committee must determine how future decisions will be made. Because the group practice without walls concept requires both a central governing organization and a site specific decision-making process, the governance committee must make initial recommendations regarding what decisions will be made by the central board and what decisions will be made by the site governing committees. The allocation of this decision making between a central and a local decision-making process will be at the essence of the group practice without walls concept.

The committee also should consider recommending an initial slate of officers and directors, and should determine a name for the new organization. The committee should make interim and final reports to the steering committee as scheduled. The steering committee should assign such other responsibilities to the governance committee as appropriate.

The composition of the governance committee should reflect the mix of participants in the overall development process. In general, the same limitations with respect to size of a committee that were present for the steering committee should be present here. Five to nine physicians and administrators should be appointed to this committee, with the number ultimately appointed being dependent upon the size and overall complexity of the process. It is also probably appropriate to have overlap between the steering committee and this committee, but new individuals who do not serve on the steering committee should be appointed to broaden participation in the overall process.

The second committee to be created is the compensation committee. As physician compensation and the impact of entering into the group practice without walls concept will have an impact on the willingness of physicians to participate, this committee will play a key role in defining the appropriate compensation system for the new group practice. The committee will be charged with collecting from all participants an explanation of their current compensation systems. The committee must then identify a compensation system that will achieve the goals of the new group. Possible components of the compensation system to be considered and analyzed include: (1) productivity, (2) equality, (3) capitation, (4) administrative compensation, (5) seniority, (6) salary. The planning undertaken by the committee should include policy discussions to insure that the incentives created by the system will foster the overall philosophy of the group with respect to group practice, quality of care and hours worked. To the extent that there are primary care physicians and specialists in the group being formed, particular attention must be paid to primary care compensation. It is the participation of primary care physicians in these multi-specialty efforts that will insure the success of the group practice without walls and every effort should be made to insure that primary care physicians are paid a fair market value for their services. The compensation committee should be selected with the same considerations given to selection of the governance committee members. A third committee to be selected is the finance committee. The finance committee will be charged with preparation of a variety of financial matters and will be required to develop the overall financial analysis for the creation of the group practice without walls. To accumulate the data necessary to analyze cash flow and physician compensation, the finance committee should obtain financial statements from all participating entities. The finance committee should develop a variety of financial models necessary for the development of the group practice and should make interim and final reports to the steering committee. The activities of the finance committee include the following:

1. ***Pro Forma* budgets and cash flow projections**. The committee must develop capital and operating budgets for the new group. The committee should consider various funding sources for the new group, including initial capital contributions, periodic contributions and funding from ancillary services. The finance committee also should develop cash flow projections and should recommend their budgets and proposed financing plans to the steering committee.

2. **Real estate**. The committee must collect all relevant documents concerning real estate of the participants, including deeds, deeds of trust and leases. The committee then must determine whether the property will be purchased or leased. The committee should supervise the valuation of the real estate for sale or lease purposes. The committee also must coordinate and direct dealings with third parties who may influence, or whose consent may be required with respect to, the real estate portion of the transaction.

3. **Capital asset valuation**. Capital assets and other personal property must be valued in order to determine contribution amounts or lease rates. The committee must decide upon a valuation methodology and coordinate the establishment of sale or lease rates.

4. **Accounts receivable valuation**. The committee should determine whether each group keeps its own accounts receivable or contributes them to the new group. An aged accounts receivable trial balance should be generated for each participant if the new group will take over accounts receivable. The committee then must develop a rationale for valuing accounts receivable for each participating physician/group and must coordinate how accounts receivable will be treated.

5. **Banking and lending relationships**. The committee first must determine outstanding liens and loans of each participant which may effect the new group. The committee then must identify areas needing discussion with lenders, meeting with lenders as necessary, and must finalize lender issues before the transaction can be completed.

6. **Joint venture issues**. The committee must identify all joint ventures and other relationships which may be affected by the transaction. After analyzing how the joint ventures will be affected by the new group creation, decisions must be made and implemented concerning the mechanics of dealing with joint venture partners.

A benefits committee also must be appointed. The benefits committee will be charged with developing a common benefits structure for the new group practice without walls. It first must establish a process to collect information about the benefit packages for each practice. These employee benefit plans include qualified retirement plans, welfare plans such as medical and life insurance plans, non-qualified plans such as deferred compensation or deferred bonus plans, and other plans for employees such as severance pay plans and fringe benefit plans. Copies of these documents must be collected. The committee must then develop an overall benefit policy for the new group. It is important that no commitment be made to any employees of the groups until benefit packages have been designed and until the package to be offered is finalized. The benefits committee must make interim and final reports to the steering committee as required by the steering committee.

The final committee to be appointed is the quality assurance and utilization review committee. This committee is charged with developing a model utilization review/quality assurance plan and should be required to examine various UR/QA programs currently in effect for each participating physician and model plans from other sources. The committee should evaluate and select a management information system which will equip the new group with necessary expertise to operate a UR/QA program for managed care. The committee should consider the parallel objectives of efficient quality medicine and attractiveness to managed care. The committee also should develop a UR/QA plan in outline form, distribute it to the steering committee and receive comments. The final program should be drafted, approved and attached to one of the operating agreements as an exhibit thereby insuring commitment to the program by participating physicians.

Implementation issues

Having established this committee structure, it is important then to begin the substantive work of creating the group practice without walls. The substantive areas that must receive attention in the development process can be described as follows:

Transaction structure

Initially, the steering committee should consider the appropriate structure to be used to put the parties together. To facilitate compliance with self-referral and antitrust requirements, this means placing all physicians and operations within one entity. The choice of entity, however, should remain up to the parties. Choices include a professional corporation, with each of the constituent physicians being a shareholder in that corporation, a partnership, where the physicians become general or limited partners in the organization, or a limited liability company whereby the physicians become members of the limited liability company. Both the partnership and the limited liability company have the advantage of "pass-through" taxation whereby the individual owners of the organization pay the tax, rather than the organization itself. To the extent that there are no ancillaries to be combined and the parties do not reasonably anticipate having ancillaries, a separate corporate structure may be considered for both the main governing organization and the separate physician sites through professional corporations. This approach, however, does not satisfy the need to negotiate collectively for managed care plans. In most instances, therefore, a single "group practice" entity will be used.

Transforming the Delivery of Health Care:
The integration process

Governing structure

The organization that is created as part of the group practice without walls development process must be governed by a governing body. This governing body should be composed of a relatively small number of individuals who will represent the group as a whole in its activities. Just as in the merger context, sufficient attention should be paid to the governance process and to selecting a cross section of participating physicians to be represented on this governing board. In general, this means a selection of a slate for board members and officers rather than a free election for the initial term of office.

The primary distinguishing factor between the merger and the group practice without walls concept is the creation of a site governing committee structure which performs a variety of decision making that would in the merged group be undertaken by the board of directors. To establish this governing structure, the steering committee should develop bylaws which contain the provisions which will specify the relationship of the various governing committees.

First, the bylaws should establish site governing committees. These governing committees should be constituted for each practice site that is maintained by the group practice. In general, all physicians who practice at a site should comprise the site governing committee and a majority of the center governing committee present at a meeting should have the ability to take action. These site governing committees should have the authority to make decisions with respect to each site and those decisions should be binding upon the medical group as long as those actions comply with all applicable laws, rules, regulations and ordinances. Because the actions of each site governing committee will bind the corporation, and the corporation will have liability therefore, the governing committee for each site should agree to indemnify and hold harmless the medical group and its other directors, officers and employees from and against any and all liabilities, costs and expenses incurred with decisions made by the site governing committee.

The decisions made by the site governing committees should be specified in the bylaws. The full range of activities that are undertaken by a group practice should be considered and allocated between the board of directors of the organization and each site governing committee. As a general matter, the following items should be considered for decision by the site governing committee regarding issues with respect to that site, but the better approach is to allow the board of directors for the group practice to have more as opposed to less decision-making authority over the following issues:

- Establishing and modifying from time to time a mechanism to divide the compensation allocable to the physicians for that site among the site physicians;

- Hiring and firing of non-physician employees that work at each site.
- Determining the salary level of non-physician employees that work at that site;
- Determining the vacation time and sick leave policies for non-physician employees who work at that site;
- Entering into managed care contracts that pertain solely to services provided at that site, with those contracts executed in the name of the group practice, but the financial impact of the contract being borne exclusively by the site which authorized the contract in question;
- Establishing vacation, professional meetings, sick leave, maternity leave policy for site physicians;
- Ordering supplies for the site;
- Making capital expenditures for furniture, fixtures and equipment for the site; and
- Determining what real and personal property will be leased at the site and the terms thereof, provided that those arrangements should be entered into the corporation on a sublease basis, with the primary lessee being the individual physicians at that site.

These types of activities give substantial operating authority to each site and should be considered as being authorized by that site on a very cautious basis, as the more decisions pushed to the site level, the less effective the board of directors of the group practice will be in dealing with these issues.

This is particularly true in the managed care arena, and in general, the board of directors of the group practice should be given the authority to bind each of the sites to contracts negotiated at the board level. In addition, the bylaws should provide that all issues not specifically reserved to the sites should be decided by the board of directors.

Compensation

Physician compensation is always a critical issue with respect to the formation of any group practice and in respect to a group practice without walls equally as critical. Physicians who enter into a group practice without walls will be interested in maximizing their own ability to direct their compensation system. Accordingly, a mechanism can be established that would give sufficient site autonomy with respect to this compensation system. In general, however, the recommended approach is to use a common system that would be administered and modified from time to time by the board of directors. If this centralized control cannot be achieved, the following mechanism can be utilized to delegate the compensation system design to the individual site levels. To determine the amount of money that is available for distribution to physicians at each site, it is important to determine the compensation pool available for distribution. First, the site specific revenues must be determined. Site revenues will include those revenues generated by a physician employed at that site and also will include any allocated general revenues that may be allocated to a specific site as determined by the board of directors. These general revenues can include such items as all other revenues that are not the revenues generated by a particular site. These allocated general revenues plus the revenues generated by physicians at each site comprise the site revenues.

To arrive at the compensation pool for each site, the costs associated with each site should be subtracted from the site revenues, along with subtracting the allocated general costs that are allocated to each site by the board of directors.

Center costs should include all operating and non-operating expenses incurred in the operation of a site, including but not limited to:

1. Salaries, benefits (including contributions under the profit sharing plan of the medical group) and all other direct costs of all employees at each site, but excluding those salaries of site physicians;
2. Obligations of the medical group under real property leases for the site or personal property leases or subleases for equipment, furniture or fixtures used at that site;
3. Real property, personal property and intangible taxes assessed against the assets of the medical group used solely in connection with that site;
4. Acquisition of real or personal property used solely in connection with the site;
5. Inventory, supplies and other items used for the site;
6. Services, supply or maintenance obligations pertaining to that site and activities taking place therein; and
7. Interest expense on indebtedness incurred by the medical group which relates solely to the site and its operations or to site physicians at that site.

Having determined the site costs, it is then necessary to determine the general costs which are not site specific that must be allocated to each site. First, general costs must be defined. General costs should be defined as all operating and non-operating expenses incurred in the operation of the group practice, including but not limited to all costs incurred by the corporation, but excluding salaries for site physicians and site costs for all sites. In essence, by defining the general costs broadly and including everything but those that are determined to be site costs, the definition of general costs will be all inclusive and will include all other costs associated with the operation of the group practice other than those from a practice of site. When general costs are determined, they must then be allocated across the various sites. In general, there are several different ways to allocate these general costs, one being allocation based upon the ratio of full-time equivalent physicians employed at a particular site, as compared to the number of total full-time equivalent physicians employed by the medical group. This type of determination will allocate general costs on a per-physician basis. Other options include allocating costs based upon the revenues of each site or allocation based upon a site, as opposed to the number of physicians in that site. Whatever method is utilized, however, the actual implementation of that method should be supervised and directed by the board of directors, so no question can be raised regarding or challenge made to the allocation process.

With the determination of the compensation pool available for allocation at each site, this type of compensation system will allow physicians at each site to determine the appropriate methodology for allocating the revenues generated by that site among themselves. The usual options with respect to designing a compensation system that are faced in the merger process are faced as well in these types of transactions. In general, however, from an administrative convenience point of view and from a group practice development point of view, physicians should, if possible, agree on a common compensation system that will encourage the physicians to work together across all sites, rather than to continue to maintain a site specific operating mentality.

Name

Just as in the merger process, it is important for the new group practice to come up with an effective name. The same principles in name selection that apply in a merger context apply here as well.

Budgets and cash flow projections for the new organization

One of the dangers of a group practice without walls development process is that physicians who desire to safeguard their autonomy will be reluctant to invest in the group practice itself and will be unwilling to contribute dollars for the overall effort. Just as in the merger, however, the group practice without walls will still require significant central operating responsibilities. These can include the central administration, billing and collection for revenues generated by physicians, a central governance mechanism and central administration. These types of activities and the activities of the individual sites themselves will require close scrutiny of the type of monetary needs that will be necessary to support sustained operations. Accordingly, consideration should be given to the development of a budget process that will forecast capital requirements and future operations with respect to the group practice. To the extent this planning is not undertaken, the practice may run into cash flow difficulties, with the attendant loss of confidence that practicing physicians may have in the system if an interruption in their own cash flow occurs. The steering committee that develops the group practice without walls therefore must encourage the participating physicians to be willing to invest in the new venture. Start-up costs must be considered carefully, as well as funding the initial few months of operations, before the revenues are received that have been generated during the first several months of operation of the group practice. Accordingly, a strategy must be developed by the finance committee to finance any potential shortfalls during the initial months of operation.

Due diligence

The participants in the group practice without walls development process must undertake an evaluation of their prospective partners. This process of exchanging information about each of the participating practices is often viewed as the "due diligence" process. This process must encourage open disclosure with respect to the details of each practice, and physicians and their administrators should be encouraged to pursue this evaluation so all facts can be known about the operations of the respective parties. This process is often viewed as particularly burdensome by physicians and their administrators who will tend to ignore the process rather than give it the attention it deserves. Entering into a relationship without conducting a thorough evaluation of the practices of the other participating groups, however, invites trouble and potential financial loss to the extent a financially troubled partner is taken into the new group practice.

Benefits and personnel

The issues raised in the benefits and personnel areas in the development of a group practice without walls are very similar to those raised in the merger process. In the group practice without walls process, there may, however, be more physicians with more plans who wish to participate and this added complexity of a multitude of plans may put severe strains on the ability of the steering committee and its benefits committee to evaluate in a comprehensive fashion the various benefit levels and options to be undertaken by the new group practice. In general, the benefit plans of all of the participants will need to be standardized in one benefit plan. In addition, existing retirement plans will not be able to be continued, and must be merged or terminated. These options are the same as those available in the merger process, yet the number and complexity of a variety of retirement plans may make it even more difficult in the group practice without walls process. In general, the group practice development process is likely to encourage a standardized approach to benefits by requiring that each practice take care of its own benefit issues and join the new group practices benefit and retirement plans that have been developed as part of the implementation process. Unlike the merger situation, where the need for consolidation of benefit plans and harmonization of the various interests of the parties is present, the group practice development process may in fact place an additional burden on the constituent practices to take care of their pre-existing plans. With respect to personnel issues, many of the same personnel combination issues faced in the merger also will be present here. The difference, however, is that while each site has control over its site personnel, a combination of the administrative functions with respect to personnel may not occur. In general, though, the same need for a combined administrative approach to the group practice requires the selection of a senior administrator and a common central administration that can deal with the overall needs of the group practice. This consolidation will be particularly difficult when the very nature of the group practice without walls is to encourage site rather than consolidated functions of the practice. This type of approach illustrates the weakness of the group practice without walls concept, where standardized personnel functions are difficult to achieve. In addition to the extent that personnel functions are handled at each particular site, there exists the risk that these types of personnel issues will be handled by individuals who are unskilled in personnel issues and accordingly will cause the corporation liability for violating one of any number of the increasingly complex laws and regulations that govern the employment workplace. Accordingly, some provisions should be made to impose liability on those specific sites for actions they may take which will violate the law.

Real estate issues

Unlike the merger, where there will be significant emphasis on combining all assets and liabilities of the constituent medical groups, the group practice without walls concept generally focuses on keeping the assets and in particular the real estate owned by the constituent medical groups out of the group practice organization. Accordingly, it is likely that the steering committee, when considering this issue, will have each site that is owned by a group lease that property to the new group practice. The primary function of the steering committee for this issue is to identify the real estate, to identify the financial details regarding this real estate and to set up a cost structure whereby the real estate, if it is owned, will be leased to the site, and if it is leased, will be subleased to the new organization. The lease rate under either circumstance will be passed through as a site specific cost in the cost accounting module to determine the physician compensation pool.

In dealing with the real estate, it is important to have the individual physician at each site be responsible primarily for that obligation. To the extent a physician leaves the group practice, the obligations with respect to real estate, whether it be through the ownership or through the leasing process, should follow that particular physician. Otherwise, if the relationship does not fully protect the group practice, it may be stuck with real estate obligations but no physicians to generate revenue to meet those obligations. The documentation of the group practice without walls should place this obligation squarely upon the individual physician and have the group practice only secondarily liable to prevent this sort of damage from occurring to the group practice itself.

Asset valuation

To construct the group practice without walls concept, it will be necessary for the new group practice to access the assets utilized by the former practice in the new group practice without walls. Accordingly, appropriate valuations must be undertaken of these existing assets. Unlike the merger process, which requires this valuation in order to combine the assets into a single group, a group practice without walls concept holds these assets at arms' length outside of the new organization. The valuation process of furniture, fixtures and equipment is undertaken to determine an appropriate lease rate that will be charged by the owner of the assets, that being the prior group practice, to the new group practice without walls. The lease costs are then allocated to the site which is using those assets. This treatment of assets illustrates another basic distinction between the merger and the group practice without walls development. By leasing these assets to the new group practice, the existing physicians have the ability to leave the group practice, to have the lease severed and to resume operation of their practice without having to repurchase or disentangle the assets from a combined group practice. Accordingly, the treatment of assets facilitates an easy exit strategy for physicians, which exit strategy is consistent with allowing individual autonomy to prevail in the group practice without walls.

Accounts receivable also must be valued on a consistent basis to determine the way in which funding will occur for start-up operations. Depending upon the budgets and financial projections that may be undertaken, these accounts receivable either may be contributed to the organization as a way of funding the start-up of that organization and as working capital, or may be retained by the individual physicians who are joining the practice to collected outside of the group practice operation. Treatment of these accounts receivable will be determined by the budgetary process and the work of the finance committee in the overall development process.

Banking and lending relationships

Creating the new group practice without walls concept requires physicians to leave their old entity and join a new one. This transformation often impacts the ability of banks and other lenders to collect on their obligations of the practice. Accordingly, many financing arrangements with banks and other lending institutions prohibit major corporate changes from taking place in a medical group without securing the approval of the bank or lending institution. A comprehensive review of the banking and lending relationships of each entity must be undertaken to determine the extent of these obligations and to secure the necessary consents that may be required to allow the transaction to go forward. Just as in the merger context, it is important to have this work done early in the development process to allow for sufficient advance notice to these institutions.

Joint venture issues

Constituent medical groups may have entered into various joint ventures as part of their operations of their practices. In the group practice without walls development process, these joint ventures must be identified and evaluated. The steering committee must undertake an evaluation of these ventures and must make decisions with respect to how they will be treated in the ongoing practice. Once again, it is important to review these relationships in advance of the closing date for the transaction, as the third parties involved will need sufficient notice of any intended modification. In addition, it is important to review the documents pertaining to these relationships, as there may be prohibitions or long-term commitments which cannot be changed as part of this process.

Licenses and vendors

As in the merger process, each of the constituent medical groups will have undertaken a variety of vendor relationships for securing services for their practice. These vendor relationships include janitorial, maintenance, software licensing and other service contracts. To the extent that the operations of each practice are being consolidated, it will improve the efficiency of the organization to centralize these relationships and to have the board of directors direct the establishment or severance of the vendor relationships. While the group practice concept conceivably could allow individual sites to evaluate these relationships, that type of inefficiency will hamper the need for the group practice to consolidate these types of relationships. Licenses also must be evaluated in the development process. To the extent that new licenses must be transferred, a list of the existing licenses must be created and these licenses must be evaluated about whether they need to be transferred, terminated or whether the new organization must apply for a new license.

Physician employment agreements

In the development of the group practice without walls concept, the principal document governing the relationship will be the employment agreement that the group practice enters into with the individual physician participants. As previously discussed in Chapter 5, the creation of a merger gives the newly merged entity the opportunity to create a "group centered" employment agreement. The reasons for the need for a centralized operation and for the group to protect itself against the individual physician are well documented. In the group practice without walls development process, however, the balance goes the other way, as the individual, rather than the group, will by definition have more autonomy. Physicians who participate in the group practice without walls will participate in the process only if their individual autonomy is protected and they have an effective exit strategy. It is this exit strategy and individual autonomy embodied in the employment agreement used by the group practice that differentiates the group practice without walls concept from the merger.

While the physician employment agreement will cover the same basic areas covered by the employment agreement used in the merger process, there are basic differences in a variety of the provisions utilized in the group practice without walls process. A discussion of those subjects and an explanation of how they differ from the merger context follows:

a. **The employment relationship**. In the group practice without walls process, the employment relationship is made subject to the bylaws which establish the site specific governing committee process. This agreement accordingly embodies the governance provisions which give autonomy to each particular site. This governance mechanism limits the ability of the board of directors to impact directly the practice of the physician.

b. **Duties**. In the group practice without walls contract, individuals have more control over their duties and if they give autonomy with respect to the type of duties they undertake, it is to a site committee as opposed to the board of directors.

c. **Compensation**. While the merger employment agreement gives the ability to design and modify the compensation system for all physician employees, the group practice contract gives that authority to the site of each physician practice location.

d. **Professional meeting time, vacation, sick leave and fringe benefits**. While the merger contract gives this authority in general to the board of directors, the group practice without walls contract generally allocates this decision to the particular site, except for pension and health benefit plans which should be uniform for the group.

e. **Administrative and practice consideration.** Both the merger employment agreement and the group practice without walls employment agreement should contain strong provisions which specify that the revenues generated belong to the group, that the group owns all accounts receivable, and that the group establishes all fees and the billing process. The merger agreement allows the board of directors of the group to have full authority to administer the business of the group practice and to provide all office space, equipment and other items necessary for the practice of the physician. In general, in the group practice without walls contract, these types of provisions are allocated to the site where the physician practices rather than to the board of directors in general.

f. **Term.** The term of the agreement also is different in the merger process as opposed to the group practice process. In the merger process, it is generally in the best interest of the group to have the ability to terminate physicians without cause on relatively short notice. In the group practice concept, because the entire structure has made an easy exit strategy for individual physicians, the concern for the group is that many physicians will leave in a short period of time, thereby dragging the group down. This concern means that physicians in the group practice without walls should commit at least to a year and that they should be prohibited from leaving prior to that time. In addition, consideration should be given to allowing physicians only to exit if there has not been previous departures by physicians within an allocated time period, perhaps six to 12 months. The concern for the group practice without walls is these physicians will leave taking the revenues and capital which they have contributed to the practice and cause significant difficulty for the remaining physicians. In making these decisions, however, the steering committee should be mindful of the need to discipline physicians for inappropriate practice behavior as well. In these circumstances, requiring a year commitment may represent a fair trade off between the need for protecting the group from departures and giving the group the ability to end an unsatisfactory relationship. Accordingly, the group practice without walls employment agreement should contain "for cause" provisions that allow the board of directors to make a determination that a physician, regardless of site location, should no longer be an employee of the new medical group. These types of termination with cause provisions should be similar to those found in the employment agreement utilized in the merger context.

g. **Effect of termination.** When the physician employment relationship ends in the merger context, the goal of the group practice is to protect itself from a physician departure and to allow the remaining physicians to survive that departure in the best economic position possible. In the group practice without walls process, however, physicians who are entering into the relationship are designing their participation in a way so as to allow them to leave the relationship if it is unworkable for them. Accordingly, much less group favorable termination provisions will be found in the group practice without walls employment agreement. The parties should specify the amount of funds that are to be paid to a physician upon departure of a physician. In addition, the parties should specify the obligations of the parties with respect to malpractice insurance and with any obligation "tail" insurance. The parties should specify access to medical records, it being understood that physicians who are leaving will recontinue their practice as a competitor of the group practice without walls and will need to facilitate the transfer of records to that new practice site. Finally, the termination provision should specify what additional payments may need to be made to the physician and the basis for those payments. Accordingly, physicians who may have contributed capital to the organization to fund its start up, may be precluded from having these funds repaid to them immediately and a payout schedule which will protect the fiscal integrity of the remaining group practice without walls members should be encouraged. Otherwise, physician departures will cause an unnecessary harsh burden upon the practice of the remaining physicians.

Restrictive covenants

In the merger development process, the need to protect the group is the primary motivating factor for the institution or strengthening of a restrictive covenant provision. Physicians who enter the merger process should do so with a commitment to the overall group, recognizing that this commitment is of critical importance to protect group practice operations. In the development of a group practice without walls model, however, physicians who are participants are most often reluctant to give up their future options. Accordingly, in most group practice without walls developments, no restrictive covenant is utilized and no liquidated damages must be paid if the physician wishes to participate in a competitive activity after termination of the relationship. To the extent physicians can be convinced otherwise, the group practice without walls concept will be strengthened, but most often given the choice and the overall design criteria for the group practice process, these types of restrictions on the ability of the physician to practice in a particular area after termination of the relationship with the group practice without walls will not be utilized.

The group practice without walls

Stock ownership and shareholders' agreements

Physicians who participate in the group practice without walls concept will be required to become owners of the new group practice entity. In this context, it is important to embody the agreements of the respective parties in a shareholders' agreement, similar in format and content to the shareholders' agreement utilized by the medical group in the merger context. The primary difference will be in the buy-in into the arrangement, such buy-in being established as part of the overall development process, and the way in which physicians may be paid upon departure. To the extent that the group practice allows an easy exit from the relationship, it should lengthen the time period during which it must make a repayment of the contribution of the departing physician. Often, however, this rationale will not be utilized, as the individual physicians who are leaving will argue that the relationship should be severed and the funds that were invested in the group practice development should be returned in order to be utilized to re-establish independent practice. This type of individual perspective demonstrates the difficulty of utilizing strong group centered provisions in the creation of the group practice without walls.

The schedule

The implementation schedule for the group practice without walls is quite similar to the development process used for the merger itself. As such, a 90 to 120 day process may be feasible, but it is likely that a longer development process schedule will be necessary for this type of project. The complexity of the development is not what causes this longer period. It is more likely the attitudes and predisposition of the individual physician participants will slow the decision making process. A suggested schedule for this development process is attached as Exhibit 3.

From an integrated delivery perspective, the group practice without walls concepts represents a limited approach for integrating physicians into a cohesive organization. By design, it appeals to the independent nature of physicians, and by design it encourages physician unilateral action rather than group action. As such, this model will not sustain testing in an increasingly integrated environment where rapid action must be taken by organizations in order to make decisions. Physicians who enter into the group practice without walls concept with the belief that it will represent the final stage of their development as a group practice will position themselves for failure. The failure will result from the inability of these participants to transition into more closely structured and centrally governed relationships that will be necessary in the integrated environment.

The group practice without walls strategy, therefore, has serious limitations. As a transitional strategy, however, it may provide a useful vehicle for physicians who have previously been independent to become accustomed to working with each other and to evolve gradually into a much more group centered relationship. The danger in creating the group practice without walls concept is that by structuring it from an individual perspective, the structure itself may doom the process to failure and that physicians who see that failure will blame the overall collaborative effort for the failure rather than the weak structure which they created.

Table 3
The group practice without walls schedule

Key: **Tasks completed (boldface text)**
Tasks remaining (normal text)
Changes from previous report are underlined

	July	Aug.	Sept.	Oct.	Nov.	Dec.
1. Steering committee meetings		31	21	12	9	7 21
2. Transaction structure:						
— Commence structure work	27					
— Preliminary report distributed to executive committee		10				
— Development of legal analysis of structure and meetings with steering committee to revise preliminary report		24				
— Present structure to steering committee		31				
— New organization structure finalized			7			
Status report:						
3. Governance						
— Governance committee commences work		10				
— Governance committee develops preliminary plan		17				
— Governance committee reports to executive committee		24				
— Governance committee gives final report on plan to executive committee			14			
— Report to steering committee			21			
— Steering committee approves plan				12		

The group practice without walls

	July	Aug.	Sept.	Oct.	Nov.	Dec.
— Governance committee selects candidates for president/medical director/board of directors				12		
— Candidates for positions approved by steering committee				19		
— Governance committee selects candidates for vice-president, secretary and treasurer				26		
— Vice president, secretary and treasurer approved by steering committee					2	
— All candidates approved by steering committee					9	
— New candidates installed						31
Status report:						
4. Physician compensation						
— Compensation committee commences work		10				
— Historical information developed		24				
— Preliminary report distributed to steering committee			7			
— Comments received re: report			7			
— Final report			28			
— Share information with steering committee				12		
— Compensation system finalized					9	
Status report:						
5. Name						
— Governance committee commences work		24				
— Governance committee reports to steering committee			14			
— Report to steering committee				12		
— Name finalized				12		
Status report:						
6. Budgets and cash flow projections for new organization:						
— Finance committee collects financial statements from existing organizations		3				
— Commence projections for combined organization		31				
— Circulate preliminary draft of projections to steering committee			28			
— Determine funding sources				5		

	July	Aug.	Sept.	Oct.	Nov.	Dec.
— Incorporate results of comments on financial statements				5		
— Finalize budgets and cash flow needs				19		
— Report to steering committee					9	
Status report:						
7. Due diligence						
— Distribute due diligence requests		10				
— Document collection commences		31				
— Report to steering committee			14			
— Review of documents			21			
— Collection of additional documents commences			28			
— Creation of schedules				26		
Status report:						
8. Benefits and personnel						
— Benefits committee develops summaries of existing plans		7				
— Identify plan issues		21				
— Develop comparison chart		28				
— Preliminary report circulated to executive committee			5			
— Report to steering committee			12			
— Present final report to steering committee for approval				2		
Status report:						
9. Real estate issues:						
— Finance committee identifies all real estate, leases and mortgages		31				
— Determine valuation method			14			
— Identify areas requiring discussion with third parties			14			
— Report to steering committee			28			
— Meetings with third parties as necessary				5		
— Finalize valuation and other real estate issues					30	
Status report:						
10. Capital asset valuation:						
— Finance committee determines valuation methodology		31				
— Finance committee determines approach			7			
— Report to steering committee			14			

	July	Aug.	Sept.	Oct.	Nov.	Dec.
— Report received and reviewed			28			
11. Accounts receivable valuation						
— Finance committee determines treatment		31				
— Develop aged AR trial balance			14			
— Develop rationale for AR valuation			21			
— Report to steering committee			28			
12. Banking and lending relationships						
— Finance committee submits search request for liens and identifies loans		10				
— Identify areas with need for discussion with lenders			7			
— Meetings with lenders as necessary			28			
— Finalize all lender issues				19		
Status report:						
13. Joint venture issues:						
— Finance committee reviews affected joint ventures, if any			7			
— Preparation of analysis			28			
— Finalize issues process				12		
— Implement process				26		
— Closing of any required consolidation						17
Status report:						
14. Physician employment and administrator agreements						
— Circulate 1st draft of physician and administrator employment agreements to steering committee				5		
— Comments regarding drafts received				8		
— Circulate revised employment agreements to steering committee and legal counsel				19		
— Discussion of revised drafts at steering committee meeting					9	
— Further discussion at steering committee						7
— Circulate execution copies to physicians and administrator						7
— All agreements returned						17
Status report:						

	Aug.	Sept.	Oct.	Nov.	Dec.	Jan.
15. Transaction documents and ancillary documents:						
— Circulate 1st draft of agreements to steering committee			5			
— Receive comments re: 1st draft			8			
— Circulate 2nd draft of agreements			19			
— Receive comments on 2nd draft of agreements			22			
— Circulate ancillary documents			29			
— Circulate all drafts				2		
— Notify licensing authority of transaction, if necessary					1	
— Receive final comments on all documents					7	
— Further discussion at steering committee					7	
— Board and shareholders meetings					13-17	
— Circulate execution copies of all documents					17	
— Execution of transaction documents					17	
— Transaction effective						1
Status report:						
16. Licenses/vendors:						
— Begin inventory of vendors and licenses	31					
— Finalize list of licenses and vendors			5			
— Begin notification as needed				16		
— All licenses and vendor contracts assigned effective this date						1
Status report:						
17. Board/shareholder/physician meetings:						
— Shareholder and board meetings to approve agreement, ancillary documents and real estate matters					17	
Status report:						

Chapter 10

The physician-hospital organization

Medical groups and hospitals are confronted increasingly with both the opportunity and the challenge to cooperate more closely in the delivery of health care. This need to cooperate will require both hospitals and medical groups to change their historical relationships with each other. To state that this new relationship created must be based upon a "partnership" merely expresses an idea. How that idea gets translated into action will often dictate how close to a "true partnership" the relationship can become. Accordingly, many details in creating the physician-hospital "partnership" are subject to negotiation. This negotiation process will dictate, in large part, the structure and nature of the relationship that is created.

A common mechanism utilized by physicians and hospitals to facilitate cooperation with each other is the physician-hospital organization (PHO). Typically, this organization is founded on the premise of maintaining the status quo of independent physician practices, organizing those practices in a network, having that network obtain managed care relationships and negotiating contracts on behalf of the network participants. This cooperative effort falls far short of the integration process by which physicians and hospitals integrate their operations, staffs and governance, as well as consolidating locations.

A PHO in its simplest and most common form keeps much of the status quo intact by allowing physicians to participate in a network, but requires little other change with respect to medical group operations. In this limited form, therefore, the PHO formation process is a first step in the larger integration that must occur in the development of integrated health care systems that will predominate in the health care delivery system of the coming decade. PHOs, if properly structured and implemented, however, are important in beginning this consolidation process, and the way in which they are structured and implemented will determine what role physicians and medical groups may have in the reorganization of the health care delivery system.

The PHO formation process can be broken down into six components. These steps in the development process are as follows:

1. **Strategic vision and leadership**. The most important aspect of the development of a PHO is the creation of a common strategic vision for the participants concerning the direction and goals of the new organization. Medical groups must be involved in the process of defining the objectives of the PHO and in the development process itself. All too often, hospitals and hospital consultants start the process, define its parameters and establish the agenda to which medical groups must react. Medical groups, physicians and group administrators must take a proactive role in this process. To be proactive, leadership must be identified who will be willing to speak on behalf of the medical community which may be invited to participate in the PHO. Strong balanced physician leadership, from a variety of perspectives, should be active in this development process and should include a significant primary care presence, as primary care physicians will be asked to play a central role in the coming integration of health care.

    This leadership must focus on creating a true partnership with the hospital with consensus decision making, and must be prepared to educate physician participants at large as the process unfolds about the benefits of participating in the PHO. In order for this education to be successful it should be from the physician perspective. Otherwise, broad-based physician support will not be forthcoming, as physicians who do not understand the necessity of change will rarely support it.

    This new collaborative effort with hospitals will challenge long-held notions of physician autonomy, as many of the issues faced in the PHO formation process will, in fact, require individual physicians to work collectively with not only the hospital, but also with many other independent physicians. It is this balancing process between autonomy and the need for group decision making that will characterize many of the organizational decisions to be confronted by the medical group leadership in the PHO formation process.

2. **Governance**. The PHO will need a governing structure to function after it is organized. The development of that governing structure will be critical in determining whether a true partnership will exist between physicians and a hospital. PHO decisions should be made on a collaborative basis, as neither party should be able to impose its

will on the other party. Proposals which give the hospital a tie-breaking vote, or which require hospital control, should be resisted.

Physicians and medical groups also should resist the suggestion that a majority vote of the directors should bind the PHO. Under this scenario, even with equal numbers of physician representatives and hospital representatives, only one additional physician vote would be needed to agree with a uniform hospital voting bloc. Two classes of directors requiring a majority of physician and a majority of hospital representatives will eliminate this potential loss of evenly split power.

Another important consideration is the role of primary care in the physician component of governance for the PHO. Primary care physicians should be given a very important role in PHO governance. While each PHO will need to decide for itself the exact role of primary care physicians, as a general matter, primary care physicians should comprise a majority of the physician representatives on the PHO board. Specialists may resist this approach, and in some cases their opposition may require that less than a majority of primary care physicians are elected to the PHO board. Over the long run, however, the organization must be attractive to the purchasers of health care which will be attracted to a primary care physician perspective. In a PHO, the structural changes which recognize this perspective should be implemented in the beginning of the process rather than dictated by the failure to sell the product of the PHO in the marketplace.

3. **Structure and ownership**. Creating effective partnerships between physicians and hospitals should mean that both physicians and hospitals invest in the organization. Those medical groups that allow a hospital to develop and own a PHO should not expect to receive an equal voice in the process, or to have it be structured in a medical group-friendly perspective. Accordingly, both the medical groups involved and the hospital should be expected to contribute to PHO activities.

The selection of the model to be used is an important factor in assessing physician access to PHO activities. While the choice of the model alone is not the determining factor in creating a true partnership between medical groups and hospitals, it can have a significant effect on that process. While there are many different approaches to organizing PHOs, the following models are representative of the options available.

FIGURE I - shows the hospital ownership of the PHO with physicians and medical groups participating pursuant to participation agreements, but having no equity ownership or membership

181

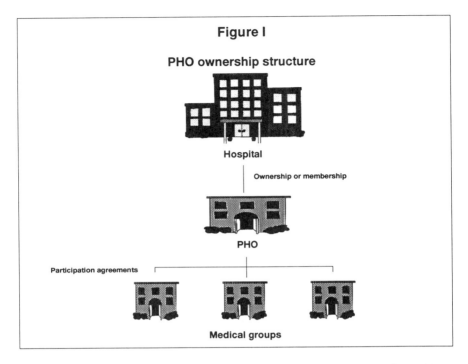

Figure I

PHO ownership structure

Hospital

Ownership or membership

PHO

Participation agreements

Medical groups

interest. While the PHO organizational documents may, in fact, allow physician representation to occur, the legal means for ensuring that selection often will rest with the hospital, rather than being within the legal control of the medical groups. Accordingly, this model is the least "physician-friendly" of the organizational structures, because physicians or medical groups have no ownership or membership interest and the governance provisions may or may not include significant physician involvement. In these models, physician representatives may in fact be selected by the hospital, may be subject to hospital approval, or if selected by physicians may be able to be removed by hospital vote. The only legal relationship that is created under this model is one of a participation arrangement between medical groups and the PHO itself, whereby the medical groups agree to participate in the managed care network formed by the PHO.

FIGURE II - describes a PHO owned jointly by, or having as its members, the hospital and a physician organization ("PO") created by physicians or medical groups. This model represents the best structure for achieving a true partnership with the hospital. A PO is created which collectivizes the independent medical groups and physicians who will participate in the PHO. As organized under a PO, physicians can have a common and unified voice by electing directors who will participate in the governance of the PHO as physician directors. The governance of the PO should be structured with the same primary care majority as found on the physician component of the PHO board. Under this model, the PO elects the physician representatives to the PHO board and the hospital elects the hospital representatives to the PHO board. Hospitals that are not accustomed to viewing their relationships with physicians as a partnership will view this model negatively, as it collectivizes the physicians and allows them to have an organized voice. Other hospitals, however, will recognize that the fragmented nature in which medical care is currently rendered in most communities must change and that an effort to organize physicians in the PHO context will facilitate the creation of a successful integrated delivery system.

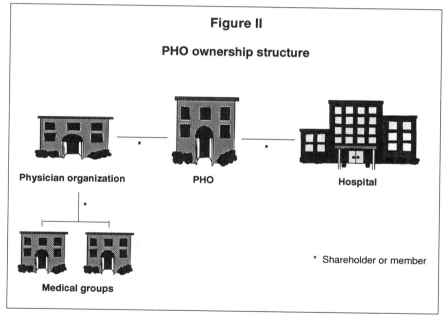

Figure II

PHO ownership structure

Physician organization   PHO   Hospital

Medical groups

* Shareholder or member

FIGURE III - illustrates joint ownership of, or membership in, the PHO by individual physicians and the hospital. While the advantage of physician ownership or membership in this model is present, the ability to organize and have the physicians speak with a collective voice is made more difficult by keeping physicians in an ownership or membership relationship directly with the PHO. This lack of organization helps perpetuate a "divide and conquer" approach and

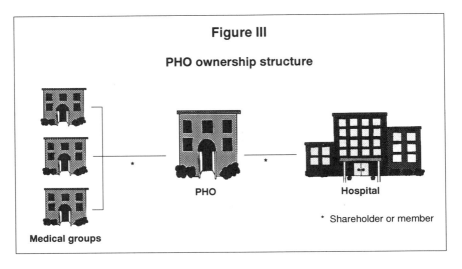

Figure III

PHO ownership structure

PHO

Hospital

* Shareholder or member

Medical groups

may be attractive to hospitals who may view it as advantageous to keep the physicians as disorganized as possible in the relationship. While it is possible under this model to collectivize physician voting by having physicians own one class of stock or membership interest and hospitals another, physicians may not arrive at a consensus as easily with this model and an opportunity to create a larger physician collaborative relationship will be lost.

In order to implement any of these structures, it will be necessary for physicians and the hospital to invest funds in the PHO. The process of raising capital will first require that a budget be created that will establish the contribution levels that will be needed to meet this operational budget. It is important before raising funds from physicians to have a good estimate of the capital needs of the organization, as the PHO should be capitalized adequately and it will be difficult to raise additional funds from physicians soon after the initial fund raising. Consideration also should be given to having two levels of physician investment. Primary care physicians are often reluctant to expend large sums of money for PHO participation and an organization which seeks to encourage primary care participation often will be required to have two levels of participation: a lower level of investment (for the same number of shares) for primary care physicians and a higher level of investment for specialists.

Another issue to be addressed in the ownership of the PHO is determining how many physicians will be invited to participate in the PHO. From a managed care perspective, a close-knit, tightly screened and well-credentialed panel will be optimum. In many communities, however, the ability to start with such a small group of physicians will be impacted by the reality that a hospital must appeal to its medical staff at large. In fact, many physicians often will take the same perspective because of their professed desire not to divide the medical community. In reality, therefore, the practical answer is for PHO development activities in many communities, all members of the medical staff are likely to be invited to participate in the network.

4. **Business plan and services**. The major risk in developing a PHO is that much effort and expense will be invested in the formation process, but when development is completed, the PHO fails because there is no business plan or, worse yet, there is no product offered by the PHO that will be purchased by its customers. The risk of operational failure for many PHOs is probably very high, given that many are formed "as the thing to do," with little regard given to the business that must be operated after formation. Accordingly, the development of a strong business plan is a critical element of the planning process for the PHO. Medical groups and administrators must be involved in this process because the way in which this product is developed and marketed will, in fact, dictate how success-ful the PHO will be. The preparation of a business plan requires development of the managed care package to be offered by the PHO to managed care companies, determination of the practice support services to be offered to participating medical groups, establishment of pricing for those services and development of the marketing plan to sell the services of the PHO. Budgets must be developed that can forecast accurately the expenses associated with PHO development. Planning must be undertaken regarding operational details to ensure that, once begun, the operations of the PHO will function smoothly.

5. **Contracting network**. As many PHOs will be formed initially to respond to the changing managed care environment, the contracting network established by the PHO will, in fact, be the principal activity during the early operational life of the PHO.

    FIGURE IV (on next page)- illustrates a typical way in which PHO managed care operations occur. The PHO negotiates terms of the managed care contracts with managed care plans. The PO, hospital and PHO contract for managed care through a managed care provider agreement under which the PO and the hospital are obligated to accept managed care contracts negotiated by the PHO, although this automatic acceptance requirement is sometimes lim-ited by PHO participants. The PO enters into network participation agreements with physicians or medical groups for all of the physi-cians employed by that group to provide services under managed

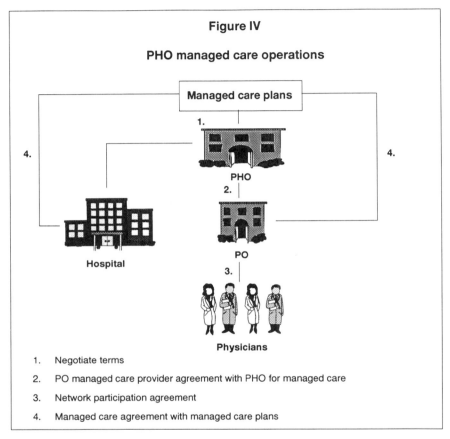

Figure IV

PHO managed care operations

1. Negotiate terms

2. PO managed care provider agreement with PHO for managed care

3. Network participation agreement

4. Managed care agreement with managed care plans

care contracts. Finally, the hospital and PO enter into managed care agreements directly with the managed care plans, as the hospital and the PO are the entities actually authorized under state law to provide the actual services, but these relationships are in fact coordinated by the PHO.

While variations to this model will occur, the basis of all organizational efforts is to have the PHO negotiate as much as it may legally do so under the antitrust laws for both the hospital and the PO. Those PHOs that are structured to deal only with physician or medical group participants and conveniently leave out the hospital are not, in fact, true partnerships. Both the hospital and the PO should agree to have the decisions made regarding their respective participation in a managed care plan made at the PHO decision making level, rather than at the individual hospital or physician level. A governance structure that allows hospital and physician services to be negotiated through the PHO governance structure will be successful in creating a medical group-oriented operational model.

From the physician or medical group perspective, a significant number of issues are raised in the PHO development process concerning how much control or autonomy will be given up by an individual practice to the PHO or PO board. For example, the issue whether individual groups can opt out of, or be required to enter into, managed care agreements will create tension between physician autonomy and the need to create a cohesive, market-driven PHO. Those situations which give more individual decision making to medical groups will, in fact, dilute the market success of the PHO organization. Allowing the PHO to commit the network to provide care will be a definite advantage in selling the managed care network to the purchasers of health care.

6. **The PHO development timetable.** The process for creation of the PHO requires the establishment of a development timetable. This schedule should be developed jointly by medical group leadership and the hospital to assure the successful implementation of the PHO project. If due attention is not paid to the schedule, the PHO committee may finish its work, but the acceptance by the medical staff at large may be limited and, accordingly, the PHO may fail. In establishing a formation strategy, the following sequence and timing of events should be considered.

   A. **Education.** The successful implementation of a PHO requires education. That education process begins with the medical staff and ends with the medical staff. Communication efforts concerning the changing health care scene and the details of PHO organization, structure and governance must be planned carefully to ensure acceptance of the PHO by physicians.
   B. **Committee selection.** Physician and medical group leadership should be involved in the establishment of committees and the committees should reflect the appropriate mix of primary and specialty care, and medical group administrators.
   C. **Delegation of authority.** From the physician perspective, it is important to establish a process by which those physicians who are involved in the PHO process have the ability to represent the interests of the physicians at large who will be likely PHO participants. Physicians on the committee must be comfortable with making these decisions on behalf of other physicians. If physicians are not comfortable with making decisions and then gathering support for those decisions by being advocates of the process with their colleagues, the

process by which decision making is made at the PHO development committee level will grind to a halt. Accordingly, physician leaders who have the ability to speak on behalf of the physicians at large should be selected.

D. **Creation of PO structure**. As part of the overall PHO development process, physicians initially should organize themselves in a physicians' organization, which will allow physicians to speak with a collective voice. The creation of the PO, however, should be undertaken in conjunction with the overall PHO development process. This simultaneous development can assist in shortening the time frame during which a successful PHO can be created, and will assist the development of a collaborative as opposed to an adversarial relationship with the hospital.

E. **Creation of PHO structure and governance**. Once the physician organizational issues have been decided, the PHO governance structure and issues associated with the creation of the PHO should be finalized, although the initial idea of a partnership with shared control should have been established previously as a fundamental precondition to being involved in the PHO development process.

F. **Creation of managed care network**. After the details of the governance and structural issues have been addressed, the PHO committee should consider the multitude of issues associated with creating a managed care contracting network, including participation agreements and basic decisions about how the network will function.

G. **Operational plan and budget**. The PHO committee should then develop an operational plan and budget in order to plan for successful operations. This process also will assist in providing guidance concerning how much capital should be raised from physicians and from the hospital.

H. **Raising capital and execution of documents**. After the preceding steps have been taken, the PHO is ready to raise its capital and actually organize itself. Documents must be distributed and the appropriate funds returned by the physician participants with the executed documents for acceptance by the PHO.

I. **Preoperational planning**. Prior to commencement of operations, the actual administrative team that will operate the PHO must be in place, and it must begin planning for future operations so a smooth start-up of operations can occur. Recruiting personnel that will operate the PHO may be part of this process.

J. **Commencement of operations**. After the governance issues have been decided, after the operational plan has been implemented with the appropriate personnel and after the capital has been raised and the PHO formed, operations should be commenced. It is clear that, despite the work associated with forming a PHO, the real work to creating a successful PHO will be the operational aspect rather than the formation phase.

The PHO process, therefore, in essence involves the creation of three legal relationships. These relationships encompass .all the development steps and issues that have been introduced above and include: (1) creation of physicians' organization; (2) creation of physician-hospital organization; and (3) creation of the managed care network. These relationships are detailed below.

Creating the physicians' organization

Creating a physicians' organization, sometimes known as a PO, is part of the overall PHO development process. It requires that several basic steps be taken by the physicians organizing this relationship. To form a PO, articles of incorporation must establish the organization, the organization must adopt bylaws, and to the extent the organization has shareholders, the control of the ownership interests must be detailed in an agreement among the shareholders. These issues and organizational steps are the same as those found in the creating of an independent physicians' organization as discussed in Chapter 8. That discussion will not be repeated here as the development of the PO should proceed as outlined in Chapter 8.

One issue that is unique in the physicians' organization development in the PHO process is the degree of independence of the physicians' organization. If a physicians' organization is being formed such as an independent practice association discussed in Chapter 8, the organizing physicians may resist the requirement that all physicians belong to the hospital medical staff or that the PO be prohibited from establishing relationships with other hospitals. If an independent approach is taken whereby other hospital relationships can be entered into by the PO, it is unlikely that a hospital confronted with that independence demand will be willing to enter into much of the collaborative decision-making process that is necessary to give physicians and hospitals an equal voice in a PHO "partnership." This is a basic and fundamental distinction between the independent physicians' organization discussed in Chapter 8 and the physicians' organization being formed as part of the PHO process. The IPA contracting network has as its main goal independence; the physicians' organization formed as part of the PHO process has as its main goal organizing physicians to allow them to speak with a collective voice in the "partnership." Accordingly, most physicians' organizations being formed as part of the PHO process will contain some requirement that the physicians are staff members of the hospital and that the PO will not enter into relationships with other hospitals.

Creating the physician-hospital organization

To create the physician-hospital organization, it will be necessary to select the structural framework for the organization. With the creation of the physicians' organization, the physician-hospital organization will typically take on the structure specified in Figure II on page 183. Creating the PHO entity will raise many of the same organizational issues, in slightly different context, that were raised in the creation of the physicians' organization.

The first task is to create the PHO entity. Typically these organizations are formed with articles of incorporation. The exact form of these articles will be specified by the law of the state in which the physician-hospital organization is formed. Just as in the creation of the physicians' organization, a determination must be made by the parties whether the organization will be for-profit or nonprofit. From an organizational perspective, the nonprofit corporation may be more consistent with the operational goals of the hospital, if that hospital is a nonprofit. The purpose of the physician-hospital organization however is not likely to be broadly charitable and qualification as a tax exempt will be unlikely. Accordingly it is most likely that the organization, if organized as a nonprofit, will be still be taxable. The decision of for-profit versus not-for-profit should be made upon business considerations and community standards. It should be recognized that the PHO itself is not likely to be the organization that will make money and create value as an investment vehicle and that the PHO will likely serve as a conduit to benefit the constitute members.

A for-profit organization has the benefit of creating flexibility with respect to the disposition of future profits if in fact they occur at the PHO level. If the decision is made to organize as a for-profit entity, further discussion should be had concerning the form of the entity. Available options include a partnership, a limited liability company and a regular corporation. The same decision making points with respect to the physicians' organization again apply here, with the recognition that the partnership may prove to have unlimited liability. The partnership form is likely to be excluded and the decision will be made between a limited liability company which has the benefit of having the constituent organizations taxed on any profits rather than having the tax paid at the PHO level, and a regular corporation which would pay tax on its profits and require the constituent organizations to pay tax on the dividends paid. Because the limited liability company is relatively a new form and because the overall profits at the PHO level are not expected to be great, most PHO developments are proceeding with the use of a regular corporation. The advent of limited liability companies does give added organizational flexibility to this endeavor because it creates a mechanism whereby the parties can come together in a form that will allow pass-through taxation for any funds that are distributed to the physicians' organization and the hospital.

Having determined the proper form of the organization, the next decisions pertain to the organizational details of the entity created. The first issue addressed is the name of the corporation. This name should be approved for use in the state and should be selected to identify the network. Because the PHO often will be used as a network for a managed care product, its name is less critical than one that must be marketed to individual employees. The name therefore should be descriptive of the organization rather than having a primary marketing focus.

The articles of incorporation should specify the categories of stock or membership interest in the organization. For example, creating two categories of interest, Class A and Class B, will allow the physicians' organization to own one class of stock or be one class of member, and the hospital to own another class of stock or be the other member. The primary difference in these two classes should be the election of categories of directors. The class held by the physicians' organization can elect the physician representatives to the PHO and the class held by the hospital can elect the representatives for the hospital. In this way the division of authority between the two classes can specify how decisions are made. If a majority of each class is required to approve decisions, the power of the organization will be evenly split between the physicians' organization and the hospital. Because there are only two entities which are stockholders or members, other alternatives such as creating one class of stock with a high vote requirement are essentially unnecessary, because a vote of the two constituent members will either be unanimous or evenly split.

The articles should prohibit cumulative voting for directors. Under the laws of many states, shareholders may vote for directors by cumulating their votes for a single director. For example, if a shareholder owning one share is voting and there are three directors being elected, the shareholder may cumulate those three votes by casting all three votes for one director. Because this voting protects minority shareholders, it is likely that this provision should be waived because there will only be two shareholders, a physicians' organization and the hospital present in the PHO.

The articles should state that, to the greatest extent required allowed by law, a director of the organization should not be liable to the organization or any of its shareholders for monetary damages for breach of a duty as a director. This section provides protection to the directors who participate in the PHO.

Transforming the Delivery of Health Care:
The integration process

The primary mechanism for specifying the governance and control of the PHO is embodied in the bylaws of the organization. While the bylaws of the physicians' organization will deal in many ways with a large number of physician shareholders or members electing a board and having that board operate the organization, the bylaws of the PHO can be much more loosely structured as the shareholders or members are only two in number and will have much more immediate control over PHO activities. Because the relationship in the PHO between the two shareholders or members is between equals, these bylaws will have a significantly different focus and purpose than the bylaws contained in the physicians' organization where a small number of directors is elected by a very much larger number of physician stockholders or members.

The difference in focus contained in the bylaws of the physician hospital organization is immediately evident in the provisions pertaining to the shareholders or members and their activities. Shareholders or members will hold an annual meeting for the PHO, and that annual meeting will consist of two entities being represented at the meeting. While many individuals may be present representing the physicians' organization and the hospital, there are only two corporate entities who will be present at the meeting. This means that collective action with respect to the shareholders or members is much more easily controlled and is much more direct than in the situation where a large number of shareholders or members exist. Electing the directors can be done at any time deemed appropriate by the shareholders or members. In most instances, the annual meeting of the PHO should probably be scheduled immediately after the annual meeting of the physicians' organization. This approach gives continuity to the overall actions of these two related organizations and, while it is absolutely not essential that this timing occur, a much smoother operation will result if in fact it does occur.

Quorum and voting requirements for the shareholders or members are also greatly simplified in the PHO process. Because there will only be two shareholders or members requiring a quorum is as simple as requiring a majority of the shareholders or members to be present. Because only two shareholders or members exist, they must both be present.

The bylaws should specify the vote required for shareholder or member action. For action to be effective, the bylaws often provide that such action must be authorized by a majority of a votes cast at the meeting. When there are two classes of shareholders or members, a majority of each class is often required. Under either circumstance where there are only two shareholders or members in the PHO, unanimous action will be required by both entities who are shareholders or members for any action to proceed.

Provisions concerning the board of directors are absolutely critical for decision making to be achieved in a fair manner for both physicians and

The physician-hospital organization

hospital participants. All powers vested by law in the PHO are exercised by or under the authority of the board of directors. Unless the corporation law of a particular state requires the action of shareholders or members on a particular issue, that issue may be decided by the board of directors. In this instance where there are two shareholders or members who elect representatives to the PHO, and those representatives are also likely to be directors in the physicians' organization or hospital, the distinction between board action and shareholder action is less important than in the physicians' organization. In general, however, from a corporate practice point of view the board should take most corporate action rather than requiring a vote of the shareholders or members.

The bylaws should specify the number of directors, their term of office and how they are elected. In general, the board should consist of equal members of representatives of both the physicians' organization and the hospital. For example, when 10 directors are selected, five may be elected by the physicians' organization and five may be elected by the hospital. The board should be as small as reasonably practical. From the perspective of the hospital, a smaller board will usually be no problem, there being two, three or four individuals in general charged with responsibility for the management of the hospital.

From the physician side of the equation, however, the decision is much more complex. While there is likely to be a relatively large physician contingent serving on the physicians' organization board, a smaller number, perhaps five, will be selected to represent physician interests on the PHO board. Making the entire PHO board larger than 10 or 12 individuals, however, will make decision making of the PHO board very difficult. A practical limit of five to six physician representatives should be placed on the number of physician representatives on the PHO board. Delegation of authority to these individuals, therefore, must be anticipated. This delegation of authority to physician PHO board members will raise questions about the appropriate role of these physicians in the PHO itself and the accountability of those physicians to the physicians' organization in the PHO process. In general, no restriction should be placed on these representatives as they vote as directors of the PHO board, even though some may wish to create more direct accountability of those physicians to the PO board of directors itself.

The second issue with respect to the physician contingent of the PHO board is the role of primary care physicians. Just as in the physicians' organization, it is likely that a successful PHO also will have a majority of its physician representatives be primary care physicians. The same issues confronted in the physicians' organization are present in the definition of primary care for purposes of selecting primary care directors. An adequate definition of primary care must be established and that definition should be consistent with the definition established by the physicians' organization. While the hospital representatives may have a significant interest in determining the definition of primary care for the PHO, in general it should be a physician's decision at the physicians' organization level which can then be translated into the PHO process. Another issue to be specified in the governance provisions with respect to directors is the term of office. In general, PHO directors will be elected each year by the physicians' organization and hospital. Because of the direct accountability of the elected directors to only two entities, it is generally preferred that the directors serve one year terms and are elected or re-elected at the pleasure of the shareholders or members. A staggered term for PHO directors is generally deemed to be unnecessary given the ability of these shareholders or members to remove directly any directors or to continue to elect directors as those organizations may deem appropriate.

Directors are usually elected by the members or shareholders. Under the most common scenario, two shareholders or members are present, the physicians' organization and the hospital, and each has the right to elect its directors to the board. Because the shareholders or members consist of the physicians' organization and the hospital, the election or selection process will be by corporate action of the members themselves rather than an actual vote. Thus, the physicians' organization would elect its representatives to the PHO board by having the board of directors of the physicians' organization select representatives to the PHO board.

PHO decision making

The manner by which the board of directors makes it decisions is a critical component of the physician-hospital organization governance mechanism. The initial issue to be decided is the necessary quorum present before action may be properly taken by the PHO board. In general, it is recommended that a majority of each class of director, both hospital directors and physician directors, need to be present for a quorum to exist. A higher quorum requirement may be utilized, however, particularly with respect to the physician component if by that higher vote requirement more primary care physicians may be necessary to be in attendance before action is taken. Having a primary care majority of the physician component of the directors of the PHO will mean that by having a higher quorum, more of them will need to be present to pass necessary or requisite corporate action. This is a way of following a high vote requirement for the primary care component of the physician directors.

Once the quorum has been specified, voting must occur. In general, to allow for consensus decision making, a majority of each class of directors present should be required before any action is taken. This majority of each class requirement makes sure that each component of the directors, physician and hospital, must vote by their own internal majority to approve an action. This voting methodology favors the physician interest because it prevents a solid hospital block of votes being joined by a single physician vote and having that majority vote of the entire board prevail. For example, on a 10 person board where five representatives are representing the physicians' organization and five representatives represent the hospital, a majority of the entire board would require six directors for action. This majority vote requirement could be met by a solid five from the hospital representatives plus one physician director. This approach defeats the consensus nature of the organization and generally should be avoided. While a higher vote requirement such as 2/3 or 3/4 vote of the entire board could ensure that more physicians would be required for a particular action, that approach is generally not as favorable as the one discussed above which requires a majority of each class of directors for action. For example, in a 10 person board, a 2/3 vote requirement for action would mean that five hospital representatives could be joined with two physician representatives to create a 2/3 vote on any particular issue. This approach again defeats the need for consensus decision making and, while it preferable to a straight majority of the entire board, still generally benefits the hospital in decision making because the hospital can be expected to vote on controversial issues with a block vote more often than the independent physician representatives.

The PHO bylaws also should designate officers of the organization. Officers generally include a chairman of the board, president, secretary, treasurer, and other officers as may be designated by the board. Often the selection of these officers alternates between physician and hospital representatives. They are elected, however, and serve at the pleasure of the entire board. The duties of the respective officers should be specified in the governing documents. Accordingly, if the president is given executive authority to operate the PHO, that authority should be specified in the governing bylaws.

The bylaws of the PHO should contain indemnification provisions that will protect directors and officers from personal liability when serving in the scope of their duties for the PHO. Indemnification rights are specified in state corporate law. In essence, directors and officers are permitted by state law and by the bylaws to be reimbursed (indemnified) for losses that may occur by reason of their service on behalf of the PHO. The provisions governing this indemnification right are often viewed as a way of encouraging individuals to serve as directors or officers by providing some protection for those individuals serving in that capacity. The extent of indemnification is a matter of state law and the scope of indemnification will be limited by those particular statutes.

The final issue to be covered in the basic organizational documents regarding governance is how to amend the bylaws. Unlike the physicians' organization where there are many individual shareholders and a board of directors that has significant delegated power, the PHO has only two shareholders or members which delegate their authority to directors whom they elect. Accordingly, the need for protection of the shareholders or members from changes in the bylaws by the directors or by one group of shareholders of the expense of the others is considerably less in the PHO context. In the PHO the shareholders or members may always amend the bylaws by vote of the hospital and physicians' organization or the board may amend the bylaws by vote of the majority of each class of directors that are elected. In either event, a majority of both physician directors or the physicians' organization and the hospital directors or the hospital will be required for amending these bylaws. Either mechanism will provide adequate protection for all PHO participants.

Shareholders' agreement

In the for-profit context, the creation of a PHO requires that the shareholder interests of both the physicians' organization and the hospital be restricted. The shareholders' agreement will govern the relationship among the PHO and its two shareholders, the PO and the hospital. The shareholders' agreement restricts the right of the parties to dispose of the stock in the PHO. It is in the best interest of all the parties to place limits on who may be shareholders of the PHO.

The shareholders' agreement should restrict the sale, transfer, assignment or other conveyance of stock in the PHO. The agreement should cover both voluntary transfers and involuntary transfers to third parties. Voluntary transfers are often permitted because of concerns that too strict a restriction on transfer may not be enforceable under state law. While a different conclusion was reached in the PO formation process, that conclusion was reached because of the need for stricter control over a professional corporation. Here a more permissive approach is probably acceptable because of the practical consideration that any attempt to sell by either party would probably signal a serious deterioration in the relationship resulting in a withdrawal from the relationship in any event.

Accordingly, a right of right refusal option is usually placed in a shareholders' agreement. Under this type of provision, a stockholder, the physicians' organization or the hospital, may voluntarily transfer the stock if it obtains a written offer from the potential purchaser. The offer must be bona fide and it must set forth certain information and be delivered to the PHO and each of the other shareholders. Upon delivery of the offer, the PHO will have a right of first refusal to purchase the stock being transferred. The PHO has the ability to purchase the stock on the same terms as described in the third party offer, including the same price and other terms and conditions. This right of first refusal will often in and of itself act as a deterrent to third parties desiring to purchase the stock. If

The physician-hospital organization

the PHO does not exercise its option to purchase, the other shareholder has the option to acquire all or part of the stock described in the third party offer and at the same price and the same terms and conditions set forth in the written offer. If neither the PHO nor the other shareholder desires to purchase the stock, it may be transferred to the party originally offering to purchase the stock. Any stock transferred by this procedure, however, is subject to the terms of the agreement with respect to future transfer, thereby allowing the PHO to maintain control of the subsequent transfer of the stock and the relationship among shareholders.

Shareholders' agreements also address the obligations of the parties if an involuntary transfer of the stock were to occur. Under these circumstances, the shareholder must offer the stock to the PHO and the other shareholders for mandatory purchase. Again, it is likely if any of these events occur that the PHO partnership will have deteriorated seriously, but from a legal perspective it is important to protect interests of the shareholders by a written agreement covering these eventualities. In general, the PHO should have the option to purchase all of the stock upon the happening of certain events, such as termination of the managed care provider agreement between the PHO and the shareholder, involuntary dissolution of the shareholder or an event of bankruptcy with respect to that shareholder. If these events occur, the effected stockholder must offer options first to the PHO and then to the other shareholders to purchase all of that shareholder's stock. The termination of the managed care provider agreement between the entity and the PHO means that the cessation of the relationship of the parties will have occurred for all practical purposes. Without the agreement to provide services to managed care enrollees in the managed care provider agreement, there is no purpose in continuing a relationship between the parties.

A principal purpose for the shareholders' agreement is to specify the valuation methodology used for the stock and to specify the purchase price. The valuation of stock is often considered the most critical aspect of the shareholders' agreement. The valuation method and the purchase price determined through that method will set forth the economic value of the stock to the parties involved. In general, the same options with respect to a valuation process as were raised in the physicians' organization are present here. The options include fair market value, a specified value or book value. The most conservative method is probably determining purchase price on net asset value. Net asset value is the per share net worth of the PHO not including good will or accounts receivable. This valuation is conservative because it only values the assets and liabilities of the PHO as opposed to the value of the ongoing business. This conservative valuation is appropriate where the primary purpose of the PHO is to act as intermediary between the providers of hospital or medical services and the managed care plan itself. A fair market value determination will result in the need for an appraisal and valuation, in the context where the parties' relationship is probably deteriorated seriously anyway. A stipulated value may place a guaranteed return on this stock when in fact the primary purpose of the investment is to facilitate a managed care response to increase the benefits to the member organizations as providers rather than investors. The valuation per share should be multiplied by the number of shares purchased to determine the aggregate purchase price of the stock. The parties should agree that the value determined under the shareholders' agreement is conclusive upon the parties. The agreement probably should allow for arbitration for the determination of the purchase price in accordance with arbitration provisions that are specified in the agreement. Any closing of the purchase should be postponed during the pendency of any arbitration proceedings. Arbitration is a method by which an element of fairness may be put into the agreement because it allows a third party to confirm that the valuation has been performed in accordance with standards specified in the agreement.

The shareholders' agreement also should specify the terms for the repayment. It should provide that the PHO or the other purchasing shareholder has the option to pay the purchase price in full at the time of the closing or to pay it on an installment basis. In general, the installment basis should allow for a small down payment at the closing (perhaps 10 percent) with the balance paid over a significant time period pursuant to a promissory note with a maturity of perhaps as long as seven years. Interest should be charged at a market rate. Specifying a longer payment period will allow the purchaser to spread out payments and lessen the impact of any purchase obligation.

The shareholders' agreement also should contain a recitation of the relationship between the physicians' organization and hospital in terms of dealing with other parties. In the nonprofit structure, the provisions probably should be placed in the network participation agreements. To create a partnership, it is likely that the parties should agree to deal exclusively with each other in that effort. Accordingly, they should probably agree that they will not form a partnership or other relationship with any other physician organization or hospital, as the case may be, regarding managed care contracting and relationships with third party payers. Allowing the freedom to deal with other organizations will damage the partnership relationship. Accordingly, it is in the best interest of both hospital and the physicians' organization to deal exclusively with each other. From the perspective of the individual participating physician, however, this provision does not mean that an individual physician who is a member of the physicians' organization is precluded from joining other managed care or physician organization efforts. As such, this freedom gives the individual physician practice greater flexibility than the physician organization itself. In general, this type of freedom is acceptable to hospitals who recognize that physicians must have the ability deal with a multitude of payers and relationships other than exclusively through the hospital. The antitrust implications of this type provision should be reviewed with antitrust counsel.

The shareholders' agreement should contain a provision which allows additional shareholders to become parties to the agreement. The control over adding additional parties should remain with the physicians' organization and the hospital. It is likely that expansion of these networks will continue to occur, particularly through adding additional hospitals in a managed care network. To keep physicians within this decision-making framework and to avoid having their vote diluted, it is important to have control over this process. In a nonprofit setting, these restrictions on adding members should be placed in the bylaws.

The final piece of the PHO organizational process in the for-profit setting is the subscription agreement. This agreement is the means of obtaining the commitment of the physicians' organization and the hospital to purchase an interest in the PHO. This type of agreement is similar to those utilized for the physicians' organization, and accordingly set forth the purchase price and formula for establishing a purchase price for the stock. The dollars to be contributed into the PHO should be specified in the agreement. Because there are only two organizations and they are corporate entities, there is usually less concern about state and federal securities issues than in the physicians' organization development process. In general, the contribution of both the physicians' organization and the hospital should be equal. The amount of the contribution should be determined by the budget prepared for the PHO and the intended scope of operations to be conducted by the PHO.

Managed care contracting network

The final step in the development of the PHO is the creation of the contracting network. Once the physicians' organization has been formed, once the PHO governance mechanism has been established and the relationships of physicians and hospitals have been set, the final developmental piece should be undertaken by creating the managed care contracting network. As one of the principal purposes for the creation of the PHO will be to organize hospitals and physicians in a contracting network, a series of contractual relationships must be created. The managed care contracting network for the PHO is illustrated in Figure 4, and requires the physicians' organization, the hospital and PHO to contract for managed care through managed care provider agreements under which the physicians' organization and hospital are obligated to accept managed care contracts negotiated by the PHO. The second portion of the development process requires that the physicians' organization enter into network participation' agreements for the physicians to provide services under managed care contracts. Accordingly, this network must be built by a series of agreements that include the following:

1. **The physician application**. This form requires physician members of the physicians' organization to provide certain practice specific information about themselves.
2. **Physicians' network agreement**. This network agreement requires physicians and medical groups to participate in the contracting network established by the physicians' organization. As such, it contains many managed care contracting type provisions typically found in managed care relationships and is quite similar to the physician network agreement used in the independent physicians' organization created in Chapter 8.
3. **Physicians' organization network agreement**. This document creates a relationship between the physicians' organization as an entity and the PHO itself. The physicians' organization agrees to provide its contracting network to the PHO who will in turn utilize this network as part of its managed care contracting network provided to managed care plans.
4. **Hospital network participating agreement**. This document obligates the hospital to provide managed care services as part of the PHO contracting network.

This structure for the development of the contracting network is discussed below.

The physician network relationship

The first step in the creation of the physician component of the contracting network is to require participating physicians to complete an application for participation in the physicians' organization which is very similar to the application for membership in the physicians' organization specified in Chapter 8. The main purpose of the application is to obtain information about the practice of the physician and to obtain authorization of the physician for the physicians' organization and PHO to make such inquiries as they deem appropriate in establishing the qualifications of the physician to participate in that network. The form should contain a release from liability of the physicians' organization and the PHO to assure that potential liability for the physicians' organization and PHO is as limited as possible.

The application should require general information concerning the physician, such as educational and training information, specialty certification, office practice information and licensure information. The application should contain a series of questions with respect to quality. Questions regarding limitation, suspension or revocation of licenses, permits or other actions should be included. Malpractice history questions should be included. CME activity and hospital and other medical organization committee activities should be listed. A listing of recognition, awards, membership in professional societies and civic responsibilities should be provided. Practice information should be detailed and participation in managed care plans should be specified. Hospital privileges should be listed. Medicare and Medicaid participation should be designated, and call group members should be specified. Insurance and liability information should be detailed along with policy limits. Medical references should be provided. The application also should contain a statement of the applicant. It should require the applicant to confirm that acceptance for membership in the physicians' organization is within the sole discretion of the physicians' organization. The application should require the physician to abide by the rules and regulations established from time to time by the physicians' organization and the PHO. The application should require the physician to certify that the information provided is accurate in the questionnaire. The application also should require that the physicians' organization be notified of any change in the information provided and should contain a release which allows the physicians' organization to consult with hospital administrators, other medical staff members, malpractice carriers and others to verify information concerning practice styles. The statement should release the physicians' organization, the PHO and their agents and employees from any liability for their acts performed in good faith in obtaining and verifying the information. Finally, the physician should consent to the release by any person to the physicians' organization of any information it may request which it deems relevant in the evaluation of the professional competence, medical practice patterns, ability to work well with others, and moral and ethical qualifications with respect to the participating physician. This consent should be followed by a release of such persons who provide this information from any and all liability.

The network participating physician agreement

The first relationship to be formed in the contracting network to be established by the PHO is the relationship between individual physician as a provider of physician services and the physicians' organization. The network participating physician agreement is an agreement between the physicians' organization and the physician in which the physician agrees to provide services to managed care plans through his or her participation in the physicians' organization. As such, it is the primary document which organizes the physicians into a relationship for managed care and is quite similar to the network agreement discussed in Chapter 8 regarding the formation of an independent physicians' organization. By setting forth a comprehensive managed care contracting relationship in this agreement, it will not be necessary to duplicate most of these provisions again in the network agreements with the physician-hospital organization or the managed care agreement with a health plan. This approach will give the physicians a negotiating advantage with managed care plans because if the provisions set forth here are not negotiated again with the managed care plan, the manner in which these' obligations are expressed will have been established by the physicians rather than the health plan.

The first series of issues that must be addressed in the creation of the participation agreement for physicians is the services to be provided by the physician and the method by which the physician becomes obligated to provide those services. To have an effective contracting network, the physician must agree to provide services under contracts entered into by the PHO. When the physicians' organization enters into a contract with a third party to provide physician services to certain groups or individuals as negotiated by the PHO, an issue arises whether the physicians' organization can bind the individual physician or whether that physician can opt out and decline to participate. From a business point of view, creating an effective contract network will mean that the PHO must obligate individual practicing physicians to participate in network arrangements as negotiated by the PHO. To the extent that this obligation arises automatically, the PHO can market its network as a cohesive whole, without the risk to the managed care plan or employer that a large number of participants may opt out of a particular arrangement that may be negotiated by the PHO. By prohibiting this opt out, a physician is obligated by the terms of the contract negotiated by the PHO to provide services in accordance with its terms and in accordance with the terms of the participating agreement with the physicians' organization.

While the business perspective of the issue of whether physicians are bound by the decisions of the PHO clearly indicates that a physician should be automatically bound, many physicians may resist that wholesale delegation of authority to the PHO. Accordingly, negotiating corridors may be developed whereby the physicians agree to provide services for contracts that contain reimbursement rates within specified corridors. This limited granting of authority can help the PHO know the extent of its network that it can offer, while at the same time provide protection to the physician that, within a given range, reimbursement will be acceptable to that physician.

The ability of the physician to become obligated by the terms of a PHO negotiated agreement in part depends upon the nature of the PO and PHO and the inter-relatedness of this issue with the antitrust laws. In general, independent competitors cannot negotiate collectively with respect to price. Accordingly, independent physicians who have not created an integrated operation or who do not assume collective risk will not be able to have the PHO automatically bind them and will require a messenger-type approach whereby any pricing terms must be negotiated directly between the HMO and each of the physicians. While a messenger can be used to facilitate these negotiations, the messenger must not communicate inter-physician pricing positions to the independent physician practices.

The options to avoid this messenger-type approach all revolve around the ability of the physicians, PO and PHO to be integrated in developing a new business which can then withstand antitrust scrutiny and negotiate prices collectively. Either a new business must be created where physicians put substantial capital at risk and integrate their practices, or a mechanism must be derived by which physicians are collectively at risk through capitation or sufficient withholds. These options all require significant funds being put at risk by participating physicians. In the capitation context, if the physician is at risk for providing care, this new business imperative of integration will have been achieved. To the extent that fee for service reimbursement is used, a significant withhold in the 20 percent range may be sufficient, if the withhold will only be paid to physicians if certain cost containment goals and operational efficiencies are achieved collectively before this money is returned. This "at risk" nature of reimbursement is a difficult and changing concept, and any final decisions with respect to this issue should be made with guidance from antitrust counsel. Accordingly, the opt in or opt out nature of contracts with managed care plans is dependent upon not only the business aspects of having a cohesive network, but also the antitrust limitations placed upon independent competitors to go forward with any particular arrangement.

When agreeing to provide services, a physician should probably be given the ability to stop taking new network patients services if that physician provides at least 30-60 days advance notice to the physicians' organization that the physician has no capacity to accept additional patients under any payer agreement. A sufficient time period should be allowed so notice can be given to managed care plans to allow those plans to remove their physicians from the subscriber list.

Because this network agreement will be signed first and the actual agreement with a managed care plan will be signed sometime in the future, it is important to consider that the participation agreement entered into between physician and physicians' organization may conflict with a provider agreement entered into with a managed care plan by the PHO. In order to protect the integrity of the managed care relationship and because each plan will be slightly different, the actual relationship will be governed in cases of ambiguity by the contract with the managed care plan. This preference recognizes the reality that it is the actual plan relationship itself that will govern the overall relationship. Creating the managed care network first, however, should give physicians and hospitals a negotiating advantage with managed care plans which are already confronted with a network agreement drafted in more favorable terms to the physicians.

While physicians will be credentialed as part of the overall physician organization development process, a network agreement should allow the physician to provide covered services to eligible persons within the scope of the practice of the physician in accordance with the terms of the agreement with the physicians' organization and the plan arrangement with managed care plan. The agreement should recognize that these physicians are only eligible to provide covered services to members of a plan upon satisfaction of credentialing requirements established by the plan.

The agreement should contain provisions with respect to the standard of care utilized by a physician to provide covered services. Accordingly, the physicians' organization participation agreement should include a provision requiring the physician to provide physician services using the standard of care required by the law in the relevant jurisdiction. In managed care contracts, physicians are often asked to agree to a higher standard of care than may be required under applicable law. Physicians should not agree to a higher standard than required by law since that could effectively increase their exposure to malpractice liability by raising the standard of care required of them. In addition, the agreement probably should contain a nondiscrimination clause. This clause would require physicians to treat patients governed by the managed care agreement no less favorably than all other patients of the physician. Illegal discrimination also should be prohibited. These provisions are often required by state or federal law. The participation agreement should require physicians to admit patients to participating hospitals, to provide encounter data in a form acceptable to both the physicians' organization and plan showing services provided to eligible persons, and to obtain prior authorization for covered services where required.

In addition to the section requiring a detailed explanation of how services will be provided for a plan, the agreement should detail provisions concerning compensation and billing. Under a participation agreement, compensation arrangements between physicians and the managed care plan may be handled in several different ways. The compensation for providing services under a third party contract are specified by the terms of that contract itself. The physicians' organization and PHO may limit their risk of nonpayment by not being responsible for making any payment to a participating provider. If the physicians' organization receives funds and agrees to pay the participating provider, however, it must avoid assuming the risk of nonpayment by the health plan. In general, it may be favorable for the physicians' organization to have these funds channeled through it or through the PHO rather than directly to the physicians. This approach may assist in the control of the managed care relationship.

Another provision with respect to payment that is often required by state law is that physicians cannot seek reimbursement from eligible persons under a plan if those persons are covered by a health plan. Accordingly, agreements often contain provisions in which the physician agrees that in no event, including nonpayment or insolvency or breach of agreement, that physician will bill, charge, collect or have any recourse against any eligible persons other than through the agreement with the physicians' organization or with the managed care plan.

Physicians are allowed, however, to bill individuals directly for any services following the date the individual ceases to be an eligible person or for copayments or deductibles as specified in a plan. When these eligible persons become ineligible for covered services, a physician may bill that patient directly. The challenge in the managed care contracting realm is to have sufficient notice from the managed care plan to determine when this coverage ceases. Accordingly, the managed care agreement negotiated by the PHO will seek to limit the ability of the health plan to delete retroactively covered individuals. This retroactive deletion would allow health plans to notify physicians of loss of coverage long after the loss occurs. Because health plans themselves often do not receive notice from employers concerning loss of coverage for individual employees on a timely basis, health plans will seek to put this risk upon participating providers. Often, the best that can be achieved in this area is a limitation on the time period which health plans may make this retroactive deletion. These limitations should be negotiated in the specific agreement with the health plan.

Payment provisions in the participating provider agreement also should contain very specific requirements with respect to the payment obligation. For instance, capitation payment reimbursement typically requires the payment of a predetermined periodic payment for specific covered services for each eligible person who is a member of a patient panel. This capitation reimbursement means the payment of a fixed sum in advance in return for the agreement by a physician to assume the risk of the volume and frequency of providing a stated range of services to those eligible persons. In order to circumscribe this risk, it is important to have several words clearly defined in this payment obligation. First, covered services must be defined accurately. The actual agreement with a managed care plan should set forth in as much detail as possible the health care services to be provided by a physician. Any ambiguity in what is covered will likely be resolved by the managed care plan in its favor.

The expression of the capitation amount is also important in that age and sex based capitation for particular services should be specified, otherwise the physician will take the risk that the patients assigned to the physician will meet the actuarial assumptions constructed by the managed care plan in determining the blended capitation rate paid to the physician. This blended capitation rate that was constructed is based on certain actuarial assumptions concerning the mix of age and sex of a particular patient panel. By breaking down a blended undifferentiated age and sex capitation amount into specific age and sex categories for reimbursement, the physician takes less of the actuarial risk undertaken by the managed care plan when it sets a fixed rate for the premium it charges to all its potential enrollees.

Finally, in the compensation area, it is important to specify that the physicians' organization itself will not be responsible or liable for any decisions to deny payments of any claims submitted by any participating physician for furnishing services that are covered or not covered to eligible persons. The physicians' organization should not be an insurer or underwriter of the responsibility of any managed care plan to provide benefits or to provide payments to any physicians. The role of the physicians' organization is to provide a physician perspective in the affairs of the physicians' organization and the affairs of the PHO. Another critical portion of the individual physician participation agreement with the physicians' organization is a section requiring compliance with laws and program requirements. Under this section, physicians agree to comply with all applicable laws and regulations that may be applicable to the practice of the physician. In addition, the physician may be required to prescribe or authorize substitution of generic pharmaceuticals when appropriate and may be required to cooperate with any program for prescribing the use of pharmaceuticals. While these provisions take away some autonomy from physicians, the purpose of the PHO is to negotiate these general program requirements with a health plan so they are fair to all participating physicians.

Another critical component for the participation agreement for individual physicians is physician credentialling. Physicians should be required to adhere to credentialling standards and procedures adopted by the PO, PHO or a payer. While this may be an open-ended provision with respect to the individual physician, the input of physicians in a representative capacity in the PO and PHO process will make this agreement fairer than if it were negotiated with managed care plans in the abstract without physician input. The agreement also should contain a provision that the physician warrants the accuracy of all credentialling information and imposes an obligation upon the physician to notify the physicians' organization of any change in any of that information. Finally, this section on physician credentialling should contain the acknowledgment of the physician that credentialling information concerning the practice of the physician will be submitted to the PHO by the physicians' organization and to any payer that may require that information.

The agreement of an individual physician to participate in the physicians' organization also should specify several key points concerning records. Clinical records should be regarded as confidential and the agreement should require compliance of all parties with applicable federal and state laws and regulations regarding such records. Physicians should maintain and furnish those records as may be required by applicable federal and state law, regulations and plan requirements. The physician should cooperate with the physicians' organization, the PHO and the plans to facilitate information and record exchanges that are necessary for the quality assurance and utilization management programs established by the physicians' organization, the PHO or the managed care plan. Finally, this section should allow the physicians' organization, the PHO, a plan or their designees with reasonable access during regular business hours to specified clinical and medical records of persons covered by a plan that are maintained by a physician. Prior to the release of such information, however, the party requesting the records must obtain the appropriate consent, or approval from the patient before such access is granted. This is an important provision to be specified in the agreement, because often this obligation is imposed upon the physician as opposed to the party who is requesting access. The agreement should place the obligation where it is most properly rests, that being on the party requesting the access itself.

The agreement should require physicians to purchase and maintain policies of comprehensive general liability and professional liability insurance. Physician participants in the physicians' organization are not employees of that organization. They maintain their own practices. Therefore, it is essential that the physician members of the physicians' organization maintain, at their own cost and expense, comprehensive general liability and professional liability insurance. These policies should be in amounts reasonably determined by the physicians' organization. In addition, the policy should provide that the insurer will give the physicians' organization written notice prior to any cancellation, termination or material alteration. Cancellation, termination or material alteration of insurance should be a default under the agreement. The physicians' organization should not be placed in the position of having to accept terms of a modified insurance policy unless it agrees to the terms of such modification. Because the physicians' organization will be composed of physicians and will represent the best interests of the physicians, the requirements imposed on physicians in this area should be reasonable. The same discretion should not be given to every health plan in its agreement with the PHO.

Transforming the Delivery of Health Care:
The integration process

Somewhat related to the insurance question is the liability issue. Liability for malpractice is always a concern in the managed care context. Often, managed care plans will require, or at least attempt to require, physicians to enter into indemnification agreements. These indemnification clauses allow a managed care plan to be reimbursed for its out-of-pocket expenses that may be occasioned by it being named as a defendant in lawsuits of professional malpractice against participating physicians. This indemnification obligation is deemed to be a "liability assumed under contract" and insurance coverage for the expenses associated with this assumed liability is often denied by malpractice carriers. Because of the lack of coverage for these indemnification clauses, physicians and the physicians' organization should try to avoid making these types of commitments. Any agreement to make these payments will often require the organization agreeing to these payments to make the payment out of their own funds rather than from insurance proceeds. The best defense to this type of situation is to include a statement that all parties should be responsible for their own liabilities. Under this type of provision, neither party indemnifies the other and neither is responsible for either the liability itself or for defending or paying for the defense of another party.

The participation agreement between the physician and physicians' organization also should anticipate the managed care company require-ment that a physician participate in grievance procedures for plan complaints. In an effort to institute grievance procedure at the physicians' organization and PHO level, the participation agreement should require the physician to cooperate with the physicians' organization in the implementation of a grievance procedure that may be established by the PO and/or PHO and to comply with appropriate corrective action taken under any of these grievance procedures. By structuring the arrangement in this way, the involvement of the PO and PHO in the grievance process is encouraged in what is typically the exclusive domain of the health plan. As such, the PO and PHO will have an expanded role in this area and the program will have a more physician focused perspective than is typically found in most health plan grievance programs. Because grievance proce-dures are often required by state law regulating health maintenance organizations, a review of that law will be necessary to determine the specifics regarding the role the physicians' organization and the PHO can have in this process.

To construct a strong contracting network for managed care pur-poses, it is also important to address the quality assurance, utilization management and rules and regulations necessary for participation in managed care plans. The goal to achieve in the participation agreement with individual physicians in the physicians' organization is to lay the groundwork for a more expanded role for the physicians' organization and the PHO in the quality assurance, utilization and management and rules and regulations established by the managed care plan. This expanded role will be a positive development for PO participants in general and physicians in particular, but will be resisted by the managed care plan in the negotiating process. As part of its obligation to maintain a quality panel of hospital and physician providers, the PHO and the physicians' organization must require that participating providers, including physicians and the hospital, comply with quality assurance and utilization management programs. This type of commitment is usually required by managed care contracts and the fact that the quality assurance program is established by the physicians' organization and the PHO should give the physician some assurance that the program will be administered in a fair manner. Under the same rationale, the physician also should agree to comply with the utilization management program established by the physicians' organization and the PHO. Finally, the physician should agree to comply with rules and regulations established by the physicians' organization and the PHO. Again, this is a typical provision required by managed care contracts. Without these requirements, the quality of the provider panel cannot be monitored or maintained, thus decreasing the ability of the PHO to contract with health plans to provide services.

While the participation agreement between physician and physicians' organization may anticipate that the physicians' organization will conduct much of the utilization review, quality assurance and other rules and regulations, in reality the administration of those programs will likely be delegated to the PHO. The physicians' organization should have the flexibility to determine where those programs should be conducted most efficiently. In general, in the division of authority between the physicians' organization and PHO, the operational aspects of the network should be conducted centrally at the physician hospital organization level. By allowing the physicians' organization to delegate its commitments under the participation agreement, the physicians' organization is given this flexibility.

The ability to amend quality assurance, utilization management and rules and regulations also should be specified in the participation agreement. In general, there are a variety of approaches that can be taken in this area. It is important to allow the physicians' organization and PHO the ability to change rules and regulations with written notice to a physician. At least 30 days advance notice should be given the physicians of any change in these programs, and the amendment should be effective at the end of that 30-day period unless the physician provides written notice of rejection during that period. If the physician does not agree to the amendment, the physicians' organization probably should have the option to terminate the agreement. During the period prior to termination, however, the rules and regulations should be conducted without giving effect to the proposed amendment. This type of provision allows the general programs of the physicians' organization and the PHO managed care network to be modified during the course of a contract year. As such, it is unfavorable to a physician as it allows modification of the rules during the course of the year. Such a provision is probably necessary, however, to allow the physicians' organization and PHO managed care network to proceed with modifications to programs without seeking amendment to the contracts with the entire physician network. This provision seeks to strike a balance between fairness to the physician by requiring advance notice and by not requiring automatic acceptance, and fairness to the physicians' organization and PHO by allowing modification of these programs without seeking the approval of every physician. It also should be noted that this provision only should apply to quality assurance, utilization management and other rules and regulations rather than the entire contract. Accordingly, it is more favorable in this respect than many managed care contracts which seek to give the managed care plan the ability unilaterally to modify other substantive provisions in the agreement, including price.

To construct the network, the physicians' organization also should require the participating physician to participate in the network for a period of time. The length of commitment of the physician to the physicians' organization contracting network should be reviewed carefully. From a marketing perspective, the ability to sell the panel to managed care plans will depend in part upon the ability of the panel to be utilized for sale of the network to employers and managed care plans. This need for a long term commitment must be balanced against the desires of the physician to maintain flexibility and the potential desire of the physicians' organization to reduce the size or modify its contracting panel by not renewing agreements, rather than being required to terminate the relationship during a longer term by establishing "cause" for the termination. In general, the initial relationship between the physicians' organization and the physician should probably be in the one- to two-year range. Any shorter agreement will not give continuity to the network which will be asked to provide care to managed care plans.

Having established a term for the initial relationship, consideration should also be given to whether the agreement and commitment should be renewed at the end of each term. In general, continuity of the network will be improved by requiring that the agreement automatically renew for additional terms unless written notice of the termination is given at least 90 to 120 days prior to the then current expiration date of the agreement. This type of automatic renewal will facilitate continuation of the network and will avoid a rather large task of having physicians sign additional participation agreements at the end of each term. Some physicians' organizations may feel that requiring this recredentialling and recontracting

The physician-hospital organization

process every year or two is an important vehicle to allow modification of the network. On the other hand, nonrenewal from a legal perspective can achieve the same goal and should be considered as the more feasible alternative.

Consideration also should be given to whether the physicians' organization should be permitted not to renew the agreement only if the physician fails to comply with certain standards. Participating physicians may be concerned that the physicians' organization will be arbitrary in its nonrenewal process. Accordingly, some physicians' organizations may obligate themselves not to renew the agreement only upon recommendation of termination by a credentialling committee and a vote of the board of directors to terminate the relationship. In general, in most physicians' organization, these additional restrictions on termination and nonrenewal should be avoided because they limit the flexibility of the organization and may create grounds for dispute in the termination context.

The relationship between the physician and the physicians' organization should be terminated if either party fails to perform under the agreement. From the perspective of the physicians' organization, it should be allowed to terminate the agreement if the physician fails to maintain adequate licensure or insurance, or violates any law. In these types of circumstances, the physicians' organization should have the ability to terminate the agreement immediately. In other types of circumstances, however, such as failure to comply with the terms of the agreement, the physicians' organization should have the ability to terminate the agreement only upon giving prior notice of the default and allowing a period of time to cure the default before the agreement is terminated.

The physicians' organization also should consider whether a provision allowing for termination of the agreement without cause should be utilized. These types of provisions permit either party to terminate without specifying any reason. In effect, if a 90 day notice period for termination without cause is utilized, the agreement is in fact a 90 day agreement as opposed to a longer two year term that may be specified in the agreement. Termination of the relationship without cause will often reduce the risk of a legal challenge to termination, but having such a short agreement for participation in the organization may reduce the effectiveness of the network for managed care plan purposes.

Consideration also should be given to the effect of termination upon the obligations of the parties. The question here is whether the obligation of the physician to continue to treat patients under managed care plans continues after the termination of the agreement. In general, provisions should be utilized which require the obligations of the parties to terminate as of the termination date of the agreement. This is a fairly limited provision with respect to obligations that may occur after termination of the agreement. Managed care plans can be expected to require a longer period of time for the transfer of their patients out of the relationship. In fact, many managed care plans require up to one year to have their patients moved out of managed care relationships with a particular provider. Because the individual employer groups and eligible persons are covered by one year agreements, many managed care plans desire to assure the coverage of those individuals under the provider panels that were initially made available to the employers and eligible persons at the beginning of their enrollment period. These provisions will likely be negotiated between the PHO and the managed care plan in terms of the extent of the ongoing relationship or obligations that are required of the physicians' organization and the physician after the termination of the agreement. Accordingly, it is prudent to place in the participation agreement with the individual physician the obligation that they will bound by any continuing care requirements as specified in the particular managed care plan.

A fundamental concept to be embodied in the relationship between the physicians' organization and the physician is that their relationship is one of independent parties. Any other relationship might impose liability on one of the parties for the action of the other. Employer-employee and agent-principal relationships should be avoided because of the liability which such relationships would create. Independent contractors are not responsible for the actions of the other party to the agreement. Physicians also should be solely responsible for exercising their judgment in medical matters.

In constructing the relationship with the physician, the physicians' organization should consider whether the relationship should be exclusive between the physicians' organization and the physician. Under the exclusivity concept, the physician would be prohibited from joining other networks. In almost every circumstance, this exclusivity will be rejected. In some instances, it will be rejected for antitrust reasons, which would limit severely the size of the panel that could be engaged in an exclusive relationship. In most other circumstances, the exclusivity will be rejected because of the need for physicians to maintain their flexibility in their practices and not limiting the organizations which they join. Requiring an exclusive commitment would probably limit the acceptance of the organization by physicians and, accordingly for marketing purposes, it is likely that this exclusivity will not be utilized.

The parties should consider, however, what should be done with the existing contractual relationships that physicians may have in the event the PHO enters into an agreement with a managed care plan. Under these circumstances, it is probably appropriate for the physician to agree not to enter into separate agreements with that payer during the term of the PHO agreement. If a physician is a party to an agreement with that managed care plan that is already in existence, the physician should either terminate the agreement with the managed care plan following the execution of the PHO agreement with that managed care plan, or the agreement should terminate at the conclusion of term of the physician-managed care plan agreement.

Finally, in the participation agreement with individual physicians, the physicians' organization should consider the interrelationship between the network that it is forming pursuant to the participation agreement and the network that will be utilized by the managed care plan. In order to encourage a managed care plan to accept the provisions of the participation agreement between the physician and the physicians' organization, it will be necessary to allow a payer to enforce the terms of the agreement. If the PHO and the physicians' organization have the direct contractual relationships with the managed care plan, that plan will likely only agree to that framework if it can assured that it can enforce compliance with its programs against the physician if the physicians' organization or PHO fails to enforce those obligations. Accordingly, the managed care plan should be allowed to enforce the agreement if the physicians' organization fails to enforce it under a third party beneficiary concept.

Network participation agreement between PHO and physicians' organization

Having created the relationship between the physicians' organization and the individual participating physician, the next step in the creation of the PHO managed care network is the establishment of the relationship between the physicians' organization and the PHO. In this relationship, the physicians' organization agrees to enter into contracts with its physician shareholders or members (pursuant to the participating physician agreement discussed previously) to provide physician services to enrollees of managed care entities who contract with the PHO.

In creating the relationship between the PHO and the physicians' organization, the first fundamental concept is that the physicians' organization will arrange for its physician services to be provided as part of the network. Accordingly, the physicians' organization should agree to arrange for the provision of physician services for the network and to eligible persons in managed care plans by entering into network participating physician agreements with each physician participant. The mechanism for creating the physician network is to require the physicians' organization to enter into a comprehensive agreement with individual physicians. The form of this individual physician agreement should be specified in creating the relationship with the physicians' organization and the PHO. In this manner, the PHO can be assured of the type of relationship the physicians' organization has with its physicians. In creating the relationship with the PHO, however, the physicians' organization should make clear that it is not actually providing care, but merely arranging it. If the physicians' organization is deemed to be providing care, it will have significantly increased malpractice risk. In addition, the physicians' organization should agree to use its best efforts to maintain the network of participating physicians with which it contracts to provide services for managed care plans. Because the PHO will rely upon the physicians' organization for its network, the physicians' organization should be obligated to use its best efforts to maintain that network. Because the network agreement with physicians will be attached to the document creating the physicians' organization-PHO agreement, it is not necessary to repeat the many provisions contained in the physician agreement in this document.

In creating the physicians' organization-PHO relationship, it also is important to specify a term and a method for terminating the agreement. The network participation agreement should probably be a long term agreement in the five- to 10-year range. The success of the PHO depends in large part on the continued availability of a qualified panel of physicians. A long term commitment indicates a desire of the parties to make the PHO successful by requiring the physicians' organization to maintain the network.

The parties also should specify a mechanism to terminate the arrangement if a party defaults. The basic principles here are that if party fails to comply with material terms of the agreement, the other party should have the ability to terminate the relationship. A 60 to 90 day cure period for any default should be provided, after which a similar time period should be provided to wind up the affairs of the parties. In many contracts the termination period is substantially shorter. The PHO, however, depends heavily on the participation of the network of providers. A shorter termination period may make impossible the continuation of the PHO through the development of another physicians' organization to take the place of the current physicians' organization. It is important that the PHO be able to maintain its agreements under the payer agreements with managed care plans, and it is important that the termination provisions of the PHO-physicians' organization agreement be long enough for an alternative relationship to be created.

The physicians' organization and PHO should consider whether a termination without cause provision should be inserted. This termination without cause would allow the parties to provide in the agreement that a one year termination could be allowed without cause even though the term of the agreement is five or 10 years. Given that the PHO relationship should be a long one, an early option to terminate without cause should not be allowed and termination during the term of the agreement only should be permitted for cause.

The physician-hospital organization

The parties' rights and obligations will terminate upon the conclusion of the agreement. This is a fairly limited commitment with respect to obligations that may occur after termination of the relationship. Managed care plans can be expected to require a longer period of time for the transfer of their patients out of the relationship. In fact, many managed care plans require up to one year to have their patients moved out of managed care relationships with a particular provider. Because the individual employer groups and eligible persons are covered by one year agreements, many managed care plans desire to assure that the provider panels that are made available to the employers and eligible persons at the beginning of their enrollment period continue throughout the term of the relationship. These provisions are likely to be negotiated between the PHO and the managed care plan.

In constructing the relationship between the physicians' organization and the PHO, it is important to establish that the parties are independent contractors. Any other relationship might impose liability on one of the parties for the actions of the other. Employer-employee and agent-principal relationships should be avoided because of the liability which such relationships would create. Independent contractors are not responsible for the actions of the other parties to the agreement.

In constructing the PHO-physicians' organization relationship, another basic design issue to be considered is whether the relationship of the parties should be exclusive. In general, unlike the physicians' organization-physician relationship, it is likely that the relationship between the physicians' organization and the PHO will be exclusive. This exclusivity would prohibit either party from contracting with another PHO or physicians' organization. This aspect of exclusivity should mean that the parties should not be able to form relationships with any other parties.

While this provision does not limit the ability of the physicians to contract individually with other health plans, some may argue that the exclusivity provisions are inappropriate and the physicians' organization should be free to construct other relationships. A basic decision should be made between the PHO and the physicians' organization about the nature of their relationship. An exclusive relationship embodies many of the partnership considerations that will frame the PHO-physicians' organization relationship. If the parties desire a true partnership with consensus decision making, the necessary corollary to that should be an exclusive relationship between themselves. If the parties desire a more arms length relationship with less commitment, the necessary corollary to that decision will be less consensus decision making at the PHO level and less partnership, given the need for the PHO to be competitive and to compete against other managed care initiatives in which the physicians' organization may participate. Advice of antitrust counsel should be obtained before final agreements are reached in this area.

Finally, the parties should permit managed care plans to enforce the terms of the PHO-physicians' organization agreement. This type of commitment is essential in creating the provider network. If the PHO has the direct contractual relationship with the managed care plan, that managed care plan will agree to the contractual framework if it can be assured that it can enforce compliance with its programs against the physicians' organization. This type of relationship means that the managed care plan should be in a position to enforce these types of commitments if they cannot otherwise be enforced.

Participating hospital agreement

The third piece in the creation of the PHO contracting network is the relationship between the hospital and the PHO itself under which the hospital agrees to provide certain inpatient/outpatient services to managed care plan eligible persons. This type of relationship corresponds to the relationship under which physicians agree to provide physician services under plans which contract with the PHO, and the agreement should contain parallel provisions to those found in both the individual physician and PO-PHO agreements. Because of the slightly different context, however, a complete discussion of the specific terms of the hospital agreement is included below.

The first area to be considered in constructing the hospital-PHO relationship concerns services to be provided by the hospital. To have an effective contracting network, the hospital must agree to provide services under contracts entered into between the PHO and the managed care plan. Some payers may require the hospital to enter into an agreement directly with the payer. Others will contract only with the PHO and rely upon the arrangement of the PHO with the hospital under a participating hospital agreement for the provision of inpatient and outpatient services. In general, the agreement between the PHO and the hospital should obligate the hospital to provide services in accordance with the PHO negotiated agreements with managed care plans and in accordance with the terms of the PHO-hospital network agreement. Allowing hospitals to opt out of the requirement to provide services on each contract will weaken the marketability of the network to managed care plans. This same consideration applies to the physicians' ability to opt out of the physicians' side of the agreement. In providing its services to managed care plans, the hospital should agree with the PHO to provide those services using the same standards as offered to any other patient. Nondiscrimination concepts should be employed which prohibit the hospital from discriminating against protected classes of individuals and prohibiting discrimination based upon the source of payment for services rendered. These types of provisions are typically found in managed care agreements, and including

The physician-hospital organization

them here will allow the parties to pre-empt much of the same discussion in the negotiations with managed care plans. In the relationship with the PHO, the hospital should agree to provide services necessary to perform its obligations and to provide such encounter data as is necessary to monitor services provided by physicians under various managed care agreements.

Another critical area to be covered in the hospital-PHO relationship is compensation and billing. The compensation arrangement depends upon the provisions of the specific managed care agreements. Detailed compensation provisions, therefore, cannot be negotiated between the PHO and the hospital, but will be found in the payer agreements. Compensation can be provided to hospitals under a variety of mechanisms, including discounted fee for service, per diem, diagnosis-related group, capitation, and various compensation provisions will be specified in the applicable managed care agreements. As a corollary to the compensation provisions, the relationship must specify that a hospital cannot seek reimbursement from eligible persons, as reimbursement to the hospital can only be made by a health plan, except for copayments, coinsurance or deductibles billed in accordance with the terms of the particular managed care plan. This type of provision is usually required by state law for the protection of subscribers or eligible persons who should not be required to pay twice for their benefits.

When an eligible person becomes ineligible for covered services, the hospital should be allowed to deal with patients directly for care that is rendered after plan eligibility ceases. The challenge in managed care contracting is to have sufficient notice from managed care plans to determine when this coverage ceases. Accordingly, the managed care agreements negotiated by the PHO should seek to limit the ability of managed care plans to delete retroactively covered individuals. Retroactive deletions allow managed care plans to notify the hospital of lack of coverage long after the occurrence of loss of coverage. Because health plans themselves often do not receive notice from employers concerning loss of coverage for individual employees, managed care plans will seek to put this risk upon the hospital. Often the best that can be achieved in this area is a limitation on the time period during which managed care plans may make this retroactive deletion. These limitations will be negotiated in the specific agreements with the health plan that are entered into by the PHO.

In structuring the service relationship with a hospital, the PHO also must make clear that it is not an insurer or guarantor of the responsibilities of any managed care plan. The parties should clarify that the PHO is neither an insurer nor a liable party responsible to make or deny payments of any claims, or to make coverage decisions. Those types of issues are the responsibility of the managed care plan and the PHO must avoid liability to the hospital, just as it avoids liability to the individual practicing physician who is a member of the network for this activity.

In creating the contracting network relationship with the hospital, the PHO should require the hospital to be bound by and comply with all applicable state and federal laws and regulations, and also should obligate the hospital to use its best efforts to require physicians to prescribe generic pharmaceuticals in accordance with managed care plans.

Just as physician licensure is a critical component to maintaining a valid network, hospital accreditation also is required for the network to be successful. Hospitals should represent that they are accredited by the standard accrediting organizations and the hospital should be required to maintain such accreditation or certification. Failure to maintain this accreditation should give the PHO the option to terminate the agreement. The hospital also should represent to the PHO that it has taken steps to determine whether physicians who are on the medical staff of the hospital are licensed in the state and have been credentialed appropriately. The PHO should be given the ability at reasonable times to review and audit credentialling files of the hospital in accordance with state confidentiality requirements. In addition, the hospital should agree to provide the PHO and the plans with a summary of credentials of each physician who is a participating physician in the physicians' organization and who has staff privileges at the hospital.

Maintaining records as part of the PHO network is also an important obligation. Clinical records of managed care participants should be regarded as confidential and the PHO and the hospital should comply with all applicable federal and state law and regulations regarding those records. The hospital should agree to furnish records and documentation and to cooperate with the PHO and managed care plans in the quality assurance and utilization management programs with respect to the release of records and information exchanges necessary for these programs. In addition, the hospital should agree to provide the PHO and managed care plans with reasonable access to specified clinical and medical records of managed care participants that are maintained by the hospital upon reasonable notice. The release or access to such records should be allowed only upon compliance with all applicable laws and regulations, including the securing of consent from the patient by the party seeking this access.

The hospital should agree to participate in the implementation of grievance procedures established by the PHO and to assist the PHO in taking appropriate corrective action. The hospital may be required under these provisions to implement the grievance procedures of the PHO and the health plan. The PHO will, if successful, be involved in these grievance procedures that are usually the exclusive domain of managed care plans. Because the PHO will have an expanded role in this area, and the hospital will be a participant in the PHO, the hospital will have more input into these programs than has historically been the case. Because grievance procedures are often required by state law regulating health maintenance organizations, a review of that law will be necessary to determine whether the PHO can have a role in this process.

Another central element to be considered in the relationship between the hospital and the PHO is the insurance and liability area. The hospital must maintain general liability and professional liability insurance. The amount of coverage will vary depending upon the current coverage limits of the hospital and the reasonable requirements of the PHO. In general, the hospital will have made this coverage decision independent of its actions or relationship with the PHO, and the PHO should be willing to accept the decision of the hospital with respect to the appropriate level of the insurance coverage that should be maintained by the hospital. The PHO, however, should receive advance notification of any modification or cancellation of the insurance policy of the hospital. The PHO should not be exposed to the risk of being responsible for the liability that may be caused by an uninsured hospital. The hospital-PHO agreement can avoid many of the problems associated with managed care contracting by not requiring that the insurer be approved by the managed care plan and by not requiring that the managed care plan specify the coverage levels. A managed care plan should not be allowed to specify these levels or requirements in its agreement with the PHO.

Another critical liability issue is whether the parties should assume some indemnification responsibilities. Because of the potential exposure for malpractice claims on the entire contracting network, it is important to have provisions in this agreement which specify the potential liability of each of the participants. Often in the managed care context, managed care plans will require or at least attempt to require hospitals to enter into indemnification clauses. These indemnification clauses allow the managed care plan to be reimbursed for its out-of-pocket expenses that may be occasioned by it being named as a defendant in a lawsuit for professional malpractice against the hospital. These types of indemnification agreements which allow for reimbursement by the hospital to the managed care plan are often not covered by the malpractice policies of the hospital. These types of obligations are often deemed to be "liabilities assumed under contract" and coverage for expenses associated with this liability is often refused by liability carriers. Because of the lack of insurance coverage for these indemnification clauses, the hospital and the PHO should try to avoid making these types of agreements. Accordingly, the agreement between the hospital and the PHO should specify that the parties are each responsible for their own liabilities. Under this approach, neither party indemnifies the other and neither party is responsible for either the liability itself or for defending or paying for the defense of another party.

The participation of the hospital in the PHO contracting network will require the hospital to participate in quality assurance and utilization management programs, as well as comply with rules and regulations established by the PHO. The goal of the PHO is to have a much more expanded role in these programs. This expanded role will be a positive development for PHO participants, but will be resisted by managed care plans in the negotiating process. As part of the obligation to maintain a quality panel of hospital and physician providers, the PHO must require the hospital to comply with quality assurance and utilization management programs. Without this requirement, the quality of the provider panel cannot be monitored or maintained, thus decreasing the ability of the managed care plan to monitor services to its eligible subscribers. To the extent that the PHO-hospital agreement does not address these issues, the managed care agreement most certainly will and it will be upon the terms of the managed care plan rather than the PHO.

The PHO agreement also should allow the amendment or modification of the quality assurance and utilization management program, or rules and regulations by providing notice in advance to the hospital of substantive amendments. Just as in the participating physician agreement, the mechanism for making these changes should be essentially fair to the hospital, by giving advance notice and by allowing the hospital to opt out of any particular change during that notice period. If the hospital rejects the amendment, the PHO should have, as it did for physicians, the option to terminate the agreement, but during the period prior to termination of the agreement, the modification should not be given effect. This type of provision is similar to what is typically found in managed care agreements, but it does provide an element of fairness to the hospital for these potential changes, particularly given the involvement of the hospital in PHO governance.

To establish a long term relationship with the hospital, the PHO agreement should specify the term of the relationship. Accordingly, a five to 10 year agreement, consistent with the physicians' organization-PHO relationship, should be utilized with automatic renewals of like periods. Success of the PHO will depend in large part on the continued availability of the hospital. A long term relationship should indicate a commitment of the parties to make the PHO successful by requiring the hospital to be a member of the network.

The agreement also should specify how it can be terminated for default. In some circumstances, such as loss of accreditation or licensure of the hospital, termination should be immediate. In most other circumstances, however, the termination should be upon a notice period of 60 to 90 days and a similar period during which the opportunity to rectify the default will be allowed. While the PHO may desire a shorter time period for termination based upon failure of performance, the fact that both the physicians' organization and the hospital will comprise the PHO means that this provision should be reasonable. The relationship also should allow the hospital the option to terminate the agreement in the event the PHO fails to cure its default.

The parties should consider, just as in the PHO-physician organizations' agreement, whether the parties should be allowed to terminate the agreement at any time without cause. For instance, allowing the parties to terminate the agreement without cause upon prior notice of one year in essence makes the agreement a one year as opposed to a five or 10 year agreement. In reality, however, the PHO relationship should probably be a long one and consideration should be given to eliminating this early option to terminate without cause by allowing termination during the five or 10 year term of the agreement only for cause.

The effect of the termination of the relationship also should be specified. In general, the provisions should specify that the obligations of the party as of the termination date consist of only those obligations which have accrued as a result of the performance of the agreement. Just as in the PHO-physicians' organization agreement, this is a fairly limited provision regarding obligations that may occur after the termination of the relationship. Managed care plans will be expected to require a longer period of time for the transfer of their patients out of the relationship. In fact, some managed care plans require up to one year to have their patients moved out of the managed care relationship with a particular provider. Because the individual employer groups and eligible persons are covered by one year agreements, many managed care plans desire to assure that coverage of those individuals at a particular hospital which was made available to employer and eligible persons in the enrollment period be made available throughout the contract period. These provisions will be negotiated between the PHO and the managed care plan, but the hospital, because it is only utilized for inpatient stays, should have more success in cutting off its post contract exposure to those patients who are inpatients at the time of contract termination than individual physicians.

The status of the parties also should be covered in any agreement between the hospital and the PHO. The parties should be independent contractors. Any other relationship might impose liability on one of the parties for the actions of the other party. Employer-employee and agent-principal relationships should be avoided because of the liability which such relationships create. Independent contractors are not responsible for the actions of the other party and the hospital-PHO relationship should be characterized as an independent contractor relationship.

The relationship of the hospital with other payers should be specified in the agreement just as it was specified in the physicians' organization-PHO agreement. The hospital should agree that in the event the PHO enters into an agreement with the managed care plan, that it will not enter into a separate agreement with that payer and that if the hospital is a party to a current agreement with that managed care plan that it will terminate that agreement as soon as possible following execution of the PHO agreement but, in any event, not later than the conclusion of the current term of that agreement. By requiring this procedure, the PHO will ensure that the hospital and physicians will work together in a network, and that the ability of a hospital to work independent of this relationship should be minimized. In constructing the relationship with the hospital, the PHO should consider whether the hospital should be prohibited from joining other networks. In general, the hospital should probably be prohibited from creating another relationship with other physicians' organizations. This prohibition should be the same as imposed on the physicians' organization. The advice of antitrust counsel must be obtained, however, before making final decisions on this issue.

The final consideration in constructing the hospital-PHO agreement is providing that managed care plans can enforce the terms of the relationship between the PHO and the hospital. This type of provision is important in creating the contractual network. In many instances, the PHO will have a direct contractual relationship with the managed care plan and the managed care plan will be more likely to accept the contractual relationships that comprise the PHO contracting network if the managed care plan has the ability to enforce compliance with that network if the PHO fails to do so.

The relationship with managed care plans

The principal purpose for the creation of the physician-hospital organization is to create and operate a contracting network for managed care plans. The relationships previously discussed have accomplished the creation of this network. The final step for PHO operations is the implementation of the business plan of the PHO by creating specific relationships with the managed care plans. While many of these relationships will be influenced by the provisions of particular state law with respect to the regulation of managed care plans, and while many HMOs will seek to create this relationship using their standard agreements, it is important for the PHO to begin with a proactive approach regarding these particular issues by setting the negotiating agenda. Creating this agenda means developing a standard contracting approach and materials for the relationship with the managed care plan. It is important, therefore, to specify the type of provisions that are acceptable to the PHO in the managed care

The physician-hospital organization

contracting environment. The creation of this relationship between managed care plans and the physician-hospital organization and its contracting network is illustrated in Figure IV on page 186.

To create this contracting network relationship with the managed care plan, it will be necessary to create a contractual relationship with that plan. The creation of this managed care relationship can occur in one of several ways. From a practical point of view, one agreement between PHO and managed care plan will centralize the relationship and will utilize the contracting network that has been formed by the PHO. In order to coordinate the efforts of both the hospital and the physicians' organizations with the PHO, this approach will make the PHO an integral party in the relationship with the managed care plan. In any type of relationship, therefore, the PHO should be a party to the principal agreement with the managed care plan. This type of involvement of the PHO will allow the PHO to structure the relationship and will allow the PHO to terminate the relationship if that decision is made. Accordingly, under any circumstances, the PHO and the managed care plan should have an agreement with each other.

In some circumstances, in addition to the PHO managed care agreement, the managed care plan or state law will require actual provider agreements to be created between the managed care plan and the physicians' organization and hospital. Under this scenario, three agreements are actually required: the first being the overall master agreement between the physician-hospital organization and the managed care plan and, secondly and thirdly, the specific provider agreements between managed care plan and physicians' organization, and the managed care plan and hospital. The rationale for these additional agreements is that because the physicians' organization, for example, will often be a professional corporation or association authorized to arrange physician services under state law, it will be necessary for that entity, as the entity authorized by state law to provide those services, to become the contracting entity for physician services. Some managed care plans also may prefer a direct contractual relationship between the managed care plan and the physicians' organization.

In addition, just as the physicians' organization as a professional corporation is the licensed entity under state law, the hospital is, in fact, the licensed entity to provide hospital services under state law. This licensure and authorization to provide these services may convince the managed care plan that a separate contract in addition to the managed care plan-PHO contract should be entered into directly by the hospital.

The actual structure of these documents therefore will be dictated by a combination of factors, including state law, the respective bargaining positions of the parties and the overall relationship of the parties. For purposes of discussion, however, it is assumed that the relationship will be embodied in one contract with the PHO and managed care plan. To the extent that these relationships must be divided into subsidiary agreements, the concepts discussed below should be incorporated as appropriate into the correct document.

In creating the relationship between the PHO and the managed care plan, the general principle should be adopted that the contract between the parties should be the comprehensive document which governs the relationship for the actual provision of care by the providers in the PHO to the members in the health plans established by the managed care company. The document therefore should supersede any additional documents that the managed care plan may require be entered into by the hospital and a physicians' organization. Because the PHO will have been formed to allow coordination between both physician and hospital interests, the contract with the managed care plan and the PHO should allow the joint governing mechanism of the PHO to speak on behalf of the constituent members of the PHO.

The services provided by the parties should form the initial basis for outlining their relationship. The health plan should solicit and negotiate health care plans with individuals and organizations. The PHO should arrange for the provision of covered services in accordance with its contracting network which has been established. These network participation agreements should be attached as exhibits to the managed care-PHO agreement and, accordingly, should be accepted by the managed care plan as the way in which care will be provided to its eligible persons. By creating the network in this fashion, the PHO will set the agenda in negotiating with the managed care plan, and make more likely the acceptance of the provisions contained in the PHO prepared agreements.

It is important from the perspective of the PHO that it be recognized as arranging for the provision of covered services as opposed to providing them. From a licensure perspective, the organizations that are licensed to provide the actual covered services must provide those services, and from a professional and malpractice liability perspective, those organizations which provide this service should have the responsibility for providing those services. Limiting the role of the PHO to an arranger of health care, as opposed to a provider, also will limit its potential liability for these services. The PHO also should not be responsible for the failure of the hospital, physicians' organization or individual physicians to provide the covered services. The health plan, correspondingly, should agree to comply with all applicable state and federal laws and regulatory requirements.

The second component critical in establishing the PHO-managed care relationship is compensation and billing.

Because the PHO will be an intermediary between the health plan and the providers, the health plan, not the PHO, should be responsible for

The physician-hospital organization

paying the physician and hospital providers. The PHO could, in fact, act as an intermediary for this compensation by which it could distribute the funds to the hospital and the physicians' organization or individual physicians, but the liability for non-payment should rest solely with the health plan rather than the PHO. A compensation schedule should be attached to the agreement showing the method of payment from the health plan to the hospital and to the participating providers, respectively.

In determining the payment terms for the provider panel, the PHO must negotiate with the managed care plan. In general, services reimbursed by the managed care plan to physicians will either be on a capitation or a fee-for-service basis. It is essential from the point of view of the participating physicians that the fee-for-service payment schedules be attached and made a part of the agreement. How these schedules are calculated and how they set forth the payment terms should be reviewed closely. In addition, the time period when such payment is made also should be specified under the agreement. For capitation arrangements, a specific date that is as close as possible to the first of every month for which services are to be provided should be when payment should be made to the physician.

The PHO should agree, just as its participating providers should agree, that it will not bill, charge or seek to collect, any remuneration, or have any recourse against eligible persons other than through the managed care plan. Reimbursement to providers is made only by the health plan except for copayments, co-insurance or deductibles billed in accordance with the terms of a health care plan. This provision is usually required by state law for the protection of eligible persons who should not be required to pay twice for their benefits. Including this obligation here will confirm what has already been established by the PHO in its network agreements with the hospital and the physicians' organization.

Another critical business point in the creation of a contracting relationship between the managed care plan and the PHO is credentialing and accreditation of the network participants of the PHO. In general, it is essential for the ability of the health plan to compete in the marketplace and to acquire contracts for managed care services with employers and other entities that the services it arranges to be provided meet a certain quality and be performed by properly credentialed providers. The PHO, therefore, should be obligated to review the credentials of physicians and the licensing and accreditation of the hospital on a regular basis. In addition, the PHO should require participating physicians to represent and warrant to the PHO that the credentialling information provided to the PHO is true and accurate, and should require participating providers to notify the PHO of any material changes in that information. Likewise, the PHO should obligate the hospital to represent and warrant that all licensing and accreditation information provided to the PHO is true and should require notification by the hospital to the PHO in the event of any significant change in that information.

Confidentiality of patient information is another central component of the PHO-managed care plan relationship. The PHO and the managed care plan should agree that the clinic records of individuals covered under the health plan should be regarded as confidential, and the PHO and health plan should agree to comply with all applicable federal and state laws and regulations regarding such records. The PHO should, subject to this obligation of confidentiality, cooperate with a health plan to facilitate information and record exchanges necessary for the managed care plan to monitor quality assurance and utilization management programs. The insurance requirements, and the liability of the participants in the managed care arrangement, are also covered in any relationship between the PHO and a managed care plan. Pursuant to the network documents created by the PHO, participating providers will be obligated to obtain and maintain comprehensive general liability and professional liability insurance. In its agreement with the managed care plan, the PHO should be obligated to require participating providers and hospitals to purchase and maintain this insurance. Many of the common problems associated with managed care contracting should be avoided by not requiring specific levels, by not requiring the insurer be approved by the managed care plan, and by not requiring that the managed care plan specify the coverage levels. All of these are common pitfalls contained in managed care contracts and the provisions of the agreement prepared by the PHO for the managed care plan should eliminate those drawbacks and place the coverage decisions within the domain of the decision making of the PHO.

In addition, this agreement will specify the liability, or lack thereof, of each party for any claims or actions that might arise out of rendering care or the managed care relationship itself. Managed care plans often insist that they should be indemnified by the provider network or providers for any loss that may be experienced by the managed care plan because of care rendered by providers. The usual lack of insurance for indemnification provisions has been discussed previously under the physicians' organization and PHO contracting network documents. The same position taken with respect to those obligations imposed upon physicians and hospitals should be set forth in this agreement. The PHO should, therefore, resist the effort of a managed care plan to require the PHO, physicians and hospitals to enter into indemnification clauses.

A PHO should take the initiative in framing the issues in this area by insisting upon provisions which specify that neither party is indemnifying the other party and that neither party is responsible for the liability itself, or for defending or paying for the defense of the other party. The argument of the managed care plan that the indemnification arrangement should be reciprocal and, therefore, appropriately placed on both parties, should be avoided. In general, indemnification clauses will favor the managed care plan, because the provider of the care, that being physicians or the hospital, will have the most potential malpractice exposure for lawsuits. Because they are more likely to be a party that may be called upon to make the indemnification payment, physicians and hospitals and their network, through the PHO, should avoid making this obligation even where reciprocity is offered.

The obligation of the managed care plan to institute grievance procedures is often required by state law regulating health maintenance organizations. A review of that law will be necessary to determine whether the PHO can have a role in this process. In general, however, a PHO should attempt to insert itself in this grievance process and expand its role over what has traditionally been the exclusive domain of the health plan. Accordingly, the agreement should propose that the PHO would require the physicians' organization and hospital to implement grievance procedures established by the PHO and the health plan. It also should require the PHO to require the physicians' organization and the hospital to comply with all final determinations made by the PHO and the health plan pursuant to these grievance procedures. While these types of provisions do not give the PHO exclusive control in this process, they attempt to insert the PHO in this process to assure fundamental fairness to the providers who are members of the PHO network.

Managed care plans have, as a prerequisite for their business operations, quality assurance, utilization management programs, and rules and regulations for the operation of their plans. Traditionally in managed care contracting, the managed care plan obligates the providers to abide by these programs, with little input, and certainly no modifications suggested by providers. The approach to be taken by the PHO should illustrate one of the benefits of being a participant in the PHO, however. Accordingly, the relationship proposed by the PHO to a managed care plan should envision a much more expanded role for the PHO in the quality assurance and utilization management programs, as well as in the rules and regulations of the managed care plan. This expanded role will be a positive development for PHO participants, but will be resisted by the managed care plan in the negotiating process.

In creating a relationship between the PHO and the managed care plan, the parties must decide how long the relationship will last. In general, in markets where managed care plans are just beginning, it is likely that the parties will prefer a one year agreement. This short term arrangement will allow the parties to begin to know each other better and their respective operations, and to evaluate whether a longer term relationship is feasible. A short term means the parties will need to evaluate quickly whether the relationship should be renewed. More mature managed care marketplaces need the stability of these longer term agreements, and it can be anticipated that as the PHO operations mature and as managed care relationships extend over a period of years, that longer term agreements will be negotiated. Until the long term nature of a relationship can be established, however, the parties will often decide that a shorter relationship, such as a period of one year, will be preferable.

Termination of the relationship is also a topic that should be considered in the establishment of the relationship. While few like to think of the impact of a potential failure of the relationship, it is important from a planning and a risk management perspective to specify termination provisions. In general, before any agreement is terminated, notice should be given before default is declared. In addition, an advance notice period, perhaps 60 days along with a 60-day period to cure, should be considered, for it will provide a long period to rectify problems associated with performance. In general, this long notice should favor the PHO and the participating providers as they will, in fact, be providing the care under the agreement. The perspective of the health plan may be different on these particular provisions and the managed care plan may attempt to negotiate a shorter period of time for termination based upon failure of performance and will likely insist on immediate termination for loss of licensure or insurance. The PHO also should have the option to terminate the agreement in the event of failure of the managed care plan to cure its default, with a shorter notice and cure period for failure of the health plan to pay for services rendered.

Another issue to be considered in the termination context is the obligations of the parties that may exist after the effective date of termination. In general, the most favorable position for the PHO to advance is that in the event of termination of the agreement, all rights and obligations of the parties will cease upon the effective date of termination, except for those which have already accrued as a result of the operation of the agreement. This is a fairly limited provision with respect to the obligations that may occur after termination of the relationship. Managed care plans can be expected to negotiate for a longer period of time for the transfer of their patients out of the relationship. Other options to consider are requiring the termination to affect all those but subscribers who are hospitalized at the date of termination and only to the extent of that hospitalization, or to require individuals to be treated until their course of illness is over. The exact nature of the ongoing relationship of the physicians and hospitals must be negotiated by the PHO as it negotiates the relationship with the managed care plan.

Chapter 11

Physician-hospital integration issues

Medical group affiliation with a hospital or management company is another major way in which the delivery of medical care is being redefined through the integration process. This combination results in the formation of a strategic alliance between medical group and hospital, or between medical group and management company. This hospital/management company provides administrative expertise and assists the physicians in their practice of medicine by providing expert business leadership.

This chapter explores the preliminary issues found in the formation of these relationship. Unless otherwise specified, the entity providing these services will be referred to as a hospital, regardless of whether the entity is owned by a hospital, a joint venture of hospital and physicians, or a management company, and regardless of whether the medical group remains a separate entity, is an independent contractor providing medical services to a hospital formed foundation, or is absorbed in a medical practice division of the hospital. Regardless of the form, therefore, physicians in this model will establish an affiliation with non-physicians to administer the practice of medicine. The three integration models, the management services organization, the medical division/employment model and the foundation model all have these preliminary issues in common.

The concept

The hospital affiliation concept usually consists of four elements. First, the hospital will acquire (by purchase or donation) most of the assets or stock of the medical practice. This acquisition of assets or stock allows the hospital to obtain the necessary supplies, furniture and fixtures to conduct its business. The advantage to the medical group and physicians is that the sale often allows these physicians to obtain cash for the equity in their practice. An acquisition will enable physicians who have spent a career building the organization, a one-time return on those efforts that would otherwise go uncompensated if the practice is kept intact. This one-time benefit will be attractive to physicians given the increasing pressures on physician compensation that are present in the medical practice arena.

The second component of the hospital affiliation concept is that the hospital will provide administrative services for physicians and capital for expansion. The hospital will assume the day-to-day administrative aspects of the business operation of a medical practice whether the medical group, the hospital or a foundation is the "provider" of medical services. By providing much needed access to capital, the hospital will provide the financial ability to renovate existing facilities and take advantage of new opportunities for ancillaries and ventures. By allowing the medical group to concentrate primarily on its medical practice, the hospital can remove the bureaucratic frustrations that physicians have about the business side of a medical practice. Management depth and economies of scale that a larger organization may provide mean that the business operation of the practice can enter a new level of sophistication.

Third, an affiliation may allow the medical group to limit or eliminate its exposure to the real estate marketplace. A hospital may be in a position to acquire the real estate of the medical group, thereby eliminating it as one of the major concerns of the medical group. In other circumstances where the medical group does not own its property, the hospital can effectively substitute its presence for that of the medical group in the lease with the owner of the property.

Fourth, the hospital affiliation concept will give the medical practice an opportunity to examine its internal workings and reorganize itself. It is this opportunity which may prove the most important long-term benefit for the future success of the medical practice, regardless of the affiliation model. Governance issues can be reevaluated. A new structure for physician relationships can be implemented. Compensation systems can be modified to reflect current and future concerns. Quality assurance and practice concerns can receive increased emphasis. All of these factors mean that the new relationship created with a hospital will enable the medical practice to transform itself to a higher level of efficient operation and vision that might be lacking without the catalyst that the affiliation may bring.

Existing administrators of a group should not view this relationship as a threat, but as an opportunity. By becoming part of a larger organization, the existing administrator can add depth to the management team. The hospital should view the existing manager as an important asset that should be incorporated into the management structure, rather than one to be replaced.

The strategic alliance

Having decided to explore seriously a hospital affiliation, the medical group should determine if the combination is in the best strategic interests of the group and if the parties have similar operational philosophies. From the perspective of the hospital, the target medical group also must "fit" with its goals. Examining whether the parties have this synergy early in the process is important, as the lack of synergy and common vision will put any transaction at increased risk for later failure. In addition, where the medical group is asked to consider an affiliation with a hospital which has already affiliated with several other medical groups, an evaluation of the "fit" with these other physicians must be accomplished.

Both the medical group and the hospital must determine their strategic goals for any combination. The same planning process that results in a strategic plan undertaken in the case of a merger between medical groups must be undertaken by a medical group and a hospital that are considering affiliation. Each party must evaluate whether the combination fits within the long-term strategy of that party. A hospital affiliation may enable coordinated approaches to medical care delivery, joint direct and managed care bids and contracts, and the development of ancillary services and projects that can make both the hospital and the medical group more competitive in the marketplace. Combinations with an entity owned by outside investors may have a different focus. Access to capital, management talent with direct experience in ambulatory care and the need to maintain neutrality in a community with respect to hospitals may all point to an affiliation with an investor-owned entity.

Medical groups that identify a need to invest in the affiliation may find ownership of a management company attractive. This combination allows a sharing of the profits obtained from management operations. While this type of affiliation may provide the same strategic and competitive advantages found in a hospital or management company-owned affiliation, it contains many of the same risks associated with independent medical practice which physicians increasingly may seek to avoid.

As part of this preliminary process, the management team used by the hospital must be evaluated thoroughly. An evaluation of the knowledge of the management team of health care and medical group/ambulatory care operations is vitally important. Medical groups must examine this issue closely, as while hospital administration often has a keen knowledge of inpatient care operations and health care in general, it often has little understanding of successful administration of ambulatory care and the practice of medicine. The proposed management team must either be familiar with ambulatory care or must recruit individuals who have an understanding of the ambulatory health care business. Where a hospital is involved in the affiliation process, the existing medical group administrator may be the one with the most significant ambulatory care experience. Management company affiliations usually do not have this weakness, as their personnel usually have extensive ambulatory care experience.

The personal character of the management team also must be probed. Are the individuals to be employed of sufficient character and integrity that they will bring credit to the reputation of the medical group as its representative in the community? An evaluation must be made whether the long-term interests of the group will be put on equal footing by the management team with the interests of the hospital. Is concern about the group's long-term success readily apparent from the management team?

The medical group also must convince itself that the management team and hospital ownership recognize that a true partnership with a medical group should be necessary. If so, the satisfaction and success of the group should be recognized as being essential to the success of the hospital in building an integrated delivery system. Recognition of the parallel incentives of both parties and the intertwining of their fates for successful operation must be understood by all parties in the relationship.

During the initial stages of discussion of any proposed affiliation, an examination of the financial condition of the hospital must be undertaken. Financial statements of the hospital must be analyzed to determine its financial credit-worthiness and strength. A weak hospital partner with inability to access capital will severely impair the future operations of the medical group. Weak financial condition of outside investors will have the same effect. A comprehensive review and evaluation of the financial health of the proposed partner is necessary to determine whether the partnership will begin and be maintained on a strong financial basis.

If the affiliation partner is headquartered in another location, the medical group must visit the headquarters. If the affiliation partner manages multiple operations, the medical group must visit those other locations and personally interview a variety of physicians and management personnel. These visits will allow a personal evaluation of the management style, personality and satisfaction of existing physicians with the affiliation. The financial health and success of other operations affiliated with the hospital should be reviewed carefully, along with the track record of expansion and provision of capital for those other operations.

The management style of the affiliation entity also should be evaluated critically by the medical group. How are the decisions to be made in the arrangement? Will the management team assigned to perform its function be given efficient autonomy to accomplish streamlined decision making? Whether a hospital or an outside investor owns the entity, the concern will be the same, as excessive involvement by another layer of management will impair the decision-making process. If the management entity is from another geographic location, that entity must recognize that providing medical services is essentially a local endeavor and that local concerns, markets, customs and values must be recognized.

The operational concept to be used by the hospital also must be probed at this early stage. What are the plans for involvement of physicians in policy decisions in the combined operations? The business philosophy of the hospital must take into account the need to work cooperatively with physicians. Together they must develop proper incentives for the physicians and hospital to work together to increase revenues and hold down expenses. The responsiveness of the hospital to the needs of physicians must be shown, otherwise a "we" vs. "they" mentality will likely develop. This dichotomy, if allowed to occur, will result in the deterioration of the overall enthusiasm and morale of physicians in the relationship, and is a particular risk in the medical division/employment model where physicians are paid a salary. The hospital, therefore, should be able to demonstrate a concrete plan, backed by experience, that it is attentive to physician needs. While a hospital can be expected to provide business leadership, it must recognize that it is, in fact, providing a "service" to the physicians in the development and furtherance of their medical practice. While it may be difficult to discern answers to these types of issues in the "sales" phase of a relationship, answers to these questions will dictate the future likelihood of success of the combined effort.

The medical group also should conduct a comprehensive due diligence investigation of the hospital. This due diligence process will require the hospital to provide certain detailed information concerning its operations in addition to the financial information previously discussed. Information concerning the critical factors such as recent acquisitions, pending investigations and lawsuits, expansion plans, relationships with other entities and any other operational issues affecting overall operations, must be requested from the hospital. The willingness to disclose this information is an important indicator of the openness of the hospital, and any reluctance to release reasonably-requested information should be reviewed with suspicion. The medical group, once receiving this information, must be prepared to evaluate it critically and must not hesitate to use outside financial experts to make a critical analysis of the information. The analysis of this information, the compilation of the results, and the report of this due diligence process, must be completed with sufficient speed so the information can be useful in making a decision whether to consummate the relationship, and in the negotiating process.

The affiliation proposal process

The development of the offer of the hospital to the medical group will proceed somewhat concurrently with the due diligence investigation. The offer often will combine the proposal to purchase the medical group at a stated price and a proposed affiliation whereby the hospital will provide a range of services for the practice of medicine. In order to make an offer effectively, the hospital should undertake a comprehensive evaluation of the medical practice of the group. This evaluation will require the hospital to spend significant effort and resources in evaluating the financial operations of the group, not only by review of financial statements, but also by interviewing management personnel and physicians who participate in the medical practice. The assets of the group should be reviewed, coupled with an evaluation of the worth of those assets. While a financial review is necessary for compilation of an offer, the review of the medical group also should evaluate the position of the group in the marketplace, an analysis of physician personalities and their willingness to cooperate in a true "partnership." These intangible factors are as important as the financial position of the medical group in assessing the future success of the new affiliation.

The hospital should consider a variety of factors before arriving at a fair purchase price for the group. While physicians most often will desire to receive funds for their practice, in other circumstances medical groups may wish to donate their assets or stock to a nonprofit entity and receive a tax deduction. In addition to the condition of the assets themselves, hospitals also will evaluate a number of competitive factors concerning the group. As the true value of the group being purchased is dependent upon the overall success of the group in the future, a realistic offer for the purchase should be something more than merely the book value of assets that have been depreciated more rapidly than their usefulness has been expended. The amount must be realistic, however, as the purchase price will have a direct impact on the ability of the entity to price its services and maintain ongoing business operations.

The factors that should be considered by a hospital and evaluated critically by the medical group include the following. Group size and mix of specialties will be important factors. Larger size groups with a comprehensive range of specialties or primary care groups with a comprehensive range of subspecialties will be more attractive than single subspecialty groups. Larger groups have the ability to become significant players in a marketplace by providing a range of services which attracts third party payers. Larger groups also can achieve economies of scales for management operations. This analysis may be tempered somewhat where hospitals are building multispecialty groups or "clinics without walls" to which single specialty groups that fit a strategic niche will be attracted.

Revenue generated by the group is another important indicator of financial success. The productivity of a group should be evaluated critically in terms of physician willingness to work and the ability to generate revenue. The balance sheet of the group, along with profitability and earnings history also must be examined. These factors will indicate the financial condition of the group and future trends with respect to revenue and profitability.

The rate of new patients coming to a group is another important factor which signals growth and a healthy outlook for continued revenue increases. The relationship of the group with its physicians should be examined by evaluating physician turnover and satisfaction with compensation. Physician employment agreements and restrictive covenants also will need to be evaluated. These factors will provide a useful evaluation of the satisfaction of the most important asset of the medical group, its physicians.

On a larger scale, the competitive position of the group in the marketplace vis-a-vis other medical groups and its relationship with hospitals must be reviewed. A group which represents the leading specialty or is perceived as the market leader by other physicians or patients in the community will be in a stronger competitive position than a group viewed otherwise, and hence, will be a more valuable partner.

The payer mix of the group also should be reviewed. Heavy dependence on Medicare may signal future steep revenue cuts, whereas a significant presence of alternative delivery systems may indicate a heavily competitive environment, with the risk of large swings in patient volume if a contract is lost. A larger number of private pay patients may indicate continued strength in revenue growth.

As this discussion indicates, the true value of a medical group is difficult to determine and is a function of the combination of a number of factors. Groups must avoid an inflated view of their self worth, even though that view is often prevalent. Outside assistance will be acquired from independent financial advisors in order for the group to develop a realistic assessment of the offer to purchase, and for the hospital to arrive at a fair price. Fraud and abuse concerns will make this independent third party evaluation necessary.

The hospital proposal will contain an explanation of how the hospital will deliver the services to physicians. Critical components of this portion of a proposal will be how the hospital and physicians will be compensated and how the new venture will be governed. The offer should contain an explanation of how compensation will be calculated, and how any bonus will be paid to reward above-average performance. The appropriateness of the assumptions used must be tested.

The way in which the hospital and physicians will govern the relationship must be reviewed. Is a board of directors established that has authority over the relationship? How are decisions that affect both hospital and medical group made? Often, a formal body that combines management and physician representatives will be effective in maintaining communication and leading to collaborative decision making. This joint body may be part of the board of directors, or an independent body that may not have any legal relationship to the governing structure of the hospital itself. However, through an affiliation agreement, this independent body is able to make decisions which will then be implemented by the administrative team.

A proposal also should contain an explanation of what obligations will be undertaken by the hospital under an affiliation agreement. Will all of the former administrative and nursing personnel associated with the operations of the medical group be hired? The hospital should be expected to perform maintenance functions to repair the facilities and pay the obligations generated by the operations of the medical practice.

The group must evaluate the proposed method of passing along overhead costs from the hospital itself. Are these costs allocated fairly to physicians? What services are to be provided and can limits be placed on the ability to pass through these costs?

The group must be prepared to analyze the proposed funding of the physician compensation pool. The receipt of funds into this pool will impact the ability of the physician to operate the compensation system. Are physicians put "on salary," are they guaranteed a certain amount in the form of a bonus, or are they at risk for the amount they receive based upon the profitability of the affiliation? Any potential change necessitated by this method of compensation must be analyzed quickly by the group. Where physicians are paid a salary, this evaluation is still necessary as physicians in that scenario become paid employees of the hospital, with future compensation pool funding still dependent on the success of the medical division.

In order to analyze accurately the financial terms of any proposed offer, the medical group will need to rely on the abilities of its financial advisors. This evaluation is critical in verifying the proposed impact on physician compensation and operations, and to provide an effective negotiating tool by analyzing the financial impact of the affiliation upon medical group profitability. The medical group leadership should commission these financial advisors to evaluate the appropriateness of the sale price. This evaluation will involve a review of the books of the medical group to ensure that all assets are included. An evaluation should be made of the financial strength and revenue generation of the group, and of the proposed purchase price in relation to that analysis. The financial advisor can break down the components of the purchase price so the group can see clearly how the various components of its operation have been valued.

This evaluation process may point out items that are overlooked or undervalued in the opinion of the medical group, and can lead to further upward negotiation of the purchase price. This financial evaluation also will be helpful as it will lead to a strategy for distribution of proceeds. This evaluation of the impact of the sale price on individual physicians can be used as an effective upward negotiating tool to the extent that proceeds are not sufficient to satisfy the needs of all the constituent physicians.

The role of the financial advisor also can be extremely helpful in the evaluation of the compensation arrangement with a hospital. A financial model should be created for operations for the next several years based upon existing operations. A comparison of the operations over a three-year period will provide a frame of reference to evaluate any proposed financial relationship with a hospital. The financial advisors then should undertake an examination of the assumptions made by the hospital in the computation of this compensation. Revenues and expenses of the group must be verified and the assumptions made concerning continued growth, and operations should be specified and evaluated. This evaluation should give the medical group the ability to quantify the "cost" that the medical group will incur in entering into the affiliation. The hospital must be able to quantify the benefits that it brings to the group in light of this financial analysis. This process may lead to further negotiations about the appropriate level of compensation to be paid to the hospital. The final component of the affiliation offer should be a proposal with respect to the real estate relationships of the medical group. The offer of the hospital with respect to real estate will depend in large part upon the real estate ownership situation. If the group owns its real estate or the real estate is owned by a partnership composed of group physicians, the offer may include either an offer to purchase the real estate or to lease it on a long term basis. In many instances, the purchase of real estate in the affiliation process is usually more desirable for the medical group. A purchase will free the physicians from significant financial obligations, will return equity to senior physicians who likely have the predominate interest in the real estate, and will remove an important business risk from the calculus of decision making that physicians must make. Most affiliation proposals will avoid purchasing real estate, given the significant capital costs associated with that investment. To the extent that the group has a significant bargaining position in the proposed relationship, however, it should seriously consider insisting that the real estate be purchased as part of the affiliation.

More often, however, the hospital will propose a long-term lease of the property whereby the hospital will assume the obligations of the group with respect to maintenance, taxes, insurance and other costs associated with the operation of the property. In this case, the establishment of rent must be reviewed closely. The hospital likely will propose a low rental rate because the rental for the property will be a practice expense, and a lower rental rate will make the business operations appear to be more profitable to the hospital and medical group if it still exists in the integration model being utilized. A high rental rate, on the other hand, with frequent escalating clauses, will likely put downward pressure on physician incomes and overall group or medical division profitability. A tradeoff, therefore, must be made with respect to the appropriate rental rate to be charged for leasing the facilities. Groups must evaluate the potential return to a hospital given by this lower rate. Groups that have a disparity in ownership, from physicians who own the real estate to those who are employed, will need to adjust the appropriate rental rate to a level which meets the concerns of both the owners of the property and the practicing physicians. Most groups, however, are driven by physician income and will be predisposed to agree to a lower return on the real property investment as a tradeoff for less pressure on physician income.

The sale of the medical group

The first component of a hospital affiliation entails the sale of the medical group to the hospital. Numerous issues are raised in the sale of the medical group. Initially, the medical group and the hospital must determine whether the sale will entail the assets or the stock of the medical group. The medical group will be required to examine very closely the impact from a tax perspective of the sale. Whether the medical group will prefer a stock or asset sale will depend on which form of transaction will result in the most tax favorable result for the group. Usually the hospital will prefer an asset sale because it will minimize the risk of the hospital assuming unknown liabilities from the medical group. A stock sale poses greater risk for a hospital because, by purchasing the stock of the medical group, it buys the whole organization, including any unknown or undisclosed liabilities. The medical group should negotiate for the type of transaction which minimizes its tax liability.

Based upon the individual circumstances of the medical group, a variety of techniques should be considered to minimize tax liability. The type of the transaction, asset or stock sale, is but one example. Receiving the payment proceeds over a period of years thus spreading the tax years impacted, and use of compensation deductions in paying physicians a portion of the proceeds as compensation, are some of the numerous options that must be evaluated. As specialized tax expertise is required to forecast accurately the tax liabilities associated with the sale, medical groups are well advised to plan to address these issues very early in the process. The results of this work will be reflected in the purchase agreement with respect to how the funds are received by the medical group or individual physician stockholders.

As part of the affiliation proposal process, the hospital will have prepared, undoubtedly, a draft purchase agreement. Preparation of this draft by the hospital is standard practice in acquisitions, as purchasers are usually given the opportunity to prepare the documentation in the format they desire. To the extent the medical group can prepare these documents, it will obtain a tremendous negotiating advantage, as controlling the word processor will allow the medical group to frame the issue in its own words.

The purpose of a purchase agreement is to set forth, in a comprehensive way, the terms and details under which the various assets will be purchased. An asset purchase agreement usually will contain a number of general areas covering various aspects of the sale.

Initially, the parties to the asset or stock purchase agreement must be set forth. In an asset sale, the principal parties to the agreement are the medical group and the hospital. Some hospitals may seek to add individual shareholders of the medical group as parties to the agreement. This approach usually is an attempt to impose personal liability on the physician-owners of the medical group for representations or warranties that later prove to be incorrect. Medical groups and physicians should resist this imposition of personal liability. In the management services model, and in the foundation model, the medical group will continue to exist and this continuing existence gives rise to the primary argument for resisting this personal liability because the continued existence of the medical group should provide a source of funding to cover any loss to the management service organization or the foundation for any breach of warranty. Whether individual physicians are added to the asset purchase agreement, therefore, is a function of the nature of the relationship between medical group and hospital that is being created and the bargaining position of the parties.

In the stock purchase agreement, the principal parties to the agreement are the hospital as the purchaser and the medical group and its stockholders. Stockholders of the medical group are parties to the stock purchase agreement because they own the stock in the medical group being sold. They must be the parties to transfer ownership of the stock to the hospital, and accordingly, face individual liability as the selling party.

In the sale of stock of a medical group, such as in a medical division/ employment model, the medical group will no longer be the operating entity and there will be no ready source of funding to cover any loss to the hospital for any breach of warranty. Accordingly, under this medical division model, the hospital will usually insist upon the creation of some fund out of which warranty claims can be satisfied, and, accordingly, will insist upon adding physicians as parties to the agreement to impose some form of personal liability on the physician.

The first section of an asset or stock purchase agreement will set forth a comprehensive list of definitions. Definitions created in this section will be used throughout the entire agreement and sufficient care should be taken to ensure that these definitions are drafted carefully. For the most part, it is particularly difficult for nonlawyers to begin to read an unfamiliar document and then be met by multiple pages of definitions. These definitions, often complex in and of themselves, add to the confusion of the situation by standing alone, out of context and with no tie-in to any larger concept. To cope with the complexity of these definitions, the recommended strategy for nonlawyers is to read the document first. After the document becomes more familiar, specific reference to the definitions then can be made and better understood.

The agreement will define the specific assets or stock to be acquired. In an asset sale, the agreement will set forth general categories of assets including accounts receivable, fixtures and improvements, equipment, furniture, automobiles and inventory. Specific detailed lists of these assets should be attached to the agreement so the parties may know precisely what is being sold and purchased. In a stock sale, an accurate description of the stock to be sold is required.

A purchase agreement also should specify the assets to be excluded and, therefore, retained by the medical group. For instance, it is important to exclude such items as the employment agreements between the medical group and its physicians (if the affiliation model selected involves the continued use of that separate medical group such as in the management services model or foundation model), the insurance policies of the medical group, managed care or other agreements which require physicians to deliver medical services specified in those agreements (if the medical group will continue to be the provider of care), corporate records of the medical group and any trade names or service marks that the medical group wishes to retain.

The purchase agreement should contain general purchase and sale language which provides that the medical group (or stockholders if a stock sale) agree to sell, and the hospital agrees to purchase the assets or stock of the medical group, as defined in the first section of the agreement. This section should make clear that excluded assets are not part of the transaction and that the assets or stock to be transferred are free and clear of all encumbrances. This lack of encumbrances or liens on the assets or stock is probably the most critical provision of an asset or stock purchase agreement for a purchaser. The hospital will be unwilling to pay for assets or stock that are subject to security interests held by third parties which will decrease the value of the assets or stock received. Much of the due diligence process prior to closing the sale will involve efforts by the medical group to clear claims on its assets or stock to make sure that good title is conveyed to the hospital.

A purchase agreement sets forth the liabilities of the medical group that the hospital will assume or agree to pay, perform or otherwise discharge. One of the main advantages of an affiliation is that the hospital will agree to assume various debts, contracts and other obligations in order to undertake its management and operational functions after the affiliation. This assumption of liabilities will relieve the medical group from most, if not all, of the liabilities on its balance sheet. It is critical, therefore, for the agreement to set forth accurately and completely, all of these obligations to be assumed by the hospital. The asset purchase agreement will provide a place for the listing of these obligations. It also will state that, unless the liabilities are specifically listed in the agreement, the hospital will have no responsibility or liability for any other obligation of the medical group. A critical aspect of preparation for the asset acquisition, therefore, is for the medical group administration to confirm that all liabilities to be assumed by the hospital are specifically listed. In a stock sale, this assumption of liabilities is unnecessary, because a sale and purchase of stock will automatically transfer to the hospital, as purchaser of the stock, the entire business of the medical group.

The asset or stock purchase agreement also will specify the purchase price, and detail the methodology for any adjustments to the purchase price. From the perspective of the medical group and its stockholders, this is the most important part of the agreement. While the purchase price may have been tentatively established during the proposal phase of the transaction, the specifics will be further detailed in the purchase agreement. The cash component of the purchase price will be specified. If the transaction is an asset purchase, the amount of liabilities to be assumed by the hospital will be specified, which will reduce the amount of cash available for distribution by the amount of the assumption.

Another component of the purchase price may be the issuance of shares to the medical group of the corporate stock of the hospital (if a for-profit entity), the management company, or the conveyance of an interest in the affiliation entity itself. In a hospital-related management affiliation, the issuance of the interest may, in fact, result from the creation of a joint venture between the medical group and the hospital whereby the medical group itself takes an equity position in the affiliation entity. In these situations, it is possible that the medical group may be asked to invest a portion of the sale proceeds in the entity. This mechanism allows the medical group to share in the growth and financial success by becoming a stockholder or partner. Of course, where a nonprofit hospital is involved, stock ownership is not available. The mix between the stock or financial interest and cash available for distribution to physicians should balance the short-term interest of providing funds to physicians and the long-term investment in the success of the affiliation which will provide an incentive to physicians to remain affiliated on a long-term basis.

The method of valuing the stock being conveyed also should be closely examined by the medical group. The issuance of stock requires that a per share value be placed upon that stock to allow conversion of a portion of the purchase price allocated to the stock component into an exact number of shares. With respect to an investor-owned hospital, this valuation may be provided by the stock market if the stock is publicly traded. To the extent there is no public market for the stock, however, a financial analysis of the company will need to be made and then translated into a per share value. The assumptions used in this valuation should be clearly specified and then tested by financial advisors retained by the medical group.

To the extent that stock ownership is in a venture created by the hospital and results in the formation of the affiliation entity itself, a conservative valuation approach should be taken since there is no history of operating results, but merely a contribution of assets by the respective parties to begin operations. In this type of affiliation, a dollar-for-dollar interest contribution should be the maximum dilution of the financial contribution of the medical group. This contribution should be reflected in an ownership interest that is directly proportionate to the dollars contributed by the hospital to the venture.

This purchase price section of the purchase agreement also should detail how the purchase price is satisfied. At the closing, therefore, the documents should specify the dollar amount of funds transferred in readily available cash to the medical group. The hospital should deliver written evidence of its assumption of the scheduled liabilities to be assumed by the hospital. The agreement also should specify the amount of the purchase price to be held pending the final reconciliation of the purchase price. Much negotiating time may be spent determining how the purchase price is, in fact, satisfied. The medical group and its stockholders will often desire to receive as much of the purchase price as possible by wire transfer or certified check on the date of closing. The hospital may seek to have the purchase price financed through the use of a promissory note. A promissory note provides a way for the hospital to acquire the medical group by minimizing the amount of cash that must be paid in advance.

As part of the settlement of the purchase price, the hospital will seek to have a portion of the funds placed in escrow. Escrowing funds can serve two purposes. The first purpose is to provide a temporary holdback pending the adjustment of the purchase price based upon the closing financial statements which value the assets of stock as of the closing date.

The use of a holdback has another purpose, however, as the escrow fund may serve as a pool from which the hospital can offset any breach of warranty that may occur after the closing. This escrowed amount is a readily available source of funds which can be offset if the hospital suffers any loss because of any misstatement of any representation or warranty. This indemnification liability offset is desired by all purchasers in order to limit their potential loss. Both the amount of the holdback and the time period of the withhold are items that can be negotiated by the parties, the medical group and its stockholders arguing for a smaller amount to be withheld over a shorter period of time, and the hospital arguing for a larger amount to be held over a longer period of time.

The purchase price section will often contain a provision with respect to adjustment of the purchase price. The purchase price established in the

The physician-hospital organization

affiliation proposal process will have been made based upon financial statements prepared as much as 180 days prior to the actual closing date of the transaction. At the closing date, a final evaluation of the assets and financial statements of the group must be made, and adjustment of the purchase price may be necessary. Changes in a positive or negative direction in financial condition will then be reflected in the final purchase price that will be adjusted effective as of the closing date. The methodology for this adjustment should be set forth in the purchase agreement along with a time frame in which this adjustment must occur. A post-closing adjustment period of 90 to 120 days is not unusual and should be expected as part of this process.

A major portion of an asset or stock purchase agreement will be devoted to representations and warranties concerning medical group operations. The representations and warranties in the stock or asset purchase agreement may be made by the medical group and its individual shareholders if they are parties to the agreement. Some hospitals may seek to impose joint and several liability on the individual stockholders of the medical group. Joint and several liability means that the hospital may recover all of the loss from any single stockholder. This expansive liability is obviously undesirable and should be avoided in the negotiation with the hospital, if possible. The ability to limit this joint and several liability will be dependent, in part, on the nature of the transaction. If the medical group will no longer exist after the closing, such as in the medical division/employment model, it is likely that a hospital will insist upon some type of individual liability. This liability could be limited by removing the joint and several liability aspect, or by limiting the total exposure of each stockholder to a reasonable amount. If the medical group exists after the closing such as in the management services organization or foundation models, it may be possible to avoid this joint and several liability.

To lessen the potential liability for the medical group and its stockholders, they may wish to employ the use of "knowledge" qualifiers through insertion of the phrase "to the best of their knowledge." Use of this phrase, in essence, shifts the burden of proof for the hospital to recover damages from proving that a violation of a representation and warranty had occurred, to proving that the violation occurred, that the inaccuracy was known to the medical group and that it was not disclosed to the hospital. This change in emphasis makes it much more difficult to recover for a breach of warranty with a "knowledge" qualifier than if the qualifier is absent.

These representations and warranties include the following general categories:

- **Authorization** (whereby the medical group states that it has taken all steps necessary for securing approval for the transaction from directors, stockholders and third parties);
- **Corporate organization** (whereby the medical group states that it is duly organized, validly existing and in good standing, and that it has the power to enter into the agreement);
- **Stock** (in stock acquisitions, whereby the medical group describes its equity structure, specifies the number of shares and warrants that the stockholders have good title to the stock);
- **Title of assets** (in an asset acquisition, whereby the medical group warrants that it has good and marketable title to all the assets, free and clear of all encumbrances, and that by the bill of sale it transfers good title to the hospital);
- **Financial statements** (whereby the medical group warrants that its financial statements, audited and unaudited, have been prepared in accordance with generally acceptable accounting principles and fairly represent the financial condition of the medical group as of the date of those statements);
- **Absence of changes** (whereby the medical group warrants that no fundamental changes have taken place in the operations of the group from the date of the execution of the purchase agreement until the date of the closing when the sale is consummated);
- **Litigation** (whereby the medical group sets forth any pending litigation against it and certifies that its insurance is adequate to cover any loss);
- **Contracts and leases** (whereby the medical group lists all written and oral contracts, leases and other agreements which are material to the business of the group);
- **Tax matters** (whereby the medical group warrants that its tax returns are true, correct and complete and have been timely filed, and whereby the group warrants that all taxes have been paid);
- **Permits and licenses** (whereby the medical group lists all permits, certificates and licenses necessary for its business);
- **Employee benefit plans** (whereby the medical group lists its benefit plans and warrants that those plans comply with all applicable rules, laws and regulations);
- **Employment matters** (whereby the medical group lists its employees who earn more than a certain amount, perhaps $50,000, and also warrants that there are no outstanding labor matters with respect to the medical group);
- **Compliance with laws** (whereby the medical group certifies that it is in compliance with all applicable laws and regulations);
- **Insurance** (whereby the medical group sets forth all applicable insurance coverage and warrants that all coverage is adequate);

- **Inventory** (whereby the medical group warrants that its inventory is sufficient for the conduct of its business, and that the inventory does not include items of below standard quality or obsolete items);
- **Environmental matters** (whereby the medical group warrants that it is in compliance with all applicable environmental laws, rules and regulations respecting hazardous or biomedical materials and wastes);
- **Regulatory, licensure or other violations** (whereby the medical group represents that it has no violations with respect to regulatory, medical or other licensing authorities);
- **Fraud and abuse** (whereby the medical group warrants that its operations and activities have been conducted in accordance with the Medicare fraud and abuse law and applicable anti-referral legislation); and
- **Brokers and finders** (whereby the medical group warrants that it has not hired a broker who would be entitled to any fee).

While extensive, these representations and warranties are standard practice in all acquisitions. These disclosures are designed to uncover past problems, to prevent the purchaser from assuming liabilities it does not wish to assume and to set up the basis for recovery if these statements later prove to be false. In the stock purchase acquisition, these disclosures are even more important because the purchaser of the stock will purchase the entire operation of the medical group including liabilities, known and unknown.

Not all representations and warranties in an asset or stock purchase agreement will pertain to the medical group. The hospital also will make representations and warranties regarding its authority to make the purchase and with respect to its operations. In the event that the hospital or management company issues stock as part of the purchase price, it will need to comply with the securities laws, and to make representations and warranties concerning the stock that is transferred as part of the purchase price. The securities laws require that all relevant information be delivered to a potential investor concerning the business operations of a company. Often, this disclosure requirement will be satisfied with the preparation of a private placement memorandum or prospectus, whereby the hospital or management company describes its business operations, its financial results and any relevant information that a prudent investor would deem appropriate to receive before making an investment decision. In addition to the representations and warranties made as part of the purchase agreement, the separate securities law disclosure will represent an independent basis of liability under which the medical group may recover from the hospital/management company.

The main representations and warranties to be made by the hospital are that it has appropriate authority to enter into the agreement and to purchase the assets or stock. Also the hospital will represent that by entering into the agreement, it does not violate any agreement, order, other provision of its articles of incorporation or bylaws, or necessitate the consent or approval of any government authority, and that the agreement will be fully binding on the hospital.

After the listing of the warranties and representations, the purchase agreement details the agreements of the parties prior to closing. The primary purpose of this section is to cover the scenario where the purchase agreement is signed on one day, and the actual closing occurs some time in the future. Where the signing of the agreement and the actual closing of the transaction occur on the same day, this section has little practical effect. This section should obligate the parties to conduct their business in an ordinary manner prior to the closing and to allow advisors, accountants, investors and other authorized agents access to the properties, books, records and personnel of either party. This provision allows the medical group and the hospital with access to information about each other to allow a more informed decision concerning the proposed relationship. This section also should contain a confidentiality provision and the agreement of the parties that any public announcements or information disclosed to third parties will receive the prior approval of all parties. Another provision to be inserted in this section which would apply, regardless of when the agreement is signed and the closing occurs, is the obligation of the hospital to hire non-physician employees of the medical group and maintain benefit plans.

Another important section of an asset or stock purchase agreement lists the conditions which must be met by both parties before each party is obligated to complete the sale. These conditions generally state that:

- The representations and warranties made in the agreement must be true as of the closing date;
- All of the conditions to be performed by the other party shall have been completed by the closing date;
- All necessary governmental approvals shall have been obtained;
- The other party must certify that approval of the board of the directors and shareholders has been obtained and that the agreement, as signed, will be legally binding and enforceable against the other party;
- All permits and licenses shall have been obtained by the other party;
- No adverse changes in the financial condition of the other party shall have occurred;
- The parties shall have entered into an affiliation agreement (management agreement, establishment of medical division or foundation medical services agreement) whereby the future operations will be governed;

- Any provisions with respect to the real estate of the group such as purchase, lease or other arrangement shall be finalized;
- The physicians shall have entered into new employment agreements containing restrictive covenants; and
- As part of the closing process, consents and copies of employment agreements shall have been made, and evidence that all encumbrances on assets or the stock has been removed.

A critical portion of an asset or stock purchase agreement will detail what happens if any of the representations and warranties made by either of the parties are untrue. This section of the agreement will provide that all representations and warranties made by a party will survive the closing and that any investigation made by the other party will not diminish or affect the representations or warranties made by the representing party. The agreement also will provide that if a party suffers loss because of breach of any representation or warranty, it will be reimbursed for its losses by the party who made the representation. This "indemnification" concept is a central feature of any asset or stock purchase agreement, as it provides a remedy to the purchaser if the purchaser is harmed because of the actions or misrepresentations of the seller. Because of the potential liability of a seller under these provisions, significant discussion may be held about the appropriateness of the indemnification requirements and the procedure for securing indemnification. Generally, the indemnification issues are negotiated on the following areas: personal liability, limitation on liability, time limit on raising claims, a materiality limit on representations and warranties and use of inheritance proceeds.

Personal liability

As discussed previously, the goal for the medical group and its shareholders should be to limit the personal liability of the individual shareholders. This will be attempted as discussed above by limiting the application of the principle of joint and several liability, by having the physicians not be parties to the agreement or by limiting their individual liability as discussed in the following sections.

Limitation on liability

Medical groups and their shareholders will desire to limit their potential liability in connection with the sale. A medical group may try to limit its liability to a fixed dollar amount or to the amount that represents the purchase price of the assets, and the shareholders may try to limit their loss to a specific amount that pertains only to that shareholder. This limitation is generally a favorable provision for sellers and medical groups and their shareholders should consider carefully whether such a limitation can be negotiated.

Hospitals will resist any attempt to limit their potential redress for any misrepresentation concerning the activities or assets of the medical group. The hospital will argue that it has relied upon the truth of the representations and warranties made by the medical group, including that the assets or stock is transferred free and clear of all other encumbrances. To deny the hospital any right of redress will limit the attractiveness of any transaction. In many instances, therefore, a hospital will resist any significant limitation on its right of redress. The extent of the limitation finally negotiated will depend upon the relative bargaining position of the parties.

Time limit on raising claims

Another favorable provision for the medical group and its stockholders imposes a time limit on the ability of a hospital/purchaser to raise any indemnification claim that is shorter than the applicable statute of limitations, which is the legal limit to enforce any claim in court. The theory is that the hospital as a purchaser will be in a position to discover any breach of warranty within a shorter period of time than the longer statute of limitations. A one or two year period would, in effect, limit the ability of the hospital to raise any claim beyond that period. This shortening of the time limit to make a claim is a favorable provision for the medical group and its stockholders, but will be resisted by hospitals that will desire the full legal limit to make any claim for reimbursement under the indemnification provisions.

Materiality limit on representations and warranties

Another significant area for the negotiation of the indemnification rights is whether a threshold of damage first must be reached before a hospital can make a claim against the medical group and its stockholders. These provisions would prohibit a hospital from making a claim unless it incurs a loss out of one event that exceeds a set limit, such as $10,000, or the losses of the hospital exceed, in the aggregate, a higher threshold limit, such as $25,000. These provisions protect a medical group from minor claims which, although technical violations of the representations and warranties are in all likelihood inadvertent and, therefore, not appropriate for reimbursement. In general, most hospitals should not be opposed to such limitations as long as the threshold of the limitation of liability does not exceed a significant amount.

On the other hand, some hospitals may take the position that any liability for misrepresentation or inaccuracy should rest upon the medical group making that representation and that the hospital, as the innocent party, should not bear any loss. Both parties will need, inevitably, to negotiate what is perceived to be a fair resolution to this issue.

Indemnification net of insurance

The medical group and its shareholders should also seek to limit their potential liability by requiring the hospital to pursue coverage under any insurance policy it may have and to have the hospital require its insurance company waive its right to seek recovery against the medical group and the shareholders for any loss the insurance company pays on behalf of its insured, the hospital.

The final significant provision of an asset or stock purchase agreement is a restrictive covenant which prohibits the medical group, and perhaps the shareholders of the medical group, from competing with the hospital/ purchaser. Restrictive covenants in the asset or stock purchase context allow the hospital another way of prohibiting competition with its activities in the ongoing relationship with the physicians. Typically, in asset or stock purchase agreements, the medical group and its physician shareholders will agree not to compete with the hospital for a given period of time that begins from the closing of the sale. The competition restricted, however, should not be drafted or construed as prohibiting a physician from admitting patients at another hospital because such a restriction could be considered a violation of the fraud and abuse laws. Whatever covenant used should be narrowly defined to not violate fraud and abuse laws.

The same principles that apply in the restrictive covenant provisions contained in employment agreements generally apply in the sale of business context. To be enforceable, a covenant must be given for valid consideration, must be for a valid purpose and must be limited to a reasonable geographic area and time. There are, however, several fundamental differences between covenants in the sale of business context and covenants in the employment context. First, courts have generally viewed more favorably the ability of a purchaser who pays value for assets or stock to restrict the future competitive activity of a seller. Courts are more likely to enforce these types of restrictive covenant provisions in an asset or stock sale context than in the employer-employee context.

The second important consideration for restrictive covenants in the asset or stock sale context is that the covenant runs from the date of closing of the sale, as opposed to the employment agreement context where the covenant runs from the point of time that the employment relationship with the physician terminates. Restrictive covenants in the asset or stock sale context only provide a limited period of protection which will end five to seven years after the completion of the sale. After the expiration of this five to seven year period after the closing of the asset or stock sale, the physician will be free thereafter to compete with the affiliation under this acquisition covenant.

The third major difference in the restrictive covenant application in the asset or stock sale context is that the covenants are generally deemed to be reasonable for a longer period of time than covenants in the employment context. Covenants deemed to be reasonable in the employment context may last in general for a maximum of two to three years. The length of time deemed reasonable in the asset sale context is longer, approaching five to seven years or more. The precise length of enforceability for all of these time periods is governed by applicable state law which varies from state to state.

Medical groups should consider the difficult position they place themselves in when negotiating these restrictive covenants. On one hand, the group and its physicians will desire to negotiate a short restrictive covenant that is extremely limited in scope. Medical groups, however, should consider the long-term purpose of entering into the affiliation, and the need to secure, in as many ways as possible, the future health, growth and security of the medical group. From that standpoint, and viewed from the group perspective, the longest enforceable time period in the restrictive covenant context, coupled with the most restrictive provisions on prohibiting competitive practice, will be deemed to be in the long-term interests of both the hospital and the medical group and/or its physicians. Medical groups should attempt to take the perspective that their future will be inextricably bound with the hospital and that anything to strengthen the stability of the affiliation will be to their mutual long-term best interests. Entering into the hospital relationship with an eye to preserving an easy exit may indicate less than total commitment to the affiliation. While some reasonable accommodation should be made of these differing views, it will be in the best interest of the group to see that the new affiliation begins on as firm a foundation as possible. While the asset or stock purchase agreement is the central document for the sale of the medical group, there are a number of ancillary documents used to finalize the transaction.

Other documents used in the sale include the following:

- **Assumption agreement**. Under this document, the hospital, in an asset sale, agrees to assume certain liabilities from the medical group and to perform those liabilities as if they belonged to the hospital.
- **Closing agenda**. In the closing agenda, the documents utilized in the relationship are set forth on a checklist to assist the parties in making sure that all items have been delivered at closing.
- **Certificate of medical group**. Under this document, the officers of the medical group warrant that representations and warranties set

forth in the asset or stock purchase agreements are correct as of the day of closing.

- **Certificate of hospital**. This document is utilized to specify that the representations and warranties of the hospital are true as of the day of closing.
- **Bill of sale**. By this document, used in an asset sale, the actual ownership of the assets is transferred from the medical group to the hospital.
- **Legal opinion for hospital counsel**. Under this document, the legal counsel for the hospital gives certain opinions regarding the transaction, primarily that the entity is a valid organization and has all necessary approvals to enter into the transaction.
- **Legal opinion for medical group counsel**. Under this document the legal counsel for the medical group gives certain opinions regarding the medical group and its execution of the agreement, primarily that the entity is a valid organization and has all necessary approvals to enter into the transaction.
- **Closing statement**. Under this document, the financial details of the closing are specified.

Chapter 12

The physician-hospital integration implementation process

he process of implementing an affiliation often is overlooked by the individuals involved. Medical groups, in particular, may have had little, if any, experience with successfully implementing a new venture of such significant size with a hospital. Uncertainty can seriously undermine the efforts of those involved to anticipate and resolve issues that might prevent a successful conclusion. In all of these transactions, however, the issues that will arise can be predicted with some certainty. Attention to the implementation process will greatly facilitate the successful consummation of a transaction. Without this attention, the transaction may drift aimlessly without direction, causing delay and additional expense. This delay creates the opportunity for loss of momentum, loss of group consensus, and for a breakdown in negotiations that may be permanent. Utilizing a letter of intent, the project schedule, the negotiating process, the medical group decision-making process, communication strategies, and the proposals for dividing the proceeds will allow the formation of a comprehensive implementation strategy by hospital affiliation participants.

Letter of intent

To implement any transaction, the medical group and hospital first must understand the scope and nature of the business transaction. In many instances a letter of intent will set forth the basic principles of the proposed transaction. Using a letter of intent serves several purposes.

First, the letter of intent will require the parties to focus on the main points on which they agree, and will require them to decide whether a basic agreement has been reached before considerable effort and expenditure of funds are made. The purchase price for the assets or the stock, the scope of the transaction, the anticipated structure and how the parties will relate to each other are all subjects which should be included in a letter of intent. The language of the letter will, by design, be vague, leaving the parties the ability to identify, and later resolve in the affiliation documents, the remaining details.

A second important reason for a letter of intent is that it serves as a psychological tool to enlist the support of physicians to accept the change. Medical leadership that announces that a letter of intent has been signed will create the impression that an important first step has been made, and this sense of progress will enable the leadership to marshal support for the transaction.

The third reason to employ a letter of intent is to allow the parties to identify those issues on which they currently agree, and to hold for further discussion those issues which cannot yet be resolved. This process of issue-narrowing and definition will allow parties to begin to work out their difficulties on issues on which they have not yet agreed. Purposefully keeping vague some of the difficult issues faced in the transaction will allow the parties to go forward in a common problem-solving mode to resolve those issues.

There may be valid reasons not to use a letter of intent, however. First, letters of intent are noncontractual, and they may be viewed as a meaningless exercise on which the parties focus undue attention. This focusing of effort can derail the process by allowing lawyers and other advisors to negotiate too heavily the language in the letter of intent. This misplaced energy may result in the entire project becoming bogged down which will inhibit the development of the necessary decision making and problem-solving spirit of cooperation. The time spent negotiating may be another significant drawback, as to the extent the parties spend weeks negotiating a letter of intent, a process is created whereby issues must be negotiated twice, as opposed to once in the final documents. Finally, a letter of intent may push issues to decision when they are not yet ready for resolution. The parties may be far apart on several substantive issues and their ability to build a consensus will take time, experience and growth in the relationships between the individual members of the negotiating teams. Prematurely rushing issues to a conclusion may result in polarization, rather than cooperation, and proceeding to negotiate a letter of intent which attempts to cover these issues may be destructive of the entire process.

Whether a letter of intent is used depends upon the facts and circumstances of each transaction. If a letter of intent is used, however, attention should be paid to the format of the letter. It is important to recognize, and the letter should state, that the letter of intent does not bind the parties to complete the transaction. Language which states the agreement to proceed is noncontractual, but represents the good faith intent of the parties to finalize the transaction, is appropriate. Otherwise, the risk arises that a binding agreement to proceed may be created in the letter which can be used as a basis for a claim of damages should the transaction later fail. It is in the interests of all parties to avoid having a contract for the affiliation arise based upon the execution of the letter.

Another important provision to be included in the letter of intent is a confidentiality provision. Both parties should agree to keep confidential all financial information and other confidential materials that are exchanged. This part of the letter should be made contractually binding on the parties and language to that effect should be added to the letter. Making this obligation binding addresses the risk that information which is exchanged in the negotiating process could be leaked to third parties or used to the detriment of the party that provided the information. This paragraph also should contain a provision that requires all this information to be returned immediately if the negotiations terminate. A final provision for inclusion in the letter of intent is an exclusivity provision. Exclusivity provisions bind both parties to proceed in negotiating their transaction, usually for a specific period of time, without negotiating with a third party. Exclusivity provisions allow the parties to proceed with some confidence that third parties will not interfere with an orderly process of negotiating or that a bidding war will not be started by one of the parties by soliciting a third party offer. This provision also should contain a reference to a continuation of the exclusivity period if the parties are proceeding in good faith toward final negotiations at the expiration of exclusivity. The time period for exclusivity should be relatively short in most instances, and should coincide with a reasonable estimate of how long the transaction will take to conclude. Including an exclusivity provision in a letter of intent is usually reasonable as the effort and expense of engaging in a transaction means that the parties should use their best efforts to complete their transaction without outside distraction. The exclusivity provision also should be made contractually binding on the parties.

The schedule

For groups to understand fully the process before them, a schedule should be prepared for the transaction which identifies the issues to be confronted, categorizes the tasks to be performed and sets an appropriate timetable in which to accomplish these tasks. Schedules serve several purposes. First, they allow all of the issues to be identified by the participants by providing an overview of the hospital affiliation process. The schedule illustrates that there is a beginning, middle and end to any transaction. Second, the schedule helps the individuals charged with implementing the transaction to plan effectively to deal with the issues and the process in a coordinated manner. This planning process will improve greatly the chance of success for implementing the transaction. Finally, the schedule helps to create a sense of accomplishment and momentum as the parties proceed through the process and accomplish the tasks contained on the list. It is important to update the schedule every several weeks to reflect this progress. During the process the schedule will need to be revised to reflect unanticipated problems, inevitable delays and other factors that will arise. Using the schedule as the operative document, however, can help minimize these disruptions and put them in the context of achieving the larger goal.

While each transaction will have issues that are unique to the parties involved, a typical transaction should be achieved in a 90 to 120 day period, beginning from the date of execution of the letter of intent. Prior to beginning the intensive implementation process, a significant period of time may have elapsed whereby the parties have identified each other, discussed in general the terms that will bind them together, and then focused more specifically on the details of their transaction. This exploratory period may last another 90 days, but may extend even over a longer period, given that knowledge of particular opportunities and relationships often evolve slowly and in response to a variety of factors.

Once the decision is made to proceed, however, the 90 to 120 day implementation period probably is ideal. A shorter period of time makes building group consensus difficult to achieve and makes covering the myriad of details necessary for successful implementation nearly impossible to accomplish. A longer period of time has its own set of risks and problems. Momentum may be lost as the parties become bogged down in detail, losing a sense of urgency to accomplish their goal and becoming sidetracked on ancillary issues that may result in loss of perspective on the strategic importance of the overall transaction. The uncertainty caused by the transaction will be increased significantly by a longer time period, as employee anxiety and turnover increases, rumors are generated, and the stress and tension about job security are not resolved. This uncertainty is inevitable in any major change, but a longer time period magnifies these negative aspects. Finally, a longer time frame will allow those who are opposed to the transaction to find ways of raising ancillary issues that may threaten progress on the transaction.

While most parties will find ample excuse to delay the process beyond this 90 to 120 day period, given the "unique" set of factors present in their situation, this argument should be resisted. Most issues faced by the parties are not unique and can be reduced to the fundamental issues which must be decided before the transaction is finalized. Those charged with implementing the transaction must be prepared to convince those who seek delay that the schedule should be adopted and followed. Often, the desire for more information and more data can mask the real motive of delaying the process which is to avoid making critical decisions. Usually, the additional information obtained by this data will not give the "ultimate" answer that those who request the data are seeking. The decision-making process should provide enough data to make decisions, but the judgment and analysis that must be employed usually will not be improved by this additional data.

The hospital affiliation timetable

The hospital affiliation will contain its own set of unique issues that must be scheduled regardless of whether the affiliation is a management services relationship, medical division/employment relationship, or foundation model. A detailed list of issues to be covered and a suggested timetable is set forth on table 3. While the exact sequence in which a transaction will be implemented often depends on the specific circumstances of each transaction, the process will fall roughly within three distinct phases.

First period
During this time period, the main goal will be to establish the framework for successful implementation of the affiliation. The parties should conduct their due diligence investigation of each other in order to ascertain detailed information regarding the other party. The parties should also establish the structure of the affiliation and the way in which the affiliation will be governed. A tax analysis of the sale of assets or stock should begin as answers to these tax questions may dictate significant changes in approach or structure. The substantive work also should begin on the physician compensation system that may be modified in light of the new relationship. Work on a number of other issues should begin, given the long lead time necessary to resolve the issues. Banking and lending relationships, licenses and vendors and identification of obligations and security interests that may preclude the group from tendering good title to the assets or stock to be sold, all must be identified. Preliminary work also must begin on the formula for distribution of proceeds to individual physicians from the sale. During this time period, the board of directors of a group should expect to meet weekly, and a smaller negotiating committee should continue its work begun during the pre-letter of intent phase. Specific committees may be utilized to examine issues such as affiliation governance, physician compensation and distribution of the proceeds. Regular communication sessions must be held with the medical staff.

Second period
During this time period, the negotiating process will begin in earnest. The preliminary tax analysis should be finalized. Documents such as the

asset or stock purchase agreement and the affiliation agreement should be circulated for review. The hospital may have prepared these documents and a process must be set up to allow the group to identify issues raised by these documents. Medical groups that take the time and trouble to prepare the first drafts of these documents will be more than rewarded with a negotiating advantage in the process. Work should be finalized on the distribution of proceeds so individual physicians will know the benefits that they can expect to receive for proceeding with the transaction. Pension plan and employee benefits work must begin as the new benefit structures must be finalized. Physician employment agreements also must be circulated during this time period, and the governing board of the new relationship must be identified. Any real estate leases that will be assigned to the hospital should have been identified in the first period and contacts with those landlords must be made during this second period. Joint ventures that the group may have entered into that will need modification will need to be identified, and issues created by those ventures resolved.

The work on physician compensation should be completed so this critical issue can be communicated to individual physicians during this time. The identification of contracts and liabilities of the medical group also must be a priority during this time period. It is in the best interest of the medical group to identify all of these relationships and to have these liabilities assumed by the hospital in the asset sale context. In the stock sale context, these contracts and liabilities also must be evaluated to determine if consent is required. Communication with vendors and other third parties must begin in order to start this assumption or approval process. The board of directors can be expected to meet weekly and shareholders will have another formal meeting for a progress report with a question and answer session during this time period. Informal lines of communication must be utilized extensively to keep physicians in the group informed. The leadership of the group also must receive feedback from these influential decision makers in order to process that input through the negotiating process.

Final period

The final period of an affiliation schedule will be intensely legal in focus. The acquisition documents and affiliation agreement must be finalized during this period. Several drafts will need to be reviewed as the negotiated changes are incorporated into these documents. Physician contracts that may be required to be signed as part of the transaction will be required to be returned (preferably within two weeks of the closing date) and a formal vote of the shareholders should be taken to ratify this sale and affiliation agreement. While state corporate law may not require that a formal vote be taken under all circumstances, it is in the best interests of the leadership of the group to require approval by the group as a whole, even if it is not technically necessary from a legal point of view.

Employee benefit plan decisions must be finalized and any changes in the pension plans or benefit structures that may be required will need to be implemented. Relationships with third parties including banks and lenders must be finalized prior to closing and any liens on assets should be removed, if required. Liabilities that need to be assigned to the hospital also must be identified and assumed. Any modifications to joint venture structures also should be concluded. Real estate leases that must be assigned should be transferred. In addition, informational sessions should be held with physicians to answer final questions and to continue to maintain morale and momentum. Finally, the board of directors must continue to meet to address such issues, expected and otherwise, as may arise in the process. The culmination of this process is on the closing date when the sale of the medical group will be finalized, the hospital will pay the purchase price, and the affiliation documents will be signed.

The negotiating process

Integration transactions between medical groups and hospitals inevitably will entail an extended negotiation process. The ability to create a situation in which both parties feel they have won, and to create a spirit of compromise, are essential elements for creating a successful combination. Unlike the sale of a house or even the sale of a business, the parties to an affiliation do not disappear after the closing. If an adversarial approach that often is taken in conjunction with a sale of a business is employed in implementing these transactions, the transaction may fail, or this confrontational approach may become the method of operation for the parties in their future relationships. All parties must recognize that the manner of negotiating will establish the foundation of future cooperation in resolving difficult issues. This spirit of cooperation to solve a problem in the acquisition phase should be encouraged by all concerned. The leadership of the parties must be cognizant of the need to utilize this approach and must monitor the approach utilized by their respective legal counsel who may use the adversarial approach. The parties must convince their respective legal counsel that an overly adversarial approach will be counterproductive in these types of transactions and that the interests of both parties can be best served by lawyers who avoid the use of a confrontational negotiating style.

Equally important in the negotiating process is the way a party decides to assemble its negotiating team. Various approaches can be taken. For example, a negotiating team representing a medical group can be selected. It will be responsible for examining documents, raising issues of concern with the other party, and providing momentum and leadership for the remainder of the group in the transaction. This negotiating committee must be small in number, perhaps not exceeding five, and should include both the group administrator as well as key physician leaders. The negotiating committee should speak for the group and should discourage other physician involvement in the negotiating process. This involvement by others not authorized to negotiate may lead to unintended signals sent to the other side, confusion in negotiating positions being created, and an undermining of positions taken by the negotiating committee. A negotiating committee may be particularly effective in the hospital affiliation process, as it allows a small group to interact with the nonphysician members of the management team of the hospital. This negotiating committee can then report to the board of directors and the physicians at large, providing the leadership as well as receiving input on significant points raised by the board or the physicians at large. From the perspective of a hospital, it will be important to select members who are sufficiently senior in the organization so they can speak with authority for the hospital.

Decision making

Inevitably in the affiliation process, conflict will arise over various issues. How this conflict is resolved will set the framework for future conflict resolution in the new relationship. A process by which conflict can be resolved effectively must be established for the creation of a healthy working relationship. Each party will have developed over the years its own conflict resolution process. For hospitals with well-defined decision-making structures, the challenge will be to integrate this process with the immensely more complex decision-making process found in medical groups. Medical group decision making may take many forms. For example, some groups may use the well-respected senior leadership to fashion and direct physician support. Others may use the team approach whereby physicians with special relationships with the constituent physician groups will be used as a liaison between those groups and the larger group. Others may use a group meeting concept where decisions are discussed in true democratic fashion, with consensus forming from those interactions.

Whatever the mechanisms that have been utilized by the respective parties, the new organization or affiliation must develop a new strategy. This strategy can be developed only by examining, in a historical fashion, how the constituent parties have made these decisions. A combination of efforts, and a balance of old and new approaches, is likely to be successful for the new effort. In the resolution of conflict, it is important that decisions be achieved by allowing all in the decision-making process to feel a part of the decision in order to secure support for decisions ultimately made. It is important, therefore, that majority votes not be used to decide critical issues. Discussion, identification of common ground and consensus building are essential for achieving these decisions. This process of consensus building at the decision-making level should not be used for all group decisions involving all group members, where attempting to build a consensus with too large a group will lead to delay and failure.

Within a medical group, decision making also should receive attention so support for the transaction can be built. Regardless of the size of a group, the medical group leadership must identify issues, propose solutions, and guide physician thinking on these issues in order to implement these decisions. While input from physicians is a necessary component to this decision-making process, the physician leadership must develop its agenda for implementing the change and, as part of that implementation process, incorporate physician feedback on various issues.

As part of the decision-making process within a medical group, discussion of issues must continue outside of formal meetings. Private discussions must be held with those who may be reluctant to support the group position, as this type of individual lobbying will be necessary to build support. This approach also allows physicians to feel a part of the process, enabling them to support with some enthusiasm decisions that are ultimately made. Without appropriate involvement of these physicians, and attention to their opinions, the risk exists that groups or individual physicians will not support the transaction and will either leave or become agents of discontent in the newly-formed organization.

Communication

To implement successfully an affiliation, significant planning must occur with respect to communication. This communication planning is multi-faceted, as it covers not only the process of informing physicians about a transaction, having the negotiating committee report to the board of directors, or having the board of directors report to its physician-staff, but also includes contact with a variety of other interested parties including medical group or hospital employees, the parties with whom a medical group has ongoing relationships, and the public at large. The rumor mills that exist in many medical groups, and in the physician community at large, are often well established and must be managed rather than ignored.

A strategy must be developed to confront this communication challenge. A central element to that strategy is the need to control information and confidentiality. In one respect, confidentiality means the ability to keep details of the transaction from those who are outside of the medical group. In order to accomplish this goal, physician leaders must impress upon the group members the need for secrecy. Details of the transaction may be discovered by the media, competitors, or other medical groups or hospitals, with the risk that the transaction may be inappropriately characterized or prematurely disclosed. All players in the process must guard against inappropriate disclosure of the details of the transaction.

An equally important concept that leadership of the parties must confront, however, is the amount of information given to various participants in the process. This control of information is critical to the success of implementation. The leadership must strike a balance between withholding information from others in the group in order to allow a clear consistent message of information when it is finally communicated, and providing sufficient amounts of information to enlist support, understanding and feedback concerning the proposed transaction.

When communication is made, the leadership must be prepared to summarize the information that is conveyed to their constituents. Information should not be conveyed in such detail that individuals who are not intimately familiar with the process become bogged down in details. Clear and concise summaries that leave out the various negotiating positions and nuances that a negotiating committee may take in the process are helpful.

Equally important as the nature of the disclosure is the timing of that disclosure. Information must be disclosed at the right time. Premature disclosure of information may cause undue alarm by focusing on issues yet to be resolved, or by focusing on a variety of options that the negotiating committee currently confronts. Raising issues that have yet to be decided, and that may prove to be difficult to resolve, also may heighten insecurity or tension if the recipients of this information are not part of the conflict resolution process. Medical group leadership should plan how information will be conveyed among various players. At the beginning of the process, the concept of the affiliation will be extremely confidential. Throughout the process, various decisions and negotiating positions that are taken also will be confidential, and the leak of that information or the mechanism by which a decision will be made may hamper the ability to form a cautious around the compromises that inevitably will be made.

While the individual context of each decision will dictate the strategy employed, leadership of the group must understand that in many situations, the complexity and volatility of many positions dictate that the information be kept confidential and that when in doubt, preference should be given to maintain confidentiality rather than premature disclosure. Seasoned leadership experienced in making changes and implementing decisions will understand the need for a cautious approach in this area.

As part of the communication plan for a medical group, sessions should be scheduled with physicians for briefing. Discussions must be held with physicians concerning proposed new employment arrangements, physician compensation and the details of the transaction. This communication, on a routine and regular basis, is important to build support for the process, and to identify danger signs which may evidence an erosion of physician support. Another critical aspect of this communication program will be to clarify to individual physicians the risks associated with not completing the transaction. To accomplish the affiliation successfully, it will be necessary to focus physicians on the larger issues confronted in the transformation of medical care delivery. Information concerning changing medical practice patterns, and the changing economies of that practice, must be conveyed to physicians. The message must be communicated that the status quo and a return to the days past are not viable alternatives, and that change and evolution inevitably will occur. This message will, if properly conveyed, convince physicians that planning for change is as important a process as any in a medical practice, and that the ability to adapt to that change, as represented by the proposed transaction, will allow their practice to operate more successfully in the changing health care marketplace.

With respect to employees, a medical group must be aware that the benefits in the proposed transaction which the physicians have so readily identified as being available to them will not be as readily apparent to the nonphysician employees. Employees will be concerned about a variety of matters. They may view the combination as a threat to job security, recognizing that affiliating with a hospital may result in loss of, or modification to, job duties. These employees also will be concerned about modifications to benefits that may arise given the combination of work forces, with minor changes in benefits being viewed with exaggerated apprehension by those employees. This employee uncertainty must be dealt with effectively by the medical group and the hospital.

A strong communication program must convey information to employees on a routine basis in a form that allows employees to have their questions answered in as timely a fashion as possible. Both group meetings and written communication programs should be utilized to enhance this effort. Without a program sufficiently attuned to employee concerns, rumors and gossip will replace facts, increasing the risk of confusion and the likelihood of harm to employee morale and employee retention. The medical leadership should develop a communication program that only deals with the basic issues of the proposed combination and that will treat, in summary fashion, many of the nuances that will have been covered in greater detail with the physicians. Broad statements about the type of relationship that will be created, coupled with more specifics about benefit changes and redirection in staffing will be the right mix of detail to satisfy these concerns. Negotiating positions or difficulties, and any recitation of problems associated with the affiliation, should not be part of this communication process, the focus being on positive information provided in a general format.

With respect to the general public, another level of the communication plan must be created. First, a plan must be developed to deal with inquiries from the media and other parties about the inevitable rumors that will arise about a pending transaction. Each of the parties to the transaction should appoint a central spokesperson who will provide information or answer questions concerning any potential relationship. The response to these general inquiries should be discussed in advance by all the parties to the transaction, with the understanding that parties will communicate with each other about the nature of the inquiry and the response given. The nature of this response must be agreed to in advance so consistent positions can be taken with the media.

In addition to this preventive strategy with respect to immediate inquiries, it is critical for the parties to spend sufficient time in the preparation and development of a plan to announce the integrated relationship. Appropriate attention should be given to the drafting of press releases, to the site of the news conference, and to the timing of that conference. In many instances, public interest will be high in the venture, and the message that can be conveyed should be planned in light of the strategic plan of the affiliation. This announcement will be one of the initial steps in a coordinated marketing plan that will be necessary to communicate the new message of the relationship to the general public and the medical community. The medical group and hospital must focus not only on the general public, but also on the medical community, given the many referral relationships that are essential to the fiscal success of many groups. Public confusion about the medical group-hospital relationship must be minimized and a consistent message must be developed for communication. The ability to plan effectively for the communication of the message of the new relationship to the community at large is a critical component to the successful launching of the new venture. Special attention must be made if the name of the group will change as part of the process. Public confusion about this name change will inevitably occur and a general awareness campaign about the new name must be planned. Without this campaign, patients may become confused in the process and this confusion may result in loss of patients to the new group until confusion is eliminated.

Dividing the proceeds

A critical part of the integration implementation process is the development of a successful plan that will inform the physician participants of the monetary benefits of going forward with a proposed transaction. In most instances, the availability of funds for distribution to the physicians will occur, where the hospital purchases most, if not all, of the operating assets or stock of a medical group. This sale usually will result in significant dollars flowing to the physicians in the medical group.

In general, distribution of the funds to individual physicians should be planned to incorporate an incentive for physicians to remain associated with the new relationship over a long period of time. A staggering of payments spread out over several years is one method of encouraging this loyalty. A vesting of benefits based on years of service will avoid immediate distribution of funds to physicians who then may be free to move elsewhere, and thereby jeopardize the long term viability of the new relationship. The following components should be considered in any proceeds distribution proposal.

Stockholder status

Most medical groups are organized as corporations, and as such will have physicians who have an equity interest in the corporation by way of stock ownership. Because the assets of the group will be sold as part of the transaction, and those assets represent value of the corporation, or because the stock of the medical group will be sold, it is appropriate to consider allocating a portion of the proceeds for distribution to physicians on the basis of stock ownership. Groups that have minimal buy-ins can be expected to allocate a small portion of the proceeds to this stock owner-ship. Groups that have significant buy-ins, or that have stock values that fluctuate over a period of time based on a valuation formula, can be expected to have a greater amount allocated based upon stock ownership. Groups that employ a fixed valuation for their stock should consider allocating a portion of the purchase price based upon that fixed valuation in order to provide a return of those funds. The reality with respect to distribution of proceeds by stock ownership is that medical groups exist because of the productive efforts of their physicians and that it is the participation of a physician in the medical group as a practicing, revenue generating physician rather than as a stockholder-investor that should be rewarded. In most circumstances, therefore, allocation of a portion of the purchase price proceeds to stock ownership is appropriate, but that amount should be limited, and not exceed amounts reasonably related to the investment of a physician in the medical group. Amounts allocated to the stock may be increased where tax advice indicates more of the acquisition price should be allocated to the stock.

Accounts receivable

As part of an asset acquisition, it is likely that a hospital will purchase assets that consist, among other items, of the accounts receivable gener-ated by individual physicians for services they have performed on behalf of the medical group. As part of a stock acquisition, the hospital purchases control of the medical group entity and, as a consequence, control of the accounts receivable. In either event, these accounts receivable will be purchased and will be in effect be "collected" at the closing by the purchase of those accounts receivable. The handling of the accounts receivable in a proceeds distribution formula will depend, in large part, upon the compensation system of the group. To the extent physicians are paid on productivity and collections, a portion of the proceeds should be allocated based upon how these accounts receivable were generated. Physicians who are otherwise entitled to payment for these accounts receivable should not be denied the benefit of those collections merely because of the sale. Accounts receivable payments, therefore, often will be part of the allocation of the proceeds. Whether a dollar-for-dollar payment to physicians should be made based upon what physicians would have received had the accounts receivable been collected in the ordinary course is a decision that must be made in light of the other competing concerns and considerations in developing a fair and effective proceeds distribution system.

Seniority

Rewarding physicians for years of service in a group is often utilized as another method for proceeds distribution. The value and contribution of physicians in building the group is often felt worthy of reward. To the extent that this seniority is not already reflected in disproportionate stock ownership, it may be appropriate to recognize those physicians who have contributed most to the development of the value of the practice. A small portion of the distribution plan probably should be utilized to reward this longevity factor.

Physician productivity

Often, the value of the acquisition will be significantly impacted by the amount of revenue generated by the practice, as opposed to being solely based on the value of the hard assets themselves. Physicians who produce large amounts of revenue for the group are, in effect, creating a disproportionate share of value for that group, which often is reflected in a higher purchase price. A distribution plan, therefore, might consider distributing a portion of the proceeds based upon the relative contribution to revenue that a physician may make to the group. If the group utilizes this plan, however, it must be prepared to deal with specific facts and circumstances that may make a uniform application of this process unfair. For example, physicians who are part of the group for only a short period of time, that may have had unusual interruptions in their practice due to illness or other factors, or that may be in the practice development mode will all seek some relief from this type of system, and often some special accommodations should be made for these factors. Whatever system is utilized in resolving these special cases, the result must be perceived as fair by all those who participate.

Signing bonus

To the extent that physicians are asked to enter into employment agreements, it is appropriate for the proceeds distribution system to include compensation for physicians who do so. In models where the medical group remains in existence, if all physicians enter into a new agreement with a restrictive covenant, it may be appropriate to allocate a portion of this purchase price to them as the "consideration" for entering into a new agreement. How this element of proceeds distribution is valued is a function of how these restrictive covenants are viewed. Some may take the position that the restrictive covenant of each physician is valued equally, and under this rationale would assign an equal value to each physician for execution of a covenant. A second position is that physicians who are higher earners and who may be subject to a higher liquidated damage provision in the covenant ought to receive more, as their value to the group is greater and their covenant, accordingly, more valuable. Other groups that have some physicians already under a covenant, but have others who are not, may wish to value the respective "freedom" that a physician gives up. Those under no covenant under this rationale would receive a disproportionate share which recognizes that they have given up "more" of their freedom. Under this theory, those under a partial covenant would receive correspondingly less because those physicians have less to "sell" in the process.

Equal distribution

Another important concept that should be employed in the development of a proceeds distribution plan is that of equality. A certain portion of the proceeds should be earmarked for distribution on an equal basis. It is important in a group practice for all physicians to recognize that they are part of a group and that contributions to the value of the group are often difficult to ascertain and not capable of reduction to precise amounts through an exact formula. An equal distribution to each physician of a portion of the proceeds will serve to reinforce the notion that physicians, as group members, have made significant contributions to the group. Groups that have less disparity in physician income will find it easier to allocate a larger portion by this mechanism than groups that have wide disparities in physician income. As an overriding concern in the development of a physician distribution plan, the medical leadership must determine that sufficient proceeds must be given to each physician to make the physician feel that he/she will receive significant benefit by continuing with the group. The various alternatives discussed above will need to be evaluated and combined in various scenarios to make sure that lower earning physicians are not penalized in the distribution system. In addition, higher earners must not feel like they are unduly "subsidizing" lower earning physicians. A balance between these competing concerns in groups where there is significant disparity of physician incomes must be achieved. This balancing of competing interests, as in a variety of other issues in this group practice setting, is a significant goal to be achieved in the physician distribution process.

TABLE 3
The hospital affiliation schedule

Key: **Tasks completed (boldface text)**
Tasks remaining (normal text)
Changes from previous report are underlined

	Sept.	Oct.	Nov.	Dec.	Jan.
1. Asset purchase, affiliation agreement and ancillary documents					
— 1st draft of asset purchase and affiliation agreements received by committee and counsel		15th			
— Meeting with hospital re: issues		25th			
— Provide additional comments re: 1st drafts		30th			
— Circulate 2nd draft of asset purchase and affiliation agreements			10th		
— Hospital receives comments on 2nd draft of asset purchase and affiliation agreements			15th		
— Receive 1st draft of ancillary documents			20th		
— Circulate 3rd draft of asset purchase and affiliation agreements			25th		
— Comments on ancillary documents				1st	
— Comments on third drafts of asset purchase and affiliation agreements				10th	
— Receive final comments on all documents				15th	
— Circulate final copies				24th	
— Closing				28th	
— Transaction effective					1st
Status report:					

The physician-hospital integration implementation process

	Sept.	Oct.	Nov.	Dec.	Jan.
2. Board/shareholder physician meetings — Shareholder board meeting to approve asset sale and affiliation agreements Status report:				23rd	
3. Formula for distribution of proceeds: — Identify alternatives — Negotiating committee structures formula — Negotiating committee finalizes formula — Report to physicians — Report to physicians Status report:		1st 15th 25th	1st 15th		
4. Governance: — Review of concept — Negotiations re: governance — Finalize affiliation governance issues — Select representatives for governing body Status report:	15th 20th	10th		1st	
5. Medical group document collection: — Document collection commences — Report to negotiating committee — Review of documents — Collection of additional documents commences — Creation of schedules Status report:	15th 31st	5th 10th			
6. Due diligence on hospital: — Telephone contacts with references — Check references — Report to negotiating committee — Receive private placement memorandum or substitute Status report:	10th 15th 25th		1st		
7. Physician employment agreements: — Circulate 1st draft of employment agreement to negotiating committee		1st			

Transforming the Delivery of Health Care:
The integration process

	Sept.	Oct.	Nov.	Dec.	Jan.
— Comments regarding drafts received		15th			
— Circulate revised employment agreement to all physicians		16th			
— Discussion session with physicians re: employment agreement (if necessary)		25th			
— Circulate execution copies to all physicians			1st		
— All agreements returned			20th		
Status report:					
8. Pension plan/employee benefits/personnel:					
— Identify plan issues	15th				
— Advisors report with respect to plans and benefits		1st			
— Advisors complete necessary decisions	15th				
— Session with physicians			1st		
— Sessions with employees			15th		
Status report:					
9. Banking and lending relationships:					
— Search results for liens received	15th				
— Identify areas for discussion with lenders		1st			
— Meetings with lenders as necessary			15th		
— Finalize all lender issues			20th		
Status report:					
10. Real estate leases:					
— Commission appraisals if purchase involved	15th				
— Identify all real estate leases/mortgages		15th			
— Identify areas with need for discussion with third parties		25th			
— Meetings with third parties as necessary			1st		
— Determine real estate purchase price			15th		
— Finalize all real estate issues				15th	
Status report:					
11. Physician compensation:					
— Review of compensation system in light of form of affiliation	15th				
— Meeting with board		15th			

The physician-hospital integration implementation process

	Sept.	Oct.	Nov.	Dec.	Jan.
— Finalize compensation formula Status report:			15th		
12. Tax analysis:					
— Tax analysis commences	12th				
— Preliminary analysis discussed with negotiating committee		1st			
— Report to negotiating committee		15th			
— Revised report due			1st		
Status report:					
13. Joint venture issues:					
— Meeting to review effected joint ventures	10th				
— Preparation of analysis	15th				
— Finalize issues process		15th			
— Implement process			1st		
— Closing of any required consolidation				15th	
Status report:					
14. Licenses/vendors:					
— Begin inventory of vendors and licenses	15th				
— Finalize list of licenses and vendors		1st			
— Begin notification as needed			1st		
— All licenses and vendor contracts assigned effective this date				1st	
Status report:					

Chapter 13

Nuts and bolts of hospital integration implementation

Surrounding any affiliation with a hospital, there are a variety of issues that must be confronted, analyzed and resolved in order to implement the project. Many of these business issues form the foundation on which the future operation can be built, and accordingly represent great planning opportunities to improve the previously standard way of dealing with these issues. A proactive approach to confront these issues early in the affiliation process will avoid unpleasant surprises near the closing date which can seriously delay completion of the transaction. Identifying these issues, assigning appropriate administrative team members to these tasks, and creating effective reporting mechanisms that allow communications to be made to group leadership on these issues, will form the basis for the successful resolution of these issues.

Real estate

In the hospital affiliation, the real estate of the medical group plays a significant factor. Unless the hospital is persuaded to purchase the real estate, the most likely scenario is that the medical group will continue to own the real estate and the hospital will lease the property from the medical group or its related real estate partnership/limited liability company.

To the extent a medical group has a strong bargaining position, however, in most circumstances it should insist that the hospital purchase the real estate from the group even if the group continues its existence as in the management services or foundation models. In addition, to the extent that the physicians become employees of a hospital medical division, the medical group should insist upon a purchase of the real estate as the independent medical group will no longer exist.

This purchase of real estate usually will be attractive for a medical group. The sale of real estate may give the medical group a solution to many of the concerns it will face in structuring its ownership and in coping with physician departures and the addition of new physicians. Another attractive aspect of the sale is that it will allow distribution of the equity in a building to individual physicians, creating more "value" in the transaction.

To the extent the medical group and hospital agree that real estate should be purchased, it is important to evaluate thoroughly the terms of the sale. Appraisals of the property are necessary to establish a fair market value. The medical group must evaluate critically the current cost of its real property occupancy on the overall profitability of the group, versus the impact new lease rates may have on profitability when the group occupies a hospital-owned building. The cost of occupying new space in a hospital-owned facility, even if that facility was previously owned by the medical group, may make the cost of practicing medicine significantly higher, thereby reducing overall group profitability in those integration models where the independent medical group exists. In any event, before evaluating and proceeding with the purchase of the real estate by a hospital, the group must plan out over an extended period of time, perhaps 10 years, the expected occupancy costs that the group will face should it move into a new building or remain in its old building subject to a new rent structure. This forecasting is necessary in integration models where the medical group remains in existence to make sure that the group does not mortgage its future for a single one-time payment to existing physicians who are entitled to proceeds at the time of a sale.

In the creation of a hospital affiliation, the hospital, in addition to taking over the business aspects of the medical practice, will assume the various financial obligations of the medical group. An important component of this assumption where there is no real estate purchase will be the willingness and commitment of the hospital to undertake to lease the property in which the medical group leased for its practice. Where the medical group leases the property, the hospital should assume the obligations of the medical group with respect to that lease. Where the medical group undertakes to lease its own property to the hospital, however, a variety of issues should be considered. Factors to be considered generally include the following:

Rent

The rent payable by the hospital to the medical group for the use of the property should be set at a competitive fair market value level. The physician entity that owns the property should receive a fair return on its real estate investment. The rent should be a function of the debt service on the building and the market rate in the community for comparable leased space. Allowing the hospital to obtain a below market rate rental bestows on the hospital a benefit at the expense of the physician-owned entity. Unless the hospital compensation formula will take into account this subsidy, hospital efforts to achieve this favorable rental rate should be resisted. To the extent, however, that rents have historically been low for a group, it may be difficult to raise the rent as part of the affiliation process without adversely affecting the physician compensation pool.

Term

The term of the rental must be evaluated in light of the length of the affiliation arrangement. While the hospital will be obligated to provide a place for the physicians to practice, the medical group will want reasonable assurances that it can have the space it owns utilized for a medical practice. The term of the real estate rental should be made consistent with the length of the affiliation arrangement or in the medical division/employment model, on a long-term basis that extends well beyond the two to three year term of the individual employment agreements. Otherwise the group may be burdened with property that it is unable to rent or may be faced with the increased amount of debt service that may result if the hospital decides to move the location for medical group operations elsewhere.

Repairs and maintenance

Because the hospital will be undertaking to provide many administrative functions for the physicians, the lease should require that the hospital will provide all necessary repairs and building maintenance in a timely fashion in order to assure an environment conducive to the quality practice of medicine. Just as the medical group will depend upon the hospital to provide good business administration, it also will rely upon the hospital to maintain the property in which the practice is undertaken.

Taxes and insurance

The lease also should require that the hospital pay all necessary taxes and insurance associated with the operation of the property. Evidence of payment of taxes should be provided to the medical group. In addition, insurance levels should be set and the type of insurance coverage should be specified. The lease also should provide that the insurance policies will specify that at least 30 days advance notice will be given by the insurance company of any cancellation or modification of the policy.

Default

The lease should require the hospital to meet specific standards of performance which, if not performed, would allow the medical group to terminate the lease. In addition, the hospital should be allowed to terminate the relationship if the medical group does not comply with its responsibilities. Because the lease will be tied inextricably with the affiliation agreement, the lease and the affiliation agreement should contain provisions allowing for the declaration of default of one agreement if there is an event of default under the other agreement. For example, if the hospital fails to fulfill its obligations under the affiliation agreement, the medical group should have the option to declare the hospital in default under the lease. Where the medical group no longer exists in the medical division models, this cross default provision will be difficult to achieve.

Physician compensation

It is no surprise that the most difficult, and potentially most divisive, issue in any medical group relationship is that of physician compensation. Hospital affiliations put the compensation system in a spotlight, as change in the compensation system often may need to be made in, or may be caused by, the process. In an affiliation, change may be required in the existing compensation system either because the system no longer, in and of itself, meets the needs of the group, because the payment mechanism used to compensate the hospital and medical group will require a change in the way individual physicians, themselves, are paid, or because the hospital, as employer, will develop a new system.

In the affiliation context, either the medical group hires the hospital, and pays a management fee, the medical group is hired as an independent contractor by the hospital-foundation, or the physicians become hospital employees and the hospital pays the physicians. Such payment obligations may not absolutely require a new system for individual compensation to be used. In addition to the political factors within a group which may at any time require a reevaluation and modification of a compensation system, the determination of whether the current system is used in the affiliation context must start with an examination of the methodology by which a group will receive funds into its physician compensation pool created under the affiliation agreement.

The compensation system, therefore, may need to be changed because of the way in which the affiliation arrangement will operate with the hospital. For example, the amount available for a physician compensation pool may be based upon the accounts receivable of a group that are collected. Groups that base their compensation system on a charge-based methodology may need to reevaluate the logistics of making that calculation in light of cash basis on which their compensation pool is funded. On the other hand, payment methodologies for medical groups in an affiliation that are based upon charges generated for services rendered each month, may likewise create the imperative to modify medical group compensation systems that are based upon collections. Alternative compensation systems are discussed in further detail in Chapter 6.

It is also possible that long-standing disputes concerning physician compensation may be brought into focus during the hospital affiliation process because of the change that is brought about by the process itself, and the ability of individual physicians to raise the compensation issue and withhold approval for ratification of the affiliation. The political landscape found in a medical group, therefore, may require a reevaluation of a compensation system as a prerequisite for approval of the affiliation. Leadership of the group must make the strategic decision whether this change will be necessary to receive widespread approval of the affiliation, or whether the magnitude of change created by the affiliation itself dictates that any modification of the compensation system should be postponed to the post-transaction period after the affiliation has been consummated.

While the nature of the compensation arrangement with a hospital may dictate a reorganization of the system for individual physician compensation, the total amount of money available for distribution to the compensation pool of the medical group will be determined pursuant to the terms of the affiliation agreement where a management services or foundation model is utilized. The actual distribution of that pool to individual physicians in those two models should be a physician decision, and while the hospital may provide a valuable consulting role based upon experience with physician compensation systems, the ultimate decision should remain with the physicians. In the medical division/employment model, compensation will be paid directly from the hospital, as the employer, to the physician, as employee. Even in this model, overall compensation to physicians should be evaluated in the establishment and review of the medical division budgets.

The payment mechanism used for the compensation of individual physicians in the affiliation context will receive the greatest amount of scrutiny of any portion of the transaction by individual group members. The physician leadership must understand that any change in a compensation system will create winners and losers, even though in the foundation or medical division/employment model physicians may have guaranteed salaries for the first several years of the relationship. These guarantees can be directed to group compensation at large, to all physicians individually or to individual physicians who may be more adversely impacted by the new system.

It is critical, therefore, to collect sufficient data and construct models which will forecast the impact that the new compensation system will have on physician income. Identifying winners and losers, and making modifications to a proposed system to address perceived inequities, will be an important part of the fluid process of designing a system that generally is perceived to be fair by all physicians involved. The analysis necessary for construction of this fair system must be started early in the process of considering an affiliation, as most physicians will not agree to support the proposed transaction until they have an opportunity to review and evaluate the potential impact on their take home pay. The negotiating committee and hospital representatives must quickly formulate the structure necessary for this work, and to create accurate models evaluating the proposals.

Banking and lending relationships

A hospital affiliation will bring about a major change in the business operation of the medical group, which means that a change in banking or lending relationships inevitably will occur. In order to assess the impact of this change, banking and lending relationships must be identified and documents that embody those relationships reviewed. This exercise is necessary because these loan documents will often contain provisions that will require the approval of the lender before any changes are made in the business of the medical group. The structure of the proposed change, the modification of the structure of the medical group, the operation of the real estate partnership, or the transfer of assets or stock may give the lender the ability to approve or veto these fundamental changes. In order to secure the approval of a lender and to formulate an effective strategy for strengthening the banking relationship, the medical group must develop an effective communication strategy to explain the transaction to bankers and must be prepared to meet personally with banking representatives. This strategy should include an explanation of the proposed transaction, the impact that it will have upon the medical care delivery capabilities of the group, the impact upon health care delivery in the community, and any available projections about the financial implications of the transaction, along with plans for future growth and expansion. The strategy to be utilized is to explain to the bankers why the proposed transaction represents a positive move for the group and, therefore, why the bank should view it as in its best interest to cooperate with any requested change. This face-to-face meeting should include the leadership of the group, along with appropriate representatives from the hospital.

Utilizing an approach that conveys information and explains the merits of the proposed transaction will assist the medical group in securing the necessary approvals. The medical group must plan to present this information a significant time in advance to allow the bankers to become familiar with the proposed transaction, and to secure the needed consent. Many lenders, particularly those who are not in the community in which the new group will operate, such as mortgage lenders, will have little incentive to cooperate quickly with these requests. Planning for this communication and consent process must be undertaken early to avoid potential delay in finalizing the transaction.

Personnel

Making effective personnel decisions will be a challenging task to all who confront it, but making effective personnel decisions for the new business arrangement will do much to ensure its success. Without sufficient attention to personnel issues, the risk will increase that while the affiliation may be completed successfully, the business operations that are conducted thereafter will be damaged seriously or impaired because the personnel function has not been addressed adequately.

In the hospital affiliation, the management functions of the group are often assumed by the hospital, meaning that non-physician employees of the medical group will become employees of the hospital. The challenge in this situation is to integrate the existing employee base of the medical group with the personnel utilized by the hospital. At the commencement of any affiliation, few if any changes will be made to the work force and the main issues for most employees, initially, will be reassurance about job security and their roles. In some contexts where groups join an existing affiliation, some personnel may be already in place and the consolidation issues raised in a merger will also need to be considered almost immediately.

Regardless of the form of the affiliation, however, the hospital should, after commencement of the relationship, conduct a thorough study of the way in which the personnel function is being performed at the medical group. This work will include efficiency studies, cost studies and other work to determine whether the employee work force is performing its function in the most efficient way possible. These studies will result, undoubtedly, in modification in the way in which personnel are used. Unlike the implementation of the merger, however, the issues raised by an affiliation are not usually on the critical path to complete the affiliation.

Who will lead the administration of the group is a major issue faced in the affiliation process. The affiliation process replaces the existing management structure in a new management arrangement. The existing administrator of the group will, of course, desire to continue in a central, if not principal, role. The ability of the administrator to continue in that role, and to become the principal representative of the hospital in the operation of the affairs of the medical group, will depend largely upon the administrator, his or her ability to impress and win the confidence of the hospital, and the relationship that the administrator has with his or her existing medical group. Despite the uncertainty which change brings, administrators should not view the relationship with a hospital as a threat to their existence, but as an opportunity to work with a new management structure that will provide much needed support for the administrator.

Employee benefits

Linked closely with the personnel issue is that of the benefits that must be provided to employees. In addition, any change in benefits that are provided to the physician staff will be viewed with great concern by the physicians who must understand the need for any proposed change. The modification of benefits will be a significant issue that must be addressed in the pre-transaction implementation phase.

The medical group and its physicians must be prepared to analyze the impact of these benefit modifications upon their existing benefit package. In particular, attention will be focused upon the pension plan of the medical group. Because the hospital will have other employees either at the hospital or at other locations, pension plan rules may require that the plan of the medical group be modified to mirror the plan of the hospital, or the medical group may be required to terminate its own plan and adopt the plan of the hospital as its own. Again, complex legal issues and the nature of the affiliation will determine if these plans must be combined.

The ability of the medical group to impact benefit design decisions in the affiliation context will be limited because of the reality that the employees of the medical group hired by the hospital will likely only be a small portion of the overall employee work force that is employed by the hospital. Changes in benefit packages in response to negotiating positions taken by a medical group may have implications for benefit costs far beyond the employees hired by the hospital from the medical group, and the ability of the hospital to react in a positive fashion may be limited given the potential impact of change that may be required to respond to the request of the medical group. In some situations, physicians who remain employees of their own medical group in the management services or foundation models will be required to adopt parallel benefit packages because of the leased employee rules which require that physician group employees receive comparable benefits to their physician employers, even if the direct employment relationship no longer exists.

There is an important role for communication about benefit issues in the affiliation process, both with respect to employees and physicians. Proposing a major change in any benefit package, particularly with respect to the pension plan, is a volatile issue and one that must be communicated fully to physician group members early in the process. Without this communication and acceptance of the benefit proposals of the hospital, opposition may develop to the entire affiliation.

Licenses and reimbursement considerations

Commencing new business operations in a hospital affiliation may impact the licenses under which a group has previously operated. As part of the implementation process, it is important to identify and categorize licenses and permits that the group currently may utilize to function. Appropriate steps should be taken to notify these regulatory agencies of the impending change. Depending on the type of transaction contemplated, many of these licenses may automatically transfer to the organization, particularly in the stock sale context. To maintain regulatory compliance for the new operation, an action plan must be developed early in the implementation process so all necessary steps will be taken regarding licenses and permits by the beginning of the start-up of the new operation. Particularly important in this area is the relationship the affiliation will have with third party payers. An analysis will need to be undertaken concerning how the new organization will be able to bill for the medical and ancillary services that are provided. In light of the basic decision about the structure of the relationship, the parties must review the legal requirements that must be fulfilled for the new organization to receive reimbursement. To the extent a change in provider number is deemed necessary, the parties must plan for any required notification and must apply for new provider numbers where necessary. Medicare intermediaries, for example, will often require a waiting period before processing the change, and the medical group should be in constant communication with the applicable intermediaries to assure a smooth transition. Interruption of cash flow and other negative implications may occur if these steps are not followed.

Third party contracts

All medical groups receive a variety of services pursuant to vendor contracts. As part of the affiliation process, the hospital will assume many of these liabilities, and it is important to develop a detailed plan to deal with these relationships.

In the affiliation context, the ongoing business relationship with third party vendors often will be undertaken by the hospital. The task for the medical group in this context is to identify correctly all relationships that must be assumed. It is in the best interest of the medical group to identify and contact these third parties, so the hospital can assume these liabilities of the ongoing business operation. The precise approach taken depends in large part upon whether the acquisition is a stock sale or an asset sale. If the acquisition is a stock sale, these contracts automatically remain with the medical group entity, with only the ownership of the entity changing. Accordingly, in most instances, receiving consents for assignment of these agreements is unnecessary.

Where the acquisition is by asset purchase, the procedure is quite different. In order to relieve the medical group from the legal liability associated with these vendor relationships where there is an asset sale, contact with these third parties must be made and liabilities of the medical group must be assumed in a formal assignment of contract developed as part of the transaction documentation. Identifying the relationships to be assigned will require the medical group to conduct a thorough review of its operations. Sufficient advance notice must be allowed in order to have the medical group make the necessary contacts with these third parties. Because these third parties will not have the same incentive as the medical group to move forward quickly, it will be the responsibility of the medical group to pursue these parties for a timely response. Most third parties will be anxious, however, to continue the relationship, and as long as the payment stream of dollars under the contract remains unmodified, these vendors often will accept the new relationship.

In asset sale contexts, the administrative team must delegate this contract assignment process to appropriate individuals on its staff. Much of this detail work requires aggressive contacting of third parties and those who are asked to accomplish this task must have impressed upon them that this process is an important part of the overall transaction.

Some of the contracts involved in the asset sale, may, by their terms, be unassignable to the hospital. In these instances, the medical group must determine if the contract provides technical medical services that only can be provided by the medical group and which should, therefore, remain with the medical group under the affiliation model being utilized. Where an assignment cannot be obtained for these practice issues, but the obligation is one that should properly be performed by the hospital under the affiliation agreement, the hospital should agree to reimburse the medical group for the costs associated with performing that contract. In other instances where the medical group is unable to secure the consent of the third party, the medical group should be obligated only to utilize its best efforts to secure such assignment and the hospital should agree, as part of the affiliation agreement, to reimburse the medical group for the obligations arising under those agreements.

Security interests

In the course of operating its medical practice over the years, medical groups will have entered into a variety of relationships whereby a third party will have extended credit or provided leased equipment. In order to secure its right to have its loan repaid, or to perfect its right to repossess the equipment if the debt is not repaid by the medical group or if lease payments are not made, these third parties will have filed liens on the property of the medical group. These security interest filings made under the uniform commercial code protect the interest of a creditor or lessor to the equipment.

These third party filings may apply to specific medical equipment purchased by the group, to equipment leased by the group (and therefore rightfully owned by the lessor) or to such general categories of assets as equipment or accounts receivable. For example, a security interest will likely have been created when a group purchased its computer with the proceeds from a loan. In this process, the group will have granted a security interest in the computer which would allow the lender, who advances funds for the purchase, to "repossess" the computer if there is a default in the loan. The theory for allowing this repossession is that the lender can then sell the equipment and take the proceeds from that sale to apply to the reduction of the debt.

In the asset sale transaction which is part of the affiliation process, the assets will need to be transferred to a new entity which will require the medical group to transfer clear title to those assets, and also warrant that these assets are transferred free and clear of all liens, encumbrances and claims. In a stock sale transaction, a similar warranty regarding the assets may be required, although clear title is not absolutely necessary in a stock sale if there is notice and evaluation of the encumbrance.

In order to convey this clear title, it is important to identify these interests immediately when the transaction begins its initial implementation phase. From the perspective of the medical group, it is important to have these security interests released, otherwise, it will violate covenants in the transaction documents requiring clear title. The purchaser of these assets, the hospital, will not be anxious to pay twice for this equipment. If the hospital receives assets, in an asset sale transaction, that are subject to a security interest, it will have paid the medical group the full value for this equipment and will at the same time be subject to losing the equipment if the secured party repossesses the equipment. Accordingly, it risks paying twice for the same assets. This risk is not the same in the stock sale context, where the encumbrance should be noted so it can be reduced from the purchase price.

Having identified these relationships which must be dealt with in order to convey clear title, medical groups must undertake an analysis to determine how these various interests may be released. Several options exist. In the case of an asset acquisition, it is possible that the secured party will agree to an assumption of the liability by the hospital for the new medical group. In this instance, a change in the security documents and a formal assumption of that liability by the hospital will occur. In other instances, these third parties may require that the debt be paid off in order to obtain clear title to a particular asset or group of assets. This, obviously, is the least favorable position in that it requires expenditure of cash to relieve these liabilities. The facts and circumstances of each case, however, will dictate whether this approach is necessary.

In some circumstances, the third party can be persuaded to give up a portion of its security in a category of assets. In this situation, a bank may have secured the repayment of a line of credit by taking a security interest in general categories of assets such as equipment, accounts receivable, furniture, fixtures or other assets. Banks are always anxious to have more than adequate security for their obligations and it may be that the bank will have obtained a security interest in a greater amount of assets than is reasonably necessary to secure the loan. Medical groups that have entered into lending relationships with banks without a critical view of the level of security given to those banks may find themselves in this situation where a bank may be oversecured. The task of getting a bank to reduce the scope of its security in the assets will be a difficult one to achieve without some payment on the bank debt. The only effective strategy that can be used here is to explain the new business plan, the prospects for the new future combined operations and the reduction in risk that will occur to a bank if the transaction occurs. Despite the use of all of these arguments, it will usually be difficult to convince a bank which will have little, if any, incentive to agree to a less secured position for itself.

If clearing title to the assets is not possible, it may be possible for the assets to be transferred subject to the liability. While this option may be available in a stock sale and be accounted for in the valuation of each shareholder's holdings, in an asset acquisition this assumption may be more difficult as the security interest may extend beyond a particular piece of equipment. For example, while a computer may be taken by the hospital subject to the security interest of a lender, it is impossible to purchase the accounts receivable of a medical group that are subject to a lien of a bank because there is no way to separate the obligation owed to the bank from their general rights in all of the accounts receivable of the medical group. It is the inability to quantify this obligation of a bank that makes these blanket security interests on accounts receivable or equipment troublesome areas that must be identified and dealt with quickly in the affiliation process. Failure to plan adequately for this issue may result in a delay of the closing because of the inability of the medical group to convey clear title to these assets.

Patient care issues

While a medical group and a hospital may be consumed with staff combination and medical practice issues throughout the transaction process, the parties must also pay attention to an analysis of patient demographics and payer mix in the new practice. The parties should identify applicable patient population demographics information, identify third party payer mix and specify collection data. This raw data should be provided to the hospital to provide strategic information about the future direction of the medical group. The development of this database will be a useful planning tool to be used in both the implementation period and in the future operation of the medical group.

Chapter 14

The management services organization model

Medical groups that are evaluating their options to participate in the integration process are faced with balancing the desire of its member physicians to maximize physician autonomy with respect to practice issues, while at the same time meeting the external demands of payers and the realities of the increasing difficulty of operating an independent medical practice. The operation of an independent medical practice places a premium on the ability of the organization to manage itself in a cost-effective manner, to develop resources for capital expansion and capital expenditures, and to form strategic alliances that access patient populations which are controlled increasingly by third-party payers.

One option that many groups consider is forming a management relationship with a management services organization (MSO). This management relationship is more than just a vendor relationship, as it requires the MSO and physicians to work together to create a more integrated approach for the delivery of medical care. Creating a management relationship often appeals to physicians because it keeps the medical group intact, does not require the physicians to be employed by the MSO, and puts the MSO in a management relationship, rather than in an ownership relationship with the physician practice. The level of integration in the management services relationship is not as comprehensive as other integration models, but it does appeal to physician autonomy by keeping the medical group ownership, governance and employment relationships with its physicians intact.

An MSO relationship may provide an approach that can address successfully many of the organizational and strategic issues confronted by medical groups in an increasingly integrated delivery system. A properly constituted MSO can bring a new discipline and business approach to the practice of medicine. Access to a management structure and management depth can supplement the single medical group manager who is often required to perform a multitude of tasks with little support or infrastructure.

An MSO can provide access to a network relationship with a hospital for managed care contracting, and access to the strength and analysis of experienced negotiators with third party payers and managed care entities. An MSO also can provide capital for future operations and new affiliations, thereby meeting the critical capital needs of groups which have heretofore been met by reducing physician income to raise these funds. In an asset sale which usually accompanies the affiliation, capital can also be generated which provides a mechanism to purchase the equity of senior physicians in the practice and to lower the amount of the buy-in needed by new physicians to become members of the group.

The concept

Three elements should be present in any proposed management services organization relationship. First, the MSO should be willing to purchase certain of the assets of the medical practice. This sale of assets provides access of physicians to the equity of the practice, which might not otherwise be available. Individual physicians who leave groups rarely are permitted to obtain a significant return on the business that they have built up for the organization because of the need not to burden the remaining practice with the debt service for buying the interests of departing physicians. The purchase of assets by the MSO from the entire group provides a one-time benefit to all physicians in the group that would not otherwise be available.

The second component of the relationship is that the MSO will provide management services for the group and access to capital for expansion. The MSO relieves physicians from being consumed with the day-to-day business operations of the practice. By providing access to capital for expansion, the MSO provides the financial ability to take advantage of new opportunities and to renovate existing facilities. By allowing the medical group to concentrate primarily on medical practice issues, the MSO removes one of the major frustrations of physicians about the increasing bureaucracy of medical practice.

Finally, the affiliation allows the medical group an opportunity to reorganize itself. It is this opportunity that may provide the most important long term benefit to the future of the medical group. Governance issues can be evaluated. The real estate investments of the group can be reexamined and more central control can be implemented. A new structure for the relationships of physicians among themselves can be implemented. Compensation systems can be modified to reflect the current concerns of the group and the future realities of compensation. Quality assurance and

The management services organization model

practice concerns can receive increased emphasis. This reorganization will allow the group to face its future on a much stronger footing.

The MSO relationship is illustrated on exhibit 1

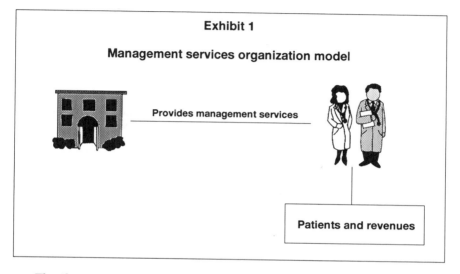

Exhibit 1

Management services organization model

Provides management services

Patients and revenues

The three components of the MSO relationship care discussed below.

The asset sale

The issues raised by the sale of substantially all of the assets of the medical group are discussed in Chapter 11.

The management services relationship

The management relationship between the management services organization and the medical group is the fundamental relationship created between the parties. It forms the basis of the ongoing partnership between the parties and creates the mechanism by which this form of integrated delivery system can prosper. Under this management relationship, the MSO agrees to provide comprehensive management services and the medical group agrees to practice medicine and to pay the MSO a management fee.

While there are many different ways to express the relationship, the most critical element of the partnership is how the parties can establish an ongoing governance mechanism. Any management services relationship that hopes to create an integrated delivery system must deal effectively with the central issue of governance and policy setting for the overall relationship and for the practice of medicine by the physicians in the medical group. Any contemplated relationship must create a "partnership" between the medical group and the MSO. Without this ability to provide management services in an ambulatory care setting in a coordinated fashion, the relationship likely will fail.

It is in the best interests of all parties to specify the details of their relationship in a management agreement. While a management agreement may take many forms depending upon the precise nature of the relationship between physicians and the hospital/management company, all agreements should include many similar concepts.

The management agreement will generally be between the MSO and the medical group. To the extent that the MSO is a newly created organization owned by the hospital, the medical group may wish to consider adding the hospital as a party to the agreement, or requiring the hospital to enter into a separate agreement whereby the hospital will guarantee the performance of the MSO under the agreement.

The management agreement will provide the mechanism by which the hospital undertakes a variety of responsibilities for physicians. In general, all agreements will follow the same outline regardless of whether a hospital-owned or investor-owned company is the affiliating party. The major provisions of the management services relationship and the implications of those provisions are described below.

First, a management agreement should contain a general explanation of the relationship of the parties. It is important to specify at the outset that the parties are independent contractors. Each party should be required to comply with all laws applicable to that party and the hospital should be required to provide such offices, facilities, equipment, supplies and personnel, as necessary, to perform its services. The physicians, on the other hand, should retain responsibility for the practice of medicine, and the group should retain responsibility for its internal agreements and finances including distribution of professional fee income and tax planning. This aspect of the MSO relationship is one of the main attractions for physicians, as the medical group retains significant autonomy and the ability to develop its relationship with its physician employees and shareholders. The parties should acknowledge, however, that their relationship will be subject to adjustment, given the application of the state and federal anti-referral laws that will govern their relationship. Under the federal anti-referral law, commonly known as the Stark Law, ancillaries such as x-ray, clinical laboratory, imaging services, pharmacy and various others which were operated by the medical group, cannot be operated by the management services organization. In order to comply with the Stark Law, the operation of these ancillaries must remain with the medical group, and be performed by medical group employees. The expansion of anti-referral laws, both at the federal level through the Stark Law, and at the state level through state anti-referral legislation, will impact the management services relationship between the medical group and the MSO.

The parties must be aware of this changing environment and must be prepared to refine their operations based upon expansion or modification of these antireferral statutes. As the statutes expand and include more operations, a comprehensive management relationship with the MSO may be difficult to achieve. While these antireferral laws were primarily designed to attack joint venture relationships among independent physicians, they have had the impact of reducing the effectiveness of a comprehensive management relationship between a management services organization and a medical group. The full impact of this legislation on the viability of the MSO integration model is yet to be seen.

This first section of the agreement also should contain provisions which explicitly set forth that payments under the agreement are not in exchange for admission, referral or other arrangements for services that may be offered by either party. This general statement will help the parties establish the ground rules for compliance with the Medicare fraud and abuse law and any applicable antireferral laws. While a recitation that the agreement is not made for the referral of patients is not conclusive on any government investigation, it is important to have this general statement of principle to establish the intent of the parties. Where the MSO organization is controlled by a hospital, heightened concern exists that the relationship established will violate the fraud and abuse laws by inducing or encouraging referrals by physician members of the medical group to the hospital which controls the MSO. It is important to structure the management services relationship to minimize this risk of attack. Accordingly, the financial projections, fee negotiations and ultimate implementation and operation of the relationship must be done on an arms-length, fair market value basis.

The parties also should consider whether they should establish a framework by which the parties can modify the agreement based upon significant legal changes in the regulatory environment for integrated delivery systems. The parties should provide that they have entered into the agreement to effect compliance with the tax exempt provisions of the internal revenue code (if applicable), the fraud and abuse law and the Stark Law.

The parties also should agree that a mechanism should be established to allow the parties to modify the agreement should any change in the regulatory and legal environment make a change necessary. First, the parties should, upon mutual agreement, have the ability to renegotiate or terminate the agreement. A dispute resolution mechanism should also be included if the parties cannot agree regarding the content of any of these legal changes or the desirability of making changes to their relationship. Accordingly, the parties can seek an advisory opinion regarding the need to restructure their relationship. By obtaining this "independent" opinion, the parties may facilitate resolution of any dispute that their respective legal counsel may have concerning the desirability of any change.

Obtaining the advisory opinion is only the first step in the process, however. The parties still must agree upon any intended change. If the parties cannot agree, they should consider specifying an arbitration process to resolve this dispute. The prospect of a stalemate is another scenario which may encourage the parties ultimately to resolve the dispute between themselves rather than allowing a third party to make that determination. The parties must make a basic decision about whether they wish to give a third party power over the fundamental basis of their relationship or whether they can resolve the dispute themselves.

The management agreement should specify how the policy-making function of the hospital-medical group relationship should occur. Clearly, this is the most important aspect of the management services organization relationship. While the hospital will be in charge of day-to-day business operations, and the medical group will be responsible for the actual practice of medicine, the two distinct entities must cooperate to set general policy for their combined operations. The mechanism to achieve this cooperation may take several forms. One option is for the medical group to establish the policy which is then implemented by the hospital. This gives physicians a predominant role in the overall operation of their practice, while eliminating or reducing the ability of the hospital to have a significant, strategic role in business operations. However, to the extent that the medical group concludes that a hospital affiliation is desirable, it also will have concluded that the medical group needs a higher level of outside involvement in its affairs. Input in strategic decisions and the ability of the hospital to have an impact on these policy decisions should be encouraged, not limited.

From the perspective of the hospital, it may prefer to make all significant policy and strategic decisions, thereby limiting the role of the medical group or physicians to that of a vendor of medical services. This approach, however, leaves the hospital without the valuable input, emotional investment and enthusiasm that involvement in issues can create in physicians who believe they have a stake in the success of the affiliation.

Under most circumstances, therefore, both parties should be prepared to share policy-making authority as this is the critical mechanism to achieve an integrated operation between the medical group and the hospital. To create a mechanism whereby representatives of the hospital and the medical group can come together to establish policy for medical group operation, a governing body, either as a formal board of directors of the management company or as a separate decision making body, should be established. This common governing body makes the policy and strategic decisions necessary for overall group operations. A combined governing body has the advantage of bringing together the respective skills of physicians and hospitals in a forum in which the parties must cooperate to achieve effective decision making. A cooperative working relationship between physicians and hospitals will lead to better decision making and will encourage the parties to work through their differences and develop a true partnership.

The voting requirements of this combined governing body must be considered carefully. Allowing a majority of board members to be hospital representatives or physician representatives may be counterproductive, as whoever holds the majority vote will feel that they are in control. An even division of voting power requires the parties to work together to build consensus.

Because most management service organizations will not have broadly charitable purposes, but will provide management services to medical group, it is unlikely that the organizations will be able to achieve tax-exempt status. Because these organizations are likely to be taxable, the only limitation on the ability of the medical group to achieve a split of control is the bargaining position of the medical group with the hospital. To the extent that the management services organization is granted tax-exempt status, however, or to the extent the medical group is unable to negotiate an equal split of control, other mechanisms must be utilized. In the tax-exempt arena, in most instances, physicians will be limited to no more than 20 percent of the board of directors of a tax-exempt entity, and a committee structure should be utilized to help physicians maintain their input necessary in the overall policy-making structure of the integrated system.

In addition, consideration should be given to how voting actually works. Where an equal number of representatives are elected by the hospital and the medical group, it is more favorable for the medical group to require a majority of each class of governing board members (one class being selected by the hospital and the other class being selected by the medical group) to vote to approve an action. This type of provision would help the medical group from losing decisions by having one physician vote with the hospital-appointed directors for board action. The parties, however, may need to rely on a majority or a super majority vote where the consensus decision making by classes of directors cannot be achieved.

From an operational perspective, the parties must consider whether utilizing the potential of a deadlocked board will fit their overall philosophy. If, from the operational and financial perspective of the management services organization both parties have the same incentives, that being to maximize revenue and to minimize expenses, it is likely that they will view the issues raised at the governing board level in the same fashion and that the potential for a deadlock will be minimized. This provision likely will be subject to extensive negotiations given different philosophies. From the perspective of the medical group, however, the optimum outcome is to be in a partnership with the management services organization and that partnership should require the parties to work together.

To the extent the medical group is unable to negotiate a position on the board of directors of the MSO, it is advisable that the types of responsibilities that are specified as the responsibility for a governing board, detailed above, be delegated to a policy-setting body rather than the board itself. Accordingly, failing the ability to have an even number of representatives on the board of directors, the next strategy for the medical group should be to establish this policy-making body which will undertake many operational decisions. While this policy committee need not be a formal, legally recognized body, such as a board of directors, it may be established by contract pursuant to the management services agreement. The validity of that body to act will be established by the terms of the agreement and will provide significant protection to the medical group in the relationship.

Regardless of the decision-making mechanism that is adopted by the medical group and the hospital, general policy decisions will need to be made. The duties and responsibilities of the governing board will be subject to much negotiation between the parties. The negotiation of the specific provisions will depend upon facts and circumstances of each situation and the relationship of the parties. In general, the philosophy should be to require that the parties make joint decisions concerning their relationship by allowing the governing board to address the full range of issues that can be confronted in the performance of the management function by the MSO. The parties should be encouraged, therefore, to be more inclusive rather than less inclusive in designating the responsibilities of this joint governing organization. The range of decisions to be made could include the following:

- **Capital improvements and expansion**. Capital expenditures for both building and equipment should be approved by this governing board.
- **Annual budgets**. Annual budgets for the operation of the group practice, including both the MSO operations and medical group operations should be approved by the governing board.
- **Determination of sanctuaried income**. Many medical groups have policies with respect to the earning of income by physicians that are not directly related to the practice of medicine. These fees may be generated by speakers' honoraria, witness fees, book royalties and other types of income. To the extent that a physician is allowed to keep these funds by medical group policy, that same policy should be considered for adoption in the MSO relationship. There is likely to be some negotiation concerning the inclusion of some of these

items in that policy. Excluding these revenues from group revenues will decrease directly the amount of management fee payable to the MSO when the management fee is based upon a revenue figure. In addition, the physician who earns the fees usually will profit greatly by having those sums paid directly to the physician rather than to the medical group, and thereby being subject to the usual overhead extraction.

- **Advertising**. Advertising and marketing operations should be approved by the governing board with the final approval being granted by the medical group. In this way, the medical group maintains the ability to veto any advertising program that it finds inconsistent with the image it wishes to create in the community.
- **Professional fees**. The governing board should be responsible for arranging legal and accounting services for the group practice operations.
- **Ancillary services**. Ancillary services provided by the MSO should be determined by the governing board. Ancillaries provided must meet a standard of a full range of services and products for group practices as that standard may exist from time to time. One of the concerns from the medical group perspective in entering into the MSO relationship would be that the hospital connection with the MSO will encourage the MSO to shift ancillary revenues to the hospital. Addressing the range of ancillary services to be provided can minimize this potential risk.
- **Payer relationships**. Decisions regarding managed care relationships should be established by the governing board. The medical group will remain the provider of medical services in the MSO model and it must be the entity which enters into the managed care relationship directly with the managed care plan. In general, this decision should be made jointly by the governing board, rather than by the medical group by itself.
- **Strategic planning and network expansion**. Strategic planning developed by the governing board is an important concept for the future success of the MSO/medical group integrated relationship. The governing board must approve additional relationships between the MSO and physicians who are not members of the medical group. This type of restriction will give the medical group some control over the expansion of the MSO relationship and the cost of that expansion should be an expense of the MSO rather than the medical group.
- **Physician location, hiring and restrictive covenants**. The governing board should be given the power to determine the locations to be utilized by physicians, any changes in those sites and the power to recommend minimum levels of staffing. The governing board should have the ability to approve variations of the restrictive covenants

contained in the physician employment contract with the medical group and act as the entity responsible for enforcement of those covenants. The governing board should be given the ability to be an active participant in restrictive covenant enforcement in the physician employment agreement. The MSO will be vitally interested in the ability of the medical group to enforce these restrictive covenants, having acquired significant assets from the medical group and being desirous of protecting its investment by insuring that physicians who consider leaving the group are not aided by the inability of the medical group to enforce a restrictive covenant through inaction of the medical group leadership.

- **Senior administrator and medical director**. The selection of the senior administrator should be subject to the approval of the governing board. In addition, the medical director should be selected by the medical group and selection approved by the governing board.
- **Grievance referrals**. The agreement should provide the governing board with the ability to act as an appeal body of matters not specifically addressed in the agreement.
- **Real and personal property leases**. Any real or personal property leases that impact the MSO or the medical group should be approved by the governing board.
- **Practice management system**. A practice management system should be established by the governing board in conjunction with the medical group. This mechanism will allow the governing board the actual ability to establish and implement a system covering these issues.
- **Credit collection policies**. The governing board should have the ability to establish credit policies for the MSO in collection of patient accounts receivable for the medical group.
- **Contracts**. Contracts for the operation of the group practice, whether entered into by the medical group or the MSO, should be approved by the governing board, or should be executed in accordance with guidelines established by the governing board.

An affiliation agreement should contain a comprehensive list of the duties, responsibilities, services and facilities to be provided by the hospital that will be implemented in accordance with standards established by the governing board. A detailed list of services provided should be present in any agreement, as parties will forget, over time, their respective obligations unless future reference can be made to a document which clearly specifies the various responsibilities. While the detailed list is important for physicians to be assured that they will receive the scope of services they have been promised in the marketing phase of the relationship, it is even more important to insist on listing quantifiable performance standards. A management agreement prepared by the hospital likely will set forth, in rather general language, the type of responsibilities to be undertaken. The task of the medical group or physicians in finalizing the management agreement is to take these general standards, which are incapable of measurement, and transform them into benchmarks of performance so hospital performance can be evaluated. Without these performance standards, no claim can be made that the hospital has failed to meet its performance responsibilities.

The administrative staff actually employed by the MSO must have the ability to perform a wide variety of management functions. This performance of management functions may be done directly by the employees of the hospital, or the concept of a small operating committe, consisting of administrators and physicians can be given the authority to conduct actual operations. The hospital in the course of negotiations will likely desire to perform these functions unilaterally, with the medical group desiring to have more physician input through membership on an operating committee. Because of the unique attributes of group practice and the limited experience that many hospital personnel have with ambulatory care operations, it is advisable to use an operating committee concept to ensure physician and medical group administrator input on day-to-day operations. This sharing of responsibilities should increase the chances for success of the relationship.

The management services to be provided by the hospital in accordance with policy established by the governing board (through the operating committee if such a committee is utilized) should include at least the general areas listed here.

- The hospital should make a specific commitment with respect to the practice facilities it will provide for the ongoing practice of medicine. Maintenance, repair and operation of those facilities also should be provided;
- The hospital should be authorized to perform its responsibilities in a way it deems appropriate, but in accordance with the general guidelines established by the governing board structure comprised of physician representatives and the hospital;
- The hospital should commit to prepare and provide annual budgets on a timely basis, and provide capital acquisition plans and goals for financial performance over the coming years;
- The hospital should be obligated to make certain capital expenditures with governing board approval. Because the dynamics of medical group operations depend upon a variety of factors, it will be difficult to specify an exact amount of capital expenditures which the hospital is obligated to make each year. Accordingly, the best approach is probably to have governing board involvement in the

process and to require the hospital to use its best efforts to add a variety of services.

- Expansion of the group practice is likely to be a critical element for the future success of not only the medical group, but also the management services organization created by the hospital. The hospital should support recruitment of physicians to the medical group according to schedules approved by the governing board and in compliance with legal guidelines.

- Annual financial statements for the operations of the affiliation should be prepared, along with interim financial statements. The hospital should agree to provide these statements on a timely basis, using accurate financial reporting standards;

- The hospital should agree to purchase necessary inventory and supplies for operations;

- Practice administration also should be performed by the hospital. The hospital should agree to bill and collect the professional fees generated by physicians and generally be authorized to use the full range of collection techniques necessary to collect these funds.

- As part of its general administrative activities, the hospital should be required to maintain patient medical records, accounting, billing and collection records, and to manage these files and records in accordance with all applicable state and federal statutes. The hospital should be obligated to preserve the confidentiality of patient medical records. Clerical, accounting, bookkeeping, computer services, printing, postage, duplicating services, medical transcribing services and payment of licenses and certification fees are additional responsibilities that the hospital should assume;

- The hospital should make commitments with respect to public relations and marketing. Effective marketing techniques will benefit greatly the overall success of the affiliation. While the medical group and physicians should be willing to rely on the marketing expertise of the hospital, the medical group and physicians should retain the right to veto marketing programs that are done without the requisite professionalism;

- The hospital can be expected to provide important assistance in the recruitment of physicians by carrying out necessary administrative tasks, including marketing the group, identifying potential candidates and coordinating the interview process. While physicians should be allowed to make the final hiring decision, the hospital can play an effective role in performing the many administrative tasks necessary to recruit physicians successfully and to provide financial support. Recruiting for the expansion of the medical group is a critical function to be undertaken by the hospital. Some arrangements may obligate the hospital to advance to the medical group recruiting costs, agency fees, relocation and interviewing expenses. Because the hospital has capital to provide these advances, the medical group is assisted in the recruitment process. Medical groups who add physicians often experience a direct reduction in the income of the existing physicians at the group. The ability of the MSO to advance these funds until new physicians can "pay for themselves" is an added benefit that can be provided by the hospital under the management services model. In general, however, these advances must be repaid in order to comply with fraud and abuse and tax-exempt requirements. Repayment can be over a period of years, if necessary, after the physician has turned profitable.

In addition, just as recruitment costs are important costs to be defrayed so income for medical group physicians will not be reduced, the start-up costs associated with bringing on a new physician present a similar problem. The hospital should be obligated, therefore, to advance the amount of any loss that is experienced by the medical group for a new physician. This loss can be defined by the amount by which the expenses associated with that new physician exceed the revenue generated by that new physician. The MSO can be obligated to advance the difference to the medical group, thereby cushioning the impact of bringing on new physicians on existing physician income. The amounts advanced, however, usually must be repaid in order to comply with fraud and abuse and tax-exempt requirements.

- The hospital should arrange for the legal and accounting services for the affiliation and should negotiate and administer managed care and direct contracts. A joint decision-making process should be implemented concerning the selection of managed care contracts and the pricing of services to be provided. The experience of the hospital in analyzing managed care contracts and responding with a well-reasoned analysis of the financial implications of these arrangements should be important responsibilities of the hospital, coupled with the commitment of the hospital to administer these arrangements once they are implemented;
- Under the management arrangement, the hospital usually will perform the personnel function for the affiliation by hiring and training all non-physician employees, and by administering the workplace routine. Salaries, benefits and working conditions of these non-physician employees generally will be established by the hospital. A mechanism must be implemented to identify problem employees and allow a vehicle for physicians' complaints about job performance of these employees, resulting in transfer or termination

of employees who have demonstrated unsatisfactory job performance;

- The hospital should be obligated to operate ancillary services consistent with legal requirements for referral relationships between
physicians and providers of ancillary services. For example, the
ownership and operation of clinical laboratories, imaging centers
and ambulatory surgery centers must be reviewed closely to ensure
compliance with federal and state anti-referral legislation. In general, a growing number of these ancillary services must be owned and
operated by the medical group in order to effect compliance with the
restrictions of federal and state antireferral legislation. Standards of
performance should be specified to assure competent management
of ancillary services that are operated by the hospital;

- The hospital should be responsible for obtaining and paying for
professional malpractice insurance. While physicians will be
requested to make an effort to ensure insurance eligibility, the
hospital should arrange for malpractice insurance, and the costs
associated with that coverage may be paid for as part of the
management services rendered by the hospital; and

- The agreement should specify the method by which the hospital will
hire the executive responsible for administration of the affiliation.
Ideally, this executive will be hired in a collaborative effort between
medical group and hospital. To manage effectively, this executive
must win the confidence of physicians, and therefore a mechanism
should be developed to allow physician input and a veto power over
undesirable candidates. While the hospital will resist limiting its
management discretion in this area, physicians must maintain a
strong voice in determining who will manage the affiliation and insist
that individuals placed in a management position have strong
ambulatory care management experience.

Another section of the management agreement should contain a
delineation of the rights and responsibilities of the medical group. The
management services model utilizes a separate medical group. The
primary function of the medical group, of course, is to provide professional
services to its patients. The management agreement should accordingly
require the medical group to render these services in compliance with all
ethical standards, laws and regulations applicable to the practice of
medicine.

The affiliation agreement should not, however, require the medical
group to perform to any particular standard of care, other than that which
may be established by state law. Phrases such as "highest quality,"
"teaching hospital quality" or others which may imply a higher standard
of care than required by state laws should be avoided. If a higher standard

of care is established by the management agreement, the medical group may be required to perform to this higher level of care in any malpractice action that occurs after the establishment of the relationship. This result is completely undesirable and may result in unnecessary liability being imposed upon the medical group.

The management agreement also will require the medical group to occupy the facilities provided by the hospital exclusively for the practice of medicine, and other physicians will be prohibited from utilizing the facilities without the agreement of the hospital. The medical group will be responsible for hiring physicians and any other technical employees for reimbursement purposes. The hiring decision and the compensation, supervision, evaluation and termination of these employees should remain responsibilities of the medical group. Fringe benefits and other employee-related expenses for the physicians also may be borne by the medical group, as well as professional dues and continuing education expenses.

Another important provision in the management services relationship will be how the hospital and medical group are compensated. Generally, the system utilized should offer incentives to both the group and hospital to conserve costs and maximize revenue. If the system fails to provide these parallel incentives, it may result in pitting the hospital against the medical group with adverse consequences to the overall success of the affiliation. If every decision becomes a "we" versus "they" decision, the overall best interest of the affiliation will not be served.

Generally, the parties may consider a variety of payment methodologies for management compensation:

A set fee

Under this reimbursement methodology, the hospital is paid for its services a flat management fee that is fixed in advance. This method will provide little incentive, and will likely produce mediocre performance given there is no incentive to generate revenues, collect fees or increase overall margin. This type of fee may qualify for the management contract safe harbor provision to the Medicare fraud and abuse law, and may be attractive from that perspective. From a business point of view, however, it is not very attractive in creating performance incentives.

Set compensation for physicians

The opposite of a set fee for the hospital is a set salary for physicians. This method is not available in a management services relationship where the medical group is the owner of the business, and it pays the hospital a management fee for the services it renders.

Gross revenue reimbursement

Some management agreements may reimburse the hospital by using a percentage of billings. While this method may be an incentive to increase overall business activities, it creates little incentive to collect the billings that are generated, or to minimize expenditures. Increasing expenses and increasing overhead are concerns for physician practices and this system does little to address those concerns.

Fee based upon collections

A reimbursement methodology based upon collections gives the hospital the incentive to both increase revenues and collections. Medical groups benefit by only being required to pay a fee when funds are received from operations. The same drawbacks with respect to attention to growing overhead are present here as were present in the reimbursement system based upon gross revenue.

Cost-based reimbursement

Cost-based reimbursement allows the hospital to calculate the costs of operations and to be reimbursed for those costs, plus an appropriate profit. Cost-based reimbursement provides little effective performance incentives. There is no incentive to increase revenues, nor any incentive to hold down expenses, as the management fee is received without any relationship to the overall profitability of the business.

Physician guaranteed performance

Hospitals also may take some risk in receiving their fee by providing commitments to the medical group that the overhead of the medical group will not exceed a certain level or percentage, or that the pool for physician compensation will be set at specified levels regardless of overall operational results. While these types of systems put great risk on the hospital and provide a "safety net" for medical groups, they may create conflicting incentives on expenditures and may give medical groups few performance incentives. Both fraud and abuse and tax exempt issues limit the use of this type of compensation.

Profit-based reimbursement

This reimbursement method allows payment of a management fee based upon the contribution of the hospital to the overall success of the affiliation. Usually, this methodology requires a calculation of the revenues generated by the affiliation. All operational expenses and non-physician employee costs then are subtracted from this revenue. The amount available after payment of these expenses is then distributed to the parties. The portion distributed to the hospital is its management fee and the amount available for distribution to the medical group is used for the physician compensation pool. This method of reimbursement increases the incentives for both parties to increase revenues while holding down expenses.

Budget determined compensation

A final compensation system for hospitals and physicians is based upon a negotiated budget determined each year. In this system, for example, the physician compensation pool can be established in a budget process that examines overall affiliation operations. This system will require an annual or biennial negotiation process in which the risk of under-budget performance or the reward of over-budget performance can be allocated to the parties. This system may create uncertainty in the reimbursement system that may cause severe stress every time compensation is negotiated. If successfully managed, however, this system may allow the relationship of the parties to adapt successfully to changing business considerations. In general, however, the management services concept requires the medical group to be at risk for operational results.

Both parties should determine whether a fair price is being paid for the services provided by the hospital in light of the need for capital and market expansion. The medical group must review the proposed compensation mechanism and seek an explanation of the fee determination with reference to projections concerning new and existing operations of the medical group. The medical group should consider seriously the use of financial experts to evaluate the proposed model. The projected compensation levels for physicians, before and after the affiliation, as well as with and without that affiliation, should be reviewed. These projections will enable the group to focus on the benefits and costs of affiliating with the hospital. The compensation system also should specify any bonus methodology. The management services agreement should provide a bonus to the parties for achieving superior results in their respective functions. The bonus methodology should be reviewed carefully. Specific, identifiable performance standards should be placed in the agreement. It is possible to provide rewards based on specific criteria regarding reduction of accounts receivable, increases in physician income, reduction in expenses or other particular indicators of management success. Another possible bonus methodology will be to examine overall operational profitability. To the extent that the affiliation exceeds budgeted revenue, the parties may be entitled to divide that excess. The ability to obtain a bonus under this methodology would give both parties the same incentive, i.e., to maximize revenues and decrease costs. The assumptions upon which this bonus methodology is based must be tested carefully with reference to prior medical group performance and the results achieved at any other hospital or management company affiliations.

While significant negotiations may take place concerning the bonus mechanism, the parties should not lose sight of the goal to allow for a fair distribution of the bonus amount. Whatever division is achieved, it is important that both parties perceive the arrangement as being fair, as neither the medical group nor hospital can afford, in the long run, to drive too hard a bargain with the other side, for to do so eventually will discourage one of the parties from performing well under the agreement.

Another significant section of the management services agreement should contain insurance and indemnity provisions. Liability and professional malpractice insurance coverage levels should be specified for both parties, and each should endeavor to name the other party as additional insured under their respective policies, if feasible. The agreement also may contain provisions whereby each party will agree to indemnify the other should the other party suffer loss associated with the combined operation. Broad indemnification clauses should be avoided as they will be uninsurable obligations. For the medical group, this uninsured obligation will impact physician income if the medical group is required to make payments under these types of provisions. If possible, only specific events such as intentional wrong-doing should be covered, if the entire indemnification concept is not omitted.

The term of any affiliation agreement also must be evaluated. In general, the term of the affiliation proposed by the hospital will be long, perhaps in the 20- to 30-year range. Medical groups, however, may desire a shorter agreement, allowing ongoing performance evaluation. To the extent that the medical group has some bargaining leverage, it should seek a shorter commitment. A longer term agreement will tie the future of the medical group to a single party and, to the extent there are no easy ways to terminate the relationship, may result in a long-term, unhappy relationship that may impact adversely the future of the physicians.

While the medical group may be able to negotiate a shorter term of the proposed relationship, it will not be without consequences. The hospital often will make an extensive capital investment by purchasing the assets of the group pursuant to an asset purchase agreement. In order to recoup its investment, the hospital will need a relationship of sufficient length to receive an adequate return on investment. A request for a shorter term agreement likely will be met with a significantly reduced purchase price for the assets because of the shorter time in which an adequate return on investment can be achieved. Given this choice, many medical groups may accept a longer term relationship, rather than accepting a shorter term agreement with a significantly reduced purchase price for assets. Critically evaluating the hospital and the proposed operation will be important in raising the comfort level of the medical group to agree to a longer term relationship.

The management services organization model

Termination provisions of the affiliation agreement also should be reviewed thoroughly. While all parties hope that termination provisions will never be utilized, and may feel that undue negotiating effort is placed on these provisions to the detriment of goodwill that has developed between the parties, it is important to look at the "worst case" scenario. Both parties must assume the worst from the other party in evaluating these provisions. The agreement should delineate clearly responsibilities of the parties and allow for termination of the agreement should either party not fulfill its obligations under the agreement. Without clear performance standards contained in the agreement and without the ability to demonstrate a failure to perform pursuant to those standards, the medical group will have little redress should the quality of performance of the hospital be unsatisfactory.

Given the long-term nature of the management agreement, however, medical groups can expect the hospital to insist upon a variety of limitations on the ability of the medical group to terminate the agreement unilaterally. Termination of the agreement by the medical group may therefore be permitted only upon a vote of the shareholders, rather than just a simple majority of the board of directors of the medical group. Other provisions, such as requiring a high vote requirement of those shareholders, or requiring a cooling off period if there is a dispute, may be suggested. In general, the medical group probably will conclude that a higher vote requirement of the shareholders is reasonable, given that termination of the agreement affects the practices of the entire medical staff, not just the leadership. From the perspective of the hospital, it will be advisable to specify reasons that may allow the hospital to terminate the agreement. However, because the main obligation of the medical group will be to practice medicine and compensate the hospital, specifying performance standards will be less critical in this context. In either context, making termination difficult will encourage the parties to work through their differences as opposed to seeking easy solutions by terminating the agreement.

While termination events are important to specify, the agreement also should specify the impact of termination on the parties. For example, parties should address access to medical and financial records, who owns them and who is entitled to access after the agreement ends. The agreement should specify how the parties will conduct business immediately after the termination and require them to cooperate to fully wind-down their relationship. How the affiliation is unwound also must be specified. Dealing with termination issues will be difficult, but it is far better to confront these issues in advance than to postpone the decisions until the parties are engaged in a bitter dispute. For example, the hospital may insist upon the repurchase of various assets that it had acquired from the medical group if the agreement is terminated. While the medical group generally should resist agreeing to these types of provisions, it should at least attempt to limit these repurchase obligations to certain circumstances, including its own default in the relationship, and should avoid making individual physicians responsible for any repurchase obligation.

A final significant provision in a management agreement is a restrictive covenant that will prohibit both medical group and hospital from engaging in competition with each other. This restriction will exist at least during the term of the agreement, and will be necessary for both parties. For the medical group, it is important to prohibit the hospital from diverting its energies to other competitors of the medical group or to those groups outside of the hospital affiliation network. This exclusivity arrangement is important for the future of the medical group, and may be particularly important to preserve the important place that the medical group has in the hospital relationship. Likewise, the hospital will request that the medical group refrain from engaging in other affiliations or in medical practice other than through the affiliation operation. This prohibition should not preclude physicians from admitting patients to other hospitals, as there is risk that such a restriction could be construed as violating the Medicare fraud and abuse law. This exclusivity arrangement for both sides, however, is in the best interests of both parties and will protect their relationships with each other.

The existence of restrictive covenants after the agreement has concluded, however, is another matter. The ending of the relationship between generally should resist agreeing to these types of provisions, it should at least attempt to limit these repurchase obligations to certain circumstances, including its own default in the relationship, and should avoid making individual physicians responsible for any repurchase obligation.

A final significant provision in a management agreement is a restrictive covenant that will prohibit both medical group and hospital from engaging in competition with each other. This restriction will exist at least during the term of the agreement, and will be necessary for both parties. For the medical group, it is important to prohibit the hospital from diverting its energies to other competitors of the medical group or to those groups outside of the hospital affiliation network. This exclusivity arrangement is important for the future of the medical group, and may be particularly important to preserve the important place that the medical group has in the hospital relationship. Likewise, the hospital will request that the medical group refrain from engaging in other affiliations or in medical practice other than through the affiliation operation. This prohibition should not preclude physicians from admitting patients to other hospitals, as there is risk that such a restriction could be construed as violating the Medicare fraud and abuse law. This exclusivity arrangement for both sides, however, is in the best interests of both parties and will protect their relationships with each other.

The existence of restrictive covenants after the agreement has concluded, however, is another matter. The ending of the relationship between the hospital and medical group should not force either party out of business by preventing either from conducting operations after the termination of their relationship. It is not reasonable to expect a medical group to refrain from practicing medicine in a given locality after the affiliation has terminated. Likewise, the hospital will resist all such efforts to be excluded from forming other affiliations after the relationship is over. Because of the significant financial investment in the medical group, the hospital likely will prevail on this issue. The parties may consider adding a provision whereby the medical group agrees not to enter into another affiliation with a third party for a year after termination. This provision will discourage third parties from interfering with the affiliation. If a medical group agrees to this type of provision, it should only apply upon default by the medical group.

Internal group matters

Critical to the success of the affiliation is the ability of the medical group to evaluate its current governing structure, and to implement successfully a reorganization of its affairs to allow for coordination of its operations in the MSO relationship. This reorganization process is discussed more fully in Chapter 16.

Chapter 15

The foundation model

A s discussed in Chapter 14, medical groups that are evaluating their options to participate in the integration process are faced with balancing the desire of its member physicians to maximize physician autonomy with respect to practice issues, while at the same time meeting the external demands of payers and the realities of the increasing difficulty of operating an independent medical practice.

One option that many groups consider is forming an independent contractor relationship with a foundation authorized under applicable state law to be the "provider" of medical services (the "foundation"). Creating a foundation relationship appeals to physicians because it keeps the medical group intact and does not require the physicians to be employed by the hospital or foundation. The level of integration in the foundation relationship is not as comprehensive as in the medical division/employment model, but it does appeal to physician autonomy by keeping the medical group ownership, governance and employment relationships with its physicians intact.

The foundation relationship may provide an approach that can address successfully many of the organizational and strategic issues confronted by medical groups in an increasingly integrated delivery system. Access to a management structure and management depth in a foundation can supplement the single medical group manager who is often required to perform a multitude of tasks with little support or infrastructure.

A foundation can provide capital for future operations and new affiliations, thereby meeting the critical capital needs of groups which have been met heretofore by reducing physician income to raise these funds. In an asset sale which usually accompanies the affiliation, capital also can be generated which provides a mechanism to purchase the equity of senior physicians in the practice and to lower the amount of the buy-in needed by new physicians to become members of the group.

The concept

Three elements should be present in any proposed foundation relationship. First, the foundation should be willing to purchase certain of the assets of the medical practice. This sale of assets provides access of physicians to the equity of the practice, which might not otherwise be available. Individual physicians who leave groups rarely are permitted to obtain a significant return on the business that they have built up for the organization because of the need not to burden the remaining practice with the debt service for buying the interests of departing physicians. The purchase of assets by the foundation from the entire group provides a one-time benefit to all physicians in the group that would not otherwise be available. The second component of the relationship is that the medical group will provide professional services on an independent contractor basis to the foundation which is the provider of services to its patients. The foundation maintains the patient relationship, billing for services and generating revenues that belong to the foundation. The foundation relieves physicians from being consumed with the day-to-day business operations of the practice. By providing access to capital for expansion for the foundation, the foundation has the financial ability to take advantage of new opportunities and to renovate existing facilities. By allowing the medical group to concentrate primarily on medical practice issues, the foundation removes one of the major frustrations of physicians about the increasing bureaucracy of medical practice.

Finally, the affiliation allows the medical group an opportunity to reorganize itself. It is this opportunity that may provide the most important long term benefit to the future of the medical group. Governance issues can be evaluated. The real estate investments of the group can be reexamined and more central control can be implemented. A new structure for the relationships of physicians among themselves can be implemented. Compensation systems can be modified to reflect the current concerns of the group and the future realities of compensation. Quality assurance and practice concerns can receive increased emphasis. This reorganization will allow the group to face its future on a much stronger footing as a provider in the foundation.

The foundation relationship is illustrated on Exhibit 1.

The three components of the foundation relationship are discussed on the next page.

The asset sale

The issues raised by the sale of substantially all of the assets of the medical group are discussed in Chapter 11.

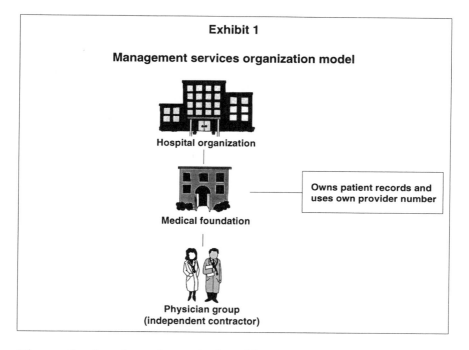

Exhibit 1

Management services organization model

Hospital organization

Medical foundation — Owns patient records and uses own provider number

Physician group
(independent contractor)

The professional services relationship

The professional services relationship between the foundation and the medical group is the fundamental relationship created between the parties. It forms the basis of the ongoing partnership between the parties and creates the mechanism by which this form of integrated delivery system can prosper. Under this relationship, the medical group agrees to provide comprehensive physician services and the foundation agrees to pay the medical group for the services it renders to the patients of the foundation.

It is in the best interests of all parties to specify the details of their relationship in a professional services agreement. While this agreement may take many forms depending upon the precise nature of the relationship between physicians and the foundation, all agreements should include many similar concepts, regardless of whether a for-profit or tax-exempt foundation is the affiliating party. The major provisions of the professional services relationship and the implications of those provisions are described below.

First, a professional services agreement should contain a general explanation of the relationship of the parties. It is important to specify at the outset that the parties are independent contractors. Each party should be required to comply with all laws applicable to that party and the foundation should be required to provide such offices, facilities, equipment, supplies and personnel, as necessary. The physicians, on the other hand, should retain responsibility for the practice of medicine, and the group should retain responsibility for its internal agreements and finances, including distribution of payments for services received from the foundation and tax planning. This aspect of the foundation relationship is one of the main attractions for physicians, as the medical group retains significant autonomy and the ability to develop its relationship with its physicians.

The parties should acknowledge, however, that their relationship will be subject to adjustment given the application of the state and federal anti-referral laws that will govern their relationship. Under the federal anti-referral law, commonly known as the Stark Law, ancillaries such as x-ray, clinical laboratory, imaging services, pharmacy and various others, which were operated by the medical group, cannot be operated by the foundation. In order to comply with the Stark Law, the operation of these ancillaries must remain with the medical group, and be performed by medical group employees. The expansion of anti-referral laws, both at the federal level through the Stark Law, and at the state level through state anti-referral legislation, will impact the relationship between the medical group and the foundation.

The parties must be aware of this changing environment and must be prepared to refine their operations based upon expansion or modification of these anti-referral statutes. While these anti-referral laws were primarily designed to attack joint venture relationships among independent physicians, they have had the impact of reducing the effectiveness of a comprehensive relationship between a foundation and a medical group. The full impact of this legislation on the foundation model is yet to be seen.

This first section of the agreement also should contain provisions which explicitly set forth that payments under the agreement are not in exchange for admission, referral or other arrangements for services that may be offered by either party. This general statement will help the parties establish the ground rules for compliance with the Medicare fraud and abuse law and any applicable anti-referral laws. While a recitation that the agreement is not made for the referral of patients is not conclusive on any government investigation, it is important to have this general statement of principle to establish the intent of the parties. It is important to structure the relationship to minimize this risk of attack. Accordingly, the financial projections, fee negotiations and ultimate implementation and operation of the relationship must be done on an arms-length, fair market value basis.

The parties also should consider whether they should establish a framework by which the parties can modify the agreement based upon significant legal changes in the regulatory environment for integrated delivery systems. The parties should provide that they have entered into the agreement to effect compliance with the tax exempt provisions of the internal revenue code (if applicable), the Fraud and Abuse Law and the Stark Law.

The parties also should agree that a mechanism should be established to allow the parties to modify the agreement should any change in the regulatory and legal environment make a change necessary. First, the parties should have the ability, upon mutual agreement, to renegotiate or terminate the agreement. A dispute resolution mechanism also should be included if the parties cannot agree regarding the content of any of these legal changes or the desirability of making changes to their relationship. Accordingly, the parties can seek an advisory opinion regarding the need to restructure their relationship. By obtaining this "independent" opinion, the parties may facilitate resolution of any dispute that their respective legal counsel may have concerning the desirability of any change.

Obtaining the advisory opinion is only the first step in the process, however. The parties still must agree upon any intended change. If the parties cannot agree, they should consider specifying an arbitration process to resolve this dispute. The prospect of a stalemate is another scenario which may encourage the parties ultimately to resolve the dispute between themselves rather than allowing a third party to make that determination. The parties must make a basic decision about whether they wish to give a third party power over the fundamental basis of their relationship or whether they can resolve the dispute themselves.

The professional agreement should specify how the policy making function of the foundation-medical group relationship should occur. Clearly, this is the most important aspect of the relationship. While the foundation will be in charge of day-to-day business operations, and the medical group will be responsible for the actual practice of medicine, the two distinct entities must cooperate for their combined operations. The mechanism to achieve this cooperation may take several forms.

From the perspective of the foundation, it may prefer to make all significant policy and strategic decisions, thereby limiting the role of the medical group or physicians to that of a vendor of medical services. This approach, however, leaves the foundation without the valuable input, emotional investment and enthusiasm that involvement in issues can create in physicians who believe they have a stake in the success of the affiliation. Under most circumstances, therefore, both parties should be prepared to share policy-making authority as this is the critical mechanism to achieve an integrated operation between the medical group and the foundation. To create a mechanism whereby representatives of the foundation and the medical group can come together to establish policy for operations, a governing body, either as a formal board of directors or as a separate decision-making body, should be established. This common governing body makes the policy and strategic decisions necessary for overall foundation operations. A combined governing body has the advantage of bringing together the respective skills of physicians and the foundation in a forum in which the parties must cooperate to achieve effective decision making. A cooperative working relationship between physicians and hospitals will lead to better decision making and will encourage the parties to work through their differences and develop a true partnership.

The voting requirements of this combined governing body must be considered carefully. Most foundations will be structured to have broadly charitable purposes, and it is likely that the organization will be able to achieve tax-exempt status. In the tax-exempt arena, in most instances, physicians will be limited to no more than 20 percent of the board of directors of a tax-exempt entity, and a committee structure should be utilized to help physicians maintain their input necessary in the overall policy-making structure of the integrated system. Physicians of the medical group also will be prohibited from serving on the compensation committee established by the foundation. If the organization is taxable, the only limitation on the ability of the medical group to achieve a split of control is the bargaining position of the medical group with the foundation.

Where the foundation is taxable, consideration should be given to how voting actually works if an equal number of representatives are elected by the hospital and the medical group. Where there are equal numbers of directors, it is more favorable for the medical group to require a majority of each class of governing board members (one class being selected by the hospital and the other class being selected by the medical group) to vote to approve an action. This type of provision would help the medical group from losing decisions by having one physician vote with the hospital-appointed directors for board action. The parties, however, may need to rely on a majority or a super majority vote where the consensus decision making by classes of directors cannot be achieved.

Regardless of the decision-making mechanism that is adopted by the foundation, general policy decisions will need to be made. The duties and responsibilities of the governing board will be subject to much negotiation between the parties. The negotiation of the specific provisions will depend upon facts and circumstances of each situation and the relationship of the parties. The range of decisions to be made could include the following:

- **Capital improvements and expansion**. Capital expenditures for both building and equipment of the foundation should be approved by this governing board.

- **Annual budgets**. Annual budgets for the operation of the foundation, including both the foundation operations and medical group compensation, should be approved by the governing board.
- **Advertising**. Advertising and marketing operations should be approved by the governing board for the foundation.
- **Professional fees**. The governing board should be responsible for arranging legal and accounting services for the foundation operations.
- **Ancillary services**. Ancillary services provided by the foundation and the medical group should be determined by the governing board. Ancillaries provided must meet a standard of a full range of services and products for group practices as that standard may exist from time to time.
- **Payer relationships**. Decisions regarding managed care relationships should be established by the governing board. The foundation is the provider of medical services in the foundation model and it must be the entity which enters into the managed care relationship directly with the managed care plans.
- **Strategic planning and network expansion**. Strategic planning developed by the governing board is an important concept for the future success of the foundation/medical group integrated relationship. The governing board must approve additional relationships between the foundation and physicians who are not members of the medical group.
- **Location**. The governing board should be given the power to determine the locations to be utilized by the medical group and any changes in those sites.
- **Medical director**. The medical director should be selected by the medical group and selection approved by the governing board.
- **Real and personal property leases**. Any real or personal property leases that impact the foundation or the medical group should be approved by the governing board.
- **Credit collection policies**. The governing board should have the ability to establish credit policies for the foundation in collection of patient accounts receivable for the medical group.
- **Contracts**. Contracts for the operation of the foundation, whether entered into by the medical group or the foundation, should be approved by the governing board, or should be executed in accordance with guidelines established by the governing board.

A professional services agreement should contain a comprehensive list of the duties, responsibilities, services and facilities to be provided by the foundation that will be implemented in accordance with standards established by the governing board. A detailed list of services provided should be present in any agreement, as parties will forget, over time, their respective obligations unless future reference can be made to a document which clearly specifies the various responsibilities.

The administrative staff actually employed by the foundation must have the ability to perform a wide variety of management functions. The foundation should undertake the responsibilities for its operation which would include at least the general areas listed below.

- The foundation should make a specific commitment with respect to the practice facilities it will provide for the ongoing practice of medicine by the medical group. Maintenance, repair and operation of those facilities also should be provided;
- The foundation should be obligated to make certain capital expenditures with governing board approval. Because the dynamics of operations depend upon a variety of factors, it will be difficult to specify an exact amount of capital expenditures which the foundation is obligated to make each year. Accordingly, the best approach is probably to have governing board involvement in the process and to require the foundation to use its best efforts to add a variety of services.
- Expansion of the group practice is likely to be a critical element for the future success of not only the medical group, but also the foundation. The foundation should support recruitment of physicians to the medical group according to schedules approved by the governing board and in compliance with legal guidelines.
- The foundation should agree to purchase necessary inventory and supplies for operations.
- Practice administration also should be performed by the foundation. The foundation should agree to bill and collect the professional fees it generates and generally be authorized to use the full range of collection techniques necessary to collect these funds.
- The foundation should be required to maintain patient medical records, accounting, billing and collection records, and to manage these files and records in accordance with all applicable state and federal statutes. The foundation should be obligated to preserve the confidentiality of patient medical records. Clerical, accounting, bookkeeping, computer services, printing, postage, duplicating services, medical transcribing services and payment of licenses and certification fees are additional responsibilities that the foundation should assume.
- The foundation can be expected to provide important assistance in the recruitment of physicians by carrying out necessary administrative tasks, including identifying potential candidates and coordinating the interview process. While physicians should be allowed to

make the final hiring decision, the foundation can play an effective role in performing the many administrative tasks necessary to recruit physicians successfully and to provide financial support. Recruiting for the expansion of the medical group is a critical function to be undertaken by the foundation. Some arrangements may obligate the foundation to advance to the medical group recruiting costs, agency fees, relocation and interviewing expenses. Because the foundation has capital to provide these advances, the medical group is assisted in the recruitment process. Medical groups who add physicians often experience a direct reduction in the income of the existing physicians at the group. The ability of the foundation to advance these funds until new physicians can "pay for themselves" is an added benefit that can be provided by the foundation under the foundation model. In general, however, these advances must be repaid in order to comply with fraud and abuse and tax-exempt requirements. Repayment can be over a period of years if necessary after the physician has turned profitable.

In addition, just as recruitment costs are important costs to be defrayed so income for medical group physicians will not be reduced, the start-up costs associated with bringing on a new physician present a similar problem. The foundation should be obligated, therefore, to advance the amount of any loss that is experienced by the medical group for a new physician. This loss can be defined by the amount by which the expenses associated with that new physician exceed the revenue generated by that new physician. The foundation can be obligated to advance the difference to the medical group, thereby cushioning the impact of bringing on new physicians on existing physician income. The amounts advanced, however, usually must be repaid in order to comply with fraud and abuse and tax-exempt requirements.

- The foundation should negotiate and administer managed care and direct contracts.
- Under the arrangement, the foundation usually will perform the personnel function for the affiliation by hiring and training all non-physician employees, and by administering the workplace routine. Salaries, benefits and working conditions of these non-physician employees generally will be established by the foundation. A mechanism must be implemented to identify problem employees and allow a vehicle for physicians' complaints about job performance of these employees, resulting in transfer or termination of employees who have demonstrated unsatisfactory job performance.
- The foundation should be obligated to operate ancillary services consistent with legal requirements for referral relationships between physicians and providers of ancillary services. For example, the

ownership and operation of clinical laboratories, imaging centers and ambulatory surgery centers must be reviewed closely to ensure compliance with federal and state anti-referral legislation. In general, a growing number of these ancillary services must be owned and operated by the medical group in order to effect compliance with the restrictions of federal and state antireferral legislation. Standards of performance should be specified to assure competent management of ancillary services that are operated by the foundation.

- The foundation should be responsible for obtaining and paying for professional malpractice insurance. While physicians will be requested to make an effort to ensure insurance eligibility, the foundation should arrange for malpractice insurance, and the costs associated with that coverage may be advanced by the foundation, but ultimately paid for by the medical group.
- The agreement should specify the method by which the foundation will hire the executive responsible for administration of the affiliation. Ideally, this executive will be hired in a collaborative effort between medical group and hospital. To manage effectively, this executive must win the confidence of physicians, and therefore a mechanism should be developed to allow physician input and a veto power over undesirable candidates. While the foundation will resist limiting its management discretion in this area, physicians must maintain a strong voice in determining who will manage the affiliation and insist that individuals placed in a management position have strong ambulatory care management experience.

Another section of the management agreement should contain a delineation of the rights and responsibilities of the medical group. Under the foundation model, the primary function of the medical group, of course, is to provide professional services to its patients. The professional services agreement accordingly should require the medical group to render these services in compliance with all ethical standards, laws and regulations applicable to the practice of medicine.

The professional services agreement should not, however, require the medical group to perform to any particular standard of care, other than that which may be established by state law. Phrases such as "highest quality," "teaching hospital quality" or others which may imply a higher standard of care than required by state laws should be avoided. If a higher standard of care is established by the professional services agreement, the medical group may be required to perform to this higher level of care in any malpractice action that occurs after the establishment of the relationship. This result is completely undesirable and may result in unnecessary liability being imposed upon the medical group.

The foundation model

The professional services agreement also will require the medical group to occupy the facilities provided by the foundation exclusively for the practice of medicine, and other physicians will be prohibited from utilizing the facilities without the agreement of the foundation. The medical group will be responsible for hiring physicians and any other technical employees for reimbursement purposes. The hiring decision and the compensation, supervision, evaluation and termination of these employees should remain responsibilities of the medical group. Fringe benefits and other employee-related expenses for the physicians also may be borne by the medical group, as well as professional dues and continuing education expenses.

Because the medical group will be an independent contractor that provides medical services to patients of the foundation, it will be necessary for the professional services agreement to contain certain requirements that will ensure that the medical group is following proper procedures for the provision of medical services to patients. Accordingly, the professional services agreement will contain provisions which will require the medical group to certify the credentials of its physicians and to require that those physicians comply with the utilization review and quality assurance standards established from time to time by the medical group, which standards are approved by the foundation. These standards must be sufficient to ensure the foundation that the medical group will monitor the performance of its physicians. Credentialing, licensing and insurability should also be specified in the agreement as being the responsibility of the medical group. In general, the goal of the professional services agreement should be to require the medical group to provide physicians, properly credentialed, and to monitor those physicians' performance of the rendering of services to the patients of the foundation.

In addition to the requirement that the medical group provide care to the patients, the professional services agreement should contain requirements that the medical group sufficiently staff its physician contingent necessary to provide services to patients of the foundation. The professional services agreement must provide that the medical group will undertake the effort to recruit, hire and maintain a sufficient physician complement to service anticipated patient volume for the foundation. The exact number of physicians to be provided should be subject to an annual medical staff development process whereby representatives of the medical group and the foundation should determine jointly, based upon anticipated needs, the available contingent necessary to service the expected patient volume. The parties will likely negotiate this particular volume, with the foundation seeking to require the medical group to provide physicians but giving no guarantee of expected patient volume. The medical group will seek guaranteed compensation and a commitment from the foundation to compensate the physicians for providing a certain level of support regardless of the actual patient volume of services rendered. This issue is likely to be negotiated by the parties, but should most successfully be handled by requiring that the parties arrive at a negotiated level each year and that the physician group will use its best efforts to provide that level, and the foundation should agree to provide a minimum compensation level to assure some corridor of potential performance to be achieved by the medical group.

Benefits and compensation for medical group physicians should also be specified in the professional services agreement. In general, the physician compensation system will be a subject that should be within the realm of decision making of the board of directors of the medical group. The compensation received by the foundation for the provision of medical services by medical group physicians should be specified in the agreement. The actual distribution of compensation to physicians should be the subject of medical group discussion, although the foundation will have an interest in the compensation system used given the incentives that compensation system may have upon physician behavior. The provision of benefits for physicians is also likely to be specified in the professional services agreement. To the extent that the employees who are non-physicians of the medical group become employees of the foundation, the retirement plans and welfare plans of the medical group will need to be a mirror image of the medical plans established for foundation employees or the medical group will be required to become an adopting employer for those plans. In either event, the medical groups' previous benefit levels may be changed and the details with respect to those benefit levels, along with the commitment of the foundation to provide benefit levels to the former non-physician employees of the medical group, should be dealt with in the agreement. A review of these benefit plans must be made prior to execution of the professional services agreement. To the extent that the medical group has non-qualified plans and items of reimbursement such as for books, subscription or continuing medical education, it may continue to provide those benefits to its physician employees with the recognition that those expenses must be taken out of the compensation that the medical group receives from the foundation.

The medical group should also agree in the professional services agreement that it and its physicians will not discriminate against individual physician patients based upon their ability to pay for the services rendered, or to otherwise engage in any discrimination prohibited by law. The medical group should also agree to treat the patients seeking urgent care at any of the foundation's facilities without regard to the ability of those patients to pay for the services they receive. The agreement also may provide that medical group physicians will provide coverage in hospital emergency rooms and will render care in those situations without regard to the ability of the patient to pay for those services. The extent of this obligation, however, should be specified in the agreement.

Medical group compensation

Another important provision in the foundation relationship will be how the medical group is compensated. Generally, the system utilized should offer incentives to both the group and foundation to conserve costs and maximize revenue. If the system fails to provide these parallel incentives, it may result in pitting the foundation against the medical group with adverse consequences to the overall success of the affiliation. If every decision becomes a "we" versus "they" decision, the overall best interest of the affiliation will not be served.

Generally, the parties may consider a variety of payment methodologies for physician compensation but the compensation system is likely to be based on the underlying basis by which the foundation itself receives its reimbursement.

Gross revenue reimbursement

Some professional services agreements may reimburse the medical group by using a percentage of billings.

Fee based upon collections

A reimbursement methodology based upon collections is another option. This approach gives the medical group the incentive to increase revenues.

Capitation-based payments

Another reimbursement methodology is to compensate the medical group on a basis of a percentage of the capitated contracts entered into by the foundation.

Physician guaranteed performance

The foundation also may take some risk by providing commitments to the medical group that the pool for physician compensation will be set at specified levels regardless of overall operational results. While these types of systems put risk on the foundation and provide a "safety net," both fraud and abuse and tax exempt considerations limit the use of this type of compensation.

Budget determined compensation

A final compensation system for medical groups in the foundation model is based upon a negotiated budget determined each year. In this system, for example, the physician compensation pool can be established in a budget process that examines overall affiliation operations. This system will require an annual or biennial negotiation process in which the risk of under-budget performance or the reward of over-budget performance can be allocated to the parties. This system may create uncertainty in the reimbursement system that may cause severe stress every time compensation is negotiated. If successfully managed, however, this system may allow the relationship of the parties to adapt successfully to changing business considerations.

Both parties should determine whether a fair price is being paid for the services provided by the medical group. For tax-exempt foundations, the internal revenue service has established three principles for compliance with its prohibition of inurement regarding physician compensation plans. These requirements are: (a) the plan must not be a device to distribute the foundation's profits, thereby creating a joint venture, (b) the plan must be negotiated at arm's length, and (c) the plan must result in reasonable compensation. In general, the internal revenue service does not view compensation systems based on net income in a favorable light.

The medical group must review the proposed compensation mechanism and seek an explanation of the fee determination with reference to projections concerning new and existing operations of the medical group. The foundation should consider seriously the use of financial experts to evaluate the proposed model. The projected compensation levels for physicians, before and after the affiliation, as well as with and without that affiliation, should be reviewed. These projections will enable the group to focus on the benefits and costs of affiliating with the foundation.

Another significant section of the professional services agreement should contain insurance and indemnity provisions. Liability and professional malpractice insurance coverage levels should be specified for both parties, and each should endeavor to name the other party as additional insured under their respective policies, if feasible. The agreement also may contain provisions whereby each party will agree to indemnify the other should the other party suffer loss associated with the combined operation. Broad indemnification clauses should be avoided as they will be uninsurable obligations. For the medical group, this uninsured obligation will impact physician income if the medical group is required to make payments under these types of provisions. If possible, only specific events, such as intentional wrong-doing, should be covered, if the entire indemnification concept is not omitted.

The term of any affiliation agreement also must be evaluated. In general, the term of the affiliation proposed by the hospital will be long, but if tax-exempt bond financing is used, the term will be limited to either two or five years. Where tax-exempt financing is not used longer terms, even to 20 or 30 years may be used. A longer term agreement generally will favor the medical group because it will no longer have the patient relationship and will be dependent upon the foundation for access to patients.

Termination provisions of the professional services agreement also should be reviewed thoroughly. While all parties hope that termination provisions will never be utilized, and may feel that undue negotiating effort is placed on these provisions to the detriment of goodwill that has developed between the parties, it is important to look at the "worst case" scenario. Both parties must assume the worst from the other party in evaluating these provisions. The agreement should clearly delineate responsibilities of the parties and allow for termination of the agreement should either party not fulfill its obligations under the agreement. Without clear performance standards contained in the agreement and without the ability to demonstrate a failure to perform pursuant to those standards, the parties will have little redress should the quality of performance of the other be unsatisfactory.

While termination events are important to specify, the agreement also should specify the impact of termination on the parties. For example, parties should address access to medical and financial records, who owns them and who is entitled to access after the agreement ends. The agreement should specify how the parties will conduct business immediately after the termination and require them to cooperate to fully wind-down their relationship. How the affiliation is unwound also must be specified. Dealing with termination issues will be difficult, but it is far better to confront these issues in advance than to postpone the decisions until the parties are engaged in a bitter dispute. For example, the foundation may insist upon the repurchase of various assets that it had acquired from the medical group if the agreement is terminated. While the medical group generally should resist agreeing to these types of provisions, it should at least attempt to limit these repurchase obligations to certain circumstances, including its own default in the relationship, and should avoid making individual physicians responsible for any repurchase obligation.

A final significant provision in a professional services agreement is a restrictive covenant that will prohibit both medical group and foundation from engaging in competition with each other. This restriction will exist at least during the term of the agreement, and will be necessary for both parties. For the medical group, it is important to prohibit the foundation from securing services from other competitors of the medical group. Likewise, the foundation will request that the medical group refrain from engaging in other affiliations or in medical practice other than through the affiliation operation. This exclusivity arrangement for both sides, however, is in the best interests of both parties and will protect their relationships with each other. This prohibition should not preclude physicians from admitting patients to other hospitals, as there is risk that such a restriction could be construed as violating the Medicare Fraud and Abuse Law.

The existence of restrictive covenants after the agreement has concluded, however, is another matter. The ending of the relationship between the foundation and medical group should not force either party out of business by preventing either from conducting operations after the termination of their relationship. It is not reasonable to expect a medical group to refrain from practicing medicine in a given locality after the affiliation has terminated. Likewise, the foundation will resist all such efforts to be excluded from forming other affiliations after the relationship is over.

Internal group matters

Critical to the success of the affiliation is the ability of the medical group to evaluate its current governing structure, and to implement successfully a reorganization of its affairs to allow for coordination of its operations in the foundation relationship. This reorganization process is discussed more fully in Chapter 16.

The legal group practice structure in MSO and foundation models

Many medical groups that undertake a management services or foundation relationship will have basic legal organizational documents in effect prior to the affiliation that were prepared by individuals to protect physician autonomy and, as a consequence, will have neglected guarding the interests of the group as a whole. For example, employment agreements will likely have been drafted to protect individual physician rights by specifying generous benefits and salaries that cannot be changed without the consent of the individual, and by making termination of the relationship difficult for the group to invoke. In these employment agreements, restrictive covenants will be non-existent, will be very narrow in scope, or will contain a small amount of liquidated damages. Concern for the right of the individual to practice medicine and the mobility of the practice of the individual will prevail against the interests the group has in guarding its patient base, and protecting it from the loss of revenue that inevitably will occur if a physician leaves the group and takes patients away from the group as a result of that departure.

The governing structure of many of these "individually focused" groups will often be non-existent, as all physicians may make decisions in a general staff meeting that allows participation by all in attendance. In other groups, a large board of directors may have been created which includes a high percentage of physician group members, and the size of this board may preclude the fast, efficient action necessary in a changing health care environment. Groups in this phase of development with a large board of directors likely will have failed to delegate sufficient authority to the administrator, physician executive, or a small executive committee that may meet between board of directors meetings.

The shareholders' agreement which governs the purchase and sale of the stock of the group is another example of how individual interests predominate in many of these "individually focused" groups. The rights of the individual are again protected, allowing the individual to have his or herstock repurchased upon departure at a favorable rate, and that requires the group to pay out this repurchase price in a short period of time. This slant of shareholders' agreement toward an individual perspective also must be examined in light of the organizational change that will occur in the management services or foundation affiliation.

Finally, many groups will have neglected over the years to formalize their relationship with their administrator, or will have done so without adequate provisions for protection of the group and for the administrator. In many situations, these key players in the operation of a group will be operating without a contract. Groups implementing a management services or foundation relationship will be presented with the opportunity, or will be required to re-examine the legal basis of their organization. In implementing the transaction, the group must proceed with a heightened awareness of the importance of protecting the group. This re-evaluation will make the group concept stronger by protecting group rights and at the same time lessening the ability of the individual to cause damage to the group. In order to implement successfully the management services or foundation relationship, and to lay a solid foundation upon which the new organization will operate, many familiar documents will need to be revised and take on a new perspective. This new group perspective must be incorporated as a common theme throughout all of these documents. As revised, these documents will serve as the legal basis for implementing change in groups from the "individually focused organizations" they may have been, to a group with centralized authority where the group as an organization is strengthened in its ability to confront the challenge of individual threats to its health and well being.

Physician employment agreements

The management services organization or foundation development process will bring into focus the relationship of the individual physicians to the medical group to which they belong, because in both of these integration models the medical group will continue to exist. To create a strong new medical group, an effective employment agreement that gives the group the power to govern its individual members must be signed by all physicians.

Individual physicians may resist the infringement upon their personal rights by this new group contract, but all group members must be convinced that by protecting the group, individual members are also protected. It is often the actions of only one individual that will create significant harm to the entire group due to the inability of the group to deal effectively with that individual.

While an employment agreement should reflect the history, personality and work philosophy of the new group, certain basic elements should be included in every document and should be designed to move the organizational structure to a different level of group development. The following paragraphs present some suggested guidelines that may be utilized in the process of revisiting the basis on which the physician-medical group relationship is maintained.

Introduction

The employment agreement should begin with introductory wording which describes the parties involved, their addresses, a legal description of the organization and the overall intent of the employment contract. The agreement should set forth that as a condition of the affiliation, the physicians and the group are being required to enter into a new agreement. In addition, if the physician is a shareholder in the group, that status should also be specified. These recitations are necessary because contracts can only be changed in a binding manner by the parties who exchange something of value. The requirement of "consideration" means that merely signing a new agreement will not be binding on the physician for such an important item as a restrictive covenant. This "value" requirement means that an affiliation will present a group with the opportunity to effect new and binding agreements by allowing physicians to receive proceeds from the transaction, or by benefiting as an employee with a new work environment or new compensation system.

General statement of employment

Each contract needs to contain a general statement that the physician and the medical group are creating an employment relationship based upon the terms and conditions set forth in the employment agreement. This general paragraph is the basis for defining the rights and obligations of the parties and specifically references the other provisions of the agreement.

Duties

The employment agreement also should contain a section which describes the duties which the physician is expected to perform. These provisions may have, in the past, been limited to describing generally the duties of the physician and requiring that these duties be performed within the policies, rules and procedures of the group that are established from time to time. While this general language should be retained, it needs to be supplemented by adding a requirement that the physician should agree to serve the group faithfully and to devote such time as may be necessary for the adequate performance of his or her duties. In addition, in light of the need for more centralized management in the group, stronger language should be placed in this section which would require the physician to perform his duties in such areas and at such times and locations as may be required by the medical group, and which would make the practice of the physician subject to such review processes and procedures as may be established by the group from time to time. These types of provisions will allow the group to adopt and modify utilization review/quality assurance programs and to review individual physician participation and compliance. This contractual basis to review physician performance will establish the legal authority for the review programs of the group and preclude later questioning of that authority by an individual physician.

Other activities

Physician employment contracts also benefit from having provisions which prohibit the physician from engaging in any activity which is determined to be detrimental to the group or which results in the physician not devoting his or herfull time to the practice of medicine for the medical group. From the perspective of the medical group, it is important to establish that the physician is devoting full time to the business of the group. It is also important for the group to obtain the agreement of the physician that he or she will not engage in other work for anyone else without the prior written consent of the medical group. Budgetary considerations, revenue projections and space allocations may all be impacted by the other activities of a physician. The group must have oversight duties on the amount of effort devoted by its physician employees. From the viewpoint of the individual physician, to the extent that the physician desires to engage in other practice related activities or independent teaching or research, specific reference to these activities should be made so no questions will arise in the future regarding the propriety of the physician engaging in these activities.

Compensation

Another major goal of the revised employment contract, both from the group and physician perspective, is to set forth the method of compensation of the physician. The compensation system for physicians will be established or modified as part of the management services or foundation development process. With regard to employment contract content, however, it is in the interest of the medical group to leave discretion to its board of directors to make modifications in the compensation system. Without this flexibility to make modifications, a new contract or amendment must be executed each time a change in the compensation system is implemented. While a flexible provision gives the individual physician less certainty in his or her relationship with the medical group, the medical group should consider this approach to enable it to respond rapidly to changes in the finances of the medical group. Historical reasons regarding group governance and lack of trust in the new organization may result in significant individual physician resistance to giving up this indicia of autonomy. Medical group leadership, however, should be aware of the significant advantages from a governance and financial operations perspective of a more flexible expression of the compensation obligation. Even in circumstances where a full delegation to the board cannot be achieved, the strategy should be used to centralize decision making about as many aspects of the compensation system as possible.

Professional meeting time, vacation, sick leave

Accrual of professional meeting time, vacation and sick leave should be contained in the personnel policies of the group. From the position of the medical group, therefore, no further obligations with respect to professional meeting time and related expenses, or with respect to additional vacation or sick leave or their accrual, should be made in an employment contract. While individual physicians may desire to see these matters set forth in writing, the group will have more flexibility to modify the policies if the board of directors is free to modify these provisions without seeking the approval of each physician.

Disability

Although many existing physician contracts spell out in detail the effects of the partial or total disability of a physician, it will be more beneficial, from the perspective of the medical group and in light of the affiliation, to specify disability provisions in a policy manual which can be updated and changed rather than in the contract. The affiliation process may also highlight weaknesses in the existing disability provisions of a group. As a general matter, groups will no longer be able to act as an "insurance" company by providing benefits out of group revenues to individual physicians. By allowing payments to disabled physicians that are in addition to the disability insurance coverage maintained by the group, income of the remaining physicians is put at risk. Physicians should be encouraged to obtain individual policies consistent with their own level of risk concerning their health that they are able to assume. Group assumed contractual obligations with respect to disability not covered by separate insurance policies should be limited.

Fringe benefits

The revised physician contract should contain a section covering fringe benefits. From the perspective of the medical group, the provision should state that the physician can participate in employee benefits generally provided by the group, but that no special fringe benefits are provided for the physician. To the extent that the group has decided to provide other fringe benefits such as a car allowance or additional life insurance, those provisions may be generally referenced in this fringe benefit provision, but the details should be established by the board of directors from time to time.

Administrative and practice considerations

The relationship of a physician with the business operations of the medical group is also an important topic to be included in a "group centered" physician employment contract. A variety of concepts should be considered for this paragraph to strengthen the ability of the medical group to manage its affairs. First, the paragraph should establish that all fees, billings and collections are to be established by and remain the property of the medical group. Departing physicians should not be able to make the claim that they are entitled to some general interest in receivable, unless this interest is specifically granted in the termination section of the agreement. Second, the agreement should specify that the group, and not the physician, has the full authority to administer the business of the group and to hire and fire all personnel. Individual physicians should not be given the authority to make these decisions. Third, the agreement should provide that all accounts and medical records are the property of the medical group and that the physician is required to keep accurate records of all professional work performed or supervised by him. Finally, the contract should state that the group will provide all office space, equipment and other items necessary for the practice of the physician, but that the group alone has the authority to determine what is necessary and what is to be purchased. All of these provisions will enable the group to operate the practice in the hospital affiliation without granting the individual practitioner a veto power over the decisions of the collective leadership of the group.

Automobiles and insurance

Physician contracts may contain paragraphs pertaining to automobiles and automobile insurance. While many of the details of automobile insurance should be determined at the board level without reference in the contracts, many groups require that their physicians maintain an automobile and appropriate insurance regarding liability and property damage, and therefore believe that such a provision is necessary in the contract. If such a paragraph is utilized, flexibility on limits of coverage should be maintained, allowing the board of directors of the group to specify from time to time the coverage levels. Regardless of whether the insurance issue is covered in the agreement or in a separate policy statement, attention to insurance is necessary, as physicians who are traveling on medical group business, even in their own automobiles, will be deemed to be doing so in the course of their employment for the group. This means that the medical group is responsible for the actions of the physician if an accident occurs while the physician is driving the automobile. In order to coordinate the coverage that a medical group may have in its umbrella policy which will cover excess liability for the group and its employees, individual physicians will be required, pursuant to the terms of those umbrella policies, to maintain a baseline of coverage before the umbrella policy takes effect. Because uninsured liability actions may pose a major threat to their financial integrity, groups undergoing affiliations should reexamine their policies on this issue, as they may have been neglected over the years.

Term

The term of the contract is one of the most important provisions to be considered in a review of the employment agreements to be utilized in the management services or foundation affiliation. A review of the principles to be employed in determining the appropriate term of a contract should be made. For example, if a contract with a long term (more than one year) is utilized, the medical group and the physician are obligated to satisfy their respective obligations for that entire stated period of time. Generally, the longer the term of the contract, the more favorable it is for the physician. Physicians who desire to leave are, in most instances, of less value to the medical group, and the medical group has little to be gained in seeking redress for the breach of the obligation of that physician to perform services for the entire term of the agreement. Physicians who decide to leave for other positions often will avoid providing adequate notice and usually feel free to do so without any great risk of liability.

If a medical group decides to terminate the services of a physician in the first year of a three-year agreement, on the other hand, the medical group will be obligated (unless it has cause to terminate the agreement, and is prepared to establish that cause) to continue to pay the physician for the full term of the agreement. While the physician has an obligation to seek new work to lessen the damages the medical group would be required to pay for the remainder of the contract term, this type of provision is in fact quite favorable to the individual physician.

It is usually in the best interest of the medical group, therefore, to provide for a much shorter contract term. In this light, a short contract term (certainly not more than one year) with liberal termination provisions as discussed below would protect the interest of the medical group by permitting the release of a physician in an undesirable situation, without having to establish that the physician, in fact, breached the agreement.

Another issue to be decided in determining the appropriate term of an agreement is whether the contract should contain language that automatically renews the contract at the end of the term, unless one party notifies the other that the contract will terminate at the end of that current term. These automatic renewal or "evergreen" clauses are usually desirable. Most medical group contracts should contain this automatic renewal provision after the parties have worked with each other for some time and a longer term relationship is anticipated. In this circumstance, the automatic renewal clause has the advantage of not requiring a new contract to be executed at the end of each term. On the other hand, it is recommended that a contract not contain this automatic renewal clause where the contract is with a new physician and the medical group utilizes a "probationary" period to evaluate the practice of the new physician. Inadvertent renewal of contracts for these new physicians should be avoided, as the end of the contract will provide a convenient time to evaluate the performance of the physician. In the implementation of the management services or foundation relationship, it is likely that most, if not all of the physicians to be retained under the new arrangement, will be existing employees of the medical groups. In those circumstances, it is recommended that the clauses prepared for those physicians contain the automatic renewal provision.

Termination

An equally important provision in the employment agreement is the provision which specifies how the contract may be terminated prior to the expiration of its term. If, for example, a physician is employed for a one year term, but the contract may be terminated on 30-days notice without any reason, the contract really has a term of 30 days, as opposed to one year. The employment contract provision which allows a contract to be terminated by either party without any reason is called a termination "without cause" provision. It is generally in the best interest of the medical group for its employment agreements to contain a termination without cause provision that has a short (30- to 60-day) notice period. The rationale for this type of provision is that it allows the medical group to sever relationships without specifying the reason for termination. In many circumstances, a medical group will prefer to avoid disclosing in a public forum the reasons for termination.

Many individual physicians and, in particular, participants in the affiliation process may view such short notice termination provisions with some skepticism. Attempts may be made to limit the discretion of the board of directors to act on this termination. In fact, some may feel that a higher vote requirement or a vote of all the shareholders should be obtained before severing a relationship without any reason. Such provisions are thought to protect the individual from the arbitrary behavior of the group at large. In general, the leadership of the medical group should attempt to resist these limitations on the authority of the new governing authority. It is likely that the collective wisdom of the board would not allow it to act arbitrarily in the termination of a physician, and most termination situations arise under a set of circumstances in which the behavior or practice style of the physician has created serious problems for the group. Because the "problem" behavior is the most common reason for the termination of a relationship by a group, physicians should be reminded that it is this type of problem rather than an arbitrary decision which causes the termination to occur.

From a legal perspective, the ability of the group to terminate the agreement in those "problem" situations is greatly enhanced if the agreement contains provisions that allow termination of the relationship without the need for giving any reason for termination. The adverse publicity or difficulty in proving behavior and practice concerns in a public forum can be minimized greatly by use of these provisions. While compromise may be necessary to have an agreement to be acceptable to the group at large, medical group leadership should guard against the tyranny of the individual rather than the tyranny of the group.

Another difficult question raised in termination sections of employment agreements is under what circumstances may the agreement be terminated "with cause." The phrase "with cause" means that the contract can be terminated at any time if a reason exists which would allow the non-breaching party to terminate the agreement prior to the conclusion of the term of the agreement. Cause provisions that specify how the medical group has failed to live up to its obligation in the contract are relatively straight forward. The interest of the physician in this situation is for the group to continue to pay the salary, provide the fringe benefits and abide by the policies and procedures established in the medical group. "Cause" in this context is often defined as the failure of the group to satisfy its obligations under the agreement.

On the other hand, the reasons the medical group may rely on to establish "cause" are more difficult to detail. The group is vitally interested in having the duties performed by its physicians in a competent manner. To the extent the physician is not performing his or her duties, the medical group has an interest in and, in fact, should be required to terminate the relationship. How the reasons giving rise to the right of the medical group to terminate the agreement are expressed will depend in large part upon the perspective of the leadership of the medical group and its balancing of individual versus group rights. In most instances, a group-centered agreement should define "cause" as:

- Willful or repeated failure of the physician to comply with the reasonable directives of the board of directors;
- Impairment due to drugs or alcohol;
- Disability;
- Loss or suspension of license; or
- Loss or suspension of hospital privileges or other practice privileges.

While some medical groups may wish to consider adding a statement that allows termination of the agreement for lack of quality of care, the difficulty in proving lack of quality in most instances means that medical groups will be reluctant to try to establish this lack of quality in a public forum such as in court. Because quality is difficult to attack, even most medical groups that decide to put this type of provision in the agreement rarely will utilize it as the basis to terminate the relationship. Terminating physicians with quality of care problems will more often be achieved by using the termination without cause provision, which allows a medical group to sever the relationship without establishing any reason or revealing physician behavior to the public.

Effect of termination

Once the agreement is terminated, the parties must specify their respective rights and obligations which arise as of the effective day of termination. As part of the affiliation process, it is important for the medical group to focus on the adverse impact that a termination has upon its fiscal health. While it is impossible to prevent a departure of a physician, medical groups should consider including some version of the following concepts in their agreements to cushion the group from the adverse effects of departure:

- A provision should be included that all uncollected charges and accounts receivable will remain the sole property of the medical group and that the physician has no rights in any of these amounts. In many instances, the departing physician will claim that revenues created from the work performed during the last several months of his or her employment should be rightfully his or hers, and that the physician should be paid for that effort when the amounts are ultimately collected. The medical group leadership should consider, however, that there are significant costs associated with a physician departure, including loss of revenue, replacement costs and start-up time for replacement physicians. The accounts receivable of the departing physician can be used to help defray the costs associated with finding a replacement for this departing physician. While this amount of money will rarely, if ever, fully compensate the medical group for the loss, it is better than the alternative of having an additional obligation to make payments to the departing physician on top of recruitment and start-up costs for the replacement for that physician.

- A provision also should be added that the physician is responsible for the payment of any malpractice premium that may be necessary to provide extended coverage to the medical group for the actions of the physician. This endorsement on a malpractice policy converting a policy from a "claims made" to an "occurrence" basis is often an expensive item for a group and this expense should be borne by the departing physician who caused this expense to occur. The rationale for imposing this expense upon the physician is that without making this transfer to an occurrence basis, the physician will be uncovered (although the medical group will retain its coverage) and, therefore, the medical group will be more likely to be the target of any potential litigation than the physician. Separate limits and different levels of coverage for the group and the physician also may impact the extent of dollars available to protect the group. The occurrence basis conversion therefore adds another layer of coverage and the cost to convert a policy to an occurrence basis is usually a warranted expense to impose on the departing physician.

- The agreement also should specify the amount of compensation owed to the physician. The exact nature of the compensation due the physician upon departure should be specified, otherwise the risk exists that a physician may claim amounts due beyond what is intended by the medical group.

- Finally, the agreement should contain references to both the obligation of the physician to resell his or her stock in the medical group upon departure pursuant to a shareholders' agreement and a reference to the obligation of the physician to be bound by the terms of any practice limitation provision that may be applicable to a physician.

Restrictive covenants

Restrictive covenants (or covenants not to compete) usually prohibit a physician from practicing medicine within a certain area (for example, a county or within a 50 mile radius of an office) for a specified period of time. Restrictive covenants often have been used by medical groups to protect the patient loyalty that the group has established over the years in the community. Often medical groups and their physicians think of restrictive covenants only where an established group hires a new physician and establishes that physician in the practice, thereby conferring a great benefit upon that new physician. Equally, if not more important, are the situations like management services or foundation relationships where the medical group engages in a new endeavor and where the success of the new effort depends upon, to a great extent, the efforts of all the constituent physicians. A management services or foundation relationship with a hospital will implicate restrictive covenants as the hospital will wish to retain the productive services of physicians during the course of the relationship with the medical group.

In these situations, a properly drafted restrictive covenant can allow the group to prevent individuals from establishing a competing practice. In many states, the legal requirements that a restrictive covenant must meet to be enforceable are generally similar, and in these states in order for a covenant to be enforceable, it must have been entered into in exchange for something of value and must be reasonable. In other states, specific statutes may prohibit the enforcement of a restrictive covenant, except in narrowly-defined circumstances or only where liquidated damages are to be paid. In designing an appropriate covenant, therefore, reference must be made to both the specific statutes in the state in which the transaction will occur and the applicable cases that have been decided in that state in order to determine specific guidelines concerning the enforceability of a particular covenant.

The process of determining what covenants are enforceable in the employment context has been impacted by the competing policies surrounding restrictive covenants. On the one hand, courts must consider the public policy in favor of allowing people to work and contribute their skills and abilities to the community. This policy, therefore, would limit the enforceability of covenants and this policy is particularly applicable in the employment context. On the other hand, courts must consider the general principle of freedom of contract and the public policy in favor of encouraging employers to hire employees in a particular community.

A great number of cases have been decided across the country concerning restrictive covenants, and a considerable body of case law has developed governing their interpretation and enforcement. In determining whether a particular covenant is reasonable and therefore enforceable, courts have applied a number of rules. The following guidelines give a brief overview of the type of considerations that will lead to more enforceability in a particular contract:

Writing required

The covenant should be in writing and signed by the physician. Oral restrictive covenants are not enforceable in many states, and in any event it is critical that the covenant be in writing and signed in order to establish clarity regarding the terms of the covenant.

Business interest protected

The covenant must be related to the protection of the legitimate business interests of the medical group. Examples of this legitimate business interest include the patient relationships and name recognition developed through the investment of the time, effort and resources of the group. Covenants must be drafted narrowly to protect only this interest.

Consideration

The covenant must be supported by valuable consideration. Physicians cannot merely agree to refrain from practicing in a particular area. This promise will not be enforceable because it lacks legal consideration, which means that in exchange for agreeing to refrain from practice, the physician must receive something with an economic benefit, such as salary or payment, a portion of which can be thought of as being given in exchange for the covenant. In the sale of assets context, the new employment agreement derives consideration from the asset purchase payments that are made as part of the acquisition. For new physicians hired by the new group after the arrangement has been consummated, the situation is simplified as the requirement of legally-sufficient consideration will be satisfied when the physician enters into an employment contract in connection with accepting the offer of employment and before the physician begins work.

In general, if improvements or strengthening of restrictive covenants are to be made in the management services or foundation context, it is important that they be done in conjunction with the consummation of the transaction. Any deviation from this procedure, such as waiting until "the dust has settled" to address the physician contract issue, may result in a court finding that the covenant was given without valuable consideration and, therefore, unenforceable. Many courts have invalidated covenants when they were entered into after the employment relationship had commenced. In order to strengthen the enforceability argument for restrictive covenants, therefore, the employment agreement should be entered into during the course of the medical group reorganization that will take place simultaneously with the effectiveness of the management services or foundation relationship.

Activity

The covenant must be reasonable with regard to the scope of activity prohibited. In order to be reasonable and, therefore, enforceable, a covenant must be drafted so it only restricts the physician from a reasonable scope of activity. Standards of what is reasonable concerning the scope of permissible activity vary from state to state. Regardless of the specific standard that may apply, however, the following guidelines should be considered. Multi-specialty groups should consider whether the group needs protection over the full range of practice encompassed in the phrase "practice of medicine," or whether a restriction limiting the physician from practicing only his specialty is sufficient. The medical leadership should determine what interests of the group need to be protected. Often this interest is one which requires the protection of the patient relationships and financial well being of the group. Because the reality of most large groups is that the physician staff member is quite specialized and only sees patients in a limited area of practice, it is prudent for the group to consider restricting the physician from practicing only in the area in which the physician worked while employed with the medical group. While a broad prohibition against the departing physician "practicing medicine" may be enforceable in a particular state, the added protection of this broad prohibition may not be worth the uncertainty it raises in the specialized practice of medicine of today. It is strongly recommended that single specialty groups limit the practice of the departing physician to the specialty being practiced for the same reasons.

Time

The covenant must be reasonable as to the time of the restriction. Time periods that extend beyond a two or three year period following the termination of an employment agreement may be suspect as being too long to protect the legitimate interest of the medical group. While the exact period of enforceability may vary from state to state, a conservative approach should be used in selecting the appropriate time period. The main purpose of a time period is to disrupt the practice of a physician who leaves a group, thereby making it impossible for that physician to transfer his or her patient population to a new competing practice.

Territory

The covenant also must be reasonable as to the territory in which the activity is prohibited. Covenants are often phrased in terms of prohibiting practice within a county or city, or within a radius of miles from an office or city. The exact extent of the territory to be restricted, however, should be based upon the business activity of the medical group. If the group draws patients from a county or series of counties or a wide geographic area, the restriction should be based upon the attraction of patients from that wide referral area. On the other hand, if the covenant extends beyond the reasonable drawing area of a medical group, it will likely be deemed to be unenforceable as not being related to the interests of the medical group that need to be protected. In most instances, a 25 to 50 mile radius from an existing office site will be sufficient to cover the bulk of most patients that are seen by the physician, and requiring that the physician practice outside of that area will disrupt the practice of that physician sufficiently to protect the interest of the group. The proper approach is to decide this issue in light of the specific facts of each relationship.

Public policy

The covenant must not be against public policy. The parties will be allowed to make agreements between themselves, except when the public interest in not enforcing the agreement outweighs this freedom to contract.

This public concern arises when enforcement of the restrictive covenant may harm the general public. An example of this type of issue and one that may jeopardize enforcement of restrictive covenants with highly trained specialists are situations where a medical group employs a specialist which is the only physician of that kind in a community. In some cases courts have ruled that the covenant was invalid on public policy grounds. These cases have concluded that if ordering the physician to honor the contractual obligation would create a substantial question of potential harm to the public, then the public interest outweighed the contract interest of the parties and the court would refuse to enforce the covenant. If, on the other hand, ordering the physician to honor the agreement would merely inconvenience the public without causing substantial harm, courts have concluded that the medical group would be entitled to have the contract enforced. The decided cases have provided limited guidance and, accordingly, great uncertainty remains in this area.

This developing area of the law will impact some groups who hire specialists that are unique in a community. While this development should not discourage medical groups from continuing relationships with these rare specialties, it does add another element of uncertainty in the already uncertain area of restrictive covenant enforcement. Because of the limitations on employment agreements in this public policy area, it may be prudent in those circumstances to have those "super specialists" sign additional restrictive covenants based upon the sale of assets itself, thereby giving an independent basis that is separate from the employment basis in which to restrict the practice of a physician.

Liquidated damages option

As an alternative or supplement to a restrictive covenant, many medical groups will consider the use of a liquidated damage provision. Liquidated damage clauses provide that a physician must pay the medical group a specified amount if the physician practices within a prohibited area or if the physician leaves the group. The rationale for a liquidated damage provision is that the exact damages caused by the departure of a physician will be difficult to establish and, therefore, a fixed amount set in advance is the only way to determine these damages. While physicians have different perspectives on establishing a liquidated damage amount, many will find these clauses preferable to an all-out prohibition against practice. It is this softened effect of liquidated damage clauses that may give physicians in leadership positions cause to consider them more seriously than is warranted. These provisions may also receive additional interest because of the mistaken belief that while restrictive covenants may be difficult to enforce, payment of liquidated damages is an uncomplicated process resulting in easy payment for the group.

Liquidated damage provisions, however, are neither easy to enforce, nor is the ability of the group to collect payment as clear cut as many physicians would believe. Liquidated damages may be attacked as vigorously as restrictive covenants and a physician who desires to practice in breach of a liquidated damage provision will have only the payment of monetary damages as the downside risk, as opposed to being put out of business by the enforcement of a restrictive covenant.

In comparing restrictive covenants to liquidated damage provisions, medical groups should consider the following. As an alternative to a restrictive covenant, the liquidated damage clause reimburses the medical group for expenses associated with recruitment and establishing a replacement in practice. Liquidated damage clauses, however, may be subject to attack, as in most states a clause is not enforceable if it is a penalty. The determination of whether the clause is a penalty or truly a liquidated damage amount is a hazy distinction and subject to varying interpretations. Because liquidated damages are only enforceable where the actual amount of damages are difficult to determine, the medical group that seeks to collect a liquidated damage provision also must meet this burden. These abstract concepts are difficult to establish in any enforcement action and disputes about the use of liquidated damage clause are likely to occur just as often as disputes concerning the enforcement of a restrictive covenant.

Other difficulties with liquidated damages exist. Often they are set at a fixed amount and do not increase over time. What may seem to be an appropriate liquidated damage amount when it is established will lessen over the years and, in many instances, may seem to be insignificant by the time a physician is prepared for departure. Second, it is very likely that with higher-paid specialties, a liquidated damage amount that approximates some significant percentage of annual income will be deemed so high that the ability to convince physicians to sign it will be jeopardized. This high liquidated damage amount provision may create serious opposition to the affiliation, causing physicians to seek to have the number negotiated downward as part of the negotiations. In an effort to accommodate the short-term interest of the wide number of physicians who may oppose a higher liquidated damage amount, the group may seriously impair its ability to protect itself in the future. A lower liquidated damage amount will encourage physicians to view departure as a less painful process, and if departure is made too easy, this ultimately may jeopardize the long term survivability of the group.

Selection of a restrictive covenant as opposed to a liquidated damage clause will depend upon the goal of the group in using these vehicles. If the goal is to prevent a physician from entering into competitive practice, a restrictive covenant clause in some fashion should be utilized. If the goal is merely to seek reimbursement for costs expended when a physician leaves, a liquidated damage provision should be considered. Most medical groups will conclude that the real goal is to prohibit competition from being created and therefore will opt for a restrictive covenant.

Stock ownership and shareholders' agreements

The way physicians buy and sell stock in the medical group is also a significant matter to be addressed in advance of the consummation of any proposed management services or foundation organization transaction. Because a medical group has existed before the consummation of the affiliation, the group will have established a mechanism by which physicians purchase and sell their stock upon their departure. The affiliation process, however, is a perfect time to reevaluate the role of stock ownership in a medical group. While all physicians who were shareholders in a group prior to the affiliation will continue to be shareholders, the group must decide the basis on which physicians new to the group should become shareholders. In many groups, a long apprenticeship and significant buy-in, where physicians buy-in over time and ultimately accumulate the same number of shares as a senior physicians, is a concept under attack. While this phase-in makes sense in terms of continuity of leadership, and in giving the new physicians the opportunity to become accustomed to the history and tradition of the group, many young physicians believe that they are entitled to equality more immediately in the medical group hierarchy. A short period of time to equal stock ownership after the physician becomes eligible for stockholder status is therefore becoming accepted practice.

While many factors may go into how a group ultimately decides its stock ownership issue, it should keep in mind the competitive realities of attracting new physicians to its practice. The goal, given these recruiting pressures, should be to minimize the amount of a physician buy-in, to allow equality in terms of number of shares owned so all physicians feel equal, and to achieve that equality over a short period of time. This goal should be easier to achieve in the management services or foundation relationship where substantially all of the assets will have been sold by the medical group as part of the affiliation.

Having decided these buy-in issues by establishing a buy-in amount and payment timetable, those decisions can be formalized in a separate shareholders' purchase agreement whereby a physician agrees to purchase shares. As an alternative to a separate document, a provision or paragraph could be placed in the employment agreement for the physician. The agreement specifies the obligation of the physician to make purchases of shares over a certain period of time. This obligation should be placed on the physician after the decision has been made to admit the physician as a shareholder, rather than at the new employment relationship stage where a final decision has not been made on the future of the physician with the group.

An equally important issue pertaining to ownership of stock is preparing for a physician departure through a shareholders' agreement. Shareholders' agreements set forth the conditions upon which the interest of a physician in the professional corporation may be sold by that physician or repurchased by the corporation. Without this agreement, there will be no binding agreement that details under what circumstances and terms a medical group will be entitled to repurchase the shares of the stock of the group from a physician.

A shareholders' agreement should cover a number of issues concerning the relationship between the individual physician and the group. The agreement should restrict the transfer of stock in the medical group by prohibiting a physician shareholder from selling, or in any other manner disposing of the stock, without complying with the terms of the agreement. This restriction is important, as it protects the group from having its stock pass to third parties without the consent of the medical group. This restriction is also important because state law often restricts ownership in a professional corporation to physicians who are authorized to practice medicine in that state.

An equally important issue to be addressed in the shareholders' agreement is the circumstances under which stock owned by a physician must be repurchased by the medical group. Shareholders who sever their relationship will desire to have their investment returned. The medical group also will want to reclaim the shares from its former employee because it does not want a physician who is not associated with the group to have the right to be active in its affairs. The shareholders' agreement should detail the events which cause the corporation to become obligated to repurchase these shares. Events which should give rise to the obligation of the medical group to repurchase the shares usually include the following:

- Death of the physician;
- Termination of the employment of the physician by the group;
- Inability of the physician to perform his or her duties as an employee, officer or director of the group for a certain period of time, perhaps six months or more;
- Retirement of the physician;
- Conviction of the physician of a criminal offense;
- An event of bankruptcy with respect to the physician;
- The entry of an order by a court that the spouse of the physician has acquired an interest in the stock under the applicable divorce or separation laws of the state; or
- The physician being found to be disqualified to practice medicine under the applicable state law.

Other events may be added depending upon the individual preferences of the group. When any one of these events occurs, therefore, the medical group is required to repurchase the stock upon the terms and at the value contained in the shareholders' agreement.

The value placed upon each share of stock in the medical group is, perhaps, the most critical provision to be found in the shareholders' agreement. Without an agreement in advance concerning the repurchase price of the stock owned by a physician, the risk of disagreement concerning value and perhaps even litigation is greatly increased. Various methods may be used to value the interests of the physician in the corporation, and, for sake of consistency, the valuation method for repurchase should be the same as the original purchase obligation.

Many issues should be considered in determining how the valuation of stock is established. One issue to be determined is whether physicians are entitled to receive value for the accounts receivable of the group. In general, physicians should not be entitled to accounts receivable as part of their stock interest in the corporation. Whether accounts receivable are paid to a departing physician should depend upon the provisions specified in the employment agreement, not the shareholders' agreement.

The group also should examine whether real estate is included in the valuation process. In general, real estate should be held in the partnership or limited liability company form, which will avoid double taxation upon sale or other disposition of the property. In any event, if the property is in the corporation, it should be valued and the valuation method should be specified as either cost or market value.

Apart from the real estate which should be valued separately, two different methods of valuing stock may be considered. First is the book value method of valuation as determined by the corporation's accountants, in accordance with either generally accepted accounting principals in the case of accrual basis medical groups, or in accordance with cash receipts and disbursements methods of accounting for those medical groups on a cash basis system. This valuation method can give a conservative value to the hard assets of the corporation which are listed at the acquisition price of the assets minus depreciation. Second, in light of the changing reality of medical practice and the sale of substantially all of the assets to the management services organization or the foundation, many medical groups may reconsider the practice of valuing the assets of the organization by determining the book value or some other valuation formula and switch to a fixed buy-in price that is not directly tied to fluctuations in value. This method of stock valuation has the advantage of eliminating financial concerns at the end of every year that might impact the stock value determination formula, and recognizes that stock ownership in the group is properly viewed as "dues" in the hospital affiliation context where substantial assets are no longer owned by the group. Just as in the front end purchase price valuation, a conservative valuation for physician departures will help attract physicians, for in the departure context, the remaining physicians must be in a position to continue practice in the medical group, while at the same time undertaking to repurchase the interest of a departing physician.

After establishing the value of the shares, the terms of payment for those shares purchased from a departing physician should be established. The medical group should be given great flexibility to determine how payment is made. The shareholders' agreement should give the group the option either to pay the full price for the shares at closing or to pay the purchase price over a number of years on an installment basis. The number of years during which payment should be made, as well as the interest charged on the unpaid balance, also should be specified in the agreement. A long period of time to repay this obligation to departing shareholders is the preferred method for protecting the interests of the group. Where the repurchase price is not large, this extended payment period may not be necessary.

Another issue that should be addressed in the shareholders' agreement is an authorization to allow insurance to be placed upon the life of physician shareholders. Life insurance can be a useful funding vehicle to allow the repayment of the capital investment of the physician at the time of the death of a physician. The shareholders' agreement, therefore, should provide that a shareholder will agree to allow the corporation to obtain insurance upon the life of the shareholder. In the event of the death of a shareholder, the insurance proceeds would then be applied to the purchase price for the shares. Where the repurchase obligation is a small amount as is often the case in the management services or foundation model, this provision is less important, but should be included regardless as a matter of good practice. Upon termination of the agreement or transfer of the stock, physicians should be given the option to purchase the insurance if the physician so decides, or the group should be allowed to maintain the insurance if the physician decides that he or she does not wish to purchase the insurance.

Finally, the provisions of the shareholders' agreement should allow for termination of the agreement if the business of the medical group ends, if the medical group becomes bankrupt, or if a number of the shareholders of the corporation die within a relatively short period of time, thereby making it very difficult to fund a repurchase of the stock.

Administrator employment agreements

During the development of the management services or foundation relationships, the status of the current administrator of the group will be brought into focus. In general, the same considerations that apply to physician employment agreements apply equally to the administrator contracts. A new employment agreement should be negotiated during this time period, however, to reflect accurately the position of the administrator in going forward with the new affiliation.

The first issue to be faced in the management services or foundation model is whether the administrator should remain an employee of the medical group or whether the administrator should become an employee of the management services organization or foundation. In general, the administrator should become an employee of the management services organization or foundation. The rationale for this is that the employees of the management services organization or foundation should be responsible to, and report to, their administrator who should be a member of the same organization. In addition, as the integrated system grows, it will be important to have the parties move toward a more integrated relationship.

While this structure may be the ideal setting, administrators in these situations are put under tremendous strain. To the extent that the hospital views the administrator as an ally, it will probably seek to have that administrator become its employee. It also may believe that by having created this employment relationship, that the administrator will be under the control of the hospital, rather than under physician control. In those relationships where the hospital believes in the need for control, there is great danger for the administrator who will be pulled between hospital administration and physicians. Hospitals in this environment often will pit the administrator against the physician and, if that does not work, effectively eliminate the administrator from that position. This approach is a tremendous mistake with respect not only to the appropriate treatment of the administrator, but also to the overall health and well-being of the new organization. In those circumstances, it is probably better for the administrator to remain an employee of the medical group, thereby being responsive to, and an advocate for, the physician leadership. While this position may be contested by the hospital, a basic decision must be made about the focus and emphasis which the new relationship will receive from the administrator. If the hospital affiliation can have strong physician input with respect to governance, it is likely that these concerns may be mitigated, but a critical evaluation of the relationship should be made before the employment of the administrator is transferred to the management services or foundation organization.

Administrators in this process are tremendously at risk given the change that is occurring in the organization. Many may find themselves without a position through attrition, personality or other restructuring. Although it may be difficult for many administrators to make the case that they should be treated differently from physicians who are in the group, administrators who are undergoing this change should not hesitate to make the argument that, in light of their position in the group that a different, longer-term contractual relationship should be fashioned. Under the management services or foundation model, regardless of where the administrator is employed, it is reasonable to request a contract with a longer term that will give the administrator job security for the transitional period.

In this context, the interest of the medical group must be balanced with that of the administrator in evaluating the appropriateness of the contractual relationship. Administrators have increasingly requested and received provisions which include a long-term notice for termination, severance pay depending upon years of service and severance benefits that extend the benefit of a contract to those administrators who are relieved of their obligations during the transition period. Because of the need to attract and retain good management talent, groups may find it in their best interest to structure these relationships to provide some security to the administrator. Of course, the actual nature of the relationship and the extent of security provided will in part depend upon the performance of the administrator prior to the affiliation. Accordingly, a reasonable balance should be struck between job security for the administrator in light of the circumstances and the need for the new group to protect itself in an undesirable situation.

As an alternative or supplement to a restrictive covenant, some may consider the use of a liquidated damage provision. Liquidated damage clauses provide that a physician must pay the hospital a specified amount if the physician practices within a prohibited area or if the physician leaves the medical division. The rationale for a liquidated damage provision is that the exact damages caused by the departure of a physician will be difficult to establish and, therefore, a fixed amount set in advance is the only way to determine these damages. A fuller discussion of the considerations applicable in the use of liquidated damages is present in Chapter 16. The standards and discussion present there are equally applicable in the medical division/employment model.

Chapter 17

The medical division/employment model

One option being considered increasingly by medical groups and physicians is a direct employment relationship with a hospital or medical center. This employment relationship requires the physician to give up the independent practice of medicine, become employed by the hospital, and be governed by an organization established to operate the physician practice within the context of the hospital. The goal of the relationship is to create an integrated approach to the delivery of health care where physician and hospital services are provided in an integrated fashion within one organization. This integration is achieved in one entity which allows for combined governance, sharing of resources and the elimination of duplicate services.

Physicians who have become increasingly concerned with security and have, given the changing nature of health care delivery, become less concerned about autonomy, find this employment relationship attractive. Yet describing this relationship as an "employment relationship" is not entirely accurate because the relationship cannot be viewed only in those terms. A true partnership among physicians and hospital personnel must be created, and this partnership must be exhibited in the creation of a strong group practice component within the hospital structure. Creating a successful relationship given the work styles, biases and prejudices of both physicians and hospitals that have developed over the years is a tremendous undertaking. Accordingly, while this model of integration may hold the most promise for combined operations, it is also the model that will put the most stress on the physician-hospital relationship, as parties who have been reluctant allies or even adversaries over the years become or are required to become true partners.

The concept

Three elements should be present in any proposed medical division/ employment relationship. First, the hospital should be willing to purchase certain of the assets or the stock of the medical practice. This sale provides access of physicians to the equity of the practice, which might not otherwise be available. Individual physicians who leave groups rarely are permitted to obtain a significant return on the business that they have built up for the organization because of the need not to burden the remaining practice with the debt service for buying the interests of departing physicians. The purchase of assets or stock by the hospital provides a one-time benefit to all physicians in the group that would not otherwise be available.

Second, the hospital employs the physician. This employment relationship requires the physician to enter into a new employment agreement that must be negotiated and finalized prior to the consummation of the transaction. Physicians who enter this new relationship will be faced with the conflict of creating a strong employment relationship and a "group centered" approach to that relationship, while at the same time trying to maintain maximum individual flexibility for the individual practitioner. Physicians who enter the employment relationship are likely to be desirous of obtaining income security, with the hospital paying a guaranteed salary plus a bonus to encourage physicians to leave the autonomous private practice that they have enjoyed over the years. This income security is often a major factor in tempting physicians to move to this level of integration, given the uncertainties and risks of the continued private practice of medicine in a free standing and independent medical group.

Finally, the third component of the medical division/employment relationship is the creation of the medical division concept itself. To be successful in the integrated environment, hospitals that hire physicians must avoid treating those physicians as employees in another department of the hospital. Two separate lines of business exist in the relationship, one being an in-patient line of business administered by hospital administration with the requisite skills for running that type of operation, and the other being an out-patient oriented relationship where ambulatory care management skills and the ability to administer an outpatient focused practice must exist. This dichotomy is a natural part of the spectrum of health care delivery. Yet, applying in-patient skills to the out-patient setting will surely prove disastrous for both the physicians who enter the relationship and the hospital which has acquired the physicians' practices. The development of a strong physician governance mechanism must be encouraged and required before the relationship is created. In light of these concerns, the "medical division" concept was created, whereby the group practice aspects of medical practice are preserved and encouraged, administrators with ambulatory care experience are given authority to administer the practice, and physicians are given significant self-governance upon a variety of issues, including, most importantly, medical practice issues. This medical division concept must be embodied in bylaws or other operative documents which can then be used to govern the operation of the medical division after the transaction with the physicians has been completed. The medical division/employment model is illustrated on Exhibit 1.

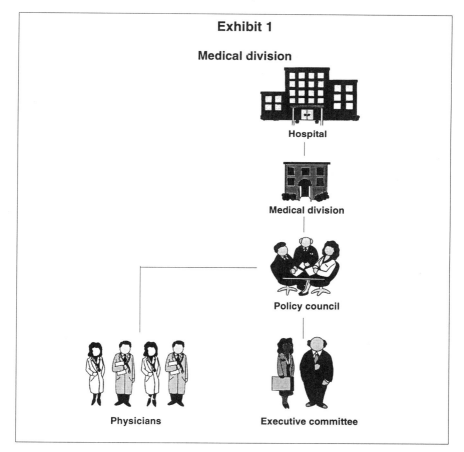

Exhibit 1

Medical division

Hospital

Medical division

Policy council

Physicians

Executive committee

The components of the medical division relationship

Creating an affiliation consists of three separate legal transactions. First, the hospital either purchases most of the assets of the medical group (which may or may not include real estate) or the hospital purchases the stock of the medical group. Second, the parties develop a governance mechanism which establishes the medical division and allows for physician self-governance. Third, the physicians and the hospital enter into employment agreements which govern the future relationship of the parties.

The medical group sale

Numerous issues are raised in the sale of the medical group. Initially, the medical group and the hospital must determine whether the sale will involve the assets or the stock of the medical group. The medical group will be required to examine very closely the impact of the sale from a tax perspective. Whether the medical group will prefer a stock or asset sale will depend on which form of transaction will result in the most tax favorable result for the group. Usually the hospital will prefer an asset sale because it will minimize the risk of the hospital assuming unknown liabilities from the medical group. A stock sale poses greater risk for a hospital because by purchasing the stock of the medical group it buys the whole organization, including any unknown or undisclosed liabilities. The medical group should negotiate for the type of transaction which minimizes its tax liability.

A complete discussion of the asset-stock transaction is found in Chapter 11.

Medical division governance

To create an effective medical division within an integrated delivery system, it is critical to establish an effective governance mechanism whereby physicians govern themselves over medical matters and the medical division is run in a group practice style rather than as an in-patient department of the hospital. Creating an effective governance mechanism is the second component of the medical division/employment model. An effective medical division governance mechanism must contain the following essential elements:

- An election process whereby physician employees elect their representatives in the governing mechanism;
- An operational approach which will ensure that group practice business concepts are employed in the medical division, rather than hospital in-patient administrative skills and
- A practice mechanism which will allow physicians to have control over medical practice affairs.

Because a medical group will not exist as a separate entity in the medical division/employment model, physicians will be at a relative disadvantage in their relationship with the hospital because they are employees of the organization, rather than owners of a separate independent medical group. Establishing an effective mechanism to embody the governance provisions is therefore essential. Several options to embody this governance mechanism are available. The one that is of most practical use, and the one that will be most likely accepted by the parties, is the use of medical division bylaws which embody the governance provisions in a bylaws setting. These governance provisions, as formulated in bylaws, can be enacted as part of the medical staff bylaws of the hospital. The legally binding nature of medical staff bylaws has been established. Accordingly, physicians will be given protection about their status in the medical division if the bylaws of the medical division are embodied in the regular medical staff bylaws of the hospital.

A second approach for the governance mechanism is to include it within the physician employment contract. This approach has some merit as it places the governance mechanism in a legally binding agreement between the hospital and the individual physicians as employees. Because the medical division/employment model no longer utilizes a medical group, the individual physician is given more protection if the mechanism is in the employment agreement and cannot be changed without amending that agreement. In general, hospitals will resist this approach and there is merit to that resistance. The rationale for this resistance is that placing the governance mechanism in the employment agreement gives unnecessary power to the individual physicians in that relationship. changes in the governance provision should be made by including physicians in that process and by requiring a majority of the medical division to approve those amendments. Giving each individual physician a veto power over this change will burden, unnecessarily, the governance mechanism process.

A third approach is to make the bylaws an independent document adopted by the board of directors of the hospital. As such, these bylaws will stand alone without any legal status to be binding on the hospital. Accordingly, this approach may be difficult to enforce if there is a dispute with the hospital, and it should generally be avoided because of the uncertainty of the legally binding nature of those commitments.

The governance provisions should contain a variety of basic concepts that will embody the relationship of physicians to the overall integrated delivery system. While many different approaches can be used, and while many of these will undoubtedly be modified by local conditions, relationships and other individual factors, all effective governance provisions should contain certain basic elements. The bylaws should specify the goals of the medical division. These goals should be broad and should include the delivery of quality, cost-effective health care services, the ability to coordinate, develop and support quality patient care, and the ability to promote, through the provision of support to other institutions, the health of the community. The purpose of the medical division also should be to encourage cooperative efforts for the integration of health care of other physician practices, to achieve efficiencies and encourage the group practice of medicine in an integrated environment, and to increase the number of physicians employed by the medical division for the benefit of the community. To the extent that the medical division is part of a tax-exempt organization, broad charitable purposes and community service should be specified to satisfy the requirements of the internal revenue service for tax-exempt organizations. While these preambles will not be dispositive of the issue of whether the medical division will have sufficient tax-exempt purposes, they are helpful in establishing that claim.

The first step in creating an effective governance relationship is to establish the medical division. The purpose of the medical division is to create the basic organization used to organize the physician relationship with the hospital. While it can be called a variety of other names, it is important that the concept remain the same, that is organizing the physicians in their relationship in the overall hospital system. Because the medical division/employment model no longer has an independent or separately incorporated medical group, it is important for physicians, both from a management and from a medical perspective, to be organized in their own division. A medical division can accomplish these goals and create the basic underlying concept of physician self-governance through a democratic process of election of representatives.

Membership in the medical division should be established by this governance mechanism. A broad statement probably should be made that any physician employed by the hospital will be a member of the medical division. While this is a relatively simple provision, some medical divisions may wish to make other refinements of this particular concept. For instance, increasingly many hospitals have employed traditionally hospital-based physicians such as radiologists, anesthesiologists and pathologists. From an integrated delivery perspective, these physicians perform a fundamentally different role than the primary care physicians who comprise much of the integrated delivery system activity undertaken by hospitals. Accordingly, primary care physicians may wish to limit the role or vote of these traditionally hospital-based physicians to give primary care physicians an appropriate voice in the governance mechanism. Other issues in constituting the membership of the medical division include whether to give part-time physicians a voice in governance, and whether only employed physicians, rather than independent contractors, should be allowed a voice. From the perspective of medical division governance, part-time physicians should be given a voice as well, recognizing that many part-time physicians will be part-time because of personal lifestyle considerations, rather than for lack of support of the medical division.

Dealing with physicians who may be independent contractors with the medical division is another matter. In general, the goal is to encourage complete integration in the medical division through the employment process. This means that from a conceptual point of view, the medical

The medical division/employment model

division should include, and give a voice to, only those physicians who have made the complete integration decision. Accordingly, it is not recommended to include as members of the medical division physicians other than employees of the medical division.

The primary right of being a member of the medical division is having the ability to vote. Voting by the medical division members is usually by majority vote, other than for election of its representatives. In general, a majority vote should be sufficient for taking action, although consideration may be given to require a higher vote requirement for amendment to the medical division bylaws or other fundamental changes in the relationship of the medical division with the hospital.

The medical division membership elects their representatives, and it is the creation of a decision-making body with delegated authority that will provide an effective governance relationship for the medical division members. The name of this organization is less important than the role which it is assigned. One such name, the policy council, embodies the concept which is the goal of this effort. The policy council can act as a governing mechanism that directs medical division governance. The policy council should have the authority specified in the bylaws to establish policy regarding the operation of the medical division and also should have the flexibility to establish and modify those policies for the management of the business and operational issues concerning the medical division. It can operate as a "board of directors," setting policy for the business and administrative aspects of the medical division, and delegating to a medical practice subcommittee, known as an executive committee, those medical practice concerns that are most appropriately handled by an all-physician body. The policy council, as such, will contain representatives elected by the medical division physicians, and should contain representatives elected by the hospital to participate in this combined governance.

How the policy council is constituted should be given careful consideration. First, the number of representatives to serve on the policy council should be established. The number of representatives should be small enough so that effective decision making can take place, but large enough so that sufficient physician representation can occur. Accordingly, a policy council which consists of seven members is recommended. Five of these members could be elected by the medical division members and two members elected by the hospital. The precise numbers of physician and hospital representatives will likely be negotiated between the parties. At the very least, physician representatives and hospital representatives should be equal so that consensus decision making can be required. To the extent that the hospital has majority control of this policy council, much of the physician self-governance concepts that are necessary for the medical division to prosper will be absent and the feasibility of that operation, as thus constituted, should be questioned.

Transforming the Delivery of Health Care: The integration process

The term of the policy council members should probably be one year. Consideration should be given to dividing the policy council into classes and having those representatives serve staggered terms. Staggering of terms will give continuity of leadership, and this continuity and experience will be important for the future stability of the medical division. Some physicians, however, may feel that initially the policy council should be elected every year in order to encourage immediate responsiveness to the needs of the physicians in the medical division. The single year term can be utilized with the understanding that, as the medical division becomes more established and stabilized, it may consider going to staggered terms to increase that stability.

Policy council members should be elected by the medical division at the annual meeting of the medical division membership. Those physicians who receive the highest number of votes are elected. This basic form of democracy, having physician employees elect their own representatives to the policy council, is a central tenant of effective medical division governance. Without this type of input, physician involvement and acceptance of the overall affiliation relationship may be damaged. Accordingly, it is critical from the perspective of effecting an integrated delivery system that the physicians are represented in a truly representative capacity.

Selection of hospital representatives of the policy council should be permitted by the hospital at its discretion. Because the hospital will be interested in appointing key members of its management team to the relationship, this discretion should be kept with the hospital. In addition, other individuals should be allowed to serve as members of the policy council without vote in an ex-officio capacity.

Having established the policy council through the election by the physicians who are employees of the medical division, it is important to establish the governance mechanism by which the policy council conducts its work. The tasks assigned to the policy council will be subject to much discussion and negotiation between the physician and medical group leadership and the hospital. The concern of the hospital in a wholesale delegation of authority to the policy council will be that the hospital remains the employer of the physicians and as such is responsible not only for the actions of the physicians, but also for the overall financial and operational performance of its employed physicians. This concern is a legitimate one, but must be balanced against the need to create an effective working mechanism through the policy council.

From a negotiating perspective, physicians and medical group administrators will seek to have final decision-making authority over a variety of issues. There are significant limitations, particularly in the compensation area, imposed by the Internal Revenue Service upon granting such final authority. In addition, the perspective of the hospital may be that the policy council should be advisory only with little real decision making in order to facilitate hospital control.

To affect a compromise between these two competing positions, the policy council can be given authority and responsibility over identified issues, but the board of directors or the chief executive officer can have a veto power over those decisions. This mechanism gives the policy council operating authority and tries to limit the ability of the chief executive or the board of directors of the hospital to changing those items only with a veto power. This veto power of the chief executive officer is limited, allowing an appeal process for any veto taken by the chief executive officer to the board of directors. A veto power permits the board or chief executive officer to veto the action and to require the medical division to come up with another alternative. This process will likely be used sparingly and should act as an effective counterweight between the desire for control by the hospital as employer, and the desire of autonomy by the policy council.

The areas of responsibility assigned to the policy council should be general in nature and should encompass the full range of operational issues that would be confronted by the operation of a group practice. Using this perspective, it will be possible to envision the medical division as an ambulatory care operation, and the kind of operational concerns that need to be addressed in the ambulatory care setting can be expressed more accurately as part of the medical division relationship. Areas of responsibility for the policy council should include the following:

A. **Capital improvements and expansion.** Capital expenditures will impact the operating results of the medical division and the need for new facilities and major capital expenditures. These type of decisions should be dealt with by the policy council.

B. **Budgets**. Annual, capital and operating budgets relating to the medical division should be subject to the review and approval of the policy council. The annual budget process will have a significant impact on medical division operations. The medical division should be permitted to develop its own budget, rather than having its fortunes dictated by the hospital financial services division. The budgetary process, however, is a collaborative one in that, while the budget for the medical division may be established by the policy council, it can only be formally enacted by the board of directors of the hospital through the overall system budget process. Because the medical division is part of the hospital, it is appropriate for the hospital board of directors to have the final word with respect to budgetary items. This limitation illustrates the inter-relatedness of the medical division with the overall fiscal operations of the hospital which is an inevitable part of the medical division relationship.

C. **Physician compensation plan**. The policy council should have the ability to establish a physician compensation plan, as the governing organization of the medical division. While physicians who are negotiating a medical division relationship will be concerned greatly about the compensation system, it is effective to have this decision making for the plan at the policy council level. While physicians may feel that this should either be an executive committee or a physician-only decision, the compensation for physicians is the largest component of the budget of the medical division, and the policy council as the overall policy body must have the controlling decision with respect to this plan. In a larger context, however, the physician compensation issue is part of the overall budget of the hospital, and as such, must be consistent with overall hospital budgetary limitations. In addition, for nonprofit facilities, physician compensation cannot be subject to final authority of physicians who are receiving that pay, and this limitation is expressed by giving the board of directors a veto power over this type of arrangement.

D. **Marketing plan**. The policy council, as the decision-making entity, should have involvement in, and have the ability to establish, the marketing plan for the medical division.

E. **Ancillary services**. The policy council should determine the type and location of ancillary services to be provided by the medical division. As health care is increasingly delivered on an outpatient ambulatory care basis, the amount of dollars associated with ancillary services performed on an outpatient basis will continue to rise. From a budgetary perspective, the more revenues generated by the medical division, the healthier the bottom line for the medical division and the more successful the division will be. Accordingly, it is important for the policy council to determine the type and location of ancillary services to be provided. This type of control allows a physician-controlled entity to safeguard the location of the ancillary services to prevent them from being combined with hospital services and taken away from the medical division operation itself. The bylaws should establish that the purpose of the medical division is to provide those ancillary services traditionally provided by group practices providing a full range of services and products. This type of standard adds an additional conceptual protection for physicians by safeguarding that a full range of ancillary services will, in fact, be provided by the medical division. The standard set forth should be a flexible one, and this full range of services should be determined at the time the decision concerning the ancillary services is made. This flexible decision making will keep intact group practice operations as they exist and evolve over time.

The medical division/employment model

F. **Strategic planning**. The policy council should develop and adopt a strategic plan containing long-term strategic planning objectives for the medical division. Strategic planning for the medical division charts the future course of that division. Accordingly, the policy council should be the entity adopting the strategic plan, and such plan should include the types of physician staffing needs, ancillary services, locations and other strategic matters.

G. **Medical division expansion**. The policy council should have the ability to direct the future growth of the division by acquisition or otherwise.

H. **Medical staff development and recruitment plan, and restrictive covenants**. The policy council should have the authority to establish physician staffing levels for the medical division by the process of the development and adoption of a recruitment plan. This power is an important element for the management of the medical division, as it establishes that the policy council itself will determine when to add physicians to the medical division. This control is quite important, for individual physicians may have different views as to when physicians should be added to the medical division. The policy council also should have the ability to review and have significant impact in the enforcement of restrictive covenants and physician employment agreements. Because the employment agreement is between the physician and the hospital, putting the medical division through its policy council as an active player in this enforcement process will be a pro-physician development.

I. **Vice president of medical affairs/medical director and senior administrator**. In order to assist in the development of a distinct medical division, it is important that the medical director and administrator who work for the medical division be accountable to that medical division. The medical director, senior administrator and other personnel should be recommended and approved by the policy council. This accountability sends a message to the employee that the services of that employee are directed by, and the employee is accountable to, the policy council. By establishing this accountability, the tendency of the employee to look to the hospital as the employer, rather than the medical division, will be minimized.

J. **Contracts**. To the extent the policy council desires to be involved in the approval of contracts regarding the business operation and management of the medical division, the policy council should have the ability to review and approve any contracts concerning those issues.

K. **Managed care**. Decisions regarding managed care participation will take on increasing importance in an integrated delivery system. Because the contract for participation in managed care plans will be between the hospital as the legal entity employing the physicians and the managed care plan, it is important for physicians of the medical division to participate actively in the approval process for these managed care contracts. Giving the policy council the ability to be involved in these decisions is therefore recommended. With the increasing use of capitation, a portion of that capitation will be paid to the hospital while another portion will be paid to the physician. The mechanism for dividing this reimbursement will ultimately determine how much physicians are paid in fully capitated systems.

The decision-making process for policy council activities should also be developed in the governance mechanism. Meetings of the policy council should be held on a regular basis. In general, a majority of the policy council members should be necessary to constitute a quorum for decision making to be taken and a majority of those present at a meeting should be required for a vote to be taken to be deemed as the act of the policy council. This recommendation is premised upon the structure where physician-elected representatives are in majority position in the policy council.

To the extent that an equal number of physician and hospital representatives are policy council members, it may be appropriate to consider other voting systems. One option is to require that, where an equal number of physician and hospital representatives are members of the policy council, the vote be based upon a majority of each class of representatives. This "consensus decision making" requires that a majority of each class approve the action. This will avoid the possibility of having, under a majority vote scenario, one member from either side join the other members on the other side of the issue. This is particularly important where there are, for example, five hospital representatives and five physician representatives, where the five hospital representatives will only need one physician representative in order for a majority to be achieved.

Another possible approach where the number of policy council members is equally divided is to require a higher than majority vote. A three-fourths or two-thirds majority will not solve the issue of having one or two physicians defect to join a hospital-lead initiative, but it will minimize the effect of having only one physician join the hospital in its decision making. Hospitals are likely to resist both consensus decision making and these high vote requirements with the argument that both physicians and hospitals are now in an integrated system where they must work together. In general, this statement is correct. In practice, old decision making and loyalties are sometimes difficult to give up. Accordingly, where there is a split of opinion, higher vote or consensus or decision making should be employed.

Where the hospital representatives comprise a majority on the policy council, physicians should question whether that type of structure is even in their best interests in going forward with the transaction. This is particularly the case where the hospital has the veto power over medical group operations. The hospital that insists that the policy council has a hospital majority is significantly concerned with the "control" aspect, and will find the needed approach of allowing physicians and medical group administrators flexibility to operate the medical division as a separate distinct business difficult to accept.

The policy council should elect officers of the policy council. In general, the policy council should have at the very least a chairman and a secretary. The chairman can serve as spokesman of the policy council and should preside over all meetings. The officers should serve for a period of one year, being reelected at the annual meeting of the policy council which immediately follows the medical division meetings.

The final critical component of effective medical division governance is how the medical division handles medical practice issues. Creating a physician-directed organization is critical for these medical practice issues to be handled effectively. Accordingly, a physician-directed body, which can be called an executive committee, should be established. While the policy council manages the business affairs and sets overall policy for the medical division, the role of the executive committee is to be involved in all medical practice issues confronted by the medical division. The executive committee derives its authority from the policy council.

The executive committee should consist of a relatively small number of physicians, perhaps five in number. The members of this committee should be physicians who are employees of the medical division. They should hold office for a period of one year and should be elected at the annual meeting of the policy council. The executive committee is charged with undertaking obligations as may be delegated to it by the policy council. In general, the executive committee will be charged with overseeing the medical affairs of the medical division. As such, it is appropriate to delegate to this executive committee those matters which involve the practice of medicine and the oversight thereof. The duties listed below recognize that division, with the policy council being involved with the business affairs of the medical division and the executive committee being involved with the medical affairs of the medical division.

The duties of the executive committee should consist of the following:

A. **Professional patient care services.** The executive committee should be responsible for the monitoring of professional patient care services. The duties of the executive committee should include ensuring compliance with applicable laws and regulations of its physicians, monitoring adequate licensure and monitoring the quality of care practice by physicians in the medical division.

B. **Hiring of physicians and allied health professionals**. The executive committee should be charged with hiring, supervision and termination of the physician employees for the medical division. This oversight function should be appropriate for an entirely physician-appointed committee such as the executive committee. By keeping the physician employment decision with the executive committee, the goal of a physician-monitored and governed practice organization is maintained. It can be expected that some hospitals will resist this type of function being given to the executive committee.

C. **Continuing medical education**. The executive committee should be responsible for monitoring continuing education compliance by physician members of the medical division.

D. **Professional insurance liability**. The executive committee should monitor professional insurance liability issues.

E. **Recommendations regarding medical staff development and recruitment plan**. The executive committee should be responsible for making recommendations to the policy council for the development of the medical staff in the development and recruitment plan.

The executive committee should meet on a regular basis. In general, because the executive committee is composed of an entirely physician-representative contingent, the usual provisions with respect to quorum and voting requirements should be adopted, requiring a majority of the members of the committee to be present for the conduct of business and requiring a majority of those present at meetings to take action on behalf of the executive committee.

The executive committee should have officers to facilitate the operation of the committee. These officers should include a chairman and a secretary. The chairman and secretary should be elected by the executive committee on an annual basis. The function of the chairman would be to preside at the meetings of the executive committee and the secretary of the executive committee should be charged with keeping permanent records of the meetings of the executive committee.

Other committees should be utilized in development of the medical division governance mechanism. Each medical staff and each medical division within an integrated delivery system will develop in a variety of different ways because of history, personality and function. With the concepts of significant physician involvement on business and medical affairs being established, and with appropriate physician input in both of these areas, other committees may be developed which will serve the function of the medical division. The ability to establish other committees to perform the functions necessary for the operation of the medical division should rest with the policy council. The policy council then should have the ability to establish and modify, from time to time, other committees necessary for the operation of the day-to-day affairs of the medical division. In general, consideration should be given to establishing at least four other committees:

A. **The operating committee**. The operating committee is a small group charged with managing the day-to-day business operations of the medical division. This committee should consist of a small number of individuals and should have a decidedly business focus. The senior administrator of the medical division probably should be selected as the chairman of this committee to reflect the business focus that the committee needs. The operating committee receives its power from the policy council which can delegate such business matters to the operating committee as may be determined from time to time. The operating committee should report directly to the policy council. In addition, in smaller medical division type arrangements, there may be no need to have this smaller operating committee function that is independent from the policy council. In general, this operating committee can perform the following functions:

- Review of managed care contracts;
- Oversight of systems development;
- Facilities planning;
- Development of collection policies and billing and collection services;
- Development of computer systems;
- Selection and training of non-physician employees and administrative staff;
- Establishing personnel policies and procedures;
- Establishing salary and benefit programs for nonphysician employees;
- Providing management services;
- Preparing annual, capital and operating budgets;
- Preparing of financial statements;
- Purchasing necessary equipment and supplies;
- Maintaining files and records; and
- Implementing public relations and marketing programs.

This day-to-day operating authority of the operating committee can be adjusted based upon the operating conditions at the medical division, with the recognition that the medical division must be operated as an ambulatory care operation as opposed to a inpatient hospital operation.

B. **Physician compensation committee**. Physician compensation is always a critical component of any governance system, whether it be in the medical group private practice setting or the medical division context. Accordingly, a separate committee to deal with those sometimes contentious issues is established. Physicians may have some flexibility with respect to compensation and system design, although overall budgetary constraints would be imposed by the system employing the physician through the medical division. Both fiscal restraints and internal revenue service guidelines will prohibit physicians from having control over the aggregate compensation amounts. This committee should provide recommendations to the policy council regarding compensation and benefits for current and prospective physician employees of the medical division and review the performance of physician employees relative to formulating incentive bonuses.

C. **Finance committee**. The finance committee reviews the financial affairs of the medical division. The finance committee should have a decidedly business composition. Accordingly, the policy council should elect members to this committee, but the senior administrator and chief financial officer of the medical division should comprise a significant portion of its membership. The finance committee derives its authority from the policy council and should be assigned such duties as appropriate by the policy council, including consultation with the operating committee regarding managed care contracts and the allocation of funds received from managed care plans. The medical division, through the finance committee, should retain involvement in managed care contracting because, in global capitation, the division of a global capitation amount into physician services and hospital services will determine the amounts of compensation received by the parties. Having significant physician and medical division input into those decisions is a critical factor in the future success of the medical division. In addition, the finance committee should be charged with monitoring financial performance of the medical division and preparing budgets, business plans and other financial materials as appropriate for review by the policy council.

D. **Quality assurance/utilization review committee**. This committee is important in fulfilling the mission of the medical division in providing quality care. Membership on this committee should have a decidedly medical perspective. The quality assurance/utilization review committee should supervise all quality assurance programs, supervise all utilization review activities and perform such other quality activities as assigned to it by the policy council. The reporting requirement for this committee is through the executive committee, which is the organization charged with the overall monitoring of the medical affairs of the medical division.

These four committees should be appointed by members of the policy council, from among the directors, officers, employees, professional advisors of the hospital and from among the physicians. Ex-officio members may also be appointed. Each committee member should serve a one-year term until the next annual meeting of the policy council. The committees should hold meetings if the majority of the voting members are present for a quorum. A majority of the voting members present at any committee should be necessary for action to be taken by the committee. Higher vote requirements should probably be resisted, given that the policy council has the ability to control the entire process. The policy council also should have the authority to remove any member of any committee, with or without cause, at any time, and to fill any vacancies in any committee.

Another section to be considered in the development of an effective medical division governance relationship is how the rules of the medical division may be modified. This amendment process is a critical item for the integrity of the medical division. The governing bylaws only should be amended by the medical division by a majority vote, and by the approval of the chief executive officer of the hospital and its board of directors. Unilateral changes of these provisions by the hospital or its chief executive must be avoided. This mutual approval process will allow the bylaws to remain an effective governance mechanism.

The final area to be considered for medical division governance is the appeal process for decisions made by the policy council. Because under at least some governance mechanisms, the decision of a policy council can be vetoed by the chief executive officer of the hospital, an appeal mechanism is necessary. The appeal can be taken by any member of the policy council directly to the board of directors of the hospital. This appeal process is important as it places the chief executive in the position of vetoing actions of the policy council only in limited circumstances and not arbitrarily. The effect of an arbitrary decision, or one that brings too many appeals to the hospital board, may be to undermine the effectiveness of the chief executive officer. Accordingly, an appeal mechanism may act as a way of ensuring significant operating authority on a variety of issues to the medical division.

The medical division physician relationship

The medical division/individual physician relationship is the third critical component for the creation of an effective integrated delivery system in the medical division employment model. The hospital will employ the physician and the physician will continue to practice medicine, receiving comprehensive support services from the hospital. The success of the hospital in the relationship will be heavily dependent upon the structure and operation of the medical division as a practicing entity. The physician employment agreement is a critical document in establishing the relationship.

As the practice of medicine becomes more group focused and as the integration of health care requires the development of systems that favor the organization, as opposed to the individual, physicians must make a transition in the way in which they view the role of the individual physician in the organization. Many medical groups have been formed and operated over the course of the previous decades with the focus of the group as an extension of the individual. This focus allowed the physicians to protect their autonomy, to maximize individual physician benefits and to defer taxes. This type of organization of a medical group placed significant limitations on the ability of the practice to act cohesively as an organization. With the creation of the employment relationship with the medical division, a premium will be placed on the ability of the medical division to act as a cohesive organization. A new relationship between the physicians and the medical division must be created to give the medical division, rather than the individual, more control.

In the medical division formation process, there is a significant opportunity to reformulate the way a medical group has traditionally operated and to refocus the relationship with individual physicians. In addition, as the hospital will purchase substantially all of the assets or all of the stock of the medical group, it will be concerned that its investment will be seriously threatened if the medical division is not structured to give the medical division more power over the individual physician. Accordingly, significant emphasis will be placed upon the relationship of the individual physician to the medical division itself.

A change in focus will often be difficult for physicians to accept, particularly those who have been accustomed to having significant autonomy within the group practice setting. In order to make the decisions necessary within the framework of the operation of the medical division in an increasingly managed care and competitive environment, it will be necessary for the medical division itself to act in a more coordinated fashion, and the ability to act in this way will be greatly assisted by changing the focus of the fundamental document that creates the relationship with individual physicians. The employment agreement, accordingly, likely will contain significant new provisions concerning the relationship of the individual physician relationship with the medical division.

Physicians and medical groups who negotiate employment agreements in this context will be faced with conflicting loyalties. On the one hand, individual physicians will seek to maintain their individual flexibility in this new relationship with the medical division. On the other hand, the need for the medical division to move in a comprehensive, cohesive fashion means a significant strengthening of group power and loss of individual autonomy. Most physicians and administrators must overcome the tendency to retain individual autonomy in negotiating these relationships. The medical division must be strengthened and this strength must come through the realization that, while the individual rights of a particular physician may be given up, the medical division, in fact, consists entirely of individual physicians and the ability of one physician to harm the remaining physicians should receive significantly increased emphasis.

A word of caution is in order, however. This group perspective is only possible where physicians have negotiated and implemented an effective governance structure that embodies a group practice perspective in the medical division with significant physician self-governance. Without this effective governance structure, it will be inadvisable to give so much power to the hospital as the employer in the physician employment agreement. Without employing the governance provisions specified in the preceding section, creating an employment agreement which gives significant favor to the hospital will effectively destroy the group practice concept necessary for a successful integrated delivery system. The agreement discussed below assumes that an effective governance provision, as illustrated earlier in this chapter, has been established.

Implementation of the medical division/employment model will bring into focus the relationship of the individual physicians to the medical division to which they belong. To create a strong medical division, an effective employment agreement that gives the medical division the power to govern individual members must be signed by all physicians. After the employment contract has been prepared, it is important to circulate a draft to physicians for discussion and revision. A process must be established to respond to concerns raised and to harmonize the responses to achieve an effective document. While some compromise can be expected with respect to the contract, caution should be exercised about weakening the contract so much that the medical division cannot deal effectively with its individual physicians.

Individual physicians may resist the infringement upon their personal rights by this new contract, but all must be convinced that by protecting the medical division, individual members are also protected as it is often the actions of only one individual that will create significant harm to the rest of the physicians due to the inability of the medical division to deal effectively with that individual.

Certain basic elements should be included in every employment agreement. The following paragraphs present some suggested guidelines that may be utilized in the process of revisiting the basis on which the physician-medical division relationship is established and maintained. While some of these issues are the same as in the management services/ foundation models where a separate medical group continues to exist, the use of the medical division concept for governance means that a separate discussion of the relationship between medical division and individual physicians should be set forth here.

Introduction

The employment agreement should begin with introductory wording which describes the parties involved, their addresses, a legal description of the organization and the overall intent of the employment contract. The agreement should set forth that as a condition of the affiliation that the physicians are being required to enter into a new agreement. The agreement should specify that the hospital has created the medical division as part of its integrated delivery system. The agreement should specify that the medical division bylaws establish a physician governance system. Under the bylaws, physician members elect representatives to the policy council which is responsible for establishing policies concerning the operation of the medical division. This policy council, as more fully described earlier in this chapter, becomes the "group practice" governing body. In addition, the agreement should specify that the policy council appoints an executive committee which is responsible for administering the medical affairs of the medical division.

Duties

The employment agreement should contain a section which describes the duties which the physician is expected to perform. The physician should agree to serve the medical division faithfully and to devote such time as may be necessary for the adequate performance of his duties. In addition, the physician should be required to perform his duties in such practice areas and at such times and locations as may be required by the policy council and the executive committee. The practice of the physician should be subject to such review processes and procedures as may be established by the policy council and the executive committee from time to time. These types of provisions will allow the policy council and the executive committee to adopt and modify utilization review/quality assurance programs and to review individual physician participation and compliance. This contractual basis to review physician performance will establish the legal authority for the review programs of the medical division and preclude later questioning of that authority by an individual physician.

Other activities

Physician employment contracts also benefit from having provisions which prohibit the physician from engaging in any activity which is determined to be detrimental to the medical division or hospital, or which results in the physician not devoting his full time to the practice of medicine for the medical division. From the perspective of the medical division, it is important to establish that the physician is devoting his full time to the business of the division. It is also important to obtain the agreement of the physician that he or she will not engage in other work for anyone else without the prior written consent of the policy council. Budgetary considerations, revenue projections and space allocations may all be impacted by the other activities of a physician. The policy council must have oversight duties on the amount of effort devoted by its physician employees. From the viewpoint of the individual physicians, to the extent that the physician desires to engage in other practice-related activities or independent teaching or research, specific reference to these activities should be made in the agreement so no question will arise in the future regarding the propriety of the physician engaging in these activities.

Compensation

Perhaps the most important function of the medical division employment agreement from the physician perspective is to set forth the method of compensation of the physician. The compensation system will be established as part of the implementation process for the medical division. The approach for the medical division/employment relationship should be somewhat different than the traditional physician employment agreement. First, because of the need to establish some security for physicians, a guaranteed base salary should be set forth in the agreement. Hospitals, as a condition of granting this base salary, may require, however, a productivity goal to be met by the physicians in order to earn this base compensation amount. If this type of productivity provision is utilized, it should give the physician a corridor of performance which can be achieved before a reduction in base compensation is affected. Second, a bonus provision should be allowed to have the policy council establish and modify the bonus compensation system from time to time. This type of provision will give the policy council significant flexibility with respect to the modification of this bonus system. While this flexibility will allow changes to be made to the bonus system as a whole, without resort to having new employment agreement or amendments signed by the parties, it should be remembered that these changes should not be used to penalize or unfairly discriminate against individual physicians. The process of modifying the bonus system should be set forth in minutes to the policy council meeting, and that bonus system and its changes should be applicable to all physicians employed in the medical division.

Professional meeting time, vacation, sick leave

Accrual of professional meting time, vacation and sick leave should be contained in the personnel policies of the medical division. From the position of the medical division, therefore, no further obligations with respect to additional vacation or sick leave or their accrual should be made in an employment contract. While individual physicians may desire to see these matters set forth in writing, the medical division will have more flexibility to modify the policies if the policy council is free to modify these provisions without seeking the approval of each physician.

Disability

The effects of the partial or total disability of a physician should be specified in a policy manual which can be updated and changed by the policy council rather than in the contract. By allowing payments to disabled physicians that are in addition to the disability insurance policy maintained by the hospital, medical division finances are put at risk. Physicians should be encouraged to obtain individual policies consistent with their own level of risk concerning their health that they are able to assume. Medical division or hospital assumed contractual obligations with respect to disability not covered by separate insurance should be limited.

Fringe benefits

The physician contract should contain a section covering fringe benefits. From the perspective of the medical division, the provision should state that the physician can participate in employee benefits generally provided by the hospital and its medical division physicians, but that no special fringe benefits are provided individually for the physicians. To the extent that the hospital provides other fringe benefits such as a car allowance or additional life insurance, those provisions may be generally referenced in this fringe benefit provision, but the details should be established by the policy council from time to time.

Administrative and practice considerations

The relationship of a physician with the business operations of the medical division is also an important topic to be included in a "group centered" physician employment contract. A variety of concepts should be considered for this paragraph to strengthen the ability of the medical division and the policy council to manage its affairs. First, the paragraph should establish that all fees, billings and collections are to be established by and remain the property of the hospital. Departing physicians should not be able to make the claim that they are entitled to some general interest in receivable, unless this interest is specifically granted in the termination section of the agreement. Second, the agreement should specify that the policy council, and not the physician, has the full authority to administer the business of the medical division and to hire and fire all personnel. Individual physicians should not be given the authority to make these decisions. Third, the agreement should provide that all accounts and medical records are the property of the hospital and that the physician is required to keep accurate records of all professional work performed or supervised by him. Finally, the contract should state that the hospital will provide all office space, equipment and other items necessary for the practice of the physicians, but that the policy council alone has the authority to determine what is necessary and what is to be purchased. All of these provisions will enable the policy council to operate the practice from the business perspective without granting the individual practitioner a veto power over the decisions of the collective leadership of the medical division.

The discipline process

This section of the employment agreement should give the policy council flexibility regarding the establishment and modification of rules and regulations pertaining to the medical division. The policy council should be given the ability to establish a disciplinary program to ensure compliance by the physicians with rules and regulations. Specific examples of disciplinary action against the physician should be set forth in the agreement which can demonstrate options, short of terminating the employment of the physician, that can be used to encourage modification of physician behavior. These options could include the following:

- Issuing a formal reprimand
- Requiring the physician to obtain treatment for a condition that interferes with the professional performance of the physician

- Limiting the performance of the professional responsibilities of the physician to the extent such performance does not meet acceptable standards of the practice
- Restricting benefits and privileges of the physician accruing under the terms of the agreement
- Temporarily withholding from physician a portion of monthly compensation to which physician is entitled under the provisions of the agreement, perhaps with a limitation that such withhold will not exceed 25 percent of the total amount of compensation, and
- Taking other action which the policy council or executive committee may deem appropriate.

Each of these options give the medical division the flexibility to design a program to encourage physician compliance, with a full range of options from issuing reprimands, to withholding salary or benefits, to taking other actions as the executive committee and policy council may determine. The jurisdiction of the policy council and the executive committee are delineated in the medical division bylaws. In general, the executive committee has the ability to discipline physician with respect to medical practice issues and the policy council would have jurisdiction over business issues.

Term

The term of the contract is one of the most important provisions to be considered in the employment agreement to be utilized in the medical division/employment model. A review of the principles to be employed in determining the appropriate term of a contract should be made. For example, if a contract with a long term (more than one year) is utilized, the hospital and the physician are obligated to satisfy their respective obligations for that entire stated period of time. Generally, the longer the term of the contract, the more favorable it is for the physician. Physicians who desire to leave a situation are in most instances of less value to the medical division, and the medical division has little to be gained in seeking redress for the breach of the obligation of that physician to perform services for the entire term of the obligation of the physician. Physicians who decide to leave for other positions often will avoid providing adequate notice and usually feel free to do so without any great risk of liability.

If a hospital decides to terminate the services of a physician in the first year of a three-year agreement, on the other hand, the hospital will be obligated (unless it has cause to terminate the agreement, and is prepared to establish that cause) to continue to pay the physician for the full term of the agreement. While the physician has an obligation to seek new work to lessen the damages the hospital would be required to pay for the remainder of the contract term, this type of provision is in fact quite favorable to the individual physician.

It is usually in the best interest of the hospital, therefore, to provide for a much shorter contract term. In this light, a short contract term would protect the interest of the hospital by permitting the release of a physician in an undesirable situation, without having to establish that the physician, in fact, breached the agreement.

In the creation of the medical division/employment model, however, the uncertainty faced by individual physicians will dictate a slightly different approach. In this context, it is reasonable to commit both hospital and individual physician to a two to three year initial term, giving the physician added security. This is a reasonable benefit for existing physicians who have been employed by the medical group for some time.

Another issue to be decided in determining the appropriate term of an agreement is whether the contract should contain language that automatically renews the contract at the end of the term, unless one party notifies the other that the contract will terminate at the end of that current term. These automatic renewal or "evergreen" clauses are usually desirable. Most contracts should contain this automatic renewal provision after the parties have worked with each other for some time and a longer term relationship is anticipated. In this circumstance, the automatic renewal clause has the advantage of not requiring a new contract to be executed at the end of each term. On the other hand, it is recommended that a contract not contain this automatic renewal clause where the contract is with a new physician and the medical division utilizes a "probationary" period to evaluate the practice of the new physician. Inadvertent renewal of contracts for these new physicians should be avoided, as the end of the contract will provide a convenient time at which to evaluate the performance of the physician. In the creation of the medical division, it is likely that most, if not all, of the physicians to be retained under the new arrangement will be existing employees of the medical groups. In those circumstances, it is recommended that the clauses prepared for those physicians contain the automatic renewal provision and that any decision not to renew by the hospital should be made by the policy council, not hospital administration.

Termination

An equally important provision in the employment agreement is the provision which specifies how the contract may be terminated prior to the expiration of its term. If, for example, a physician is employed for a one year term, but the contract may be terminated on 30 days notice without any reason, the contract really has a term of 30 days, as opposed to one year. The employment contract provision which allows a contract to be terminated by either party without any reason is called a termination "without cause" provision. It is generally in the best interest of the medical division for its employment agreements to contain a termination without cause provision that has a short (30 to 60 day) notice period. The rationale for this type of provision is that it allows the medical division through the policy council to sever relationships without specifying the reason for termination. In many circumstances, the policy council will prefer to avoid disclosing in a public forum the reasons for termination. If this type of provision is used, it should be made by the policy council, not the hospital that makes the termination decision.

Many individual physicians and, in particular, participants in the creation of the medical division may view such short notice termination provisions with some skepticism. Attempts may be made to limit the discretion of the policy council to act on this termination. In fact, some may feel that a higher vote requirement or a vote of all the physicians should be obtained before severing a relationship without any reason. Such provisions are thought to protect the individual from the arbitrary behavior of the policy council at large. In general, the leadership should attempt to resist these limitations on the authority of the policy council. It is likely that the collective wisdom of the policy council would not allow it to act arbitrarily in the termination of a physician, and most termination situations arise under a set of circumstances where the behavior or practice style of the physician has created serious problems for the medical division. Because the "problem" behavior is the most common reason for the termination of a relationship, physicians should be reminded that it is this type of problem, rather than an arbitrary decision, which causes the termination to occur. From a legal perspective, the ability of the policy council to terminate the agreement in those "problem" situations is greatly enhanced if the agreement contains provisions that allow termination of the relationship without the need for giving any reason for termination. The adverse publicity or difficulty in proving behavior and practice concerns in a public forum can be minimized greatly by use of these provisions. While compromise may be necessary to have an agreement to be acceptable, the decision-making process should guard against the tyranny of the individual rather than the tyranny of the group. If the hospital, rather than the policy council, retains the ability to terminate without cause, a different approach is in order. In that situation, the hospital should not be given the ability to terminate a physician unilaterally without cause.

Another difficult question raised in termination sections of employment agreements is under what circumstances may the agreement be terminated "with cause." The phrase "with cause" means that the contract can be terminated at any time if a reason exists which would allow the non-breaching party to terminate the agreement prior to the conclusion of the term of the agreement. Cause provisions that specify how the hospital has failed to live up to its obligation in the contract are relatively straight forward. The interest of the physician in this situation is for the hospital to continue to pay the salary, provide the fringe benefits and abide by the policies and procedures established in the medical division. "Cause" in this context is often defined as the failure of the hospital to satisfy its obligations under the agreement.

On the other hand, the reasons the medical division may rely on to establish "cause" are more difficult to detail. First, the policy council, not the hospital, should make this determination. With this approach, the physician-directed policy council can make this difficult decision and the definition of "for cause" can be drafted to give the policy council more flexibility. If there is no effective physician-focused governance, however, "for cause" should be defined very narrowly to favor the individual physician.

The policy council is vitally interested in having the duties performed by its physicians in a competent manner. To the extent the physician is not performing his duties, the policy council has an interest in and, in fact, should be required to terminate the relationship. How the reasons giving rise to the right of the policy council to terminate the agreement are expressed will depend in large part upon the perspective of the leadership of the policy council and its balancing of individual versus group rights. In most instances, a medical division centered agreement should define "cause" as:

- Willful or repeated failure of the physician to comply with the reasonable directives of the policy council;
- Impairment due to drugs or alcohol;
- Disability;
- Loss or suspension of license; or
- Loss or suspension of hospital privileges or other practice privileges.

While the policy council may wish to consider adding a statement that allows termination of the agreement for lack of quality of care, the difficulty in proving lack of quality in most instances means that the policy council will be reluctant to try to establish this lack of quality in a public forum such as in court. Because quality is difficult to attack, even most that decide to put this type of provision in the agreement rarely will utilize it as the basis to terminate the relationship. Terminating physicians with quality of care problems will more often be achieved by using the termination without cause provision, which allows the policy council to sever the relationship without establishing any reason or revealing physician behavior to the public.

Effect of termination

Once the agreement is terminated, the parties must specify their respective rights and obligations which arise as of the effective day of termination. As part of the medical division development process, it is important for the medical division to focus on the adverse impact that a termination has upon it. While it is impossible to prevent a departure of a physician, consideration should be given to including some version of the following concepts in agreements to cushion the medical division from the adverse effects of departure:

1. A provision should be included that all uncollected charges and accounts receivable will remain the sole property of the hospital and that the physician has no rights in any of these amounts. In some instances, the departing physician will claim that revenues created from the work performed during the last several months of his employment should be rightfully his, and that he or she should be paid for that effort when the amounts are ultimately collected. The parties should consider, however, that there are significant costs associated with a physician departure, including loss of revenue, replacement costs and start up time for replacement physicians. The accounts receivable of the departing physician can be used to help defray the costs associated with finding a replacement for this departing physician. While this amount of money will rarely, if ever, fully compensate for the loss, it is better than the alternative of having an additional obligation to make payments to the departing physician on top of recruitment and start up costs for the replacement for that physician.

2. Consideration should be given to adding a provision that the physician is responsible for the payment of any malpractice premium that may be necessary to provide extended coverage to the medical group for the actions of the physician. This endorsement on a malpractice policy converting the policy from a "claims made" to an "occurrence" basis is often an expensive item some may wish to impose upon the physician with the rationale that, without making this transfer to an occurrence basis, the physician will be uncovered (although the hospital will retain its coverage) and, therefore, the hospital will be more likely to be the target of any potential litigation than the physician. Separate limits and different levels of coverage from the hospital to the physician may also impact the extent of dollars available if no physician coverage is available. The

occurrence basis conversion therefore adds another layer of coverage. This issue is likely to be negotiated heavily. In general, if the medical group did not impose this obligation upon the physician previously, the hospital should not impose this obligation. If the insurance coverage of the medical group does not require a tail payment, the transition to the medical division model should not cause the individual physician to take on any additional financial obligation based upon the later actions of the hospital or the medical division.

3. The agreement also should specify the amount of compensation owed to the physician. The exact nature of the compensation due the physician upon departure should be specified, otherwise the risk exists that a physician may claim amounts due beyond what is intended by the hospital.

4. Finally, the agreement should contain references to the obligation of the physician to be bound by the terms of any practice limitation provision that may be applicable to a physician.

Restrictive covenants

Restrictive covenants (or covenants not to compete) usually prohibit a physician from practicing medicine within a certain area (for example, a county or within a 50 mile radius of an office) for a specified period of time. Restrictive covenants have often been used by medical groups to protect the patient loyalty that the group has established over the years in the community. Often medical groups and their physicians think of restrictive

Chapter 18

Legal issues

I n any merger or hospital affiliation, the parties involved will be confronted with myriad legal issues. To implement any transaction successfully, it will be necessary for the parties to employ experienced legal counsel to design and implement the merger or affiliation in light of specific legal issues encountered in the health care industry. While relying on legal counsel for advice with respect to these issues, physicians and administrators from medical groups and hospitals can assist the process greatly by having a general familiarity with pertinent legal issues. Physicians and administrators, with their knowledge of the business relationship to be formed, can use this familiarity with the legal framework to improve the quality of the assistance they provide to legal counsel. As a team, physicians, administrators and legal counsel can solve the inevitable problems and achieve their common goal of implementing the transaction.

This chapter provides an overview of some of the most common legal issues encountered in the implementation of mergers and hospital affiliations. As such, it treats a multitude of complex legal issues in summary fashion. Since each issue is subject to extensive treatment in a number of comprehensive sources, the goal of this chapter is to provide only an introduction of these issues to non-lawyers involved in the merger/ hospital affiliation process.

Because mergers and hospital affiliations are essentially two different types of transactions, the legal issues described below will have different impacts, depending on whether the transaction involves a merger or a hospital affiliation.

The legal issues associated with a merger revolve primarily around the combination of two medical groups into an integrated whole. It is this creation of a unified entity that, in many ways, allows for easier solutions to many of the difficult legal problems that arise in the health care industry. This result is predicated principally upon the reality that where two competitors existed before, only one exists after the merger. The integration of two former competitors may minimize otherwise troublesome fraud and abuse, anti-referral and antitrust issues. The creation of a single integrated group will immunize much (but not all) of the activity that would have been suspect or legally risky if the parties had remained separate. From a legal perspective, an integrated large group practice is a preferred model of delivery. These legal advantages, coupled with other business factors, point to the continued growth of integrated group practice as a favored form of medical care delivery.

Hospital affiliations, on the other hand, present their own unique set of legal problems. While the integration of hospital and medical care delivery is certainly a concept that should be encouraged for, among other reasons, economies of scale, the method of health care delivery and the overall improvement of quality, the legal system, in general, views such combinations with more suspicion where hospitals and physician do not totally integrate their operations. This combination without full integration creates particularly difficult issues in the fraud and abuse area and in the increasingly prevalent type of legislation which prohibits physician self-referral, which is commonly known as Stark-type legislation. Hospital affiliations, therefore, must be crafted with the recognition that, in many areas, non-integrated relationships (between hospitals and medical groups) need to be structured with particular emphasis on the technical provisions of these laws.

Medicare fraud and abuse

Perhaps the single most troublesome legal issue confronting parties to a merger or hospital affiliation is raised by the Medicare fraud and abuse law. In the merger context, the concern for the parties is evaluating whether the other party has engaged in conduct that might have violated the fraud and abuse law. Careful evaluation of the activities of the other group is necessary, because the combination of the groups means that the liabilities of one group are assumed automatically by the other group. In the hospital affiliation context, while the actions of the parties in the past should be scrutinized, it is the affiliation design itself that may create potential liability for the parties. The ongoing affiliation of hospital and medical group may create a number of opportunities for potential violations of the fraud and abuse statute which may be increased by the design of the affiliation itself.

History

In 1972, Congress enacted a statute (the Fraud and Abuse Act) aimed at preventing kickbacks and bribes for referrals in the Medicare or

Medicaid programs (collectively, "Medicare"). The statute prohibited solic-iting, offering or accepting kickbacks or bribes in connection with the provision of services reimbursed by Medicare or Medicaid, or rebates of any fee or charge for referrals. Violation of the original statute was a misde-meanor and was punishable by a fine of up to $10,000 or imprisonment for up to one year, or both. The statute was amended in 1977, and the term "remuneration" was used to expand the definition of "kickback," "bribe" and "rebate." The provision was further clarified by specifying that it applied to actions "directly or indirectly, overtly or covertly, in cash or in kind." In addition, the penalty was upgraded from a misdemeanor to a felony.

In 1987, Congress passed legislation which added two new provisions to the law which address anti-kickback provisions of the Fraud and Abuse Act and consolidated the Medicare and Medicaid provisions. As an alternative to criminal prosecution under the Fraud and Abuse Act, the Office of the Inspector General of the Department of Health and Human Services (the "Inspector General") was granted the power to exclude providers from participation in the Medicare program if it was determined that the party engaged in a prohibited kickback arrangement. The 1987 legislation also required the Inspector General to issue regulations, known now as "safe harbors," specifying certain payment practices that would not be subject to criminal prosecution under the anti-kickback law or would not be used as a basis for exclusion from the Medicare program.

The current anti-kickback provisions of the Fraud and Abuse Act are contained in §1128B(b) of the Social Security Act (42 U.S.C. §1320a-7b(b)) and provide, in part, as follows:

(a) Illegal remunerations

(1) Whoever knowingly and willfully solicits or receives any remunera-tion (including any kickback, bribe, or rebate) directly or indirectly, overtly or covertly, in cash or in kind --

    (A) in return for referring an individual to a person for the fur-nishing or arranging for the furnishing of any item or service for which payment may be made in whole or in part under subchapter XVIII of this chapter or a state health care pro-gram, or

    (B) in return for purchasing, leasing, ordering, or arranging for or recommending purchasing, leasing, or ordering any good, facility, services, or item for which payment may be made in whole or in part under subchapter XVIII of this chapter or a state health care program, shall be guilty of a felony and upon conviction thereof, shall be fined not more than $25,000 or imprisoned for not more than five years, or both.

(2) whoever knowingly and willfully offers or pays any remuneration (including any kickback, bribe, or rebate) directly or indirectly, overtly or covertly, in cash or in kind to any person to induce such person

  (A) to refer an individual to a person for the furnishing or arranging for the furnishing of any item or service for which payment may be made in whole or in part under subchapter XVIII of this chapter or a state health care program, or

  (B) to purchase, lease, order, or arrange for or recommend purchasing, leasing, or ordering any good, facility, service, or item for which payment may be made in whole or in part under subchapter XVIII of this chapter or a state health care program,

shall be guilty of a felony and upon conviction thereof, shall be fined not more than $25,000 or imprisoned for not more than five years, or both.

Prohibited conduct, therefore, includes not only remuneration intended to induce referrals, but also conduct that induces the purchase, lease or ordering of goods, facilities, services or other items reimbursed under Medicare.

As a reading of the statute indicates, it is broadly worded, and nearly impossible to apply to particular factual situations. While the obvious situations where someone pays money for a referral clearly violate the statute, the potential liability for engaging in complex business relationships such as a hospital affiliation is more difficult to determine.

Cases interpreting fraud and abuse act

Unfortunately, the decided cases which interpret the Fraud and Abuse Act are few in number and offer little real guidance to those parties who desire to comply with the law. For example, in *United States v. Greber*, 760 F.2d 68 (3d Cir. 1985), the defendant physician received referrals from other physicians to provide diagnostic services. After receiving payment from Medicare for the diagnostic services, the defendant would remit 40 percent of his fee for those services to the referring physician. The defendant labeled these payments "interpretation" or "consulting" fees, even though some of the referring physicians had done neither. The issue decided in the case was whether or not a payment which is only partially for the purpose of inducing referrals violates the anti-remuneration provisions of the Fraud and Abuse Act. The court upheld the conviction, determining that the statute was violated if any purpose of the payment was to induce referrals. As the statute included "remuneration" among its prohibitions, where previously only "bribes" and "kickbacks" were prohibited, the court stated that use of the term "remuneration" implies a situation in which a service was rendered. The purposeful addition of this term in the statute indicates legislative intent that the statute apply to these situations, and, therefore, implies that a violation can occur when a service was actually rendered in addition to a referral.

A second case also has construed the Fraud and Abuse Act broadly. In United States v. Kats, 871 F.2d 105 (9th Cir. 1989), the defendant was a 25 percent shareholder in a clinic that sent specimens to a laboratory for diagnostic purposes. This clinic received a 50 percent kickback of the fees for tests it referred to the laboratory. In an appeal to the Ninth Circuit Court of Appeals, the defendant argued that the trial court incorrectly allowed the jury to convict, even if it found that the referral of services was not a material purpose of the payments. The court rejected this defense and instead followed Greber which held that if one purpose of the payment was to induce referrals, the Medicare statute is violated.

In *United States v. Bay State Ambulance and Hospital Rental Service Inc.,* 874 F.2d 20 (1st Cir. 1989), Bay State, an ambulance company, put an official of a city-owned hospital on its payroll as a "consultant." The official was involved in the administration of the ambulance service contract for the city and used his influence to secure a new ambulance service contract for Bay State. Bay State provided the official with cash and two new automobiles. The issue confronted by the court was whether a payment can violate the Fraud and Abuse Act even though there is no indication that the payment exceeds the fair market value of services rendered by the payee. The court rejected the defendant's "fair market value" argument and instead focused on the element of "inducement." The court held that any amount of inducement to channel potential Medicare business is illegal, regardless of whether there were other reasons for payments, and regardless of whether the payments are in amounts reasonable to compensate the payee for such other purposes or services. The argument that the payment was fair market value and, therefore, permissible, was rejected.

The final important case is *The Inspector General v. Hanlester Network et al.* The decision in this case is the most significant reported, because it deals with joint ventures and is the only decision to deal in-depth with an interpretation of the Fraud and Abuse Act. In this Department of Health and Human Services proceeding, certain physicians set up limited partnerships in clinical laboratories. Partnership shares were sold primarily to physicians who were likely to refer business to the labs. Many of the physicians did indeed use the labs for their tests. The profits for limited partners came from the proceeds of the labs, but the amount of compensation to each partner was not related to the amount of business he referred to the labs. Partners were not required to refer any business to the labs, although it was in their best interests to do so. However, the Vice President of Marketing (the agent in charge of selling partnership interests), represented to some potential limited partners, who later became partners, that referrals were an "off the record" condition to share purchase. She was not authorized to make such a representation and was actually told that to do so would be illegal. Following a decision by an Administrative Law Judge favoring the providers, the government appealed to the administrative Appellate Panel.

The Appellate Panel reversed the decision of the Administrative Law Judge, finding in favor of the government. In its decision, the Appellate Panel concluded that the statute is violated whenever a party knowingly and willfully offers or pays anything of value, in any manner or form, with the intent of exercising influence over the judgment of a physician so as to cause the referral of Medicare-related business. The Appellate Panel focused on a strict interpretation of the statute and concluded the statute does not require proof of an agreement precluding provider choice, rejecting that theory propounded by the Administrative Law Judge.

Although the Administrative Law Judge did not conclude there was any direct payment to any physician, nor any guaranteed flow of business to the manager of the laboratory, the Appellate Panel concluded that these factors did not prove that the parties had not knowingly or willfully solicited or received "remuneration —in return for" referrals. The Appellate Panel noted that the statute focuses on the "substance, rather than the form, of any transaction or relationship." Moreover, the Panel concluded that "the absence of a guarantee of referrals does not mean that referrals, once made, are any less 'in return for' remuneration, where there is an intentional connection between the referral and the remuneration."

The Appellate Panel concluded that the Administrative Law Judge erred in concluding that section 1128 B(b)(2) proscribes only offers of agreements or agreements precluding provider choice. The Appellate Panel focused on the statutory language and found that "induce" means more than mere "encouragement," which the Inspector General proposed to be sufficient to constitute a violation. The Appellate Panel concluded that "induce" means "an intent to exercise influence over reason or judgment in an effort to cause a desired action."

The Appellate Panel then examined the finding of the Administrative Law Judge that "remuneration" is defined as paying an equivalent for services and the need for some quid pro quo for an agreement. The Administrative Law Judge had also concluded that the phrase "including any kickback, bribe, or rebate" evidenced an intention to limit the kinds of remuneration to "traditionally unethical" arrangements and that, therefore, the "remuneration" language reflects an intention prohibiting only agreements which preclude provider choice. The Appellate Panel rejected these arguments and held that the phrase "remuneration" means "anything of value employed with the proscribed intent of inducing referrals." The Appellate Panel cited Bay State and Kats in holding that, in the ownership setting, an illegal inducement may consist of an opportunity to earn money on the investment, if a non-incidental purpose of providing that opportunity is to induce referrals, and that the result is the same whether or not the referrals were specifically required or even took place.

All of these decisions taken together provide little guidance for evaluating the appropriateness of mergers or affiliations from a fraud and abuse perspective. The cases demonstrate that the courts will construe the Fraud and Abuse Act very broadly and that a violation will be found to exist in many circumstances where a non-incidental purpose of the relationship is to induce referrals, and regardless of whether or not the referrals actually took place. This broad interpretation means that there is risk in undertaking any relationship where Medicare business is involved and that medical group mergers and hospital affiliations will be subject to this risk. While obvious referrals and kickback activities clearly violate the statute, as shown by all of the decided cases involving clearly illegal activities, less obvious activities are more difficult to evaluate. Careful analysis of any merger or affiliation must be made, therefore, to avoid an overly simplistic answer that either all activity is illegal or that no activity, short of the obvious violation, will be prosecuted successfully.

Safe harbor regulations

In light of this statutory and case law, and in an effort to provide a "safe harbor" for certain activities, Congress, when it passed the Medicare and Medicaid Patient and Program Protection Act in 1987 (Pub. L. 100-93, 101 Stat. 680 (1987)), required that regulations be issued to specify various payment practices which would not be considered a violation of the Fraud and Abuse Act, even though the practices in question might technically violate the Act.

The final regulations issued on July 29, 1991 (56 Fed. Reg. 35952) set out eleven different categories of conduct which fall within the protected range of conduct. To the extent a health care provider or business engages in one of these eleven categories of activities, any compensation received or given by the provider or business will not be deemed "remuneration" under the Fraud and Abuse Act and will, therefore, not be found to violate the Act. Failure to qualify for safe harbor treatment does not mean that a violation of the Fraud and Abuse Act has occurred; rather, it means that the activity must be evaluated under the case law and the provisions of the

Fraud and Abuse Act itself. The following safe harbors are most relevant to mergers and hospital affiliations:

1. **Investment interests**. The safe harbor regulations exclude from coverage under the Fraud and Abuse Act payments that are a return on an investment, such as a dividend or interest income, made to an investor as long as all the criteria within one of two specified categories are met. One category involves interests in publicly traded companies with more than $50,000,000 in undepreciated net assets. Most investment interests owned by medical groups will not be in companies of this size and, therefore, will not qualify for this safe harbor.

    The second investment safe harbor requires that all of the following eight criteria be met:

    (a) No more than 40 percent of the investment interests of each class of investment may be held in the previous fiscal year, or previous 12-month period, by investors who are in a position to make referrals or furnish items or services to the entity.
    (b) The terms on which an investment interest is offered to passive investors who are in a position to make referrals or furnish items or services to the entity must be the same as the terms offered to other passive investors.
    (c) The terms on which an investment interest is offered to an investor who is in a position to make referrals or furnish items or services to the entity must not be related to the previous or expected volume of referrals or items or services furnished to the entity.
    (d) There is no requirement that a passive investor make referrals, influence referrals, furnish items or services to the entity, or otherwise generate business as a condition for remaining an investor.
    (e) The entity or the investor must not market or furnish the entity's items or services to passive investors differently than non-investors.
    (f) No more than 40 percent of the gross revenue of the entity in the previous fiscal year or previous 12-month period comes from referrals or items or services furnished or other business otherwise generated from investors.
    (g) The entity must not loan funds or guarantee a loan for investors who are in a position to make referrals or furnish items or services to the entity if the investor uses any part of the loan to obtain the investment interest.
    (h) The amount of payment to an investor in return for the investment interest must be directly proportional to the amount of

the capital investment of that investor. (This capital investment includes the fair-market value of any preoperational services rendered by that investor.)

The regulations make clear that the term "investor" includes not only the health care provider, but also any entity who holds the investment interest indirectly by having a family member hold such investment or by holding a legal or beneficial interest in another entity (such as a corporation, trust or holding company) that holds the investment interest.

In the merger context, this safe harbor means that the participating medical groups must evaluate in the due diligence process whether or not the investments owned by either group fall within the safe harbor. Ownership of investment interests must be evaluated carefully to determine any potential liability. In the hospital affiliation context, where the ownership of the management organization or the physician-hospital organization is held in part by physicians or a medical group, the ability of that interest to qualify for this safe harbor must be determined. Because both the hospital and medical group will be deemed to be potential referral sources, neither the 40 percent ownership or referral requirements will be satisfied if they are the only owners of the organization. In the hospital affiliation context, therefore, ownership of the physician hospital organization by both groups will disqualify the investment interest for investment safe harbor treatment. Therefore, the ownership structure of such an entity must be evaluated using the general principles of the Fraud and Abuse Act.

2. **Space rental**. Providers or businesses who lease real property at amounts above or below fair market value are exposed to the risk that the amounts paid or received will be deemed to be in exchange for referral of Medicare patients. The safe harbor regulations, therefore, provide an exclusion for payments made by a lessee to a lessor for the use of leased premises as long as the following conditions are met:

   (a) The lease is in writing and is executed by the parties.
   (b) The lease specifies the premises covered by the lease.
   (c) If the lease is intended to provide the lessee with access on a periodic basis, rather than a full-time basis, the lease must specify the exact schedule during which access to the facility by the lessee will be allowed, along with the exact rent for such intervals.
   (d) The term of the lease must be for not less than one year.
   (e) The aggregate rental charge must be set in advance, must be consistent with fair market value as determined by an

arms-length transaction, and must not be determined in a manner that takes into account the volume or value of any referrals of Medicare business between the parties.

"Fair market value" is defined as the value of rental property for general commercial purposes. The fair market value of the premises also is not to be adjusted to reflect the additional value a prospective lessee or lessor would ascribe to the property in light of the proximity or convenience to sources of referral or other business, payment of which is made in whole or in part by Medicare.

For mergers and hospital affiliations, the usual scenario with fraud and abuse implications is the relationship between a hospital and a medical group where the medical group leases its space in a hospital-owned complex or the hospital leases the medical group-owned property. In either of these situations, the parties must be able to document that the rental rate is set in accordance with true marketplace rental rates with reference to external sources of proof of those market rates. It should also be noted that the rental rate must be established in advance. Therefore, percentage leases which vary based upon revenues are not permissible. In addition, the parties must examine items that are typically "passed through" to a tenant, such as taxes, utilities and maintenance costs. These costs also should be established in advance to the extent that these items can vary based upon the action of landlord or tenant and are not set by independent third party action.

3. **Equipment rental**. The safe harbor regulations also contain a provision for equipment rental. The requirements of the equipment rental safe harbor, as well as the considerations for mergers and hospital affiliations, are essentially the same as those in the lease of real property. Payments made by a lessee to a lessor of equipment are afforded safe harbor protection as long as they meet the following criteria:

    (a) The lease must be set out in writing and executed by the parties.
    (b) The lease must specify the equipment covered by the lease.
    (c) If the lease is for a periodic interval of time, rather than on a full-time basis, it must specify the exact schedule, the precise length and the exact rent for such use.
    (d) The term of the lease must be for not less than one year.
    (e) The aggregate rental charge must be set in advance, must be consistent with fair market value as determined by an arms-length transaction, and must not be determined in a manner that takes into account the volume or value of referrals of business between the parties.

"Fair Market Value" for equipment rental purposes is determined as the value of the equipment when obtained from a manufacturer or professional distributor. The value must not be adjusted to reflect the additional value that any prospective lessee or lessor would give to the equipment because of its proximity or convenience to sources of referral or other business, payment to which is made in whole or in part by Medicare. In mergers and affiliations, rental rates charged between hospitals and medical groups for equipment must be established with reference to these third party sources, and evidence of these comparisons should be kept for any future inquiry or investigation.

4. **Personal services and management contracts**. The safe harbor regulations also address personal services and management contracts. These arrangements are defined very broadly to include any relationship of any agent to a principal (other than an employment arrangement). Management contracts are often used in the hospital affiliation context where the medical group engages the hospital to provide management services for the operation of the group. Relationships qualify for safe harbor treatment as long as they meet the following criteria:

   (a) The agreement must be set out in writing and signed by the parties.
   (b) The agreement must specify the services to be provided by the agent.
   (c) If the agreement is less than on a full-time basis, it must specify the schedules, length and exact charge for those services.
   (d) The term of the agreement must not be for less than one year.
   (e) The aggregate compensation paid to the agent must be established in advance, must be consistent with fair market value for those services in an arms-length transaction, and must not be determined in a manner that takes into account the volume or value of any Medicare referrals between the parties.
   (f) The services performed must not involve counseling or promotion of any activity which violates any other law.

"Fair market value" is not defined in this safe harbor. The comments to the regulations, however, specify that this fair market value determination is made utilizing the same standards as found in the leasing context. As in the leasing context, two aspects of this safe harbor receive the most attention by parties to a hospital affiliation designed to comply with these provisions. First, the compensation arrangement must be consistent with fair market value. The parties must establish, by reference to industry standards for an arms-length transaction, the fee to be paid to the hospital in a management affiliation, or to the medical group in an independent contractor or foundation model. The parties cannot, by themselves, determine what an appropriate compensation arrangement would be. They must refer to the industry standard of compensation for the type of affiliation in question in order to establish a benchmark for determining the appropriate arms-length compensation. The parties, therefore, should employ the services of an independent party to review the compensation arrangement to ascertain whether or not it is consistent with established practice in the industry. By obtaining this third party review, the parties will have established an important frame of reference from which to base their activities.

The other significant issue in management contract safe harbor provisions is the requirement that the compensation be set in advance. Many compensation arrangements outside of the safe harbor context involve percentage arrangements that vary depending upon the activity or size of the business. The management contract safe harbor, however, expressly eliminates the ability of the parties to rely on this accepted industry practice. In order to qualify for management contract safe harbor protection, therefore, the parties must establish the compensation amount in advance and avoid using a percentage arrangement which can vary and can be reviewed after the performance of the services for the period in question. By making volume, pricing and other cost assumptions, it is possible for the parties to establish in advance the aggregate amount of compensation that would be due the parties. Once this calculation has been made, it is then possible to express the management fee as a fixed dollar amount in the agreement. The work papers, assumptions, and reference to third party experts utilized in deriving this global fee should be retained for future reference in order to demonstrate that the parties have appropriately calculated this fee in advance. Many proposed affiliations will avoid calculating the management fee in advance because the ability to forecast accurately these operations is limited. Safe harbor protection will not be available if this decision is made.

5. **Sale of practice**. The sale of a physician's practice to another practitioner is also addressed by the safe harbor regulations. Because of the restrictions in the safe harbor, however, its practical application is limited. Payments made in conjunction with the sale of a practice qualify for safe harbor treatment as long as they meet the following criteria.

   (a) The period from the date of the agreement until the closing of the transaction is not more than one year.
   (b) The selling practitioner must not be in a professional position

to make referrals to or otherwise generate referrals for the purchasing practitioner after one year from the date of the first agreement pertaining to the sale.

The sale of practice safe harbor is limited in several important respects. First, with respect to practitioner-to-practitioner sales, the safe harbor only applies if the selling practitioner is removed from the practice no later than one year after the date of the closing. Retirement or relocation to another geographic area are the only two scenarios where this safe harbor provision could apply. The usual merger or acquisition scenario would not qualify for this safe harbor.

The second limitation of this safe harbor is that it does not cover hospital purchases of medical practices. Therefore, the acquisition by a hospital of the practice assets of a medical group must be analyzed under the provisions of the Fraud and Abuse Act. Comments to the final safe harbor regulations suggest, however, that another safe harbor may be issued in the future with respect to hospital recruitment activities.

6. **Employees**. The safe harbor provisions contain a broad exemption for amounts paid by an employer to an employee in a bona fide employment relationship. As long as the payments are made for the employment of the individual in the provision of covered services or items under Medicare, these payments are not subject to review under the Fraud and Abuse Act. This safe harbor, which repeats the exemption set forth in the text of the Fraud and Abuse Act, is significant in several respects. First, it means that in a merger, where two groups are combined, a compensation system which pays physicians as physician employees will qualify for safe harbor protection. Medical groups may design their compensation systems without fear of fraud and abuse liability for physicians who are bona fide employees. In the hospital affiliation context, this employee safe harbor means that those hospitals which directly employ physicians in a foundation model will have significant flexibility with respect to the method in which they pay physicians. While tax considerations for non-profit foundations will place limits on the total amount of compensation payable to physician employees, these foundations will be able to make payments to physicians of various specialties based upon industry standards without fear of fraud and abuse liability. It is this employee exemption which makes the foundation model of directly employing physicians attractive. It should be noted, however, that the employment safe harbor will not apply in foundation models in which the medical group remains an independent entity and is either: 1) an independent contractor for the foundation which itself is the provider of medical services; or, 2) is the provider

which, by management contract, retains the hospital to provide services to the medical group. While this factor alone should not dictate the selection of an employee-based physician-hospital organization, it is a very helpful provision for those who wish to qualify for safe harbor treatment the payments to physicians for the work they perform.

On September 21, 1993, seven additional safe harbors were proposed, but the final regulations have not yet been published. These additional proposed safe harbors address rural investments, investments in ambulatory surgery centers, group practice investments, physician recruitment, obstetrical malpractice, insurance subsidies, referrals for specialty services and cooperative hospital service organizations.

The Ethics in Patient Referrals Act of 1989

Federal and state legislation which may restrict the ability of physicians to refer patients to physician-owned ancillary services also may impact mergers and hospital affiliations. Transactions must be structured, therefore, to comply with these laws and regulations, with the recognition that, over the next several years, an expansion of the scope of these laws is likely. From a regulatory compliance perspective, however, the outlook for medical group practices to own and operate ancillary services within the medical group, and to remain in compliance with applicable law, appears to be quite good. Neither existing legislation, nor any in the foreseeable future, would expand the prohibition against physician ownership of a particular ancillary or service, if that activity is conducted solely within the group practice setting. Ventures likely to be affected by these laws are those which attract unrelated physician investors outside of an existing group practice into a setting which combines physician investment and referral activities. In addition, these laws on self-referral may impact significantly the ability of hospital affiliations to coordinate the operation of various ancillaries in the operation of the affiliation. Transactions must be structured, therefore, to comply with these various laws and to allow a mechanism to be developed which will give the parties flexibility to deal with a changing legal regulatory environment.

In 1989 Congress passed legislation known as the Ethics in Patient Referrals Act of 1989 (42 USC §1295nn). The original proposal for this legislation was made by Congressman Pete Stark, and was based on his belief that the Fraud and Abuse Act did not adequately address the situation wherein a physician referred business to an entity in which he had an ownership interest. While the original Stark proposal would have affected all types of joint venture arrangements, the legislation enacted in

1989 addressed only physician ownership of, and compensation arrangements with, clinical laboratories.

The Omnibus Budget Reconciliation Act of 1993, enacted August 11, 1993, expanded the prohibition of referrals beyond clinical laboratories. (This amendment to the original Act will be referred to as "Stark II"). Under Stark II, effective January 1, 1995, the Stark prohibitions are extended to apply to all referrals for "designated health services." Stark II defines designated health services as any of the following items or services:

1. clinical laboratory services;
2. physical therapy services;
3. occupational therapy services;
4. radiology or other diagnostic services;
5. radiation therapy services;
6. durable medical equipment;
7. parenteral and enteral nutrients, equipment and supplies;
8. prosthetics, orthotics and prosthetic devices;
9. home health services;
10. outpatient prescription drugs; and
11. onpatient and outpatient hospital services.

In the event that a physician, or the immediate family member of a physician, has an ownership or investment interest in, or a compensation arrangement with any entity, the prohibitions of Stark II apply with respect to referrals by the physician to the entity for any designated health services. These prohibitions affect both the physician and the entity. First, the act prohibits a physician from making a referral to the entity if Medicare reimburses the entity for its services. Second, the entity may not make a claim for reimbursement under Medicare or request payment from any individual or third-party payer. The statute contains an outright prohibition against these ownership or compensation arrangements, unless the activity of the physician, or the ownership of the physician in the entity is subject to exemptions contained in the law.

In structuring transactions where this legislation is likely to come into effect, reference must be made to detailed exceptions contained in the legislation which permit certain ownership or compensation arrangements. The exceptions relevant in the merger or hospital affiliation context are discussed below.

The first significant exemption applies both to the ownership and compensation prohibitions. This exemption exists for physician services personally provided by another physician practicing in the same group as the referring physician. The definition of "group practice" is critical to determine the scope of this exemption. "Group practice" is defined in Stark II as a group of two or more physicians legally organized as a partnership, professional corporation, foundation, not-for-profit corporation, faculty practice plan or similar association that meets the following requirements:

1. Each physician, who is a member of the group must provide substantially the full range of services which the referring physician routinely provides (including medical care consultation, diagnosis or treatment) through the use of shared office space, facilities, equipment and personnel. This requirement is satisfied if each member of the group individually furnishes substantially the full range of services he or she furnishes through the group practice.

2. Services of group members are provided through the group and fees for such are billed in the name of the group and treated as receipts of the group. This second requirement is met if the group practice attests in writing to its Medicare carrier, that at least 85 percent of the aggregate services furnished by all physician members of the group practice are furnished or billed by the group practice.

3. The overhead expenses and the income from the practice are distributed in accordance with methods previously determined by the group.

4. No physician who is a member of the group may directly or indirectly receive compensation based on the volume or value of referrals by the physician (except that a physician in a group practice may be paid a share of overall profits of the group, or a productivity bonus based on services personally performed or services incident to such personally performed services, so long as the share or bonus is not determined in any manner which is directly related to the volume or value of referrals by such physician).

5. Members of the group must personally conduct no less than 75 percent of the physician-patient encounters of the group practice.

6. The group must comply with any other standards that the Secretary of Health and Human Services may impose by regulation.

For faculty practice plans, these requirements only apply with respect to services provided within the faculty practice plan. Accordingly, many group practices and faculty practice plans will find that the services provided by other physicians will fall within this exemption.

A second important exemption from the ownership and compensation prohibitions of the Stark legislation exists for groups providing designated health services (other than durable medical equipment, (excluding infusion pumps) and parenteral and enteral nutrients, equipment and supplies) in their offices. In order to qualify for this exemption, in-office designated health services must meet the following three requirements. First, the services must be furnished by the referring physician, a physician who is a member of the same group practice or employees of the group practice personally supervised by physicians in the group practice. Second, the services must be provided in the same building where the other physician services are provided, or, in the case of a group practice, in another building utilized by the group for the provision of services some or all of the group's clinical laboratory services, or for the centralized provision of the group's designated health services (other than clinical laboratory services). Third, the services must be billed by the physician performing or supervising the services, the group practice of which the physician is employed, or by an entity that is wholly-owned by the physician or the group practice.

Designated health services performed in entities owned by physicians and combined pursuant to a merger will qualify for this in-office ancillary service exemption. Designated health services performed in entities that may be combined with hospital entities in a hospital affiliation, however, will not qualify for this exemption. This failure to qualify for an exemption may require that some hospital affiliation models comply with the Stark II legislation by keeping the ownership and operation of the entity within the medical group.

The third and final significant exemption exists for certain bona fide employment relationships. An employment relationship is exempt if (i) the employment is for identifiable services, (ii) the amount of the remuneration under the employment is consistent with the fair market value of the services and is not determined in a manner that takes into account (directly or indirectly) the volume or value of any referrals by the referring physician, (iii) the remuneration is provided pursuant to an agreement which would be commercially reasonable even if no referrals were to be made to the employer, and (iv) the employment meets such other requirements as the Secretary of Health and Human Services may impose by regulation, as needed, to protect against program or patient abuse.

Some hospital affiliation models which use employment arrangements with physicians may qualify for exemption under the bona fide employment exemption. Affiliation models in which the medical group remains a separate entity owned by physicians will find difficulty complying with the law if the ownership and operation of the entity to which referrals will be made is shifted to a non-medical group-owned entity.

Antitrust

Mergers and hospital affiliations often involve a combining formerly competitive entities. The joining together of these competitors raises antitrust concerns.

The health care industry was long viewed as being exempt from antitrust attack.

Transforming the Delivery of Health Care: The integration process

After several decades of antitrust litigation in the health care field, however, it is now clear that medical groups and hospitals are subject to antitrust scrutiny to the same extent as any other business or industry. While the scope of antitrust issues faced in the health care industry is exceedingly broad, this section will focus on several significant issues encountered by medical groups and hospitals contemplating a merger or affiliation. All participants in these ventures should recognize, however, that after the transaction is finalized, their ongoing operating will be subject to the entire range of antitrust laws. Accordingly, guidance for ongoing operational issues should be obtained from competent antitrust counsel.

While there are a number of Federal and state antitrust statutes, the following three separate Federal antitrust provisions are most likely to impact mergers and hospital affiliations:

Section 1 of the Sherman Act (15 U.S.C. §1)

Section 1 of the Sherman Act provides that "every contract, combination in the form of trust or otherwise, or conspiracy, and restraint of trade or commerce among the several states, or with foreign nations, is hereby declared to be illegal."

Section 2 of the Sherman Act (15 U.S.C. §2)

Section 2 of the Sherman Act provides that "every person who shall monopolize, or attempt to monopolize, or combine or conspire with any other person or persons, to monopolize any part of the trade or commerce among the several states, or with foreign nations, shall be deemed guilty of a felony."

Section 7 of the Clayton Act (15 U.S.C. §18)

Section 7 of the Clayton Act provides that "no person engaged in commerce or in any activity affecting commerce shall acquire, directly or indirectly, the whole or any part of the stock or other share capital and no person subject to the jurisdiction of the Federal Trade Commission shall acquire the whole or any part of the assets of another person engaged also in commerce or in any activity affecting commerce, where in any line of commerce in any section of the country, the effect of such acquisition may be substantially to lessen competition, or to tend to create a monopoly. No person shall acquire, directly or indirectly, the whole or any part of the stock or other share capital and no person subject to the jurisdiction of the Federal Trade Commission shall acquire the whole or any part of the assets of one or more persons engaged in commerce or in any activity affecting commerce, where in any line of commerce in any section of the country, the effect of such acquisition, of such stocks or assets, or of the use of such stock by the voting or granting of proxies or otherwise, may be substantially to lessen competition, or to tend to create a monopoly."

These provisions of the Sherman Act and the Clayton Act are brief and are written in such vague terms that they provide little guidance concerning the applicability of the law to a particular set of circumstances. In the years since these laws have been passed, however, a significant amount of antitrust litigation has occurred. This litigation provides some indication of how these general statutes will be applied to specific circumstances. Various economic theories of competition and other "rules of thumb" also have been developed to aid in the analysis. It is clear, however, that the application of these broad antitrust statutes to particular activities remains a difficult process. It is also clear that analyzing specific circumstances requires reference to the general statutes as well as to the case law that has interpreted the statutes. Antitrust analysis, therefore, is not an exact science and requires the use of legal counsel, well experienced in the application of antitrust law to particular factual situations.

Discussion of antitrust principles in the context of medical group mergers and hospital affiliations is broken down into a discussion of issues raised in these two fundamentally different transactions.

Antitrust analysis of medical group mergers

In the merger of medical groups, the primary issue is whether the merger violates §7 of the Clayton Act, which prohibits acquisitions which substantially lessen competition or tend to create a monopoly, or §2 of the Sherman Act, which prohibits monopolization or attempts to monopolize. Medical group mergers involve the consolidation of competitors in the same line of business. This antitrust legislation will prohibit the merger of medical groups which concentrate market power in an impermissible fashion. Horizontal mergers of medical groups must be analyzed by determining the organizations' market power and by analyzing the increase in market concentration resulting from the proposed merger. This process involves a three-part analysis. First, the appropriate market for the services offered must be determined. This "product market" must include those services which are viewed by the consumer as interchangeable, and accordingly, which are able to be combined into one service market. To determine the product market in the medical group merger context, it is necessary to undertake an analysis of the practice of medicine and related ancillary services. From the medical group's perspective, a larger product market means that a potential combination of activities has a smaller impact than if the product market is defined more narrowly. Medical groups will argue that the product market for medical services includes the practice of medicine and related ancillary services provided in an outpatient setting. General medical care plus ambulatory surgery, imaging services and other ancillaries could be combined together in this larger market to view ambulatory care as a whole. Those seeking to challenge a medical group merger, however, will argue for a much narrower product market definition. Thus, if two cardiovascular surgery groups are merging, a challenge to that merger would seek to define the appropriate market as cardiovascular surgery as opposed to wider product definitions which might be cardiology, medical practice or ambulatory care. The selection of a product market will have a critical impact in determining the appropriateness of the merger. While a number of product markets have been determined in antitrust litigation, there is little guidance for this determination in the health care industry. Parties involved in a horizontal merger of medical groups, therefore, must make their own analysis of the appropriate product market.

The second step in determining the appropriateness of a merger is defining the geographic market. The extent of a geographic market for the relevant product must be determined so that the impact of any combination can be judged with reference to all competitors within that particular geographic area. Again, as in the product market definition, the perspective of the purchaser of medical services must be considered, as those patients in the appropriate geographic area must be convinced that they can obtain similar services from other substitute medical groups. Other medical groups in this geographic area must have the ability to provide the relevant service to these patients. Again, there is little case law to guide medical groups in determining the appropriate geographic market. Medical groups seeking to uphold the validity of any merger will argue for a wide geographic drawing area for patients, since the larger the geographic area and greater number of competitors from within that area, the less of an impact a potential merger would have on the market. Those seeking to challenge a merger will argue for a smaller geographic market. A smaller market will include fewer competitors and, thus, the impact of any combination will be greater when measured over a smaller area. A combined analysis of the geographic market, urban concentrations, patient statistics, patient origin information and the drawing power of medical groups must be made in order to paint an adequate picture of how medical care is delivered in a particular geographic area. Groups who seek to evaluate the appropriateness of any merger, therefore, must examine their patient statistics as well as the geographic patterns in which medical care is delivered in their area.

The final step in determining the impact of a particular combination on the market is to determine the impact of the combination on market power. In this process, the market concentration before and after the merger must be compared, and the potential change in market power must be evaluated to determine whether it will violate the Clayton or Sherman Acts. A merger creating a group controlling an unduly large share of the relevant market, and which results in a significant increase in the concentration of groups in that market, is likely to lessen competition and could lead to an antitrust violation.

In an effort to provide some certainty to these somewhat vague standards, the United States Department of Justice issued merger guidelines. These guidelines measure market concentration with the use of the Herfindahl-Hirschman Index (known as HHI). To use the HHI, the following process must be undertaken. First, the market shares of the various competitors in a particular product and geographic market must be determined. Once determined, a before-merger and after-merger market share calculation are made. Under both calculations, the market shares of each competitor in the relevant market should be squared (multiplied by itself). These squared numbers are then added together to determine both premerger and postmerger indicators of market concentration. Under these guidelines, the Justice Department has developed the following general rules of thumb:

(a) Where the HHI is below 1,000 after the merger, the merger is unlikely to be challenged.
(b) Where the HHI after the merger is between 1,000 and 1,800, the merger in question will not likely be challenged if the increase in HHI from before the merger to after the merger is less than 100 points. Increases of more than 100 points may be challenged, depending on the existence of other factors.
(c) If the HHI after the merger is above 1,800 points, an increase of 100 points or more from the premerger to postmerger HHI will likely result in a challenge. Increases of less than 50 points are not likely to result in a challenge. Those between 50 and 100 points may be challenged, depending upon other factors including the nature of the service to be provided, the existence of barriers to entry into a particular market -- including licensure and cost-of-capital considerations -- whether or not the merger will promote competitive efficiencies and whether or not a new service is being offered.

Not all courts have been convinced, however, that the merger analysis propounded by the Justice Department should be applied in every situation. In fact, several significant merger cases brought by the Justice Department in the hospital merger area have resulted in decisions reaching opposite conclusions. In *United States v. Rockford Memorial Hospital Corporation*, (717 F.Supp. 1251 (ND'Ill. 1989) affirmed, NO. 89-1900 (7th Cir. 1990)), the court determined that a hospital merger between two nonprofit acute care hospitals violated both §7 of the Clayton Act and the Sherman Act. A decision rendered about the same time as the Rockford case, however, in *United States v. Carilion Health System* (707

F.Supp. 840 (W.D. VA. 1989) affirmed, 892 F.2d 1042 (4th Cir. 1989)), held that §7 of the Clayton Act did not apply to mergers of nonprofit entities and that, under the Sherman Act, the merger was permissible because of the broad geographic market. The court concluded that there was not an unreasonable restraint of trade.

From the point of view of a medical group, these hospital cases, again, provide little guidance in determining the appropriateness of any merger. While most medical group combinations will not result in undue concentration, the appropriateness of any merger must be evaluated by medical groups and their counsel by analyzing the geographic and service markets. An evaluation of the antitrust risks involved in a particular transaction can then be made.

Antitrust analysis in hospital affiliations

Hospital affiliations often result in the creation of a joint venture, and joint ventures require a separate analysis under §1 of the Sherman Act. If the hospital affiliation results in a structure which leaves the medical group as an independent entity, the parties will not be totally integrated, and a joint venture analysis of the antitrust risk of that arrangement must be made.

While §1 of the Sherman Act prohibits combinations and restraints of trade, several different standards are utilized to determine the appropriateness of activity. Certain activities which have been determined by the courts as having no commercial or economical justification are deemed "per se" illegal. This per se analysis means that the courts have determined that these activities have no procompetitive aspects and that merely proving these activities have occurred is sufficient to find illegality. No proof of the economic justification for these activities is permitted. Two of the activities deemed by the courts to be per se illegal are price fixing and division of markets among competitors.

Other actions not deemed per se illegal are judged under a rule of reason standard. Under this standard, the procompetitive purposes for a particular behavior are reviewed, and the economic justification of a particular activity may be deemed to outweigh the negative impact it may have upon competition. Therefore, the rule of reason analysis can be used to justify a variety of activities by competitors who wish to combine or cooperate in some fashion.

To determine whether per se illegality or a rule of reason analysis applies to a hospital affiliation, it is necessary to determine whether the hospital affiliation integrates the parties' activities in a way that will be allowed under a rule of reason analysis. Integration can be in the form of a merger where the competitors fully integrate their business activities and, since they are now a single entity, are no longer able to conspire or restrain trade. In a joint venture, partial integration makes only certain limited activities permissible, while unintegrated competitors are not allowed to engage in any anticompetitive activity. The determination of whether parties to a joint venture have integrated is a factual question, and the organization of each particular hospital affiliation must be reviewed to determine whether or not the parties have truly combined operations. If this economic integration occurs, a rule of reason analysis will apply, and it will be much more difficult for any party to challenge successfully the practices of the affiliation. Hospital affiliations which combine the administrative aspects of the medical practice for centralized billing, centralized personnel and employees, joint billing and collection, and joint utilization review and quality assurance, with the offering of new prepaid products, risk sharing in the venture and joint marketing, will present a strong argument that the parties have partially integrated their activities. If most or all of these factors are present in the management services or independent contractor model of hospital affiliation, the venture more than likely will be determined to be partially integrated and the activities of the venture more than likely will withstand antitrust attack under a rule of reason analysis.

Under this integration analysis, therefore, several common antitrust issues must be considered in the hospital affiliation. How well those issues withstand antitrust attack will hinge upon the integration determination. For example, in the price fixing area, if the affiliation does not have sufficient business integration, or if it fails to offer new products to the market, it will be illegal for parties to agree among themselves regarding prices to be charged for services provided by the parties. To the extent, however, that establishing prices is necessary for the activities of the venture to provide new services and the activities of the venture have been integrated, this agreement on pricing may be permissible. In the market division context, if the primary purpose of a venture is to divide markets among competitors who are not integrated, the activity will most likely be viewed as per se illegal. If, on the other hand, an integrated venture can establish that the division of markets is necessary for procompetitive reasons, the market division may be upheld. Market division issues, such as bidding on managed care contracts and other direct contracting initiatives, will be subject to this type of analysis.

Finally, in light of these antitrust concerns, hospital affiliations must also consider the issue of the size of their venture. There are two concerns in particular. First, if the venture becomes too large and all-inclusive of physicians in a community, it may be viewed as either having monopoly power or attempting to monopolize, and hence, as violating §2 of the Sherman Act. It could also be viewed as substantially lessening competition, thereby violating §7 of the Clayton Act. Second, an affiliation that excludes competitors in order to gain monopoly power may violate the

Sherman Act if access to a market for that competitor is precluded and if that access is crucial for those competitors to compete in that market. While these size issues are often not a problem in hospital affiliations, it is important to seek competent antitrust counsel early in the process to determine whether further antitrust analysis should be undertaken in the design of the affiliation.

Statements of Enforcement Policy. On September 15, 1993, the Department of Justice and the Federal Trade Commission jointly issued six Statements of Antitrust Enforcement Policy in the Health Care Area (the "Statements"). The Statements address mergers among hospitals, hospital joint ventures involving high-technology or often expensive medical equipment, physicians' provision of information to purchasers of health care services, hospital participation in exchanges of price and cost information, joint purchasing arrangements among health care providers, and physician network joint ventures. The Statements establish "safety zones" within which an entity will not be challenged absent extraordinary circumstances, by the Department of Justice or the Federal Trade Commission. The Statements do not address mergers of medical groups and deal only with the physician network component of hospital affiliations. The Statement concerning physician network joint ventures does not apply to relationships between an integrated medical group and a hospital, but rather, applies to independent practice association, preferred provider organizations, and similar physician network joint ventures used by physicians to market their services to health insurance plans and other purchasers. The Statement defines its subject as "a physician-controlled venture that jointly markets the services of its member physicians" and specifically states that other types of health care network joint ventures are not addressed by this policy statement.

Regardless of its direct applicability, however, the policy statement on physician network joint ventures reiterates the emphasis given in the traditional analysis to size of the geographic markets, financial risk and market power of the venture.

A final antitrust issue that should be considered by the participants in the planning stage of any merger or hospital affiliation is the potential applicability of the Hart-Scott-Rodino Antitrust Improvements Act of 1976 (15 U.S.C. §18(a)). This legislation requires that the parties to certain transactions notify the Antitrust Division of the Department of Justice and the Federal Trade Commission in a premerger notification filing. This filing must be made at least 30 days prior to consummating certain mergers, acquisitions or joint ventures. In general, transactions which meet certain threshold requirements are subject to this filing requirement. These threshold requirements generally provide that, if one party to a transaction has total assets or annual sales of $100 million or more and the other party to a transaction has total assets or annual net sales of $10 million or more, premerger notification will be required if, as a result of the acquisition, the acquiring party will hold 15 percent or more of the voting securities or assets of the other party, or if that person would hold an aggregate total amount of voting securities or assets in excess of $15 million. The specifics of the premerger notification rules and the precise manner in which these threshold amounts are calculated are set forth in detailed regulations interpreting the Hart-Scott legislation. If major parties are involved in mergers or hospital affiliations, a review of those detailed provisions should be made to ascertain whether a Hart-Scott-Rodino filing is required. Since the cost of making a filing by the acquiring person and the penalties for failure to file are substantial, these regulations should be reviewed in any transaction of significant size.

Tax exempt organizations

While most medical groups are for-profit organizations and pay income tax on their earnings, many hospitals with which medical groups may form affiliations will be non-profit and exempt from income taxation. Mergers of medical groups most often do not involve issues of tax exempt organization law. Yet, on the other hand, medical group affiliations with hospitals that are tax exempt require that in the structuring of any transaction, the law regulating the activities of tax exempt organizations be reviewed thoroughly. Other tax exempt principles, with respect to the operation of the venture after it has been formed, will also be impacted, but the primary focus of the following discussion is on those issues which the parties must become familiar in order to implement a hospital affiliation.

From the medical group perspective, medical group leadership must be familiar with these concepts in order to understand thoroughly the position of the hospital with respect to the organization of any affiliation. This understanding is necessary in order to negotiate effectively a mutually successful organizational relationship. From the perspective of the hospital, however, it will be necessary to structure the transaction to avoid jeopardizing the tax exempt status of the entire hospital organization. The risk for the hospital, of course, is exceedingly great should a particular structure be challenged. Accordingly, hospitals can be expected to be more conservative in the view of an appropriate structure, as the risk of being incorrect will largely fall upon the hospital which could lose its exempt status in any challenge of its activities.

Most hospitals qualify for tax exempt status under §501(c)(3) of the Internal Revenue Code, although many city or county hospitals are exempt because they are instrumentalities of state or local government. Internal Revenue Code §501(c)(3) exempts organizations that are organized and operated exclusively for religious, charitable, scientific, or educational purposes. In structuring a hospital affiliation model, a tax exempt hospital will be faced with the issue of whether or not to use its existing corporation or of forming another corporation. If the hospital has already undergone a corporate reorganization, it may have a corporate entity which already is tax-exempt, and it may be able to incorporate the activities of the affiliation into that organization. On the other hand, it is possible that the corporations utilized by the hospital in its existing structure do not fit within the activities contemplated for the hospital affiliation organization. In this case, it will be necessary for the hospital to form a separate corporation. The issue then faced by the hospital is whether or not this corporation should be a for-profit organization or a not-for-profit organization. If the subsidiary is a non-profit organization, it must also meet the charitable, scientific, educational or religious purpose test in order for it to qualify for 501(c)(3) status. In order to make this determination, the activities of the subsidiary must be analyzed to determine whether or not it meets the charitable purpose test.

In addition, in order for the Internal Revenue Service (IRS) to grant 501(c)(3) status, the hospital will be required to submit an application for exemption which will detail the purposes of the organization and set forth certain other information as required by the IRS. The review process undertaken by the IRS of the charter and purposes of the organization must be completed before tax exempt status is granted. If the hospital makes the determination to use a for-profit corporation, no qualification with the IRS is necessary and the activities of the for-profit subsidiary will be taxable to the extent that it generates a profit. For-profit subsidiaries of hospitals which are tax exempt themselves, however, must still comply with several basic rules concerning the relationship of non-profit organizations to other parties. Thus, both in the not-for-profit and for-profit subsidiary arrangement, the organization which affiliates with medical groups must meet, among other requirements, two basic tests which limit the activities of these organizations. They are the inurement test and the private benefit tests and are discussed below.

Non-profit hospitals which are exempt from federal income taxes are governed by laws and regulations which, in large part, are designed to ensure that the charitable assets of the organization are dedicated exclusively to furthering public purposes. Section 501(c)(3) organizations must be entities, "no part of the net earnings of which inures to the benefit of any private shareholder or individual." Activities which violate this prohibition are referred to as "private inurement" or "inurement." The inurement prohibition applies to more than just the "net earnings" of the organization, as value may be transferred to the benefit of an individual in a variety of other ways, as well, and that transfer may violate the inurement prohibition, even if the amounts transferred are quite small. The prohibition against inurement generally applies to a certain class of persons, who, because of their special relationship with an organization, have an opportunity to control or influence the activities of that organization. The persons specified are those who have a personal and private interest in the activities of the organization, and are commonly referred to as "insiders." The IRS has taken the position that all physicians on the medical staff of a hospital, either as employees or as individuals with close professional working relationships with the hospital, are insiders and are, accordingly, subject to the inurement rules.

While medical staff physicians are subject to the inurement prohibition, those regulations do not prevent, in and of themselves, payment of reasonable compensation for goods or services to those medical staff members. The inurement requirements are designed to prevent dividend-like distributions or expenditures to benefit private interests. Payment of reasonable salaries to physicians, as hospital employees, generally do not give rise to inurement. In addition, physicians who are providing services to, or on behalf of the hospital as independent contractors, may also be paid reasonable compensation for those services and not have those activities give rise to inurement.

To avoid the inurement prohibition, therefore, the hospital affiliation process must be negotiated at an arms-length basis between the exempt organization and the physicians. Terms of the venture must be commercially reasonable. The facts of each particular case must be analyzed to determine whether or not an affiliation arrangement satisfies the inurement requirements, and must also be examined, as a whole, to determine whether or not this arms-length process has been achieved.

The second major test to be considered in non-profit hospital affiliations is entitled "the private benefit test." This principle of tax exempt organization law specifies that the hospital is not considered to be organized and operated exclusively for exempt purposes, unless it serves a public rather than a private interest. To be exempt, therefore, the hospital must not be organized or operated for the benefit of private interests. This private benefit prohibition applies not only to insiders, subject to the more strict inurement prohibition, but to all kinds of individuals and other entities. The presence of private inurement violates both the private benefit and private inurement requirements, but the absence of inurement does not mean that there is the absence of private benefit. Inurement, therefore, is a subset of private benefit test. The presence of a single non-charitable purpose, if substantial in nature, will destroy the non-profit exemption, regardless of the number of charitable purposes.

The IRS views that there is some private benefit present in all physician hospital relationships. The private benefit which accrues to physicians, however, is generally considered incidental to the overwhelming public benefit which results from having a combination of the hospital and professional staff available to serve the public at large. For the private benefit to be incidental, the IRS looks at several factors. It first examines whether or not a reasonable relationship exists between the activity selected by the hospital and its non-profit purpose. It also considers whether or not the activity selected is necessary to achieve the purpose of the organization and, accordingly, whether or not the benefit is only the consequence of and, therefore, incidental to, the accomplishment of the exempt activity.

The IRS must also consider whether or not the individual benefits are excessive in amount and whether or not the organization confers more private benefit than is necessary to accomplish the non-profit charitable purpose. In order to establish that the private benefit is incidental, the non-profit hospital will need to establish that negotiations were undertaken at arms-length; that individual physician's payments are reasonable; that the hospital keeps control over the affairs of the affiliation; and that limits are placed upon the risk assumed by the hospital.

In Rev. Rul. 69-545, the IRS indicated a number of factors that would support an arguement that a hospital benefits the community, rather than serving private interests. In a hypothetical example in the revenue ruling, a hospital was controlled by a board composed of independent civic leaders, it had an open medical staff, it had an active, open and accessible emergency room, serving everyone without regard to ability to pay, and it treated all patients able to pay for their care, including Medicare and Medicaid patients. The revenue ruling indicated that the hospital in the example served public rather than private interests. In contrast, in a second example, five physicians who owned a for-profit hospital sold their interest in the hospital for fair market value to a non-profit hospital that they controlled, which hospital generally served only patients of those physicians. The new non-profit hospital was not exempt due to the excessive private benefit to the five physicians.

In Rev. Rul. 83-157, the IRS ruled that a non-profit hospital may, under certain narrow circumstances, be able to demonstrate sufficient community benefit to qualify for exemption without operating an emergency room. For example, where a state agency determines that an emergency room would be unnecessary and duplicative, or where a specialty hospital does not generally treat emergency medical conditions.

In 1993, the IRS published a technical instruction program for IRS agents spelling out factors that are significant in determining whether an integrated delivery system (IDS) can qualify for tax exemption. An IDS, for purposes of the IRS publication, is a health care provider (or one component entity of an affiliated network of providers) created to integrate the provision of hospital services with professional medical (e.g. physician) services. The IRS publication cites the following factors as important considerations in evaluating an IDS application for recognition of exemption for purposes of determining whether the IDS will benefit the community:

(i)   integration of medical functions for purposes of greater efficiency and reduced cost to the public,

(ii) increased accessibility of health care services to medicaid and charity care patients,

(iii) research and education functions of the IDS, and

(iv) control of board of trustees of the IDS by independent community members.

As discussed above, in order to achieve tax-exempt status, in addition to community benefit standards, an organization must benefit public rather than private interests. In the 1993 IRS publication described above, the IRS indicates that an organization may provide benefits to private individuals, provided those benefits are incidental, both quantitatively and qualitatively. To be qualitatively incidental, private benefit must be a necessary concomitant of an activity which benefits the public at large. To be quantitatively incidental, the private benefit must be insubstantial in the context of the overall public benefit. In the IDS context, one of the most important factors is whether assets being purchased from physicians to create the IDS are being purchased for fair market value. In analyzing whether private inurement exists, the IRS will look at the influence that private individuals have over the IDS and the fairness of purchase prices or compensation paid to individuals by the IDS. The focus of the IRS is to determine whether any arrangements suggests dividend-like sharing of charitable assets or expenditures for the benefit of private interests.

The structure of hospital affiliations between medical groups and non-profit hospitals must comply with these basic principles in order to protect the non-profit status of the hospital. While the standards used in the analysis of these non-profit questions depend, to a large degree, upon the facts and circumstances surrounding each particular transaction, it is clear that the IRS increasingly will scrutinize the activities of physician-hospital ventures. While many ventures can properly be structured between physicians and hospitals, it is also clear that a new environment exists for all who participate in the planning and implementation of these ventures. Recent IRS activity, including the issuance of In General Counsel Memorandum 39862, issued on December 2, 1991, illustrates the the IRS applied heightened scrutiny in the joint venture context.that the IRS will apply. While this General Counsel Memorandum pertained solely to joint ventures relating to the sale of an existing hospital department revenue stream to individual investors, the issuance of this the memorandum does signal heightened IRS interest in physician-hospital relationships in general. While the revenue stream transactions described in the General Counsel's Memorandum appear clearly excessive, it is unclear how far this new level of scrutiny will proceed. Physicians who negotiate with hospitals, however, should place the General Counsel Memorandum in perspective, and not be negotiated into less advantageous positions based upon vague references to this memorandum. Many hospital negotiators may attempt to use the existence of this General Counsel Memorandum to their advantage, but it should not be misused, and those physicians who negotiate with hospitals should be reluctant to accept, at face value, the analogy of this General Counsel Memorandum to most medical group-hospital affiliations.

Under standards set forth in the 1993 IRS publication described above, the IRS granted exempt status to two major integrated delivery systems in 1993. In granting the exemptions, the IRS cited the factors described above in determining each IDS would benefit its respective community, and that neither IDS created other than incidental private benefit or private inurement.

Tax considerations

As is the case with most business transactions, tax considerations will play an important part in determining the structure of a merger of medical groups or an affiliation of a medical group with a hospital or management company. Although tax considerations alone rarely drive a health care merger or affiliation, the tax implications of a merger or affiliation can either be very advantageous to the parties or they can be disastrous. The goal is to address the tax issues inherent in a proposed transaction early enough in the negotiation process to ensure that positive planning opportunities can be identified, potential pitfalls can be avoided, and the parties' expectations are realized in terms of net after-tax dollars.

This section initially will address the tax implications arising out of two types of combinations becoming more common in the health care industry: a tax-free merger of medical groups, and a stock sale or asset sale to a hospital or management company. Next, tax issues which must be faced in choosing the entity that will hold any real estate owned by the combining groups or their physicians will be examined.

Type of transaction

A variety of ways exist in which two or more medical groups can join forces to achieve the advantages available to larger groups. Typically it is the goal for the medical groups to combine into one of the existing groups with no tax incurred by the medical groups or their physician owners. This goal usually can be realized through a fairly straightforward application of state merger statutes and the nonrecognition provisions of the Federal tax law. For simplicity, the discussion of tax-free mergers in the following two paragraphs will focus on the merger of two or more medical groups organized as corporations. However, it should be noted that combinations involving partnerships can be structured to provide results similar to tax-free mergers of corporations.

In a tax-free merger, the physician shareholders: (i) recognize no taxable income upon the consummation of the merger to the extent that they receive stock or securities in the combined entity; (ii) recognize capital gain (and sometimes ordinary taxable income) to the extent they receive money or property other than stock or securities of the combined entity; and, (iii) they have a "carryover basis" in their stock in the combined entity. The physician shareholders are subject to tax to the extent they receive cash or other property. "Basis" is an income tax concept that allows the measurement of the gain or loss recognized upon the sale of an asset. Taxable gain or loss is measured by subtracting the basis in an asset from the proceeds of the sale of the asset. A carryover basis means that a physician shareholder's basis in the stock of the combined entity will equal his basis in the stock of the old, separate entity, reduced by the amount of cash or other property received in the merger and increased by the amount of capital gain recognized in the merger. For example, assume that Group A is being merged into Group B. Each shareholder of Group A will receive shares of Group B plus $30,000 in cash in exchange for his Group A shares. If a former Group A shareholder had a basis of $50,000 in his Group A shares, he would recognize $30,000 of capital gain on the merger and would have a basis of $50,000 in his Group B shares ($50,000 basis in Group A shares - $30,000 cash received + $30,000 in capital gain). At a later time, if he were to leave Group B and have his shares redeemed for $60,000 in cash, he would recognize $10,000 in capital gain ($60,000 amount realized - $50,000 carryover basis). Although a tax-free merger is normally used to combine medical groups, an affiliation of a medical group with a hospital or management company is typically structured as a taxable acquisition of stock or assets. With an asset sale, the medical group will sell its assets, subject to its liabilities, to the hospital or management company in exchange for one or more cash payments and possibly assumption of liabilities. Under this scenario, the medical group will recognize taxable gain to the extent that the cash received plus the amount of the debts assumed exceeds the basis of the group in the assets. If the medical group is a pass-through entity -- an S corporation or a partnership -- the medical group itself will pay no taxes, but its physician owners will pay tax on their relative shares of the gain of the medical group. If the medical group is a C corporation, the medical group will pay taxes on the gain and distribute the net proceeds to its physician owners. Creative tax planning is necessary to avoid (or at least minimize) the double taxation normally attendant upon the distribution by a C corporation to its owners, once at the corporate level on the gain, and a second tax on the dividend to the shareholders. The medical group, therefore, will characterize all, or a portion of, the distribution to the physician shareholders as compensation, which is deductible by the corporation. In seeking to make these payments, groups must avoid unreasonable compensation to their physicians, as well as distributions that closely track share ownership. For instance, it is easier to justify a distribution method that is based upon production, as opposed to a distribution process based on relative shareholdings.

With a stock sale, the hospital or management company does not buy the assets from the medical group, rather it buys the stock in the medical group from the shareholders. Since the medical group itself is not a party to this transaction, it does not recognize taxable gain or loss. However, the shareholders of the medical group will recognize taxable gain to the extent that the cash or property received exceeds their basis in their stock.

In either event — asset sale or stock sale — the key to the transaction often lies in the allocation of the purchase price. In a typical transaction, the hospital will be paying consideration for several things:

- the "hard" assets such as office and diagnostic equipment;
- the excess of the value of the medical group over the value of its hard assets or "goodwill";
- the agreement of the medical group and/or its physicians to perform medical services;
- the agreement of the medical group and/or its individual physicians not to compete with the hospital; and
- a favorable lease.

The goal of the hospital or management company is to structure the transaction so that a large portion of the payments produce income tax deductions. This allows a portion of the purchase price to be underwritten by the government. The goal of the medical group is to maximize the net after-tax cash to its physician owners. With the changes in the tax laws implemented in 1986, the goals of the medical group and the hospital have become more compatible. Payments for the hard assets of a business produce depreciation deductions to the purchaser and generally produce capital gain to the seller. Payments for consulting agreements and noncompetition agreements produce deductions as ordinary and necessary business expenses for the payer, but produce ordinary income to the recipient. Payments for goodwill are not deductible by the hospital, but produce capital gain for the medical group. Payments for a physician shareholder's stock are not deductible by the hospital, but produce capital gain treatment for the physician shareholder.

Legal issues

Prior to the 1986 Tax Reform Act, there was a large differential between the capital gains tax rate and the tax rate for ordinary income. At present, the capital gains rate for individuals is only 11 percent lower than the maximum ordinary income tax rate. Due to this rate differential, physician shareholders will want to maximize the portion of the consideration eligible for long term capital gain treatment and should be aware of the allocation of the purchase price among the assets being purchased. To increase the likelihood that the respective allocations of the purchase price by the parties will be respected by the IRS and the courts, the allocation should be reasonable and it should be made a part of the definitive agreement. Further, in the case of an asset sale, the parties should agree to file IRS form 8564, Asset Acquisition Statement, consistent with the agreed-upon allocation.

It is important that the advisors to any medical group considering an affiliation with a hospital have a firm grasp on the amounts and timing of the tax payments which must be made by the medial group and by its physician owners. If at all possible, the transaction should be structured so the medical group and its physician owners will have received enough cash at all times from the transaction with which to pay the taxes caused by the transaction, as it is very unpalatable for physicians to have no cash to pay these taxes.

A significant issue which must be considered when structuring a transaction is depreciation recapture. For instance, assume a medical group sells its operating assets for which it has a $1 million adjusted basis to a hospital for $150,000, at closing, plus the hospital's promissory note for $1.35 million payable over five years in equal installments. Assume further that the medical group originally paid $2 million for these assets, but had claimed depreciation deductions of $1 million, thus reducing the group's adjusted basis in the assets to $1 million. The medical group has a gain of $500,000 on the sale ($1.5 million purchase price - $1 million adjusted basis). However, all of this gain is attributable to the depreciation deductions claimed in prior years. All of this gain is "recaptured" in the year of sale. Recapture income is not eligible for the installment method of accounting in which capital gains are recognized as the payments are received. At a 38.62 percent tax rate, the medical group will incur tax liability of $193,100, but have only $150,000 with which to pay these taxes. Careful planning can avoid such unpleasant surprises.

Real estate

For years, physicians and medical groups have been investing in the real estate occupied by their practices, with varying degrees of financial success. If one or more of the medical groups considering a merger, or if the medical group considering an affiliation with a management company or hospital, owns real estate, it must be determined at an early stage whether or not the real estate will be a part of the transaction. Often, the circumstances may dictate that the medical office building of one of the parties should be sold and vacated. Other times, the management company or hospital may desire to purchase the real estate. In other cases, it is best for the combined entity to lease the real estate from a partnership of some or all of the physician members.

What type of ownership structure should be used? As a general rule, the real estate ownership interest should not be held by the entity engaging in the practice of medicine. Partnerships (general or limited) are almost always the superior choice of entity for holding a real estate investment , such as a medical office building. First, partnerships are pass-through entities. They do not pay tax themselves. Rather, the taxable income, or loss, earned by the partnership is reported directly on the partner's tax returns. Thus, if partnerships — unlike C corporations which require payment of tax at the corporate level and payment of tax at the level of the individual physician on the dividend — have taxable income, only one layer of tax is imposed at the individual level. Also unlike C corporations, if the partnership incurs losses, these losses are not trapped at the corporate level, but may be passed through to the individual physician.

Second, unlike S corporations, partnerships allow partners to include their share of the losses of the partnership in their basis. Medical office buildings typically are built or purchased mostly with borrowed funds and with relatively little of the cash of the owners. Partners in a partnership and shareholders of a corporation can only claim losses to the extent that they have basis in their investment. Partners can claim a share of the debt of the partnership in their basis, but shareholders of a corporation cannot claim a share of the debt of the corporation in their basis. Being able to claim a share of partnership losses in their basis greatly enhances the ability of the partners to shelter their income with tax losses generated by the real estate investment, due to interest and depreciation deductions.

Finally, partnerships are more flexible than S corporations. S corporations can only have a single class of stock. Each share of stock must have the same rights as to dividends and proceeds upon liquidation. Partnerships are not burdened by the single class of stock rules and can structure the allocations of taxable income and loss, and the distributions of cash to reflect differing economic interests. As discussed in Chapter 8, partnership agreements can be drafted to provide for preferred returns that (1) protect the investment of those partners who have invested significant capital, and, (2) allow new partners to participate in the future appreciation of the real estate with relatively little additional capital required. Such flexibility is impossible to achieve with C corporations or S corporations.

These factors make real estate partnerships an integral part of the merger decision. Caution should be exercised when dealing with the tax aspects of partnerships. When more than one-half of the interests of a partnership are transferred in a twelve-month period, that partnership is terminated for tax purposes. Tax termination can have positive results such as loss of an unfavorable tax election made in prior years, but can result in harmful consequences, such as the recognition of taxable income by the partners. The accountants and tax counsel should be consulted to determine if tax termination will occur, and, if so, what the consequences will be.

One other ownership vehicle bears mentioning: limited liability companies. A limited liability company or LLC is an entity that is governed like a corporation with limited liability to the partners and free transferability of interests, but taxed like a partnership. Limited liability company statutes have been enacted in several states and are under consideration in several more. Limited liability companies can be attractive vehicles for holding real estate. Depending upon the particular state statute, it may be advisable to organize the real estate holdings of a medical group in a limited liability company.

Employee benefit issues

In any medical group merger, the groups involved must address employee benefit plan issues. Employee benefit plans include, but are not limited to: qualified retirement plans, such as pension plans, profit sharing plans, 401(k) plans and employee stock ownership plans; welfare plans, such as medical plans and life insurance plans; non-qualified retirement plans, such as excess benefit plans and deferred compensation or deferred bonus plans; and other plans which benefit employees, such as severance pay plans and fringe benefit plans.

As discussed in Chapter 6, the groups must first decide what should be their overall benefit policy. In making this policy decision, it is important to consider the possibility that (even if there is no merger) there may be significant and unavoidable changes from year to year in the costs of any benefit plan (especially medical insurance). On the other hand, there may be some efficiencies of scale which may contribute to overall lower merger costs.

Once the overall policy is established, the group or committee must decide how best to implement this policy with respect to each type of plan offered. Implementation issues differ depending on the type of plan involved. With respect to all plans, however, the groups must not make any commitments to any employees until the benefit plans have been designed and until it is clear what will be offered under all plans.

Qualified retirement plans

Each group may have one or more pension plans, profit sharing plans, or 401(k) plans which are qualified plans under Internal Revenue Code §401. The groups generally have three choices with respect to organizing the qualified retirement plans of the surviving group. First, the groups may decide to combine and merge the separate retirement plans of each group into one or more retirement plan(s) that will cover all members of the surviving group. Second, the groups may terminate all or some of the separate retirement plans of each group and either bring affected individuals into existing plans maintained by the other group or create one or more new retirement plans covering all members of the merged group. Third, the groups may opt to continue to maintain the separate retirement plans of each separate group and continue to cover only separate group members under each plan even after the merger. This latter option may also be used as a temporary solution during a transition period after which one of the other options are chosen.

There are both legal and business issues to consider when deciding whether or not to merge the retirement plans of each group, terminate existing plans, or maintain separate retirement plans covering only the members of each group prior to the merger.

Nondiscrimination rules

First, IRS rules and regulations require that qualified retirement plans not discriminate in favor of "highly compensated employees." "Highly compensated employee" is a specially defined term, but in most physician groups can be assumed to generally include any employee who earns at least a specified amount; as of 1994 this amount was $66,000 and will be indexed up each year. In order to satisfy these rules and regulations, plans must pass very complex "nondiscrimination tests" which have many exceptions and conditions, some of which relate specifically to mergers and acquisitions. A plan, which seemingly does not discriminate, may not pass these tests, so any medical group anticipating a merger should consult a lawyer specializing in employee benefits for advice on how best to structure the employee benefit plans of the merged group. One nondiscrimination test is the Internal Revenue Code §401(a)(26) minimum participation test. Under this test, a retirement plan must benefit the lesser of 50 employees or 40 percent of all employees of the employer. The definition of "employee" also includes partners in a partnership and certain "leased employees" who work on a routine basis with the physicians, but who technically are the employees of another entity. The Code §401(a)(26) test may cause problems if a small medical group merges with a large medical group and the combined group wishes to maintain separate retirement plans for each group involved in the merger. Because each retirement plan separately must satisfy the §401(a)(26) test, the retirement plans of the small group may not be able to pass this test, and the merged group would not have the option of continuing to maintain separate plans for each pre-merger group.

A second nondiscrimination test is the Internal Revenue Code §410 test. This test is very complex, but generally, it compares the percentage of non-highly compensated employees and highly compensated employees who benefit under a retirement plan. If the ratio of these percentages is less than 70 percent, non-highly compensated employees must receive actual average benefits that are at least 70 percent of the actual average benefits received by highly compensated employees and meet certain other rules promulgated by the IRS. Under this Code §410 test, all plans that are the same type of plan are tested together. For instance, if each of two medical groups maintains a profit sharing plan and they merge into one medical group that continues to maintain both profit sharing plans, these two profit sharing plans must be tested as one plan for purposes of Code §410. This test may pose particular problems for a merged medical group wherein the retirement plan of one group covers a disproportionate number of highly compensated employees and provides larger benefits than the pre-merger retirement plan of the other group.

In addition to considering the number of employees covered under a retirement plan pursuant to Code §401(a)(26) and the respective benefits provided to highly compensated and non-highly compensated employees under Code §410, Code §401 also provides that retirement plans may not discriminate in favor of highly compensated employees with respect to certain other rights and features provided under a retirement plan. For instance, if a retirement plan allows plan participants to receive distribution of their benefits in a lump sum, this option must be available to highly compensated employees and non-highly compensated employees on a relatively equal basis. Therefore, if a medical group maintains separate plans for different individuals, all the features of each plan must be examined to determine whether or not they are available, in the aggregate, to a nondiscriminatory group of individuals.

Internal Revenue Code rules and regulations also provide that certain rights or features of a retirement plan may not be taken away from an individual once they have been provided, at least with respect to benefits that the individual already has earned. A medical group which has decided to merge retirement plans of each group into one retirement plan covering all individuals of the merged group must include certain rights and features contained in the pre-merged plans at least with respect to benefits earned before the merger.

Plan termination

Another set of special and complicated rules applies when a retirement plan is terminated. Again, a medical group should consult a lawyer specializing in employee benefits before deciding to terminate a retirement plan. A benefits consultant can also be used to assist with all of the forms, employee communications, and benefit calculations necessary, should a retirement plan be terminated.

One rule pertaining to retirement plan terminations is that all benefits accrued in a retirement plan as of the date of termination must be made 100 percent vested. In certain cases, 100 percent vesting must also be extended to individuals who terminated prior to the Plan's termination. Therefore, a medical group which opts to terminate a retirement plan, either before or after the merger, must be sure that assets are available to 100 percent vest all affected plan participants. In addition, the plan must distribute benefits from a terminated plan within a limited amount of time. In deciding whether or not to terminate a retirement plan, the groups must determine whether or not they want plan participants to receive this retirement money while they are still working with the medical group. Although any new plan could be drafted to allow a distribution from a terminated plan to be "rolled over" into the new plan, participants cannot be forced to make such a rollover.

Finally, before a decision is made to terminate a plan, it is important to analyze the plan's investments to make sure they can be liquidated without undue penalties or charges, or otherwise handled so that distributions can be made to participants.

Frozen plans

Rather than terminating the pre-merger groups' retirement plans, the merged group could opt to "freeze" some or all of these retirement plans and simply provide that no further benefits will accrue under these plans. If a retirement plan is frozen, the assets stay in the plan and are distributed as provided under the plan, which typically means distribution occurs upon the participant's retirement, disability, death, or separation from service. It is often very difficult to maintain a frozen retirement plan without violating the nondiscrimination rules; therefore, a medical group should get expert advice from a lawyer specializing in employee benefits before seriously discussing this frozen plan option.

Welfare plans

The groups also must decide what types of welfare plans to provide for the merged group, what benefits to offer under these plans, and whether or not to self insure these plans, or provide these benefits through an insurance company. Welfare plans, for our purposes, include health, accident, dental, life insurance and disability plans, as well as Internal Revenue Code §125 cafeteria or flexible spending account plans. Unlike qualified retirement plans, welfare plans generally are funded out of the general assets of the employer or through insurance contracts so there are few legal issues associated with merging plan assets or terminating plans and distributing assets; rather, the main concern will be merely to take appropriate steps far enough in advance to prevent any gaps in benefits coverage.

Welfare plans generally are easily amended, so the merged medical group usually can readily change the existing welfare plans for the combined group. However, plan changes may not be so easily accomplished if retiree benefits are involved in circumstances where unconditional promises were made to an employee prior to his or her retirement.

If the merged group opts to provide some type of a self-insured medical plan (which may include certain "minimum premium" insurance arrangements), that plan must comply with the nondiscrimination rules of Internal Revenue Code §105. Similarly, if the merged group opts to provide a cafeteria plan, this plan must comply with the nondiscrimination rules of Internal Revenue Code §125. These nondiscrimination rules are similar to some of the retirement plan nondiscrimination rules.

Another important consideration for the merged groups is ongoing COBRA/medical plan coverage, both for individuals who terminate employment premerger and individuals who terminate employment as a result of the merger. Governmental regulations and certain case law indicates that the merged group (even in an asset acquisition) may have responsibility for providing ongoing COBRA coverage. The necessity for making arrangements in advance to provide ongoing COBRA medical coverage is underscored by the fact that such coverage may not be easy to obtain if the individuals on COBRA are incurring higher than average medical expenses.

Non-qualified retirement plans

The separate groups also may provide non-qualified retirement plans. These plans generally consist of employer promises to pay benefits upon the occurrence of certain events and usually benefit only certain highly compensated employees. Non-qualified retirement plans do not receive the same favorable tax treatment as qualified retirement plans and, therefore, are not subject to the Code §§401(a)(26), 410 or 401 nondiscrimination rules. Typically, these plans are funded out of general assets and, therefore, there are few legal issues associated with merging plan assets or terminating plans and distributing assets. Non-qualified retirement plans occasionally provide that a merger or some similar event will affect the plan. For instance, the plan may provide that if a merger occurs, the plan will terminate and benefits will be distributed. Therefore, medical groups anticipating a merger should carefully review the non-qualified plans of each group for any such provision.

Other employee benefit plans

Medical groups must also review other types of employee benefit plans, such as severance plans and fringe benefit plans, and determine what plans to offer to the combined group. Some severance plans are drafted to allow for severance pay after a merger even though the employee remains employed by the surviving group. Severance plans should be reviewed for such language and amended to delete these provisions, if possible.

Affiliated service group and related issues

If a medical group has an affiliation with a hospital or other outside entity, the medical group and the hospital or other entity may be treated as a single employer for purposes of determining whether or not an employee benefit plan is eligible for favorable tax treatment and satisfies the various nondiscrmination rules. This single employer determination will occur if the medical group and the hospital or entity are members of the same "controlled group" or "affiliated service group" under IRS rules and regulations. Even if these entities are not members of the same controlled group or affiliated service group, other IRS rules and regulations covering "leased employees" may require that employees of the hospital or other entity, who perform services for the medical group be treated as employees of the medical group for purposes of determining if the employee benefit plans of the medical group are eligible for favorable tax treatment.

These controlled group, affiliated service group, and leased employee rules pose concern for medical groups anticipating a hospital or similar affiliation, particularly with respect to the nondiscrimination rules and regulations of Internal Revenue Code §410. Code §410 requires that: 1) the ratio of the percentage of non-highly compensated employees who benefit under the plan, to the percentage of highly compensated employees who benefit under the plan, be at least 70 percent, or, 2) the plan both benefit a nondiscriminatory class of employees and provide actual average benefits to non-highly compensated employees which are at least 70 percent of the actual average benefits received by highly compensated employees. If a medical group and a hospital or other entity are members of the same controlled group or affiliated service group, all employees of both the medical group and the hospital or entity must be included when performing this Code §410 test. For example, assume a medical group includes ten employees, two highly compensated employees and eight non-highly compensated employees, all of whom benefit under the retirement plan of the group. Assume further that the medical group is in the same affiliated service group as a management organization that employs 75 non-highly compensated employees and two highly compensated employees, none of whom are covered by the medical group plan. The plan of the medical group will fail to pass the first prong of the Code §410 test because the ratio of the percentage of non-highly compensated employees who benefit under the plan, to the percentage of highly compensated employees who benefit under the plan, is less than 70 percent. The second prong of the Code §410 test is more complex, but the plan also would fail this prong because the plan benefits a discriminatory class of employees by benefiting such a small percentage of non-highly compensated employees compared to the percentage of highly compensated employees included under the plan.

This example illustrates that even though the plan of a medical group benefits all of its employees, the plan may not qualify for favorable tax treatment if the medical group is a member of a controlled group or affiliated service group. A similar result may occur if hospital employees are determined to be leased employees of the medical group because these leased employees must be counted when determining whether or not the benefit plans of the medical group satisfy the nondiscrimination rules.

The controlled group, affiliated service group, and leased employee rules are very complex and are in a state of great flux, but the following is a generalization of these rules.

Controlled group rules

Under Code §414, by reference to Code §1563, there are two basic types of controlled groups: parent-subsidiary and brother-sister. Generally, a parent-subsidiary controlled group exists where one parent organization has at least an 80 percent ownership interest in another organization. If one of these two organizations has at least an 80 percent ownership interest in a third organization, all three organizations are members of the same parent-subsidiary controlled group. For this purpose, and for purposes of the brother-sister controlled group rules, an organization or entity includes a corporation, association, partnership, sole proprietorship, trust or estate.

A brother-sister controlled group is much more complicated to describe than a parent-subsidiary controlled group, but generally requires that five or fewer entities taken together have at least an 80 percent ownership interest in two or more organizations. The entities comprising the 80 percent ownership also must have at least a 50 percent identical ownership interest when taken together. An identical ownership interest is like the common denominator of ownership. For instance, if Smith owns 40 percent of partnership A and 80 percent of corporation B, and Jones owns 20 percent of partnership A and 10 percent of corporation B, Smith's identical ownership in A and B is 40 percent and Jones' identical ownership in A and B is 10 percent. Together, Smith and Jones have an identical ownership interest in A and B of 50 percent. Any entity considered for the 80 percent ownership requirement must also be considered for purposes of the 50 percent identical ownership requirement. In addition, any entity taken into account under the 80 percent test must have at least some interest in each organization tested. These brother-sister controlled group rules are best expressed by way of an example taken from the IRC §414 regulations.

Example. Unrelated individuals A, B, C, D & E own the following interests in sole proprietorship F, GHI Partnership, and corporations M, W, X, Y & Z:

	F	GHI	M	W	X	Y	Z
A	100%	50%	100%	60%	40%	20%	60%
B		40%		15%	40%	50%	30%
C					10%	10%	10%
D				25%		20%	
E		10%			10%		

Based on this ownership interest, there are four brother-sister controlled groups: GHI, X and Z; X, Y and Z; W and Y; and F and M.

Affiliated service group rules

Generally an affiliated service group under Code §414(m) may exist anytime one service organization performs services for another service organization and there is some ownership interest between the two organizations. A service organization is an organization which performs services as its principle business. A medical group or hospital almost always will fit this definition of a service organization. The actual affiliated service group rules are very complex and are referred to as the A-org and B-org tests. Any medical group that is considering having services performed by an outside group, or is considering preforming services for another organization, should employ an employee benefits specialist to check these rules.

Where an organization, whose principle business is to perform management functions, performs such management functions for another organization, these two organizations also will be members of an affiliated service group. This affiliated service group will exist even where there is no ownership interest between the two organizations. This test is of particular concern to a medical group which utilizes a management organization for some or all of the administrative work of the medical group. Again, the rules are complex and should be tested by an expert.

Leased employee rules

An employee will generally be considered a leased employee of a recipient organization under Internal Revenue Code §414(n) if the individual is not an employee of the recipient organization, but performs services for the recipient organization on a substantially full-time basis for at least one year, and these services are of the type historically performed by employees. In addition, these services must be performed pursuant to an agreement (written or unwritten) either between the recipient organization and the individual, or between the recipient organization and another entity, the leasing organization. There are exceptions to this rule, for instance, where the individual is covered under a certain type of plan maintained by the leasing organization.

Corporate practice of medicine

In some states, statutes exist which prohibit corporations, other than professional corporations which employ physicians, from practicing medicine. While these statutes do not impact a merger between two medical groups, this legislation may affect the way in which hospital affiliations are structured. These statutes must be reviewed to determine the extent to which hospital-controlled organizations may hire or relate to physicians.

In several states, legislation which expressly prohibits a corporation from practicing medicine is sometimes construed to prohibit non-physicians or non-professional corporations from having an employment relationship with physicians. In other states, legislation may not expressly prohibit the corporate practice of medicine, but licensing statutes of physicians may otherwise be construed to prohibit a physician from having a direct employment relationship with non-physicians. Reference to specific legislation in a particular state must be made in order to determine this issue.

In hospital affiliation models where the medical group remains intact and is the provider of medical services, the corporate practice of medicine statues should not impact negatively the affiliation. Under these types of structures, physicians remain the provider of medical services to patients, they retain the provider number, they enter into agreements to provide physician services in managed care, and the services are all provided through a professional corporation owned and controlled by physicians.

Other types of hospital affiliations, however, may bring a particular corporate practice of medicine statute into consideration. For example, a hospital foundation which directly employs physicians as employees may be viewed as the employer of these physicians for corporate practice of medicine purposes, and such a relationship may be prohibited. To the extent these statutes prohibit this type of relationship, the parties must resort to the utilization of a professional corporation which employs the physicians. This professional corporation could be owned by the physicians at large or owned by a smaller group that could be more easily "controlled" by the hospital.

In the independent contractor hospital affiliation model, where the hospital becomes the provider of services and subcontracts various medical services to be provided by the medical group, the corporate practice doctrine also may apply. In this type of organization, the hospital affiliation should recognize expressly that it is unable to practice medicine. It, however, retains the right to have the patient relationship, to have provider numbers so it will receive directly reimbursement for services rendered by physicians, and to have in its own name the managed care arrangements required by employers and managed care entities. It is this funnelling of control through the hospital-affiliated corporation that may be impacted negatively by some corporate practice statutes. A review of these statutes and their precise limitations on the organizational structure, therefore, must be made.

Chapter 19

Financial planning, forecasts and projections

In order to assess accurately the financial impact of any merger or hospital affiliation, it is necessary to compile a variety of financial projections that will enable the participants to gauge the impact of the proposed venture. These financial forecasts and projections serve several useful purposes. First, projections can assist the parties to understand their current financial situation better. This base-line knowledge is sometimes lacking in medical groups and it may require undertaking in a major transaction for the groups to obtain a better picture of their current financial position. Existing statements, therefore, may need to be revised with the help of outside financial experts, who can clarify the existing financial condition of a group.

Another benefit of financial projections is that they assist in the evaluation of the proposed transaction. In order to evaluate the offer price for any type of transaction, it will be necessary to conduct an analysis of the offer with reference to the existing situation of the group, followed by an analysis of the details of the offer. Forecasts can be used to clarify whether or not an appropriate price is being paid, and to identify those areas of an offer which may need further negotiation.

Financial projections also can be used to forecast the future operations of the combined organization or affiliation. It is critical to understand both the current situation of the group and the operations after the transaction has occurred. This analysis can assess the benefits associated with proceeding. Accurate financial modeling must compare not only past operations with future operations, but also should compare the operations of the new combination versus the operations of the group during that same time period, if the transaction does not occur.

Finally, forecasts can be used to provide useful data about the ability of a medical group to make financial decisions concerning the admissions of new partners, the need for new capital and the impact of any future capital requirements. These projections will enable the individual physicians in the group to evaluate the future capital contributions they may need to make, and also will provide the merged group or hospital affiliation with an indication of future capital needs to be supplied either internally or by third parties.

In any merger or hospital affiliation, regardless of its structure, accurately prepared financial projections must address a variety of these concerns. These projections and forecasts must be prepared by financial advisors, who are capable of collecting, processing and placing the data in appropriate models, enabling the information to be conveyed in a logical and understandable format. A description of the various types of projections are detailed below.

Physician compensation models

As critical as any component in a transaction is the impact the merger or hospital affiliation may have on physician compensation. In order to win the support of individual physicians for any proposed change in their operations, the question that must be answered is "How will this proposed change effect my compensation?" Once the implementation process gets underway, answering that question must become a high priority.

In the merger context, two groups often will be combining separate compensation systems into a new system. In this situation, it is likely that all physicians will experience some change in their income due to modifications in the system. It is important to gather data concerning the operations of both groups, to compile historical information concerning operations and the compensation systems in effect, to present that information with an historical basis of compensation for existing physicians, and then to forecast the change of the new system into the future. In the hospital affiliation context, a new compensation system may or may not be implemented. Regardless of the system used, however, the impact of the affiliation must be presented at the individual physician level. This future forecast will be scrutinized most closely by individual physicians.

The presentation of data concerning compensation systems can take many forms. Each of the following forms can be used to express the data in slightly different ways, providing information to the physician in a comprehensive manner.

Table 4 presents compensation data for the merger or hospital affiliation by projecting the impact of the new combination. This physician by physician presentation of data allows a physician to make the comparison for the first year of the operation using, as a base-line, the projected compensation during the first year, if no merger or affiliation occurred. The projection can be made over a two-year period with the first year broken down into three different scenarios for the new operation. A conservative scenario can utilize the least optimistic forecast of the new operation. Minimal growth in revenues can be forecast, and conservative assumptions can be made concerning the ability to control increases in expenses. A moderate scenario can use what is believed to be the most accurate assumptions concerning revenue increases and expense control. This forecast should be the most likely portrayal of the impact that the combined organization will have on physician income. An aggressive scenario can be created which assumes significant, yet reasonably achievable, increases in revenue and productivity of physicians, while, at the same time, forecasting quantifiable cost savings. Finally, this format can project a second or third year, using the most likely scenarios to give physicians a forecast into the future. Accurate projections beyond the second year, however, may be difficult to make given lack of data and the limited ability to forecast both expenses and revenue in a changing health care environment. In any event, this document will provide the most sought after data for physicians by providing a comparison of compensation projections for the merger or hospital affiliation versus remaining in the original form of business.

Another important presentation for physicians considering a transaction is an historical-based presentation of compensation. This presentation shows compensation for the year prior to the transaction, the anticipated compensation during the current year and compensation for the year when the transaction is effective. Table 5 presents this information assuming that the merger or affiliation does not occur. Table 6 contains the same type of information as Table 5 except it assumes that the transaction occurs. In both of these tables, the comparison is made between the first year when the transaction is deemed effective versus the last year full data is available (referred to as "Transaction Year Minus 2"), and the current year estimated on current trends ("Transaction Year Minus 1").

The final comparison that can be made with respect to this data is shown on Table 7, which takes the raw numbers of total compensation and presents that data using the differences between the numbers, rather than the numbers themselves. This presentation compares the difference between the compensation in the commencement year of the transaction, assuming the transaction does not occur, to the various conservative, moderate and aggressive scenarios, assuming the transaction occurs. Finally, Table 6 examines compensation in the year after the transaction is effective by comparing compensation if the transaction did not occur, with a moderate scenario, assuming the transaction has been completed. The presentation of this data utilizing the difference in numbers provides another useful way for physicians to gauge the costs or benefits of proceeding with the merger or hospital affiliation.

To construct the physician compensation scenarios in Tables 4 through 7, it will often be necessary to demonstrate to physicians the derivation of the various compensation assumptions. This data presentation will allow physicians to have confidence in the methodology used to construct the by-physician data, and is particularly applicable in the merger context or in the affiliation context where physicians are paid on a basis in which they share the risk of group operations.

Table 8 illustrates the process by which the compensation pool for distribution to the physicians is calculated. Regardless of the compensation system selected, there must be an aggregate amount of dollars available for distribution to physicians. Only those amounts of revenues in excess of expenses can be distributed. For any transaction, the compensation pool without the transaction, and the compensation pool taking into account the implementation of the transaction, should both be calculated. Table 8 illustrates this calculation if the transaction does not occur, and compares the compensation pool for the previous year to the compensation pools in the year in which the transaction is effective using conservative, moderate and aggressive assumptions.

Table 9 is calculated in the same fashion except that the compensation pool is derived by assuming that the transaction has occurred and that the merger or hospital affiliation proceeds according to budget. Under both Tables 8 and 9, assumptions must be made with respect to the productivity of physicians and the revenues generated, and revenue generating activities, including fee for service income, HMO participation and ancillary income, should be calculated. The collection rate for these revenue production figures should be applied to arrive at net operating income. Expenses should be subtracted from those revenues to arrive at net operating income from which compensation pool amounts can be derived.

Determination of merger combination basis

In the merger between two medical groups, it is necessary to value the number of shares of all of the physicians, and then convert that value according to the determined plan of share ownership to arrive at the number of shares to be owned by each physician in the new medical group. In order to compute the amount of the contribution of the various physicians, the basis for combining the shareholdings of the various physician members of the new combined group must be determined. For example, if an equal ownership philosophy is selected by the groups, it will be necessary to determine how that equalization will be accomplished. The ultimate decision about how the shareholdings will be combined will depend upon the disparity of value and ownership both between the groups and among the various shareholders of each group. The respective ownership interests of the group members must be valued in order to determine alternative scenarios of combining ownership. These calculations can be made and presented in table format by examining the net book value (net assets minus liabilities) of the respective groups. To portray this comparison accurately, the financial statements of the groups must be converted to the same format. This conversion is necessary to make sure that assets have been valued in accordance with standard procedures, that all assets have been depreciated using the same schedules, and that liabilities have been recorded in the same fashion. Once any required conversion has been made, the respective values of the shareholdings of each physician should be determined.

As Table 10 illustrates, the net book value of the professional corporations has been determined. Under this illustration, because an equal ownership per physician is desired, a per shareholder dollar value has been derived. Because Medical Group II in this illustration has a higher net book value per shareholder, it is necessary to equalize ownership at the lowest common denominator. Hence, a payment of $30,000 will be made to the shareholders of Medical Group II to equalize the ownership of the assets in the professional corporation.

As part of the merger process, it also will be necessary to evaluate accounts receivable to be contributed to the merged organization. Because most groups conduct their affairs on a cash basis, it is likely that a separate valuation of the accounts receivable must be made, as these receivables will not appear ordinarily on the financial statements. In valuing accounts receivables, the same discount factor should be used for both groups to reduce the value of the accounts receivable to a net basis, and then the value held by each group should be compared. Any suggested differences in accounts receivable valuation should be scrutinized carefully and not be permitted unless there are compelling circumstances. If the parties determine that contributions for individual physicians should be equal, it will be necessary to equalize ownership at the lowest common denominator, resulting in additional payments to be made to the physicians in the group which has the higher per shareholder accounts receivable value. In Table 10 the contribution level is established at $150,000 per physician.

With the method of comparison illustrated in Table 10, it will be possible to compute the amount of contribution each physician must make to the new organization. This can then be translated into the numbers of shares of stock to be held by all individual physicians after the merger. By utilizing this type of analysis, it will be possible to evaluate various assumptions and principles concerning the contributions of physicians to the merged corporation. These scenarios can be used to arrive at the scenario which best approximates the ownership philosophy of the new group.

Affiliation fee evaluation

In transactions which involve an affiliation between the medical group and a hospital, it will be necessary, where physicians are not paid using a salary mechanism for the group to evaluate critically the cost of the management or affiliation fee and the impact of that fee upon physician compensation. The hospital fee proposal will have been constructed, in part, through the systems utilized by the hospital, but also, in part, by a review of the existing financial condition of the medical group. In deriving an affiliation fee, a model should be constructed which will make assumptions about group revenues and expenses as impacted by affiliation operations. To the extent that the hospital takes over the existing business operation of the medical group, the historical cost experience of that medical group will be critical to a determination of an accurate estimate of operations. Assumptions with respect to increases of revenue and the impact of changing legislative initiatives on physician reimbursement must also be factored into the equation. Assumptions used in the construction of the model must be tested thoroughly. Revenue projections must be realistic in light of conditions in reimbursement, as well as local competitive conditions. Conservative estimates on revenue growth should be made in order to improve the accuracy of the projection. Expenses must also be forecasted accurately based upon a realistic assessment of increasing costs over the next several years.

With these assumptions, it will be possible to project a net revenue figure from which the expenses in running the practice, plus the affiliation fee, can be subtracted before arriving at a net amount that will be distributable to the physicians. Table 11 illustrates this process where both physicians and hospitals share the risk of operations. Any proposed subsidy of operations by the hospital should also be reflected in Table 11. By undertaking this analysis, a more accurate assessment can be made of the appropriateness of the level of the fee to be charged by the hospital. Without a detailed examination of the numbers used to construct the fee, medical groups will have little idea concerning how they can expect their future operations to be impacted by the affiliation with the hospital.

Basic financial planning documents for the new organization

In order to plan for the commencement of the new operation, it will be necessary to prepare financial statements, budgets and cash flow projections. These basic financial planning documents are critical in accessing the future of the operation, as well as providing planning documents by which the organization can be managed after the transaction is completed.

Financial planning, forecasts and projections

With respect to the financial statements, a balance sheet which contains assets, liabilities and shareholders equity must be prepared. These statements should be prepared in accordance with standard financial practice. In addition, an income statement should be prepared. This income statement which examines revenues and expenses, and derives net operating income, should be prepared on an historical basis to indicate the previous year's activity, the existing year and at least one year into the future of the new transaction. An example of this type of an income statement is found at Table 12.

Another important planning document is a cash flow projection. In order to determine the cash needs of the organization for operations, for borrowing needs and for making payments to any physician shareholders, the hospital or other entities, it will be necessary to predict the cash flow of the organization. A month-by-month statement of anticipated cash receipts based upon a realistic assessment of the billings and collections should be made. The cash requirements, including salaries of physicians, employee salaries, benefit payments, insurance, vendor payments and all other payments necessary to be made in any given month should be set forth. By using this cash-in/cash-out methodology, it is possible to assess the cash position of the group during any given month. This planning is necessary in order to avoid unpleasant surprises with respect to operations and to limit the need for borrowings to the extent expenditures can be planned in a comprehensive fashion. Table 13 illustrates this process.

Real estate evaluation

Determining an accurate financial assessment of the impact of a particular proposal regarding real estate is as complex as any part of a merger or affiliation. While a particular transaction may involve the sale and purchase of real estate which will require appraisals and a calculation of the purchase price, the more complex issue from a financial projection perspective is that which requires a reorganization of real estate holdings by combining the holdings of two medical groups, and by accounting for the addition of new partners in the real estate holdings of that combined group. A series of calculations must be made, therefore, to assess the financial implications of scenarios which combine the real estate of respective medical groups or add new physicians to an existing partnership. For purposes of discussion, it is assumed that the real estate is owned in the partnership form.

In order to begin analysis of how real estate may be combined, the first step in the process is to determine the respective interests of the existing partners in the partnership, because before any combination can occur, the relative values of the interests of respective owners of the property must be determined. This first step is known as "marking to market" the capital accounts (or ownership interest) of the existing partners, as illustrated on Table 14. First, assume that all property is to be liquidated. The fair market value of the property is determined as of a recent appraisal, with this value being used as the amount to be realized in the assumed sale of the property. An amount realized will be determined by adding up the respective assumed sale prices of each parcel.

Then liabilities relating to all the parcels must be satisfied. Any loans associated with acquisition of the property including prepayment penalties, any notes that have been issued with the property as security, and any obligations to partners who have departed, retired or died, will need to be added to arrive at a cumulative amount of liabilities. These liabilities must be subtracted from the amount realized to obtain a net amount available for distribution to the partners. This net amount is the increased equity amount in the partnership that is available for distribution.

The net amount available for distribution to partners must then be allocated to the individual physicians. First, the capital account balances of the existing partners should be listed. This amount will be obtained from a review of the financial statements of the partnership and the tax returns that have been filed for the partnership. These existing capital account balances serve as the floor upon which the appreciation of the property will then be distributed. Appreciation, meaning the net amount of increased equity available for distribution on the assumed sale of the property, will then be allocated among the partners. Each physician will, in accordance with the terms of the partnership agreement, be allocated the appreciation of the property. In the event that the partners share equally in all appreciation of the property, the net amount available for distribution will be divided by the number of partners and the amount allocated equally to all existing partners. Table 14 illustrates this equal distribution. If a different ownership arrangement is present, the appreciation must be divided according to the percentage interests of each of the physician partners in accordance with the terms of the existing partnership agreement. This appreciation, once allocated, is then added to the existing capital account balances of the partners to arrive at a new "mark to market" capital account balance for each of the existing partners. The end result of this process is to show the full value of the partnership as of the date when a combination must be considered.

Once the interests of the partners for the real estate combination have been determined, the parties must decide how the real estate will be combined and how new partners will be admitted. This process requires financial modeling to show the financial impact on the operation of the partnership and on the costs associated with each physician making contributions, or receiving payments, as a result of the combination of the real estate. While there are many combination possibilities, depending on the facts and circumstances of each merger and the desires, goals and strategic aims of the partners, all of these can be illustrated using the same financial analysis. It is this financial modeling that will enable accurate decisions to be made concerning the impact on the partnership, as well as impact on the individual physicians.

Having determined the respective values of the partnership interests, and having made certain basic assumptions about the method of ownership, it will then be necessary to assess the cash needs of the partnership by examining the operations of the parcels of property to be combined. Table 15 illustrates this process. This exhibit represents an evaluation of the properties and the cash flow associated with the operation of this real estate venture.

First, it will be necessary to determine the rental income for the respective parcels. The rent to be established should be viewed, first, with an examination of the rent currently being charged the medical group by the partnership. A review of the marketplace in order to establish a fair market value rental, must be made, and the parties should agree that all parcels to be combined should be valued using the same standard in the determination of the appropriate rental to be charged. This rental review may result in the conclusion that either above or below market rates are being paid for a particular parcel, and this determination may require an adjustment of the rental amounts to be charged that will be phased in as of the date of combination of the ventures. Having determined the rentals for the respective parcels, these aggregate rental amounts will be totalled and the total income for the partnership will be determined.

The next step in this process illustrated in Table 15 is to determine the partnership expenses, including taxes, insurance, utilities, maintenance, repairs, janitorial services, groundskeeping and appropriate capital reserves. These expenses will be based on historical operating costs associated with the property, as well as projections of increases in those costs over the years that are subject to the cash flow projection. These amounts will be totalled to arrive at a total operating expense amount which will be subtracted from total income to arrive at the cash available for debt service. Debt service will usually consist of mortgage payments for the mortgage of the property, any promissory notes that may be issued with respect to medical group operations which may be secured by a mortgage on the real property, and promissory notes to retiring, departing or deceased physicians. The total debt service then will be compared against the cash available for servicing that debt. To the extent that the debt service payments exceed cash available for debt service, there will be a cash flow deficit. To the extent cash available for debt service exceeds total debt service there will be positive cash flow to the partners. In the event there is a deficit, the partnership must make plans to require capital contributions of the partners to make up for that deficit.

Transforming the Delivery of Health Care:
The integration process

Before a model can be constructed for combination of the real estate, taxable income of the partnership must be calculated. The determination of taxable income is necessary, as it will impact the capital accounts of the partners, effect the dollar values assigned to those interests, and effect the way in which those interests are valued to arrive at a combination proposal. Table 16 illustrates the determination of taxable income. This determination begins with the cash flow or deficit from the partnership calculated in Table 15. Depreciation and amortization are then subtracted, as they are noncash items. The next step is to calculate the amount of principal repayments made in the debt repayment process. All of these items are combined together to arrive at a taxable income figure. In the illustration in Table 16 the amount of taxable income results in a loss for the year, and that loss is subtracted from the capital account balances during the course of that year.

The final step in this real estate modeling process is the calculation of the combination scenarios whereby real estate will be combined together in one operation, or whereby additional physicians will be allowed to join and their contribution levels established. Table 17 illustrates this process. While many scenarios may be prepared, all should follow the same general format as illustrated below. First, all partners, new, old and otherwise, should be listed with their capital account balances that have been marked to market, using the procedures outlined in Table 14. After listing these capital account balances, it will then be necessary to adjust them by any profit or loss from the taxable income or loss computation that has been calculated pursuant to Table 16. Next, this amount will be further adjusted by the cash flow of the partnership which has been calculated pursuant to Table 15. To the extent there is a cash flow deficit, each of the partners will need to make up the amount of the deficit by making an additional capital contribution. The method by which these contributions shall be made needs to be determined by the partners, and will be a function of the decision concerning how the partnership will make additional funding available for operations.

Finally, as illustrated in Table 17, the method by which individual partners will make contributions to the partnership should be determined. To the extent that physicians with less ownership interests will be required to make contributions, that contribution level should be set forth in the projection. In addition, those physicians who have large capital account balances, who may have them reduced as part of this process, will be shown as having received these funds. These payments and distributions will then be aggregated to arrive at an ending balance which represents the capital account balance for those physicians at the end of the year. This ending balance will be used as the starting basis for future annual modifications to the partnership, to be made based upon the formula adapted by the partners to combine the real estate. As a summary of the activity that takes place through this process, the final column of the projection in Table 17 should indicate the net amounts of distributions or contributions that will be required of each individual partner. In summary fashion, the financial workings of the real estate partnership can be illustrated to all participants, who will then be able to determine on an aggregate and individual level, the appropriateness of the proposed combination methodology.

TABLE 4
Projected compensation / merged medical groups
or as a result of hospital affiliation
(in thousands)

	Year 1 non-merger projection	Conservative scenario year 1	Moderate scenario year 1	Aggressive scenario year 1	Moderate year 2
Physician 1	$ 250	$ 240	$ 250	$ 260	$ 290
Physician 2	$ 275	$ 290	$ 310	$ 330	$ 320
Physician 3	$ 250	$ 260	$ 270	$ 280	$ 280
Physician 4	$ 300	$ 310	$ 330	$ 350	$ 360
Physician 5	$ 300	$ 310	$ 330	$ 350	$ 360
Physician 6	$ 250	$ 250	$ 260	$ 270	$ 260
Physician 7	$ 275	$ 260	$ 280	$ 290	$ 300
Physician 8	$ 300	$ 300	$ 320	$ 330	$ 320
Physician 9	$ 225	$ 220	$ 230	$ 240	$ 250
Physician 10	$ 200	$180	$ 190	$ 200	$ 190
TOTAL	$2,625	$2,620	$2,770	$2,900	$2,930

TABLE 5
Projected compensation without transaction,
commencement year
(in thousands)

	Total comp. commencement year	Actual income commencement year minus 2	Difference	Current year (commencement year minus 1)
Physician 1	$ 250	$ 230	$ 20	$ 225
Physician 2	$ 275	$ 250	$ 25	$ 240
Physician 3	$ 250	$ 250	-0-	$ 250
Physician 4	$ 300	$ 280	$ 20	$ 275
Physician 5	$ 300	$ 280	$ 20	$ 275
Physician 6	$ 250	$ 200	$ 50	$ 210
Physician 7	$ 275	$ 270	$ 5	$ 280
Physician 8	$ 300	$ 290	$ 10	$ 300
Physician 9	$ 225	$ 200	$ 25	$ 200
Physician 10	$ 200	$ 210	($10)	$ 220
TOTAL	$2,625	$2,460	$165	$2,475

TABLE 6
Projected compensation with transaction, commencement year

	Total comp. commencement year	Actual income commencement year minus 2	Difference	Current year (commencement year minus 1)
Physician 1	$ 250	$ 230	$ 20	$ 225
Physician 2	$ 310	$ 250	$ 60	$ 240
Physician 3	$ 270	$ 250	$ 20	$ 250
Physician 4	$ 330	$ 280	$ 50	$ 275
Physician 5	$ 330	$ 280	$ 50	$ 275
Physician 6	$ 260	$ 200	$ 60	$ 210
Physician 7	$ 280	$ 270	$ 10	$ 280
Physician 8	$ 320	$ 290	$ 30	$ 300
Physician 9	$ 230	$ 200	$ 30	$ 200
Physician 10	$ 190	$ 210	$(20)	$ 220
TOTAL	$2,770	$2,460	$ 310	$2,475

TABLE 7
Projected net changes in compensation comparisons transactions versus non-transaction forecast (in thousands)

	Comparison non-transaction to transaction (conservative)	Comparison non-transaction vs. transaction (moderate)	Comparison non-transaction vs. transaction (aggressive)	Comparison non-transaction vs. transaction plus one year (moderate)
Physician 1	$ (10)	$ 0	$ 10	$ 40
Physician 2	$ 15	$ 35	$ 55	$ 45
Physician 3	$ 10	$ 20	$ 30	$ 30
Physician 4	$ 10	$ 30	$ 50	$ 60
Physician 5	$ 10	$ 30	$ 50	$ 60
Physician 6	$ 0	$ 10	$ 20	$ 10
Physician 7	$ (15)	$ 5	$ 15	$ 25
Physician 8	$ 0	$ 20	$ 30	$ 20
Physician 9	$ (5)	$ 5	$ 15	$ 25
Physician 10	$ (20)	($10)	$ 0	$ (10)
TOTAL	$($5)	$ 145	$ 275	$ 305

TABLE 8
Derivation of compensation pool /
no transaction scenario (in thousands)

	Year prior	Implement. year conservative	Implement. year moderate	Implement. year aggressive
Total Net Production	$10,000	$10,200	$10,400	$10,600
Capitated Production	$1,000	$1,000	$1,100	$1,200
Ancillaries-other services	$2,000	$2,000	$2,100	$2,200
Collection rate	95%	95%	95%	95%
Other income	$100	$100	$100	$100
Operating income	$12,450	$12,640	$13,020	$13,400
Revenues	$12,450	$12,640	$13,020	$13,400
A/R accrual adjustment				
Expenses	$7,000	$7,300	$7,300	$7,200
Net operating income	$5,450	$5,340	$5,720	$6,200
Compensation ratio	99%	99%	99%	99%
Compensation pool	$5,395	$5,287	$5,663	$6,138

TABLE 9
Derivation of compensation pool /
transaction implementation (in thousands)

	Year prior	Implement. year conservative	Implement. year moderate	Implement. year aggressive
Total Net Production	$10,000	$10,400	$11,000	$11,500
Capitated Production	$1,000	$1,200	$1,500	$2,000
Ancillaries-other services	$2,000	$2,100	$2,200	$2,300
Collection rate	95%	95%	95%	95%
Other income	$100	$100	$100	$100
Operating income	$12,450	$13,115	$14,065	$15,110
Revenues	$12,450	$13,115	$14,065	$15,110
A/R accrual adjustment				
Expenses	$7,000	$7,300	$7,200	$7,100
Net operating income	$5,450	$5,815	$6,865	$8,010
Compensation ratio	99%	99%	99%	99%
Compensationpool	$5,395	$5,757	$6,796	$7,930

TABLE 10

Illustration of combination of
shareholder interests / merger
(assumes Medical Group I = 10 physicians,
Medical Group II = 11 physicians)

Net book value of professional corporation		
Current net book values		
Medical Group I	$200,000	
Medical Group II	250,000	
Contributions to new organization		
Medical Group I ($20,000/shareholder)	$200,000	
Medical Group II ($20,000/shareholder)	220,000	
Difference payable to Medical Group II	$ 30,000	
Net Accounts Receivable		
Current Net Receivables		
Current accounts receivable		
Medical Group I	$1,500,000	
Medical Group II	2,000,000	
Contributions to new organization		
Medical Group I ($150,000/shareholder)	$1,500,000	
Medical Group II ($150,000/shareholder)	$1,650,400	
Difference payable to Medical Group II	$ 350,000	
Total Payments to Medical Group II		$ 380,000

TABLE 11
Derivation of affiliation fee

	Year 1	Year 2
Revenues		
Medical Services	$12,000,000	$13,000,000
Ancillary Services	2,000,000	2,200,000
Expenses		
Employee Costs	5,000,000	5,300,000
Administrative	1,000,000	1,100,000
Property	3,000,000	3,200,000
Net Income	5,000,000	5,600,000
Management Fee	500,000	560,000
Amount Available for Physician Compensation	4,500,000	5,040,000
Salary Guarantee	250,000	250,000
Net Physician Compensation Amount	4,750,000	5,290,000

TABLE 12
Income statement
(in thousands)

	2 yrs. prior	One year prior	Transaction year	One year post merger transaction
Revenues				
Net patient revenues	$5,000	$5,300	$5,700	$6,000
Other revenues	$ 200	$ 200	$ 200	$ 200
Total revenues	$5,200	$5,500	$5,900	$6,200
Expenses				
Physician expenses	$ 300	$ 400	$ 500	$ 600
Non-physician salaries and benefits	$1,000	$1,200	$1,400	$1,400
Medical supplies and expenses	$ 250	$ 250	$ 300	$ 300
Building expenses	$ 400	$ 400	$ 450	$ 450
General/adminis-trative expenses	$ 900	$ 950	$ 950	$ 850
Total operatingexpenses	$2,850	$3,200	$3,600	$3,600
Net operating income (NOI)	$2,350	$2,300	$2,300	$2,600

TABLE 13
Cash flow projection
(6 months)

	Month 1	Month 2	Month 3	Month 4	Month 5	Month 6
Beginning Cash	200,000	200,000	100,000	100,000	100,000	150,000
Revenues	$1 M	900,000	800,000	900,000	$1 M	$1.1 M
Expenses	600,000	700,000	700,000	600,000	600,000	600,000
Physician Compensation	400,000	400,000	500,000	400,000	350,000	400,000
Borrowings	-0-	100,000	400,000	-0-	-0-	-0-
Ending Cash	200,000	400,000	-0-	-0-	150,000	250,000

TABLE 14
Medical properties partnership
example of mark-to-market calculation
as of _____, 19___ based on _____, 19___

ASSUMPTION: Deemed Liquidation

Amount Realized		
Parcel 1	2,000,000	
Parcel 2	1,000,000	
Parcel 3	1,000,000	
		4,000,000
Liabilities		
Mortgages - Parcel 1	1,000,000	
- Parcel 2	400,000	
- Parcel 3	300,000	
Note to retiring Dr.	100,000	
Note to departed Dr.	200,000	(2,000,000)
Available forDistribution		2,000,000

Summary by Partner

	PPV	Appreciation	Total
Partner 1	200,000	100,000	300,000
Partner 2	200,000	100,000	300,000
Partner 3	100,000	100,000	200,000
Partner 4	100,000	100,000	200,000
Partner 5	100,000	100,000	200,000
Partner 6	100,000	100,000	200,000
Partner 7	50,000	100,000	150,000
Partner 8	50,000	100,000	150,000
Partner 9	50,000	100,000	150,000
Partner 10	50,000	100,000	150,000
Totals	1,000,000	1,000,000	2,000,000

TABLE 15
Medical properties partnership
example of cash flow
based on _____, 19___ appraisal

	Year 1	Year 2	Year 3
Rental Income			
Parcel 1	250,000	275,000	300,000
Parcel 2	100,000	125,000	150,000
Parcel 3	100,000	125,000	150,000
Total Income	450,000	525,000	600,000
Operating Expenses			
Taxes	50,000	60,000	60,000
Insurance		10,000	10,000
10,000			
Utilities	40,000	50,000	50,000
Maintenance/Repairs	25,000	30,000	20,000
Janitorial		10,000	12,500
12,500			
Groundskeeping	10,000	12,500	12,500
Reserves	5,000	5,000	5,000
Total Operating Expenses	(150,000)	(180,000)	(170,000)
Cash Available for Debt Service	300,000	345,000	430,000
Debt Service			
Mortgage	200,000	200,000	200,000
Demand Note (7)	50,000	45,000	40,000
Note to Retiring Dr.	50,000	50,000	40,000
Note to Departed Dr.	100,000	100,000	100,000
Total Debt Service	400,000	395,000	380,000
Cash Flow (Deficit)	(100,000)	(50,000)	50,000

TABLE 16
Medical properties partnership
example of taxable income
based on _____, 19___ appraisal

	Year 1	Year 2	Year 3
Cash Flow/(Deficit)	(100,000)	(50,000)	50,000
Less Depreciation & Amortization	(50,000)	(50,000)	(50,000)
Plus Principal Repayments			
Mortgage	25,000	30,000	35,000
Note to Retiring Dr.	40,000	40,000	40,000
Note to Departed Dr.	30,000	30,000	30,000
Note	5,000	5,000	5,000
Taxable Income	(50,000)	5,000	110,000